D0866179

A Guide to the Architecture of Minnesota

David Gebhard
Tom Martinson

The John K. Fesler Memorial Fund provided assistance in the publication of this volume, for which the University of Minnesota Press is grateful.

The contribution of the McKnight Foundation to the general program of the University of Minnesota Press, of which the publication of this book is a part, is gratefully acknowledged.

Contributions to the Bicentennial Exhibition of Minnesota Art and Architecture and its supporting publications were provided by the following individuals and organizations:

Allstate Sales Corporation
Area Vocational-Technical Institute #916
Bauer Brothers Salvage Company
Charles A. Weyerhaeuser Memorial Foundation
Chevrolet Motor Division—General Motors Corporation
Dayton Hudson Foundation
Dayton's
Elizabeth W. Musser
Ellerbe Inc.
Ford Motor Company
Fruehauf Trailer Division, Fruehauf Corporation
General Mills Foundation
GMC Truck & Coach Division
Grotto Foundation
International Harvester Company
Iten Chevrolet
Knox Lumber Company
Land O'Lakes
Mack Trucks, Inc.
Mary Livingston Griggs and Mary Griggs Burke Foundation
Metropolitan Transit Commission
Minnesota American Revolution Bicentennial Commission
Minnesota Humanities Commission
Minnesota Motor Transport Association
Minnesota State Arts Council
Minnesota White Trucks, Inc.
National Endowment for the Arts
National Endowment for the Humanities
North Central Publishing Company
North Central Trucks, Inc.
Northprint Company
Otto Bremer Foundation and affiliated Bremer banks
Patrick and Aimee Butler Family Foundation
The Saint Paul Foundation
The Schubert Club
Thermo King Sales & Service of St. Paul
Town & Country GMC, Inc.
University of Minnesota, Regents Reserve Funds

A Guide to the Architecture of Minnesota

David Gebhard
Tom Martinson

Published by the
University of Minnesota Press,
Minneapolis, for the
University Gallery of the
University of Minnesota and the
Minnesota Society of Architects

Printed at the North Central Publishing
Company, St. Paul.

Published by the
University of Minnesota Press,
2037 University Avenue Southeast,
Minneapolis, Minnesota 55455,

and published in Canada
by Burns & MacEachern Limited,
Don Mills, Ontario

*Library of Congress Catalog Card Number
75-36032 ISBN 0-8166-0773-7*

Jacket photo:
Ice Palace, St. Paul Winter Carnival, 1886.
Courtesy of the Minnesota Historical Society.

Designed by Marc Treib

to Dimitri Tselos
the first to open our eyes critically
to the architecture of Minnesota

Contents

Foreword

This book was conceived from its inception to supplement and augment the Bicentennial exhibition, *The Art and Architecture of Minnesota*, organized and presented by the University Gallery in conjunction with the Minnesota Society of Architects. The exhibition was more than three years in the planning stages, and at every step our desire was to publish something other than an exhibition catalogue — something at once less ephemeral and more comprehensive yet not boring that ubiquitous person, the "interested layman," with heavily erudite prose. In the end we decided to publish *A Guide to the Architecture of Minnesota*. Long a priority of the Minnesota Society of Architects, such a guide seemed to us to be the sort of publication which would most nearly meet our needs.

We offer the fervent hope that this volume will help Minnesotans to see things and buildings never truly perceived before — and will encourage them to think more than once before bulldozing the past and near-past away. For example, a few buildings described in the text have been razed since the manuscript for the guide was completed. (By the time the information reached us, the production of the guide was well under way, and we were unable to modify the text to indicate which buildings had been destroyed.) All that is past is not gold, but neither is it dross simply because it has been poorly maintained or has gone out of fashion. We have not been able to provide a town-by-town, street-by-street guide, but we have included the broadest possible selection of interesting houses, public buildings, and landmarks from the various regions of the state. The guide contains succinct but vital information, and it is our hope that with this volume in hand the weekend traveler will be able to explore a new facet of Minnesota's cultural heritage.

Have buildings of interest been overlooked? We welcome letters from readers who wish to call our attention to important omissions or to any errors in the text. The information and suggestions supplied by readers will be kept on file and reviewed for possible inclusion in a subsequent edition of the guide.

This undertaking could not have come to fruition without the dedicated help of the Historic Resources Committee of the Minnesota Society of Architects. Among students at the university our special thanks go to Terry Pfoutz and to Peter Petzling, a researcher *extraordinaire* whose enthusiasm never flagged, even in the face of the most tedious detailed tasks. Of the University Gallery staff, Lyndel King, assistant director and acting director, and Susan Brown, curator and editor, demonstrated their abilities as museum professionals of the highest caliber, coping with daily crises with aplomb. Finally, we would like to thank Mrs. Georgia DeCoster, architecture coordinator of the Minnesota State Arts Council at the beginning of our project and later executive director of the St. Paul-Ramsey Bicentennial Commission, for her unstinting help and support.

A Guide to the Architecture of Minnesota serves as a companion volume to Rena Coen's *Painting and Sculpture in Minnesota, 1820–1914*, which was also published in conjunction with the Bicentennial exhibition. We hope that together these books will initiate a new awareness and reassessment of Minnesota's cultural heritage.

Barbara Shissler
Director
University Gallery
University of Minnesota

Daniel J. Sheridan
Executive Director
Minnesota Society of Architects

Acknowledgments

The authors wish to express their thanks to the institutions and the individuals whose efforts and support have made this guide possible.

For the sponsorship of the guide:

The University Gallery, University of Minnesota, Minneapolis, and Barbara Shissler, director

The Minnesota Society of Architects, St. Paul, and Daniel J. Sheridan, executive director

For contributions in research, editing, and production:

The staff of the University Gallery, including Lyndel King, assistant director and acting director; Susan Brown, curator; Peter Petzling and Terry Pfoutz, research assistants; Hayden Valdes, design assistant; Anne Morrison, production assistant

The members of the Historic Resources Committee of the Minnesota Society of Architects, including William W. Scott, chairman, *Taylor's Falls*; William Broderson, *Northfield*; Brooks Cavin, *Minneapolis*; Foster Dunwiddie, *Edina*; Basil Filonowich, *Roseville*; Ernst Ibs, *Minneapolis*; Alan Lathrop, *Minneapolis*; Duane Stolpe, *St. Paul*

For production and general editorial assistance:

Gerald M. Kimball, Lawrence J. Sommer, *Duluth*; Marjory Martinson, Harold Sand, *Edina*; N. C. Van Guilder, *Faribault*; Lorie Halstensgaard, Debbie Lund, *Fergus Falls*; Mrs. Albert A. Jacobson, *Hastings*; Clint Blomquist, *Hopkins*; Tom Anding, Gail Bronner, Dorothy Burke, Michael Cronin, Richard Heath, Charles Nelson, Dana Noonan, John Rauma, Herbert Scherer, Donald Torbert, Gordon Wagner, Jon Walstrom, *Minneapolis*; Lauren Soth, Robert Warn, *Northfield*; Mrs. John R. Hill, *Rochester*; Georgia R. DeCoster, Lila Goff, Virginia Kunz, Eileen Michels, Marvin J. Pertzik, B. Warner Shippee, Bonnie Wilson, Carole Zellie, *St. Paul*; Ruth Ann Collins, Patricia A. Gebhard, *Santa Barbara*; Richard Heiny, *Schroeder*; Elizabeth Scobie, *Sleepy Eye*; Donald Lovness, *Stillwater*; John D. Olsvik, *Two Harbors*; Mrs. Charles Kelly, *Wayzata*; Mrs. Thomas Newcome, *White Bear Lake*

The Northwest Architectural Archives, University of Minnesota, *Minneapolis*; the Minnesota Historical Society, *St. Paul*; the Minneapolis Public Library, History Collection; the Municipal Information Library of the City of Minneapolis

Photographic Credits:

The sources of text illustrations by photographers other than the authors are noted in the captions. All other photographs in the text are by Tom Martinson or David Gebhard. The photograph of the St. Paul Winter Carnival Ice Palace of 1886 on the jacket of the hardbound edition and on the cover of the paperbound edition of the book is reproduced through the courtesy of the Minnesota Historical Society.

A Guide to This Guide

In this guide we have brought together a broad survey of Minnesota's architecture from the early decades of the nineteenth century to the present. The built-in limitation of such a survey is that it presents only buildings which are still standing. Like other states, Minnesota has lost a good number of its major monuments so that the picture which we have today is in some respects neither representative nor accurate. Still, enough remains, especially in the smaller communities, so that we can gain a sense of the past and the near-past. Our hope is that the guide will encourage readers to go out and really look — to experience our architectural inheritance — and above all to sense how we have transformed an area of deciduous and coniferous forests and grass-covered prairies into a new and very different man-made environment.

We have attempted to be as impartial in this survey as possible, admitting a variety of styles and man-made environments which we have reservations about, and we have tried to provide a reasonable sample of Minnesota's architectural inheritance from all parts of the state. But we are well aware that we have certainly missed some important buildings, and even some towns, which perhaps should have been included, and we hope this can be corrected when the guide is revised and updated in the years ahead. We all still have a lot to learn about our architecture and how we have transformed the environment of our state.

Probably the most controversial part of the guide is its coverage of the twentieth century, especially the years from 1920 on. We are not only friendly to the aims and the results of Period architecture — we are at times enraptured with it. And the same holds true for the Zigzag Moderne of the 1920s and the Streamline Moderne and the PWA Moderne of the 1930s, styles which until recently we were all taught to despise. Buildings in these styles are historically important and are equally significant in the quality of their design. While we are in no way unsympathetic to the architecture of the past four decades (especially the 1960s and 1970s), we have tried to look at it as critically as we have looked at the architecture of the earlier periods.

We certainly make no claim that very many of the hundreds of buildings discussed in the guide are major High Art objects, but they do provide reliable clues to Minnesota's environment at any given moment. Finally, it must be admitted that we have listed certain kinds of buildings and groups of buildings in places outside the Twin Cities metropolitan area which we have omitted from the listings for Minneapolis and St. Paul. The reason for this is that we could be much more selective in the metropolitan area in presenting its environmental transformation than we could be in the smaller communities. The character of small communities outside the metropolitan area is frequently established by a few key building types. In the downtown commercial area these are often a Beaux Arts bank building, a Streamline Moderne theatre of the 1930s, and a post office of the 1920s or 1930s. On the outskirts of town the major landmarks are typically a railroad station, grain elevators, and a water tower. Occasionally public buildings such as county courthouses or schools assume some importance in establishing the sense of a place, but most public buildings (with the exception of post offices) do not count for much. Almost invariably the most interesting domestic architecture in small Minnesota communities was built before 1900.

Geographic Organization. We have divided the state into eight geographic areas, with the Twin Cities area as the starting point. For ease of reference we have used key abbreviations for each of the areas (M, Metropolitan; SCV, St. Croix Valley; C, Central; A, Arrowhead and Iron Range; NW, Northwest; MRV, Minnesota River Valley; SE, Southeast; SW, Southwest) and have arranged the cities and communities in each area in alphabetical order.

Maps. Individual maps are provided for the large urban areas. (All maps are oriented with the top to the north unless otherwise noted.) In the Minneapolis, St. Paul, and Duluth areas we have divided the communities into a number of smaller units. We would recommend that the reader obtain a standard highway map of the state and probably detailed street maps of Minneapolis, St. Paul, and Duluth to supplement the maps in the guide.

Format of Entries. The heading of each entry contains the original name of the building (if we know it), its current name or use, the date of the building, the name of the architect, and the street address. The symbol • is used in the text to denote buildings that are illustrated in the Photohistory or Glossary sections.

In many instances the dating of a building poses problems. Is the "correct" date the date when the building was completed, or is it the date of the architect's sketches and drawings? Wherever possible, we have listed the year when the design was first conceived, and if that year is not the same as the year of completion we have listed both years. One might think that the existence of a date inscription on the building itself would settle the question, but it does not. Such dates may indicate when the building was started or when it was completed — one can rarely be certain. In a number of cases we have obtained the date of a building from correspondence or from historical records (local newspapers and the like). If such dates and the evidence in support of them seem reasonable, we have accepted them, but in most instances we have not had the opportunity to examine the supporting evidence critically. If no information about the date of a building is available, we have inserted approximate dates, based upon our general knowledge of Minnesota, the history of specific communities, and our awareness of architectural styles and their chronology. An approximate date is thus our reasonable guess about the date of a building, nothing more.

Each of the entries contains a brief note providing information about the building (style, characteristics, and so on). We have sought to list only those buildings which can be seen from a public street, road, park, or lake. The listing of buildings in the guide must not be construed as permission to trespass. We emphasize that in no way does the listing of any private building in the guide constitute permission to enter the grounds or the building. In general, visitors who wish to see the interior of a private building should first consult the architect, not the owner.

Federal, state, county, and city public buildings are usually open weekdays from 8:00 A.M. to 5:00 P.M., but it is always best to write or call in advance to arrange a visit. A number of historic buildings that are open to the public are listed in the guide. Information about these buildings is included in the introduction to the area or in the numbered entries.

Photographs. Many of the buildings discussed in the guide are illustrated in photographs accompanying the text. The illustrations of buildings described in the numbered entries are keyed to the text through the captions (the number preceding the identification of the building refers to the number of the corresponding text entry). The illustrations in the Photohistory and Glossary sections are keyed to the text through the coded geographic and building designations included in the captions. In these designations the first element is a shortened reference to the geographic area, the second is the number assigned to the city or the community in the Index to Geographic Areas, and the third is the number of the text entry in which the building is discussed. For example, the caption for the photograph of the Rice County Courthouse in the Photohistory section bears the designation "SE-22-4," which means that the discussion of the building is found in the text for the Southeast area (SE), under Faribault (22), in entry 4.

Architectural Styles. The major architectural styles referred to in the text of the guide are discussed and illustrated in the Glossary section. A general description and a list of characteristics are given for each style.

D.G.
T.M.

Index to Geographic Areas

Metropolitan

St. Croix Valley

Central

Index to Geographic Areas

Arrowhead and Iron Range

Northwest

Minnesota River Valley

Index to Geographic Areas

Southeast

Southwest

A Guide to the Architecture of Minnesota

Introduction

"The close of the first century of American Independence naturally called for some extraordinary and imposing commemoration of the great event, and when it was proposed to celebrate it by an International Exhibition, in which the American Republic should display to the world the triumphs it has achieved in the noble arts of peace during its first century of national existence, and in which these triumphs should be compared in friendly rivalry with those of other and older nations, there was general and cordial response of approval from the entire country. Out of this sentiment the International Centennial Exhibition was born." (James D. McCabe, *History of the Centennial Exhibition,* Philadelphia, 1876.)

A hundred years have now elapsed since the famous and much admired Philadelphia Centennial Exhibition was held, and it goes without saying that in many ways the mood of the country in its bicentennial year is vastly different from what it was in 1876. Yet there are major points of similarity: In 1976 Americans are again taking a backward glance into the past with some nostalgia for what is felt to have been a remote and simpler Golden Age, and again their outlook is conditioned by strong opposing elements. In 1876 the optimism of material progress, laissez-faireism, and big-is-better was pitted against the belief that the simple rural life was correct and virtuous and that the city, commerce, and industry were, perhaps, inevitable but also that they were in essence evil, just as in 1976 there is fear of what a destructive effect excessive government and large-scale business could have on the individual.

Minnesota in 1976 beautifully mirrors the two worlds which America now finds itself in. The Twin Cities area is a dynamic and energetic urban world which is fully committed to the rationalism and materialism of this and the past century. Minnesota's rural areas and small towns, though intermeshed in the agricultural economic scene of the moment, are still basically nineteenth century and anti-urban. One way to gain a meaningful perspective on the state in 1976 is to see how the environment of Minnesota has been reordered from the early 1800s to the present: What was it like in 1800? What changes had taken place by 1876? And, finally, what is being done with this environment today?

Minnesota's physical environment in 1800 consisted of a mixture of rolling prairie lands, forested river valleys, and deep coniferous forests. From a European settler's point of view the region's three great assets were the open prairies which could be converted into productive

Robert House, 1853, St. Paul. Razed. Photo: Minnesota Historical Society.

farmlands, its thousands of acres of timber which could be profitably harvested and milled, and the natural transportation corridors of its rivers which gave access to the land and its resources. There were also major assets for the Native Americans in that the rivers, lakes, and land provided food and objects of trade.

The Eastern Sioux, the Ojibway (Chippewa), and the Winnebago who lived in parts of Minnesota in 1800 showed great flexibility in adapting themselves to the physical and climatic environment of the place. For the winter months they gathered into villages composed of domed and peaked wigwams. The domed wigwam was constructed of a frame of saplings bent over and tied together at the top, and the oval form was covered with mats woven from cattails or skins and other materials. The conical or pointed lodge had a framework of poles, arranged in a circle ten to sixteen feet in diameter, tied at the top. When insulated with grass and hung with inner linings, these structures created enclosures which provided warmth and a sense of seclusion from the world outside. During the summer months when life was spent out of doors, other kinds of dwellings were used — simple conical bark houses with frames of saplings, small conical lodges, and later the classic skin-covered tepee as we know it.

The Sioux, the Ojibway, and the Winnebago were not the first to live in this geographic region. Previous peoples, particularly along the Mississippi and other river valleys, had built permanent villages, had cultivated corn and other crops, and had constructed ceremonial earth enclosures and burial mounds laid out in various geometric shapes and effigies of birds, bears, humans, fish, and serpents. The sites of many of the prehistoric Native American villages and sacred areas were in many instances the same as those which were used by the Europeans when they first entered the region and began to select locations for settlements. The first European "architecture" in Minnesota closely followed the dwelling types which were then in use by the Native Americans — bark-covered summer wigwams, in some cases conical enclosures, and later tepees. Such dwellings were built, usually for temporary summer occupation, by the French, English, and American fur traders.

Traditionally we have always tended to conceive of architecture only in the sense of permanent structures, but certainly our experiences of the past thirty-odd years with mobile homes and prefabricated buildings should have convinced us by now that architecture has to do with the conscious reordering of an environment and that little of what we build is indeed permanent. A village of temporary structures, a sacred burial site, a portage trail, and one of the early Federal Government Roads of the 1850s are each a form of architecture as much as any permanent building is.

Quantitatively the first highly significant examples of the European/American tradition in architecture in Minnesota were not buildings (temporary or permanent), but the large-scale reordering of a place in the form of a fort such as Fort Snelling (1820–24), a new town such as St. Paul (1847), a milling compound, or simply the clearing of land and the establishment of a farm complex with its specific areas for crops, pasture, vegetables, the farmyard, and the eventual grouping of buildings. In most of these cases what counted was not the individual buildings but the overall man-made pattern which was imposed on the landscape. Thus, the history of architecture in Minnesota (or elsewhere in most of the United States) has far more to do with land speculation, the laying out of new towns and farms, the construction of roads, and the development of railroads and the adjacent lands than with the passing fashions of architectural styles or even the previous backgrounds of the new settlers.

Minneapolis Public Library, 1889, Minneapolis. Long and Kees. Razed. Photo: Minneapolis Public Library.

The early sites selected for settlement tended to reflect more deeply the specifics of environment than did the sites which came into being after the introduction of the railroad. The first settlements, such as those at Mendota and St. Paul, were trading communities closely tied to the transportation line of the river. The land around and behind these settlements had little direct relationship to the existence of the towns. On the other hand many of the pre-1860 towns and villages, such as Taylor's Falls and Stillwater along the St. Croix, were closely tied to the natural resources of the hinterland, its timber, the availability of energy in the form of waterpower, and the connective transportation link of the river. By the early 1850s and 1860s these fur-trading and lumber-milling river towns were joined by two other types of communities — those which combined the elements of water transportation and waterpower in the development of major shipping and processing points for wheat and other grains (Winona and Hastings), and those which became centers for the small-scale processing of grain and for retail sales to the inhabitants of the surrounding agricultural lands (Faribault and Rochester). Then, shortly before the Civil War, three other town types began to develop: the railroad town as a storage and distribution center (Kasson and Pipestone); the railroad town as a storage, distribution, and processing center with a substantial source of energy (Moorhead and Fergus Falls); and finally the highly economically specialized community such as the lumbering town (Aitken) and the iron ore mining or shipping town (Virginia and Two Harbors).

Another pre-1900 town type which has frequently been discussed is the ethnic town — the communities founded and developed throughout Minnesota by such ethnic groups as the Germans, the Swedes, the Norwegians, the Finns, and others. The existence of towns with distinct personalities of their own owing to the historic ethnic background of a group is to a large degree a myth. When these ethnic groups settled in Minnesota, their town plans tended to be similar to those of any other community in the establishment of a main street as the retail commercial center and in the placement of public and religious buildings and dwellings, and the architectural styles of the buildings accurately reflected whatever was fashionable at the moment. Perhaps the only feature which might in some cases be pointed out as distinguishing one kind of town from another is the style of the churches. The Germans and other central Europeans often built large-scale brick churches, which in many instances seemed purposely out of scale with the community; the churches of the Swedish and Norwegian Lutherans also projected a very strong physical image, but usually the prominence of the Lutheran churches was in their siting, not in their physical size.

It has also been argued that there was a far greater predilection for brick and stone as building materials in the German and central European settlements than in any of the other ethnic communities. Perhaps there is a grain of truth in this assertion, but the use of masonry as a building material, particularly for dwellings, did not lead to anything approaching a distinct architectural style. A house whose walls are of brick or stone is more likely to be simple in its form, openings, and detailing than is a house with a wood frame and wood sheathing, but that is as far as one can go.

Guaranty Loan (Metropolitan) Building, 1888–90, Minneapolis E. Townsend Mix. Razed 1962. Photo: Jack Boucher, HABS.

On the whole, the plans of Minnesota's nineteenth-century towns were generally arbitrary in their relationship to their respective sites. The gridiron scheme, which was applied almost universally, generally ignored the specific features which established the character of a site unless there was simply no way to surmount them. The streets, almost always laid out in a north/south, east/west orientation, rolled over hill and dale, lakes and rivers. In a few cases exceptions were made — for example, in Winona, St. Paul, and Minneapolis, the grids parallel the Mississippi River, which is the dominant natural feature.

Nevertheless, the grid scheme was an advantageous one in many ways. It could be easily laid out by anyone who could work with a compass and a transit. Since land was a major commodity, the grid

Guaranty Loan (Metropolitan) Building. 1888–90, Minneapolis. E. Townsend Mix. Razed 1962. Photo: Jack Boucher, HABS.

pattern was useful in that it facilitated the sale and resale of it and the preparation of the necessary legal descriptions. Of equal if not more importance, the gridiron urban plan is a never-ending scheme predicated on the principle that land use is ever changing (ideally to increasingly intensive use) and therefore has no fixed center. A courthouse or city hall square or a site for a school or a park might be set aside in the original layout of a community, but this need not fix the area as the permanent center of the community.

By far the majority of Minnesota's villages, towns, and hope-to-be cities were parsimonious in setting aside parkland and places for public buildings. Few of them, at least during the early years of their existence, sought to utilize lakes, streams, and riversides as public amenities. There are occasional exceptions: New Ulm early set aside extensive land for parks, and Red Wing developed what amounts to a civic center reaching from the hillside courthouse into the downtown area. But it should be remembered that Minnesota's record of nineteenth-century town building was neither any worse nor any better than that found in most of the other states and that by the early twentieth century Minnesota's major cities had embarked on extensive park programs, incidentally becoming models for the rest of the country.

Like the architectural styles in other midwestern and western states which were in essence frontier areas throughout much of the nineteenth century, the styles employed in Minnesota tended to be provincial and late in arriving. Thus the first permanent buildings of architectural pretense which were built in Minnesota reflected, as one would expect, the classical Federal and Greek Revival Styles. The Henry H. Sibley House (1835) and the Jean B. Faribault House (1834), both at Mendota, are dwellings that with a few changes in detail could have been built near Philadelphia or elsewhere in the east around 1800. They are essentially Federal in style with a slight sprinkling of Greek Revival details. These two dwellings are provincial in the sense that they do not mirror the latest fashion which one would find in the major East Coast cities such as New York, Boston, or Philadelphia, although houses identical to these were still being built in the 1830s in upstate New York, western Pennsylvania, and on into Ohio and Indiana.

By the 1850s, especially in the settlements along the Mississippi and St. Croix rivers, the Greek Revival entered in full force. Though we attach the label Greek to the styling of these houses, most of them are in fact Federal with a few Greek details — pedimented windows, heavy and wide entablatures, recessed doors with paneled engaged Greek piers, occasional Greek columns (although many of them are really Roman Tuscan), and even a few examples of triglyphs and metopes and dentil moldings. In plan these houses are almost always either of the late eighteenth-century side-hall type or have central halls with two sets of rooms on each side. A few, like the Parker House (1856) at Marine on St. Croix, assume Grecian garb in full with a two-story columned porch.

The commercial and industrial buildings of the 1850s and 1860s were as a rule not styled at all. Their image tended to be simple and utilitarian, but like the houses they did refer back to commercial and industrial buildings of the early 1800s. The proportions, scale, and type of window and door openings and the form and pitch of the roofs often looked back to a much earlier period. A few of them, like the Washburn B Mill (1865, now destroyed) in Minneapolis, related directly to the classical tradition.

From the 1860s on there was increasingly rapid change in architectural packaging (styling). By the end of the 1860s the Greek fashion was all but dead, and it was replaced first by those styles and moods which were literary and pictorial — the Gothic and the Italianate. These were joined by the brief avant-garde rage for Orson Squire Fowler's "octagonal mode" of building. Of these fashions of the 1860s only the Italianate came to be widely used. The most common Italianate house was really a Greek Revival box which began to place more and more emphasis on the vertical as opposed to the horizontal; it replaced the Greek gable with a low-pitched hip roof, usually with wide overhangs and above all with pronounced brackets to support the roof. The fullest expression of the style came about in the Italian Villa Style — usually a two-story L-shaped house with a three-story tower in the middle of the L.

The Gothic, the most literary of the styles, was always a rarity on the frontier. Several of Minnesota's best-known Gothic dwellings are not really Gothic at all; the Le Duc House (1856–62) at Hastings and the St. Julien Cox House (1871) at St. Peter have basically Italianate designs with a decorative overlay of the Gothic. Minnesota does have a few of Fowler's octagonal gems, the most impressive being the Octagonal House (1857–58) in Hastings and the Lawther House (1857) in Red Wing, but the rage for this style of house was virtually extinguished by the 1880s. The circle and the octagon did continue on in popularity in Minnesota for barns, and the years immediately after 1900 witnessed a renaissance of round barns with domed roofs.

The Gothic saw its fullest use from 1860 on in church architecture. As in residential architecture the style was first simply applied to Federal/Greek plan and proportioned buildings, later the proportions were "verticalized," and finally the plan, disposition, and design of the tower became more correctly Gothic. The Gothic, particularly Ruskinian Gothic, was also employed for educational institutions and on occasion for commercial blocks (printers and newspaper publishers especially seemed to favor it).

By the middle of the century there was almost universal agreement that the Italianate was *the* correct style for county courthouses and other governmental buildings. The first Minnesota Capitol Building (the first territorial capitol, 1851–53) was Grecian with a drum and dome. In 1872 and again in 1878 the original building was enlarged and remodeled into the Italianate, reflecting the change in taste which had occurred in less than twenty years. The Italianate also became the dominant style for commercial buildings, and variations of the style continued to be built through the 1890s.

Other mixtures and new styles burst forth in the 1870s. The French Second Empire Style with its mansard roofs and end or central pavilions was a rage for ten or fifteen years, during which it was used for business blocks (often mixed with the Italianate), schools, and private residences. The French Second Empire designs provided a way whereby one could continue the classical tradition of balance and control but at the same time could be picturesque and fashionable. This dualism can be seen on a large scale in the Alexander Ramsey House (1868–72) in St. Paul and on a small scale in the McKusick House (1868) in Stillwater.

By the early 1880s it is no longer easy to separate the styles which came and went and which so often intermingled in a single building. The pure, spindly Eastlake Style is not found very often in either residential or commercial buildings in Minnesota. Usually it was combined with another style — in churches with the Gothic (but then pure English Eastlake is Gothic) and in residences often with the Queen Anne.

It was the Richardsonian Romanesque which at long last thrust Minnesota onto the national architectural scene. The central figure in this preeminence was the designer Harvey Ellis and especially his work in LeRoy Sunderland Buffington's office. As a designer Ellis was of the caliber of John Root and Stanford White, and he had the added advantage of being a superb renderer who could make even a dull building look impressive. By the mid-1890s Ellis, Long, and Kees and others were well on their way to converting downtown Minneapolis and St. Paul into Romanesque Revival areas, and the style quickly became fashionable for public buildings and commercial establishments in even the smallest of towns. The early part of the 1890s was a period of great building activity in which many of Minnesota's courthouses of the late 1860s and 1870s were replaced and numerous new ones were built; as a result, by 1900 the majority of Minnesota's courthouses were Romanesque in style.

The Queen Anne Style was often used in designs for dwellings by the same architects who worked in the Romanesque for other types of buildings. Considering the intense building activity of the 1890s it is surprising that Minnesota, which by this time was keeping up with the latest fashions, did not plunge itself into the Shingle Style. Instead there was an almost direct leap from the Queen Anne to the turn-of-the-century Colonial Revival. And by 1900 the major urban centers of Minnesota had fully embraced the ideal of classicism in the Beaux Arts, especially after the construction of Cass Gilbert's Capitol Building, which was designed in 1893–95.

Except for the most northern reaches of the state Minnesota was by 1900 a transformed environment. The region was now crisscrossed by railroads, small to large cities existed along every major river, an immense acreage was under cultivation, most of the rich and extensive timber forests were gone, and the Twin Cities of Minneapolis and St. Paul had emerged as a major urban center. Up to 1900 the distinction between the rural, small town, and urban areas was not great. The business districts and residential neighborhoods of large cities throughout the nineteenth century tended to be enlargements of those of the smaller cities and towns, and the styles of architecture encountered along the streets of Red Wing, Pipestone, or New Ulm were reduced versions of those in the large urban centers of Duluth and the Twin Cities.

There were a number of reasons for this nineteenth-century similarity. At first most designs came from the hands of carpenters or builders or from one of the numerous pattern books published during the century. By the late 1880s, however, the major business blocks and large residences in both small towns and large cities were beginning to be designed by professional architects — generally architects who operated out of Minneapolis or St. Paul. Since these architects were in close touch with changes in architectural fashion in the east, by the 1890s there was little or no time lag between the acceptance of a style in New York or Philadelphia and the utilization of it in Minneapolis or St. Paul.

Another reason for the similarity between the major and small urban environments until about the turn of the century is that the nineteenth century was a period of establishment and rapid growth for both of them. New buildings of all types were being built throughout the state. By 1900 the typical town or city contained buildings ranging in style from the Italianate through the Romanesque, and although the frostings of style did indeed change markedly from decade to decade all of these styles generally fitted comfortably together; they were almost always of the same scale, and they employed the same building materials. The typical rural farm dwellings of wood or brick with a slight touch of the Italianate, the Eastlake, the Queen Anne, and finally the turn-of-the-century Colonial Revival could be found along the residential streets of Minneapolis or Mankato.

Thompson House, 1865–67, St. Paul, Razed
Photo: Minnesota Historical Society.

The period from 1901 through 1918 was one of consolidation of the rural and urban scenes and marked the beginning of a sharply developing contrast between the large urban environments and the rest of the state. The Twin Cities and to a degree Duluth assumed a new economic role in business, manufacturing, large-scale milling, and processing. The urban world found itself increasingly divided into a series of classes, each with its own life-style. The upper middle class increasingly turned toward the use of historic architectural garb — the Colonial, the English, or the French — in suburban dwellings. Much of the middle middle class followed suit, but there was also a contingent which looked uneasily at the city and desired to return to the image of the simple life represented architecturally in the Craftsman Style, the California bungalow, and the Prairie School, all of which enjoyed a brief period of popularity.

Out of this brief encounter (involving only the few years from about 1908 to 1917) came the largest single group of buildings of consistently high quality in Minnesota's architectural history. Louis Sullivan's bank at Owatonna, George W. Maher's extensive work in Winona, and above all the houses, small banks, and other structures designed by Purcell and Elmslie (of the firm of Purcell, Feick, and Elmslie) pushed Minnesota once more onto the national architectural scene, as the work of Ellis had done in the 1880s.

Alongside the few Prairie Style buildings was an increasing number of boxy two-story stuccoed Craftsman houses and single-floor bungalows. These dwellings were produced almost exclusively by builder-speculators, and the suburban residential streets of Minneapolis and St. Paul were lined with them by 1920. Though not objects of beauty (and certainly not high art objects) the builders' houses were intelligently planned, reasonably well built, and made of materials which weathered well (stucco,

Christ Church, c. 1860, St. Paul, Razed.
Photo: Minnesota Historical Society.

brick, and wood); their mechanical cores, plumbing, and heating were excellent. In plan, the two-story Craftsman houses generally had an entrance at the side of the front, the living room across the front (usually with a sun room or an open porch), and the dining room and the kitchen at the rear. The stairs, the front entrance hall, and the rear entrance were often joined together in a tight communication center. The characteristic Craftsman bungalow divided itself down the middle with the family public space (living room, dining room, and kitchen) on one side and the bathroom and one or more bedrooms on the other.

The simplicity and the sparseness of the Craftsman houses did not hold any deep appeal for the upper middle class, and this segment of society followed the lead of the eastern cities in demanding buildings which openly commented on America's own past (Georgian or Federal) or its roots in Europe (English Tudor, French Provincial, Renaissance, Italian, or otherwise). Though the details and in some cases the forms of the buildings were derived from the past, their plans, mechanical cores, structure, and materials were highly workable and "modern." And the visual vocabulary of these houses did not place any intense intellectual demands on their users or those who comprehended them because their point of reference was pictorial, not literary.

By the early 1900s there was a contingent of Minnesota architects (among them Clarence H. Johnston, Sr., the firm of Hewitt and Brown, and William Channing Whitney) who had acquired the ability and the finesse to manipulate the variations of historical imagery. But some Minnesotans brought in major talent from the east and from Chicago — McKim, Mead, and White to do the new Minneapolis Institute of Arts, Burnham and Company to do buildings in Duluth and planning in Minneapolis, Ralph Adams Cram, Bertram Goodhue, and Shepley, Rutan, and Coolidge to create the correct Medieval forms, and so on.

The City Beautiful movement represents one of the high points of this pictorial tradition. The grand boulevard and the axial pattern of urban streets with squares and circles express a sense of rationalism and of man's power and control which was identical to that found in industry, business, technology, and science. The language which the movement employed — the classical tradition derived from Rome, the Renaissance, and the Baroque was a language which was openly understood by all (or almost all). The use of classical forms suggested that there was indeed an acknowledged truth, just as there was an almost universally accepted belief in science and technology. Architectural fashions come and go, but always man seems to return to the classical forms.

Minnesota did not get very far with any of the vast City Beautiful urban schemes, but a beginning was made in St. Paul with the Capitol and its surroundings, in Minneapolis with the development of the Gateway district, and in Duluth with the core of its Civic Center. There was enough in the way of building activity throughout Minnesota to ensure that by 1918 nearly every major town and small city had acquired one or more classical monuments in the form of a bank on Main Street, a library, or a county courthouse. Though these classical buildings have been derided by architectural modernists since the 1930s, it is remarkable how impressive they seem today, even when unsympathetically converted to department stores or restaurants.

During the late 1920s and 1930s building activities in the state were sporadic. The small towns generally remained static, and in some cases they actually began to decline. The changes most evident in the downtown areas or on the main streets of the small communities were the occasional modernization of existing storefronts, the injection of incandescent and neon signing, and the construction of federally funded post offices, water or power plants, and (in th

Decker House, 1912–13, Wayzata. Purcell and Elmslie. Razed.

Madison State Bank, 1913, Madison. Purcell and Elmslie. Razed.
Photo: William G. Purcell.

1930s) new schools, town halls, and recreation buildings. There was of course a major change in the manner in which the large and small communities were connected to the rural hinterland and with one another, brought about by the proliferation of the automobile and the development of highways. Gradually through the 1920s the federal, state, and county road systems were expanded, and increasingly one entered a town via the auto, not the train. The projection of the highways into the towns encouraged the spilling out of industrial and commercial activities, and eventually such activities created the familiar commercial strips.

Resortism, which had its beginnings well before 1900, began to surface as a major industry in Minnesota after the advent of the auto. It existed earlier at Lake Minnetonka, west of Minneapolis, and at White Bear Lake, northeast of St. Paul, because of the close proximity of these areas to the cities and because of the excellent rail connections. But it was in the 1920s with the advent of upper-middle-class and middle-middle-class ownership of the auto that families found they could own or rent cottages at the lake with comparative ease. Resortism in Minnesota produced endless variations on the theme of lakeshore cottage colonies, and it saw the construction of hotel-lodges on the northern lakes and along the north shore of Lake Superior. During this period resortism was almost entirely directed toward the urban population of the large cities. Architecturally, most resort buildings were plain and utilitarian; if they cultivated any image, it was that of the rustic frontier. From 1910 on one could purchase precut log cabins (usually not built of whole logs, merely employing half-cut logs as a surface dressing). Very few of the resort lodges or colonies of cabins ever reached the design level of Naniboujou Motor Lodge and Resort (east of Grand Marais) on the north shore of Lake Superior, where the architect brought the Rustic

Presby House, 1898, St. Paul. Razed. Photo: Minnesota Historical Society.

nd the Zigzag Moderne (Art Deco) to- ether in a single composition.

eriod architecture reached a peak dur- g the 1920s and 1930s as the clients, rough increased travel and knowledge, nd the architects, through much more gorous academic training and exposure Europe, began to set a standard which as impressively high. The suburban reas of Minneapolis and St. Paul blos- med forth with Colonial, English eorgian, English Tudor, and French orman houses and even occasional lediterranean/Spanish dwellings of hite stucco with tile roofs. Like the eriod houses of the years 1900–20, ese later houses were beautiful nachines for living," and their uses of e past seldom if ever compromised eir functional requirements.

istoric forms continued to be used for mmercial buildings in the 1920s, but e American Skyscraper Style with Art eco (Zigzag Moderne) detailing became the preferred style for the major office buildings in the Twin Cities. The Rand Tower (1928–29), now the Dain Tower, in Minneapolis and the Ramsey County Courthouse and the City Hall (1931–32) in St. Paul are major examples of this style not only in Minnesota but in the nation. Although an important monument of the 1920s, the Foshay Tower (1926–29) in Minneapolis was in a way a Period building; it was modeled after the Washington Monument, but it was Moderne in its overall design and detailing.

We tend to think of the 1930s and the impact of the Great Depression as being basically a period of architectural dol- drums. This was indeed true in terms of the quantity of buildings constructed, but it was a highly fascinating decade as far as design is concerned. The federal financing of the PWA program provided funding for public buildings and en- vironmental improvements which had an immense impact on the state.

Gateway Pavilion, 1916, Minneapolis. Hewitt and Brown, Razed. Photo: Minneapolis Public Library.

Introduction

Bridges, new roads, and parks were built from the northern lakes to the southeastern cities of Red Wing and Winona. New post offices, schools, and armories were constructed in cities of all sizes. In style these were normally PWA Moderne (that is, classical with a nod toward the Moderne). Without exception these public buildings were beautifully crafted; they made use of native materials, and in many cases they were embellished with Art (relief sculptures and murals) which emanated from the Federal Arts Project. Impressive examples of this legacy of architecture of the 1930s can be found in towns such as Alden in the Alden Municipal Building (1938) and at the University of Minnesota in the Bell Museum of Natural History (1940) and Coffman Memorial Union (1940, now remodeled).

The Moderne came to be used for certain types of commercial buildings in the state. For instance, because of its strong connotations of modernity and hygiene it was selected for the Forum Cafeteria as early as 1929. In its Streamline phase the Moderne became *the* style for bars, small clinic buildings (including dog and cat hospitals), and fast-food establishments. Often the Moderne married itself to some historicism, as in the White Castle hamburger shops, in which an image of a castle was presented via white porcelain panels and stainless steel — the best, as always, of the past and the present. The hygienic symbolism of the Moderne made it a natural for the residences of physicians and dentists, and almost every Minnesota town of any size seems to contain at least one white stucco Moderne house from the middle or late 1930s.

New building types oriented toward the automobile slowly came to the fore in Minnesota during the 1920s and 1930s. Service stations, like the fast-food establishments, utilized the Moderne and Period architecture. In the 1920s the brick-pier-and-canopy service station was a popular form, supplemented by

White Castle, 1935, Minneapolis. Razed 1975.

exotic forms such as Pueblo Revival; in the 1930s some oil companies turned to the image of the station as an industrial product — a Moderne box of porcelainized panels — and others experimented with the Colonial and English Cottage styles. By the end of the decade the large urban areas were on the way to creating auto-oriented supermarkets and, in a few instances, neighborhood shopping centers which ranged in imagery from the Streamline to the Colonial Revival.

A few motion picture theatres were built in the Twin Cities shortly after 1910, but many more appeared during the years 1920 through 1941. A few were in the realm of motion picture "palaces" — for instance, the Baroque Minnesota Theatre (1927, now gone) in Minneapolis and the exotic Chateau Theatre (1927) in Rochester. The depression years of the 1930s were the high point for theatres in Minnesota, as was true elsewhere in the United States. New theatres were built,

Little House, 1913-15, Deephaven. Frank Lloyd Wright. Razed 1972.

and old theatres were modernized to bring their images up to date. In style all of these theatres were Streamline Moderne, and the latest of them (constructed in about 1940) were auto-oriented with adjacent parking lots.

The number of High Art Modern buildings constructed in Minnesota before World War II was limited. Wright produced his well-known Willey House in Minneapolis in 1934, and a few Minnesota architects like Elizabeth and Winston Close and Robert Cerny produced a scattering of Modern houses in the Twin Cities. With the upswing in house construction between 1939 and 1942 the almost universally proposed form was the Colonial and specifically the eighteenth-century New England Colonial of the two-story variety or the single-floor Cape Cod cottage. Minneapolis and St. Paul suburbs such as Edina and Highland Park acquired numerous examples of these white clapboard, stone, and shingle Period houses.

In the postwar years the differences between the urban center of the Twin Cities (and the smaller one at Rochester) and the rest of the state became greater. The smaller communities remained basically static in their downtown areas. Meanwhile they did acquire new schools (usually in the postwar International Style), and in some of them a limited amount of new speculative housing was built on the periphery. By the mid-1960s the highway patterns had in many cases been changed so that the major freeways went around rather than through the communities. Shopping centers then were built at the edges of the towns, causing a decrease in the use of the old central business districts.

The general ossification of the small rural towns was, of course, a national phenomenon, and so were the changes which came about in the urban Twin Cities area — the horizontal spread of suburbia over the landscape, the creation of large-scale enclosed suburban shopping centers (Southdale, built in 1954–56 near Minneapolis, was the firs in the nation), the construction of corpo rate office structures and industrial complexes, and the development of ne patterns of urban freeways. Coupled with these optimistic and positive tran formations of the Twin Cities urban world was a negative view of its architectural past. Minneapolis almost, but not quite, succeeded in obliteratin its nineteenth- and twentieth-century past in the downtown area. In the nam of urban renewal old buildings were tor down right and left until in some sections nothing was left but bare earth. The urban freeway system transforme the city even more, and Minneapolis today is radically different from what was before 1960.

Architecturally the late 1940s through the early 1960s were a period of doldrums. The fashionable Corporate International Style brought forth dozens upon dozens of brick, concrete, and met boxes, which at best can be regarded a typical of the times and in most instances deserve no more than a passin yawn. There were a few distinguished exceptions such as Skidmore, Owings, and Merrill's H. J. Heinz Building (194 in St. Paul and General Mills Headquar ters Building (1957) outside of Minneapolis, Saarinen and Saarinen's Christ Lutheran Church (1949) in Mi neapolis and International Business Machines Building (1957–58) in Roche ter, and Marcel Breuer's church (1954 61) at St. John's University in College ville.

Domestic architecture fared much better, for after the war there was a brief renaissance, encouraged to a marked de gree by the Walker Art Center. This museum had initiated its Everyday A Gallery in 1940, and it had built its fir Idea House in 1941, preceding by sever years the houses which were built by th Museum of Modern Art and by the ca study program in Los Angeles sponsor

Minnesota Theatre, 1927, Minneapolis. Graven Mayger. Razed. Photo: Anthony Lane/Minneapolis Public Library.

by the magazine *Arts and Architecture*. By the mid-1950s Minnesota had a small contingent of apostles of the Modern in domestic architecture — Elizabeth and Winston Close, Carl Graffunder, Norman Nagle, and several others. The orientation of this group was not toward the West Coast and its post–World War II woodsy tradition but toward the Harvard-oriented school of Gropius and Breuer. Small pockets of Modern housing came into being in University Grove and on Stonebridge Boulevard in St. Paul and near Upton Avenue and Minnehaha Creek in Minneapolis.

The vast majority of single-family housing was contractor-produced speculative housing. The typical dwelling of the immediate post–World War II years was small (usually not over 1,400 square feet) and was a single story or one and a half stories in height; usually the garage was separate. These dwellings were placed on lots that were fifty to sixty feet wide. Although the lots were quite stark when the dwellings were first built, now most of them are enhanced with mature plantings. On the whole the buildings and the sites seem to work well, and visually they are quite pleasant.

The past ten years have been as different from 1965 as the 1950s were from the 1920s and 1930s. Changes have been reflected in all aspects of the environment, from city planning to a markedly changed view of the past and radically different architectural fashions. Although talked about for a long period of time, regional and statewide planning as a reality did not come about until the end of the 1960s. The transformation of downtown Minneapolis and St. Paul is almost totally a product of the past ten years. And the architectural fashion of the thinly sheathed metal International Style box (large or small) has come close to being replaced by forms which are openly more monumental and in certain ways more traditional. The brick cut-into box is currently the rage, and on the whole the quality of these recently constructed buildings is remarkably high. Clients and architects in Minnesota have not yet fully embraced the idea of reusing or recycling the past, nor have they yet departed from the traditionally serious view of themselves and their imagery. (The humor and satire of Robert Venturi and Charles Moore do not seem to be around yet.) And like their compatriots elsewhere in the country, they are just beginning to think about the requirements of environment and energy.

The Minneapolis and St. Paul metropolitan area provides probably the clearest example in Minnesota of what can be accomplished in the urban environment of a more or less typical American city. The citizens, the planners, and the architects of the Twin Cities have learned much about this process of transformation over the past ten or fifteen years, and the observant visitor is well rewarded by the opportunity to see the recent reworking of an environment and also to obtain a glimpse of Minnesota's past, which has in so many ways set the stage for this transformation.

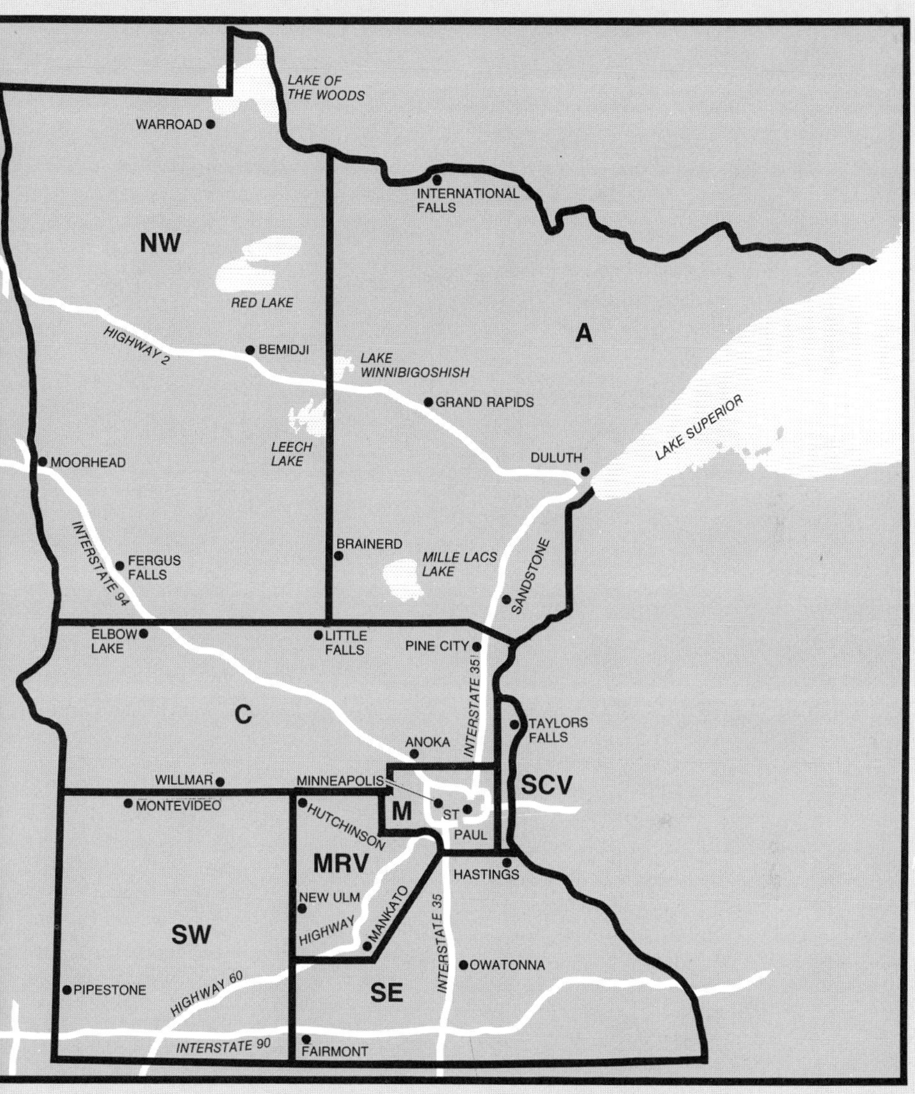
LAKE OF THE WOODS
WARROAD
INTERNATIONAL FALLS
NW
RED LAKE
A
HIGHWAY 2
BEMIDJI
LAKE WINNIBIGOSHISH
GRAND RAPIDS
LAKE SUPERIOR
LEECH LAKE
MOORHEAD
DULUTH
INTERSTATE 94
BRAINERD
MILLE LACS LAKE
FERGUS FALLS
SANDSTONE
ELBOW LAKE
LITTLE FALLS
PINE CITY
INTERSTATE 35
C
TAYLORS FALLS
ANOKA
WILLMAR
MINNEAPOLIS
SCV
MONTEVIDEO
M
ST PAUL
HUTCHINSON
MRV
HASTINGS
NEW ULM
MANKATO
HIGHWAY
SW
OWATONNA
PIPESTONE
HIGHWAY 60
SE
INTERSTATE 90
FAIRMONT

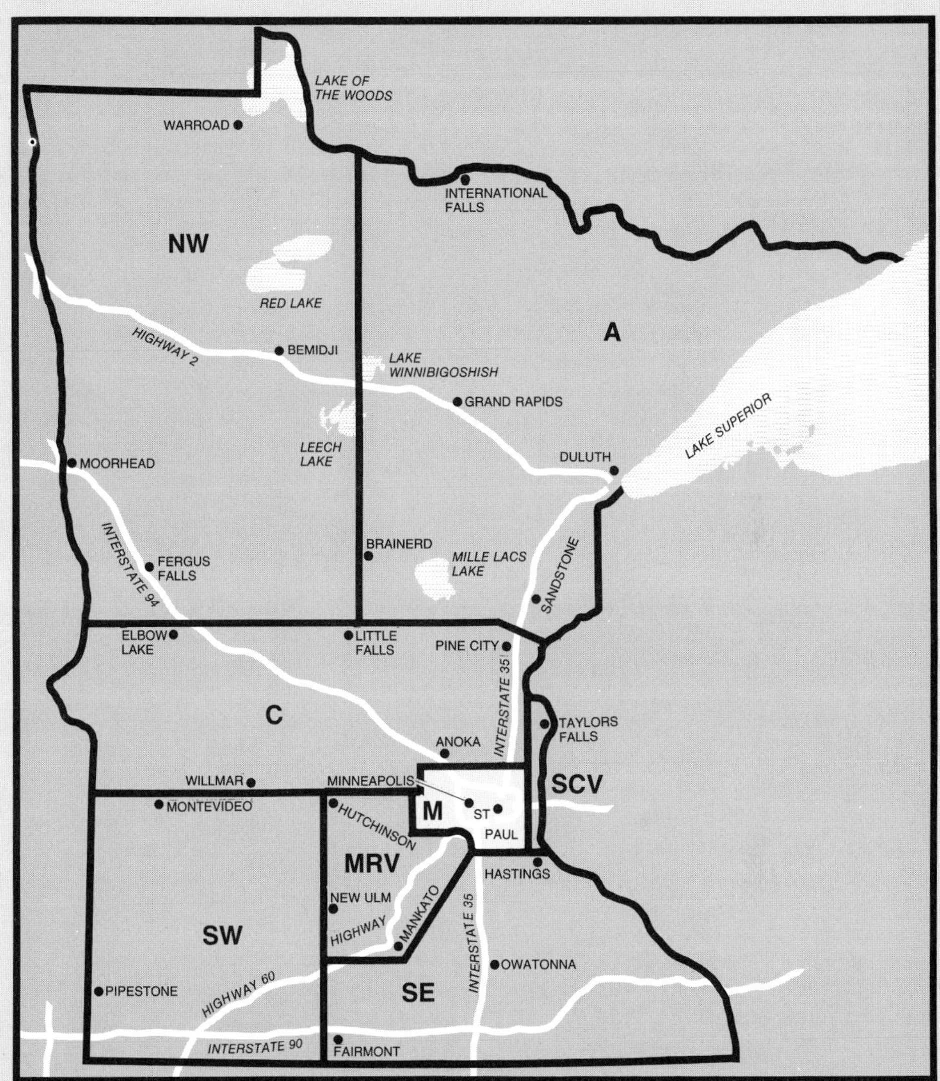

LAKE OF THE WOODS
WARROAD
INTERNATIONAL FALLS
NW
RED LAKE
A
HIGHWAY 2
BEMIDJI
LAKE WINNIBIGOSHISH
GRAND RAPIDS
LAKE SUPERIOR
LEECH LAKE
MOORHEAD
DULUTH
INTERSTATE 94
BRAINERD
MILLE LACS LAKE
FERGUS FALLS
SANDSTONE
ELBOW LAKE
LITTLE FALLS
PINE CITY
INTERSTATE 35
C
TAYLORS FALLS
ANOKA
WILLMAR
MINNEAPOLIS
SCV
MONTEVIDEO
M
ST PAUL
HUTCHINSON
MRV
HASTINGS
NEW ULM
SW
HIGHWAY
MANKATO
INTERSTATE 35
OWATONNA
PIPESTONE
HIGHWAY 60
SE
INTERSTATE 90
FAIRMONT

M-1 Minneapolis

Minneapolis, "City of Lakes," was first settled in 1848–50, and in 1854 the first of its streets were platted. A town government was established in 1858, and the community became an incorporated city in 1866. In 1872 the communities of St. Anthony and Minneapolis were unified. An important factor in the selection of this site for the city was St. Anthony Falls and the power which it made available for milling operations. With the hinterland of agricultural land lying to the west, Minneapolis quickly overtook St. Paul to become the principal commercial city of the state.

The character of Minneapolis was captured in 1871 by Ledyard Bill in *Minnesota, Its Character and Climate:* "It is perhaps, par excellence, the most wide-awake and flourishing city in the State; and, while not over a dozen years of age, exhibits, in the elegance and cost of its private dwellings, its spacious stores, its first-class and well-kept hotel, the Nicollet House, its huge factories and thundering machinery — driven by that more than Titanic power of the great and wonderous falls — evidence of solid prosperity."

Both St. Anthony and Minneapolis were initially platted with their principal streets running parallel and perpendicular to the Mississippi River, which at St. Anthony Falls ran on a northwest/southeast axis. When the city reached south to Grant and 14th Streets, a new gridiron oriented to the cardinal points of the compass was laid out. The pattern of growth in the city during the 1880s, 1890s, and early 1900s repeated the pattern found elsewhere in the United States. Commercial strips began to develop along the streets which were used by the horse-drawn streetcars beginning in 1873 and by the electric street railway lines beginning in 1889. Predictably there was a close financial relationship between those who owned and operated the street railway systems and those who speculated and developed land. Like other urban street railway systems in the United States, the system in Minneapolis was more often in the red than in the black, but this mattered little to backers who were able to make money on their investments in land. Even so, by the early 1900s Minneapolis and St. Paul had developed an impressive urban railway system which crisscrossed the cities and extended eastward as far as Stillwater on the St. Croix (1899) and westward to Lake Minnetonka (1905). Again following the national pattern, this system slowly deteriorated, and the last streetcars were replaced by buses in the mid-1950s.

In the beginning Minneapolis had little in the way of parks and open spaces. For a city which was to become nationally renowned for its parks, Minneapolis was slow to get started. Its first parkland (Murphy Park) was acquired in 1857, but the city did not get around to developing the area until 1880. In 1883, over the heavy opposition of the city council and organized labor, the voters of the city approved an extensive system of parks. The new Board of Park Commissioners appointed the well-known landscape architect Horace W. S. Cleveland to prepare a plan, which he presented later the same year. He proposed a ring of boulevards: Lyndale Avenue to the west, Lake Street to the south, a new boulevard (never built) east of the university, and a boulevard to the north (15th Avenue). Parts of the shores of Lake Harriet and Lake Calhoun were also to be developed. Few of the specifics of the plan were ever carried out, but Cleveland's proposals led to the later development of an extensive system of parks. Between 1883 and 1905 land was acquired and the major elements of the system were laid out. The period from 1906 through 1935 (when the parks were under the direction of Theodore Wirth) was one of consolidation and development. The enthusiasm for parks increased as it early became apparent that the creation of parks provided (as had been forecast) an incentive for home building.

During the 1940s and 1950s little new land was acquired by the park system, and the existing parks were only marginally maintained. In the late 1960s Robert Ruhe, the new superintendent of parks, brought in the landscape planning firm of Garrett Eckbo and Associates to revamp the system. Since then, new park shelters have been built, small neighborhood parks have received renewed attention and additional ones have been created, trees and shrubs have been planted, and the roadways through the parks have been narrowed to reduce their use as major thoroughfares. This revitalization of the parks has reflected the increased numbers of people now using the parks. Since the urban environment of Minneapolis is almost completely built up, the possibilities for expanding the park system are limited. Nevertheless, some development is taking place along the Mississippi River, and a few new neighborhood parks are being acquired. Meanwhile, urban renewal has opened up additional spaces and has injected greenery in the downtown area.

A far-reaching transformation of Minneapolis has occurred with the emergence of the urban freeway system. In the early 1930s a plan to construct a belt-line highway around the Twin Cities was initiated. Part of the plan materialized before World War II with the construction of Highway 100 below the southern boundary of Minneapolis and west of the city through Edina, St. Louis Park, Golden Valley, and Robbinsdale. But the main period of freeway building occurred in the 1960s. By 1967 Highway 35W plowed through the residential area of Minneapolis, and between 1964 and 1968 Highway 94 was built just south of the downtown area. A new ring road (Highways 494 and 694) was laid out farther from the urban core during the 1960s. The impact of the freeway has been to transform that which already existed and to encourage the growth of suburbia in all directions. Unfortunately, those who designed the system showed little concern for historic preservation or for the negative aspects of noise and air pollution.

Since 1967 Minneapolis, St. Paul, and the various suburbs have been part of the Metropolitan Council, a regional planning and coordinating agency which was established by the state legislature. The major question facing this planning body is how to control the unplanned expansion of suburbia over the rich farmlands which surround the Twin Cities.

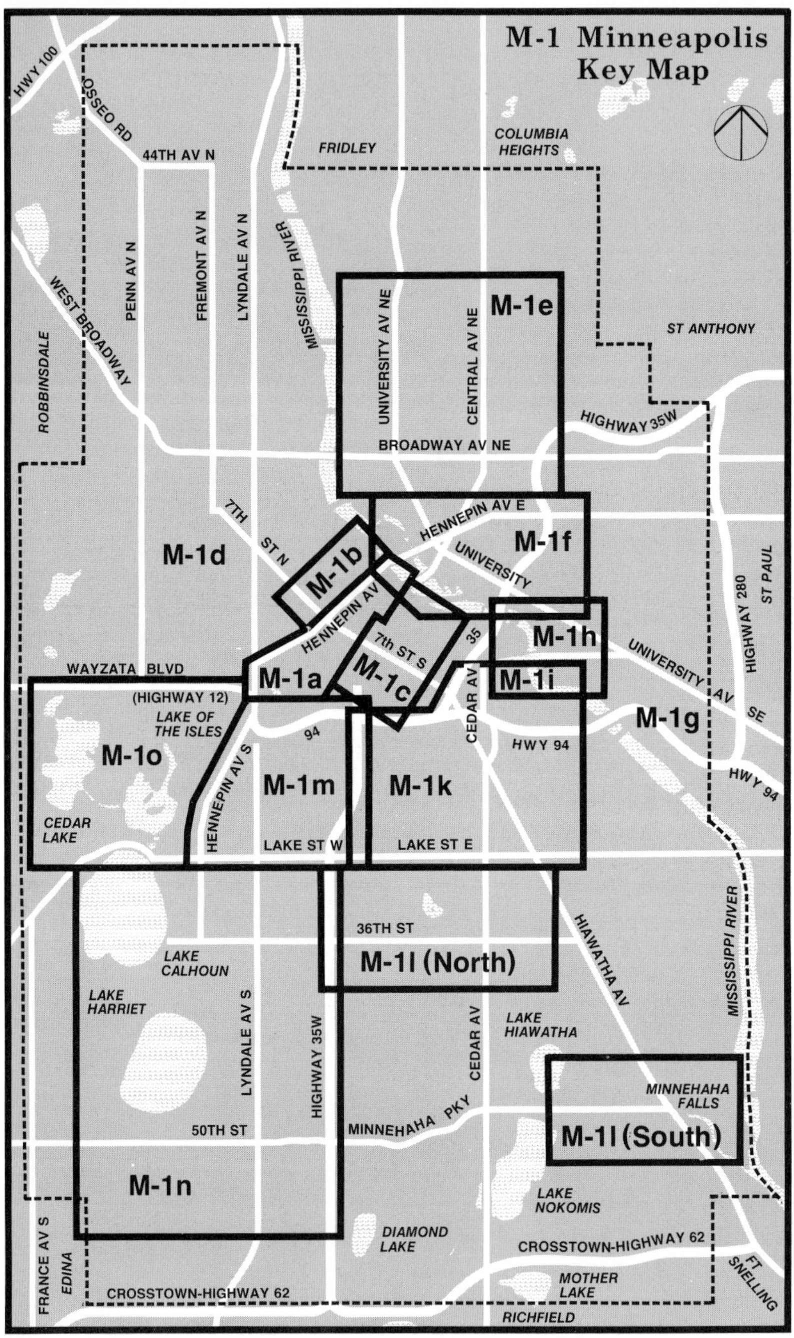
M-1 Minneapolis
Key Map
HWY 100
OSSEO RD
44TH AV N
FRIDLEY
COLUMBIA
HEIGHTS
PENN AV N
FREMONT AV N
LYNDALE AV N
MISSISSIPPI RIVER
WEST BROADWAY
ROBBINSDALE
UNIVERSITY AV NE
CENTRAL AV NE
M-1e
ST ANTHONY
HIGHWAY 35W
BROADWAY AV NE
7TH
ST N
M-1d
M-1b
HENNEPIN AV E
M-1f
UNIVERSITY
HENNEPIN AV
HENNEPIN AV
7th ST S
35
M-1h
HIGHWAY 280
ST PAUL
UNIVERSITY
AV
SE
WAYZATA BLVD
(HIGHWAY 12)
M-1a
M-1c
CEDAR AV
M-1i
LAKE OF
THE ISLES
94
HWY 94
M-1g
M-1o
HENNEPIN AV S
M-1m
M-1k
HWY 94
CEDAR
LAKE
LAKE ST W
LAKE ST E
36TH ST
M-1l (North)
HIAWATHA AV
MISSISSIPPI RIVER
LAKE
CALHOUN
LAKE
HARRIET
LYNDALE AV S
HIGHWAY 35W
CEDAR AV
LAKE
HIAWATHA
MINNEHAHA
FALLS
50TH ST
MINNEHAHA PKY
M-1l (South)
M-1n
LAKE
NOKOMIS
DIAMOND
LAKE
CROSSTOWN-HIGHWAY 62
FT
SNELLING
FRANCE AV S
EDINA
MOTHER
LAKE
CROSSTOWN-HIGHWAY 62
RICHFIELD

M-1a Downtown

)owntown Minneapolis is the product of hree economic booms — in the 1880s, he 1920s, and the period from the late 950s to the present. Each of these ursts of activity reflected strong at-empts to mold or remold certain aspects f the city into specific urban forms. Dur-ng the 1880s speculative logic man-fested itself in the gridiron scheme for treets and division of land. The open aissez-faireism of the times prompted he construction of buildings, each ighly independent of the other. Certain unctional planning considerations aturally entered into the picture — the ffice blocks clustered together on Hen-epin, Marquette, and 2nd Avenues; najor retail stores loosely gathered hemselves together on Nicollet Avenue; varehouse and similar activities were ocated east and north of 4th Avenue North and northwest of 1st Avenue Iorth; and the concentration of milling ctivity occurred along the Mississippi River northeast of 1st Street. Public uildings (including churches) were reated as private buildings, and they vere placed here and there throughout he downtown district. None of the major ublic buildings of the time — the old ederal Courthouse, the city hall and ourthouse, the public library — had any reen spaces around them, nor did they ace onto any public parks — there were one. It was then an all business, no rills world.

ike other American cities, Minneapolis vas stirred by the Chicago World's Fair ity Beautiful movement. Horace Cleve-and's 1893 plan for the city suggested ne construction of several large and pacious boulevards in the downtown rea. In 1906 a comprehensive City eautiful plan was drawn up by the Minneapolis architect John Jager (in ooperation with C. B. Stravs, C. E. dwins, and F. E. Halden). The Jager lan projected a group of public uildings around a large open square ounded by 3rd and 4th Avenues and 3rd and 4th Streets) and a five-block "public concourse" which terminated at another square with public buildings (bounded by 11th and 12th Avenues and 3rd and 4th Streets). This paper plan was followed between 1909 and 1917 by an even larger City Beautiful scheme set forth initially by the master himself, Daniel H. Burnham, and carried on after his death by Edward H. Bennett. The only part of their scheme which was fully carried out was the opening up of the Gate-way district, so that a more respectable and impressive entrance (from the rail-road station) might be provided. This area was to have been lined on both sides by Classical government buildings. The only building of this ambitious project which was actually constructed was Hewitt and Brown's Pavilion in Gateway Park (1916). World War I put an end to such "extravagant nonsense," as it was then labeled, and laissez-faireism once more asserted itself. It was during the 1920s that such buildings as the Foshay Tower, the Rand Tower, the North-western Bell Telephone Company building, and others were built. By 1930 Minneapolis, like Chicago and New York, had (in a minor way) its own skyline of skyscrapers.

The third "renaissance" began after World War II and is still going on. Abundant wealth, federal urban renewal funds, and a strong spirit of optimism and belief in the future prompted the adoption of a new set of plans for the downtown area. The first proposal en-visioned leveling the area around Washington Avenue up to 4th Street, constructing a freeway in the center, and then surrounding it in a military fashion with International Style boxes devoted primarily to governmental activities. The freeway idea was thrown out, and the use of the new buildings was mod-ified to include a mixture of public and private functions. Since the 1950s held the past in contempt, Minneapolis lost several of her major architectural monuments in the upward and onward rush for modernity — among them the famed Metropolitan Building of 1884–89 (E. Townsend Mix), Long and Kees's Public Library Building (1889), Hewitt and Brown's Gateway Building (1916), Larson and McLaren's Woolworth Store Building (1939), and others. In the rebuilding of the Gateway area, and on south on Nicollet, Marquette, and 2nd Avenues, it was not the new civic buildings which eventually emerged as the new dominant monuments but the private commercial buildings. In the Gateway itself the major landmarks are now the Northwestern National Life Insurance Building and the Federal Reserve Building. Farther uptown, there is no structure which can hold a candle to the IDS Tower. While it is true that the new Hennepin County Government Center in the eastern section of the downtown area cannot be missed, its image (except for those who know) could just as well be that of another corporate office building.

One of the greatest pluses of the renewed activities of the 1950s and 1960s has been Nicollet Mall — one of the few in the country which really works, esthetically, functionally, and financially. The current urban renewal proposals to extend the mall and other redevelopment activities down Nicollet Avenue to Loring Park will be a great asset to the city. Equally significant for the downtown area are the "skyway" pedestrian bridges which were planned in the 1960s. The skyway system presently connects the northwest side of Nicollet Mall with the south side of Marquette Avenue and on across 2nd Avenue.

On the negative side, the destruction of Hennepin Avenue and Lyndale Avenue where they joined at Loring Park and the conversion of this area into a freeway has eliminated one of the most handsome downtown spaces Minneapolis had. The relationship of the two green areas, Loring Park and The Parade, with the Basilica of St. Mary at the north end, the small triangle of terraces and steps (with Lowry's statue) on Lowry Hill to the south, and the groups of buildings stepping up Lowry Hill — St. Mark's Cathedral, the Groveland Avenue Hotel, and Hennepin Avenue United Methodist Church on the east side and the Walker Art Center and the North American Life and Casualty Company on the west side — formed a successful urban composition which is rarely found in American cities.

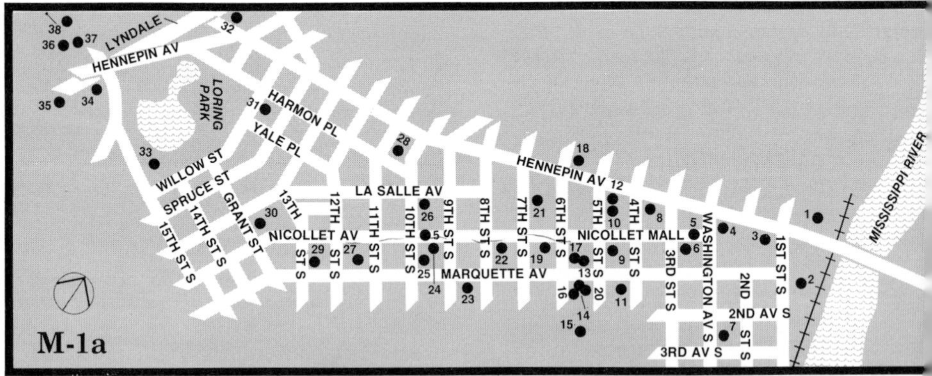

1 **Great Northern Passenger Station,** 1912
Charles S. Frost
Foot of Hennepin Avenue

The entry into most American cities was, until the late 1920s, via the railroad. The two decades from 1895 through 1915 were a heyday for the construction of Beaux Arts Classical railroad stations throughout the United States. The Minneapolis station hardly represents a high point in this architectural mode — it is cold and lacks the visual wealth of classical detail that exists in the work of McKim, Mead, and White, Daniel Burnham, and others. Still, its main waiting room is grand and dignified, as is its row of columns along Hennepin Avenue. The station and Hewitt and Brown's Gateway Pavilion (now gone) were to have been two elements in Burnham's and Bennett's City Beautiful plan (1909–17) for lower downtown Minneapolis.

2 **Post Office,** 1931–33
Magney and Tusler
100 1st Street South

The monumental Moderne on a grand scale. The Minneapolis post office indicates how this style, which we tend to think of as characteristic of the Depression years of the 1930s, was actually a product of the boom of the late 1920s. The building forms a northern visual terminal for the open space of the Gateway district.

3 **The Towers Condominiums,** 1964
John Pruyn
15–19 1st Street S

Every self-respecting urban renewal scheme of the 1950s and 1960s proposed bringing people back into the central core of the city — especially the middle middle and upper middle classes. These towers, plus those at 312 Hennepin (designed by Miller, Melby, and Hanson, 1972–73), were built to serve that purpose.With the openly flamboyant new buildings around they form a quiet urban backdrop, and on the ground level they contribute to the open space of the Gateway district.

4 **Northwestern National Life Insurance Building,** 1963
Minoru Yamasaki and Associates; Sasaki, Walker, and Associates (landscape architects)
20 Washington Avenue S

One of Yamasaki's columned, lacy buildings; a lively period piece of the late 1950s and 1960s. Its atmosphere — that of an Islamic palace — is reinforced by its fountains, terraces, and gardens. Note the interior sculpture by Harry Bertoia.

5 **Nicollet Mall,** 1958–62; 1967
Lawrence Halprin and Associates
Nicollet Avenue between Washington Avenue S and 10th Street S

The first study for the mall was made by Barton, Aschman Associates, and the planning and design were carried out by the Halprin firm. It differs from most other malls in that it is a drive-through affair, primarily for public transit. The street winds through planted areas and widened sidewalk space. The street furniture includes fountains and waiting kiosks. Sculpture, another hallmark of American downtown malls, is to be found in adjoining plazas: "Thrice" by Charles Perry, "Time Being" by Paul Granlund, and "Arcturus" by Dimitri Hadzi. The Nicollet Mall is generally conceded to be one of the most successful malls in the country. This is owing in part to the way it has been closely related to new construction and the revamping of existing buildings, to the elevated skyway bridges across adjoining streets, and to the fact that the linear nature of Nicollet still retains some motor traffic.

6 **Federal Reserve Bank Building,** 1968–72
Gunnar Birkerts and Associates
250 Marquette Avenue

Engineering and visual theatrics expressed through a huge catenary arch. Though it will be dated quickly, its drama, like that of the Foshay Tower, will make it last.

7 Federal Office Building, 1911–12; addition, 1927
James Knox Taylor
200 Washington Avenue S
Beaux Arts City Beautiful classical realized in a one-story building.

7 Federal Office Building.

8 Minneapolis Public Library, 1959
McEnary and Krafft
300 Nicollet Mall
The Cerny plan of the 1950s called for a number of municipal government buildings to be constructed along a northwest/southeast axis. The library was one of the earliest of those buildings. In design it is a pure 1950s product, tinselly and light, in quality hardly a fair replacement for Long and Kees's 1889 Romanesque Revival Public Library Building (which was torn down at this time). In front of the new building is John Rood's sculpture, "The Scroll."

9 Times Building,
1899
57 4th Street S
A miniature Beaux Arts commercial building with a rusticated base, a shaft of three arches, and an elaborate entablature for the capital. (The original building was constructed in 1884, and it was remodeled and added to several times before the major alterations of 1899.)

10 Northern States Power Company Building, 1963–64
Pietro Belluschi; Ellerbe Architects
414 Nicollet Mall
First there was the thin-skinned glass box in the late 1940s and 1950s, and then in the late 1950s and 1960s the popular approach was to close in the box and provide thin narrow windows, arranged in repetitive fashion. The NSP Building is of the latter variety.

11 Farmers and Mechanics Bank Building (now Spaghetti Emporium), 1891; 1908
Long and Kees
115 4th Street S
A rich Beaux Arts pile; the ground floor loggia was originally open, thus adding to the deep shadow patterns of the façade.

12 Lumber Exchange Building (now Upper Midwest Building), 1885
Long and Kees
425 Hennepin Avenue
This and the Masonic Temple up the street are the last of the large Richardsonian Romanesque Revival office blocks still standing in Minneapolis. The interior has been drastically remodeled over the years, but except for changes on the street level the Lumber Exchange looks as it did in the 1890s.

13 Federal Reserve Building (now National City Bank), 1922
Cass Gilbert
73 5th Street S
On top of Cass Gilbert's Beaux Arts composition Larson and McLaren added an office block (1955) in the Corporate International Style of the 1950s; in 1974 Cerny and Associates again revamped the building.

14 Bank Building, 1925
Gage and Vanderbilt
517 Marquette Avenue
The Egyptian Revival has always been a minor exotic style in America, and most of the examples of it were constructed before 1900. In this case an old building (1895) was remodeled into an Egyptian pylon in the mid-1920s. It has now been all but ruined by a pedestrian skyway (1969) which plunges right into its façade.

15 First National Bank Building, 1959
Holabird, Root, and Burgee; Thorshov and Cerny
120 6th Street S
The Miesian metal and glass cage, via Skidmore, Owings, and Merrill; introduced for the first time on a large scale into the Twin Cities.

16 Rand Tower (now Dain Tower), 1928–29
Holabird and Root
527 Marquette Avenue

The Zigzag Moderne (Art Deco) office tower of the late 1920s. Holabird and Root of Chicago did numerous designs such as this throughout the Midwest. The Foshay Tower, the Northwestern Bell Telephone Building, and the Rand Tower dominated the skyline of downtown Minneapolis through the mid-1950s. Note the relief sculpture and the architectural ornamentation.

17 Farmers and Mechanics Bank, 1941
McEnary and Krafft
88 6th Street S

The Moderne of the 1930s applied to a small bank building: a near-perfect compromise between the dignity and reserve of the classical and the desire for modernness. A new tower was added to the building in 1961.

18 Masonic Temple Building (now Merchandise Building), 1888–89
Long and Kees
528 Hennepin Avenue

An eight-story Richardsonian Romanesque Revival building. Originally its two corner towers were crowned by swirling-patterned onion domes. The general effect of the building is ponderous, in part because variety, not simplicity, was cultivated. The building, like the Lumber Exchange, is a major downtown monument, and it sits waiting for sensitive renovation.

19 Donaldson's Department Store Building, 1945–47
Larson and McLaren
601 Nicollet Mall

A five-story section of the store was repackaged in the Moderne of the 1940s with horizontal bands of glass-brick windows and thin geometric lines on the surface of its new skin of thin stone. The new styling is identical with that which was then being produced in everything from autos to electric razors — even the contrast of its smooth surfaces against the script lettering is indicative of the period.

20 First National/Soo Line Building (now Soo Line Building), 1914
105 5th Street S

The classical orders (plus other details) applied to the tall office block.

21 Forum Cafeteria, 1929
George B. Franklin
36 7th Street S

The Zigzag Moderne (Art Deco) at its best — all black glass and a silvered metal. A similar, less exuberant Moderne cafeteria, Miller's Cafeteria (by McEnary and Larson, 1935), disappeared in the post–World War II years, and the Forum is the only one left.

•22 IDS Center, 1968–73
Philip Johnson and John Burgee; Edward F. Baker
80 8th Street S

The IDS Tower has replaced the Foshay Tower as *the* landmark of Minneapolis. In scale it has no equal; its fifty-one stories are 775 feet high, and in addition to office space it provides a nineteen-story hotel, a parking garage for 525 cars, and the famous eight-story interior Crystal Court. Its slightly angled surfaces remind one of a late 1960s Mercedes-Benz radiator grill — all well done and expensive. As a rational solution to the special needs of the downtown area the tower itself (not its lower levels) poses many questions, but it is difficult to question its success as a symbol.

23 Foshay Tower, 1926–29
Magney and Tusler; Hooper and Janusch
821 Marquette Avenue

"When a skyscraper is also of unusual design," noted a public relations release in 1929, "such an added feature [as a unique design] serves only to make it more outstanding — it often then becomes a landmark — widely known," and indeed the Foshay Tower has become widely known over the years. If Adolf Loos could submit a Doric column as a building in the Chicago Tribune competition, why not be more American and use the obelisk form of the Washington Monument for a building? Like most skyscrapers of the 1920s, the Foshay Tower married utility and business with historic imagery. It has "certified aerial beacons," a two-level basement garage, banks of elevators, and other conveniences. Within this 447-foot, 32-story tower is a mild array of Zigzag Moderne ornamentation.

24 Young-Quinlan Building, 1927
Magney and Tusler; Frederick Ackerman
901 Nicollet Mall

The Forum Cafeteria represents the way-out wing of the Moderne of the 1920s; this building stands at the other extreme — it is delicate, refined, and French. Note the exterior relief sculpture.

25 Mural, Schmitt Music Center Building, 1972
Jill Sprangers
88 10th Street S

A bare side-wall of the brick building is now covered — in black and white — with a version of the musical score of Ravel's *Gaspard de la Nuit*. It contains one error.

26 Kate Dunwoody Hall, 1964
Brooks Cavin
52 10th Street S

The interior spaces are oriented around a fountained interior court lighted by an extensive skylight; externally the low three-story building with its plain brick walls and arched openings is suggestive of the Colonial Revival.

27 Orchestra Hall, 1974
Hammel, Green, and Abrahamson; Hardy, Holtzman, and Pfeiffer; Cyril M. Harris (acoustical consultant)
1111 Nicollet Avenue

There seems to be general agreement that the hall itself is highly successful, especially in its acoustics. As a design, the building seems committed in several different directions — to the exposed-ducts-and-pipes school (nonmonumental forms of the early 1970s) and to the more traditional brick vocabulary of the 1960s. The lobby expresses the former, the auditorium the latter. To the west is Peavey Park Plaza, a sunken park which intervenes between the Orchestra Hall and the Westminster Presbyterian Church. At the moment its effect is overwhelmingly concrete, but maybe nature, in the form of trees and shrubs, will win out.

27 Orchestra Hall.

28 First Baptist Church, 1887–88
Long and Kees
Northwest corner 10th Street S at Harmon Place

A Romanesque Revival church with a Gothic tower (a new, not very successful open spire has been added to the tower). When built, it was described as modified Gothic in style — but if it is Gothic, it is Gothic with a dose of Richardsonian Romanesque. Articles written about the church when it was dedicated noted that it formed "a splendid pile."

29 Westminster Presbyterian Church, 1896–98
Charles S. Sedgwick
1201 Nicollet Avenue

Loosely English Gothic, with its rose windows and paired towers. The parish house and chapel added in 1936–37 (by Magney and Tusler) along 12th Street are more correct in their interpretation of the English Gothic. Formerly there was an especially fine Sunday School room in the building designed by Purcell, Feick, and Elmslie — the room is still there, but the fireplace, the windows, the bookcases, and the furniture have been gradually eliminated over the years.

30 Hamburger Shop, 1935
Southwest corner Nicollet Avenue and Grant Street

During the 1930s Minneapolis and St. Paul were dotted with five-cent hamburger stands. Often, like the White Castle stands, they were in the image of a miniature castle, achieved in hygienic white glazed brick or porcelain panels. Though these hamburger shops always had a small counter space, they were fundamentally designed as places where one could buy hamburgers "to go" (in the White Castle shops the hamburgers were placed in their own white cardboard castle boxes). Two other hamburger shops — we hope they are still there — are located nearby on the southwest corner of 10th Street and 7th Avenue South and on the southwest corner of 10th Street and Grant Street.

31 **Smith House** (now a mortuary), 1887
William Channing Whitney
1403 Harmon Place

A rare surviving Richardsonian Romanesque dwelling in red sandstone.

32 **Basilica of St. Mary,** 1907–25
Emmanuel L. Masqueray
Hennepin Avenue at Lyndale Avenue

Both the Minneapolis and the St. Paul cathedrals are magnificently sited. The location of the Minneapolis basilica worked out far better when Hennepin Avenue and Lyndale Avenue were not freeways, for then the church looked down Hennepin and Lyndale, with the open space of Loring Park on one side, at the classical terraced shrine with Lowry's statue on the hill (the shrine and the statue have been removed). The Neo-Baroque imagery of the basilica is meant to overawe — as an object in space and internally — and it succeeds admirably in its goal.

32 Basilica of St. Mary.

33 **Loring Park Shelter** (1889) and **•Pavilion** (1906)
Southwest corner Harmon Place and Willow Place

Two popular images for park buildings — the shelter in Eastlake and the pavilion utilizes the turn-of-the-century exoticism of the California Mission Style.

33 Loring Park Shelter.

34 **Cathedral Church of St. Mark (Episcopal),** 1908–11
Hewitt and Brown
519 Oak Grove Street

English Gothic imagery, much simplified, both internally and externally; within there are two windows by Charles Connick.

35 **Hennepin Avenue United Methodist Church,** 1914
Hewitt and Brown
511 Groveland Avenue

Atop the broad "Akron" type of auditorium is a highly picturesque adaptation of the central octagonal lantern from Ely Cathedral in England.

36 **North American Life and Casualty Company,** 1946–47
Lang and Raugland
1750 Hennepin Avenue

An early post–World War II Corporate International Style building. Its high point, then and now, is the stone buffalo on the terrace (by John K. Daniels, 1948).

37 Walker Art Center, 1969–71
Edward Larrabee Barnes
Vineland Place at Lyndale Avenue

Barnes sheathed the exterior of the building in dark bronze glazed brick. In form it appears as a series of blank rectangular volumes; internally the principal exhibition spaces are arranged as alternating steps, each overlooking the other. Functionally, and as a designed object, the building is unquestionably the major post–World War II monument in downtown Minneapolis. The first building for the Walker Art Center was built in 1928, and in style it was Byzantine/Spanish. This in turn was remodeled in 1940 to convey the new image of the institution as a gallery of avant-garde modern art, architecture, and design. The 1969–71 building brought all of this up to date. Next door, connected to it by a glass wing, is Ralph Rapson's Guthrie Theatre (1962–63). The auditorium functions well. Externally the building had a charm of its own with its complex pattern of fins; their removal in 1974 has hardly helped the exterior of the building.

37 Walker Art Center.

38 Parade Hockey Rink, 1973–74
Adkins-Jackels Associates
Kenwood Parkway at Emerson Avenue S

Curved walls of brick with wood above enclose an indoor hockey rink. Its modest form does not protrude onto the open space of The Parade.

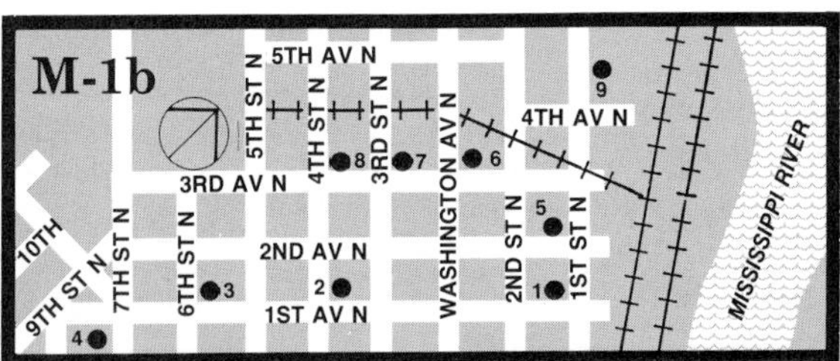

M-1b Downtown to the West

1 Minneapolis Van and Warehouse Company Building, 1904
Cass Gilbert
106 1st Avenue N

A smooth-skinned red brick cube. The low relief reveals with pointed arches cut into the surface and the windows with pointed arches give the whole a mildly Gothic appearance.

2 Newell Store Building, c. 1890
W. H. Dennis
300 1st Avenue N

Richardsonian Romanesque made classical by the use of Renaissance ornamentation. Next door, at 314 1st Avenue North, is a small four-story building which is also Romanesque.

3 **Butler Brothers Warehouse** (now Butler Square), 1906, 1973–74
Harry Jones; Miller, Hanson, and Westerbeck
100 6th Street N

An impressive example of the conversion of an existing structure to new use. The interior is now organized around an eight-story skylighted court; the original heavy wood timbering has been cleaned and left in place. Joseph Michels in his Wood's Chocolate Shop (1975) has added what is really needed in the building — a lightness of touch and a little humor. The external renovation has been well done, except that the glass should not have been brought close to the exterior brick surface — the narrow vertical panels needed the depth which existed in the original design.

3 Butler Brothers Warehouse (now Butler Square).

4 **Greyhound Bus Terminal** (now Uncle Sam's Nite Club), 1936
Lang and Raugland
29 7th Street N

A two-story Streamline Moderne building which awaits restoration. Band windows and curved corners, once resplendent with stainless steel trim and glass brick.

5 **Commercial Block,** 1890
106 2nd Avenue N

A four-story store and office block in the Italianate Style. The walls are divided into panels by the slightly projecting engaged piers.

6 **Commercial Block,** c. 1890
Northeast corner 3rd Avenue N and Washington Avenue N

As a design, certainly one of the most successful versions of Richardsonian Romanesque to be found in the Twin Cities. Some of the windows terminate in slightly pointed arches.

7 **Hayer Building,** 1886
Joseph Haley
250 3rd Avenue N

A six-story building of rough-surfaced limestone; classical in composition with each floor treated as a horizontal band.

8 **Commercial Block,** 1887
324 3rd Avenue N

Three recessed arches rise from the ground and are carried up three floors; the top floor is punctuated by a band of small windows. Coupled columns occur on the piers which support the main arches.

9 **Warehouse Building,** 1896
428 1st Street N

Richardsonian Romanesque with an arched, recessed staircase, the design of which would seem to have been taken directly from Richardson's earlier work in Boston.

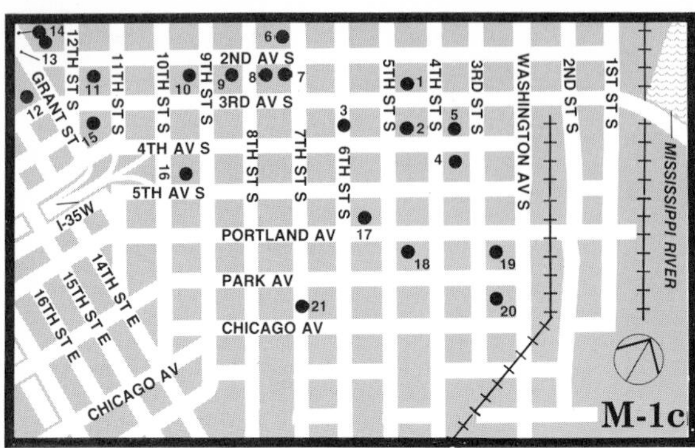

M-1c Downtown to the East

1 **Northwestern Bell Telephone Company Building,** 1930–31
Hewitt and Brown
224 5th Street S

A twenty-six-story example of the American Perpendicular Style (Zigzag Moderne) of the late 1920s, which was perfected in New York by Raymond Hood. Its set back, vertical shaft design was the rage throughout the United States by 1930. The present equipment on the roof is all post-1960, and it hardly helps the design.

2 **City Hall and Hennepin County Courthouse,** 1888–1905
Long and Kees
Northeast corner 3rd Avenue S and 5th Street S

2 City Hall and Hennepin County Courthouse.

Richardson's Allegheny County Courthouse in Pittsburgh served as the prototype for this design by Long and Kees. Although the courthouse in Minneapolis does not reveal the strength found in Richardson's work, it is still one of the great monuments of the nineteenth-century Romanesque Revival. Its tower once commanded the city's skyline, but now the whole building is like a top, dwarfed by the Hennepin County Government Center on the other side of 5th Street. The interior court is well worth a visit. Don't miss the outrageously overscaled sculpture, "Father of Waters," by Larkin Goldsmith Mead.

3 **Hennepin County Government Center,** 1967–73
John Carl Warnecke Associates; Peterson, Clark, and Associates
Southeast corner 3rd Avenue S and 5th Street S

An expensive piece of early 1960s sculpture enlarged beyond belief, the new Hennepin County Government Center is meant to be an impressive high art object. Two L-shaped volumes almost meet, separated only by glass which covers parts of the interior court. Sixth Street plows through the building on another axis (as in the 1920s City of the Future), compounding the apparently tenuous connection of the building to its site. Symbolically and factually the building poses many problems — worst of all, it has visually destroyed the neighboring courthouse. As a symbol the building suggests the preeminence of bureaucracy, but civic virtue is nowhere to be found, within it or without.

4 **Chamber of Commerce Building,** (now Grain Exchange), 1900–1902
Kees and Colburn
400 4th Street S

A ten-story Sullivanesque office block which shows early utilization of the steel frame.

5 **Flour Exchange,** 1892–93, 1909
Long and Kees
310 4th Avenue S

An early office block which developed out of the Chicago School of Burnham and Root, Adler and Sullivan, and others. Though the arched entrance is Richardsonian with a nod to Sullivan, the building's simplicity and the amount of wall space given to windows points to the work of John Root and others. The first four floors were built in 1892–93, and the upper floors were added in 1909. The brick surfaces of the building are now painted and the visually important cornice (1909) has been removed.

6 **Baker Block,** c. 1926
Larson and McLaren
706 2nd Avenue S

A richly detailed façade, more Byzantine in spirit than anything else, although when it was built it was described as both Gothic and Romanesque. Like many similar Period Revival commercial blocks of the 1920s, the Baker Block was sheathed in an ornamental surface of terra-cotta and brick with a low glaze, and it has held up very well both esthetically and physically.

7 **Lutheran Brotherhood Building,** 1954–55
Perkins and Will
701 2nd Avenue S

This was the first large-scale example of the post–World War II Corporate International Style buildings constructed in Minneapolis. The ground floor of stone is recessed, so that the thin, fragile box of metal and glass above it seems to float over the site. The rounded corners suggest that this Chicago firm hadn't quite thrown aside the Streamline Moderne of the 1930s and 1940s.

8 **Minneapolis Club,** 1907, 1911, 1920
Attrib. Hewitt and Brown
729 2nd Avenue S

Collegiate Gothic in brick, just right for the image of an exclusive upper-class club.

9 **St. Olaf's Catholic Church,** 1953–54
Thorshov and Cerny
805 2nd Avenue S

The bland 1950s making a real effort to be modern. The main architectural interest of the complex is • the "Chapel on the Street" (at 824 2nd Avenue South), designed in 1971–72 by Frederick Bentz–Milo Thompson and Associates. Within one finds a superb geometry of wood culminating in circles.

10 **Service Station** (now abandoned), c. 1925
Southeast corner 2nd Avenue S and 9th Street

A two-pier service station covered by a Japanese turned-up tile roof with miniature dormers.

11 **Ivy Tower,** 1930
Thomas R. Kimball
1115 2nd Avenue S

An office tower squeezed down to a small size. The detailing of the building and its rough pebble surfaces suggest Vienna rather than New York. A very urbane building.

12 **Minneapolis Auditorium and Convention Hall,** 1925–27
Croft and Boerner
Grant Street E between Stevens and 3rd Avenues

A looming bulk which cannot be overlooked — not a very handsome building, except in its lush, almost Spanish Revival terra-cotta ornamentation. The new additions to the building are even worse than the original. What is needed is a replanning of the avenues around the auditorium and above all the introduction of substantial planting material.

13 **Wesley Temple Building,** 1928
A. B. Boyer
123 Grant Street E

A thirteen-story Zigzag Moderne office building — the angular, stylized human heads set in the lower part of the façade are well worth a visit.

14 Wesley United Methodist Church, 1889–90
Warren H. Hayes
1st Avenue S and Grant Street E

Richardsonian Romanesque with a large Akron-plan auditorium.

15 Minneapolis Area Vocational-Technical Institute, 1932, 1940
Edward Enger
1101 3rd Avenue S

The Zigzag Moderne with pre-Columbian ornamentation. The interest in pre-Columbian architecture was strong during the 1920s, and it readily crept into Moderne ornamentation.

16 House, c. 1870
913 5th Avenue S

The only Italianate dwelling still existing in the downtown Minneapolis area. The house is of the central-gable type with a single-story porch across the front.

17 Minneapolis Armory, 1935–36
P. C. Bettenburg
500 6th Street S

A PWA Moderne auditorium with great commanding eagles over the main entrance. Within are examples of Federal Art Project murals (in the Trophy Room) by Elsa Jemne and Lucia Wiley.

17 Minneapolis Armory.

18 Minneapolis Star and Tribune Building, 1946–47
Larson and McLaren
425 Portland Avenue S

What we see today is the 1946–47 remodeling of an existing building. The architects used the vocabulary of the Streamline Moderne — alternating bands of brick and black granite, glass bricks, and elevator doors with symbolic ornamentation.

19 Northern Implement Company (now Pittsburgh Plate Glass Company), 1910–11
Kees and Colburn
616–622 3rd Street S

A Richardsonian Romanesque building, simplified along the lines of Sullivan's Walker Warehouse in Chicago.

20 Advance Thresher and Emerson Newton Plow Buildings, 1900, 1904
Kees and Colburn
700 and 708 3rd Street S

Two six-story blocks treated as a single composition. The design is essentially classical, but the placement of ornament and the composition of three recessed bays which continue up to the top floor is Sullivanesque.

21 Hennepin County Medical Center (Metropolitan Medical Center), 1972–75
Liebenberg, Kaplan, Glotter Associates; S. C. Smiley and Associates; Thorsen and Thorshov Associates
7th Street S at Park Avenue

A bewildering composition of boxes suspended over smaller boxes, bridges and parts of buildings going over streets. A highly styled and restless piece of 1970s architecture.

M-1d North Side

Minneapolis north and west of the Mississippi is an old residential area which has been sliced up in various ways by commercial strip development. As early as 1875, a streetcar line with horse-drawn vehicles extended up Washington Avenue North to Plymouth Avenue North. By 1892 the northern area, like the northeastern section, was crisscrossed with street railway lines and commercial (primarily retail) developments. Within the northern section there were several large parks: North Commons (Golden Valley Road and Morgan Avenue North), Farview Park (26th Avenue North and Lyndale Avenue North), and Folwell Park (Logan Avenue North and 36th Avenue North). At the city limits to the west is the extensive Theodore Wirth Park (acquired in 1889, 1907, and 1911). At the city's northern boundaries Webster Park and Victory Memorial Drive (1920) constitute extensive green belts which are mainly used by those living outside the area. Though there are other small nooks of greenery, the northern section of the city never obtained its full share. This is presently being remedied by the provision of open spaces around new school projects, new public housing, and some new neighborhood parks.

1 **Sumner Field Housing Project,** 1938
Magney, Tusler, and Setter
Dupont and Emerson Avenues N between Olson Memorial Highway and 11th Avenue N

The only PWA Public Housing Project built in the Twin Cities during the Depression. It consists of absolutely plain two-story brick boxes with flat roofs, arranged around open spaces. The present maturity of the plantings and the well-kept appearance of the project help to divert attention from the military dullness of the project. Nearby, reaching to Plymouth Avenue, are a number of public housing projects including Thorshov and Cerny's 1960 Lyndale Homes Housing Project, and Close Associates' housing for the elderly (1959–61).

2 **St. Joseph's Catholic Church,** 1885–86
Carl Struck
1127 4th Street N

Severe German Romanesque in brick, with a slight hint of the then-current Richardsonian Romanesque.

3 **Franklin Junior High School,** 1972
Thorsen and Thorshov
1501 Aldrich Avenue N

Le Corbusier and the English New Brutalists, with a bang.

4 **North Branch, Minneapolis Public Library,** 1894
Frederick Corser
1834 Emerson Avenue N

Gothic, not late nineteenth-century American Gothic but English Arts and Crafts Gothic of the late 1880s.

5 **Graffunder House,** 1949
Carl Graffunder
1719 Xerxes Avenue N

A Minnesota version of the woodsy, post-World War II San Francisco Bay tradition.

6 **North Star Elementary School,** 1974–75
Hammel, Green, and Abrahamson
2400 Girard Avenue N

A two-story horizontal volume punctured by large-scale concrete pylons with semicircular ends. The building is set in a block-long berm with courtyards below the grade.

7 **Birdhouses,** date unknown
Southeast corner 33rd and Sheridan Avenues N

A real village of birdhouses, set on top of a garage.

7 Birdhouses.

8 **North High School,** 1971–72
Caudill, Rowlett, and Scott; Larson and McLaren.
Northwest corner Fremont and 17th Avenues N

The Neo-Fortress Style; two-story cut-out boxes and courtyards; all well done.

9 **Public Housing for the Elderly,** 1971
Zejdlik, Harmala, Hysell, and Delapp
1314 44th Avenue N (at Humboldt Avenue)

Apartment units of six-story brick units; the upper three floors are pulled out and overhang the floors below; three angled glass units connect the brick-sheathed units. Well scaled for this section of the city.

M-1e Northeast

Northeast Minneapolis is fundamentally a neighborhood of middle-middle-and lower-middle-class single-family housing. The areas on and around East Hennepin Avenue and Central Avenue are commercial, and industrial and commercial uses occur along parts of the Burlington Northern Railroad tracks and along the river. The street railway system reached up into the area quite early and by 1900 had established an east/west, north/south grid which provided excellent service. Small neighborhood shopping areas developed along these routes, especially at points where two lines met. The southern half of this section of Minneapolis has six well-distributed neighborhood parks, and to the north is the extensive Columbia Park (acquired in 1892), Deming Heights Park, and the system of linear open space provided by St. Anthony Parkway.

From the beginning the single-family housing was almost exclusively builder-designed. Most of it was built from 1900 through the early 1920s. The single-family housing around much of St. Anthony Boulevard and north to the city limits was built in the late 1920s and early 1930s or after World War II. The houses of this period tend to be vaguely English with suggestions of half-timbering, stuccoed walls, gables, and steep roofs. Some are bungalows, others have two stories. The post–World War II single-family houses are smaller, and almost all of them have only one story. Units of public housing are to be found at 1717 Washington Street Northeast (1971), at 311 University Avenue Northeast (1962), and at four other locations.

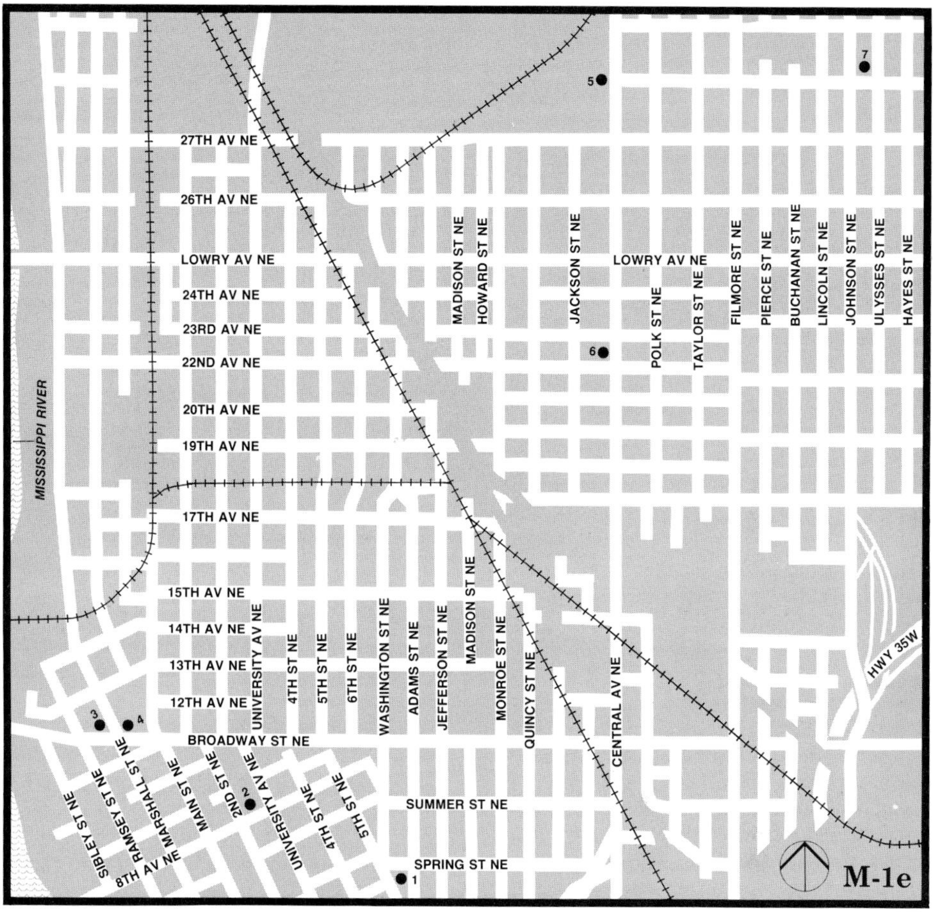
27TH AV NE
26TH AV NE
LOWRY AV NE
24TH AV NE
23RD AV NE
22ND AV NE
20TH AV NE
19TH AV NE
17TH AV NE
15TH AV NE
14TH AV NE
13TH AV NE
12TH AV NE
BROADWAY ST NE
SUMMER ST NE
SPRING ST NE
MISSISSIPPI RIVER
MADISON ST NE
HOWARD ST NE
JACKSON ST NE
LOWRY AV NE
POLK ST NE
TAYLOR ST NE
FILMORE ST NE
PIERCE ST NE
BUCHANAN ST NE
LINCOLN ST NE
JOHNSON ST NE
ULYSSES ST NE
HAYES ST NE
UNIVERSITY AV NE
4TH ST NE
5TH ST NE
6TH ST NE
WASHINGTON ST NE
ADAMS ST NE
JEFFERSON ST NE
MADISON ST NE
MONROE ST NE
QUINCY ST NE
CENTRAL AV NE
HWY 35W
SIBLEY ST NE
RAMSEY ST NE
MARSHALL ST NE
MAIN ST NE
2ND ST NE
UNIVERSITY AV NE
4TH ST NE
5TH ST NE
8TH AV NE
M-1e

1 **Webster Intermediate School,** 1973–74
Frederick Bentz-Milo Thompson and Associates
425 5th Street NE

Angles, wedges, and cut-out openings in a pristine white brick building. The interior with its open plan, bridges, and different levels suggest a fanciful and playful world for its occupants; serious architecture, but with a suggestion of gaiety for the child. Probably the finest school design in Minnesota.

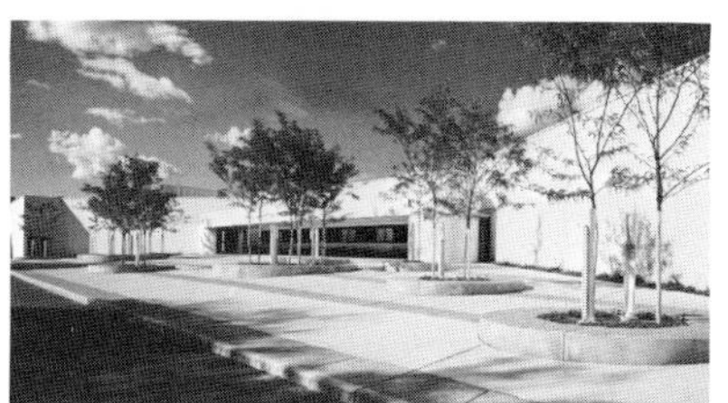

1 Webster Intermediate School. Photo: Denes A. Saari.

2 **St. Anthony of Padua,** 1861
804 2nd Street NE

Gothic revival in stone with a modern Romanesque front.

3 **Grain Belt Brewery,** 1870s and later
1215 Marshall Avenue NE

The main building is in the French Second Empire Style, the warehouse building is in the Italianate Style, and the office building is Richardsonian Romanesque. Taken together, they are a picturesque nineteenth-century assemblage.

4 **Northeast State Bank and Park,** 1974
Hirsch Associates; Arvin W. Malin (landscape architect)
77 Broadway NE

A commendable example of multiple land use; the park area is used for automobile parking from 9:00 to 3:00 daily, but the rest of the time it is a neighborhood park for children. The paved surface has been patterned to form a variety of children's play areas.

5 **Shoreham Shop, Soo Line,** 1912
Kenyon and Maine
Northwest corner 28th and Central Avenues NE

The Prairie idiom applied to a railroad repair shop building.

6 **Northeast Branch, Minneapolis Public Library,** 1971–72
Hammel, Green, and Abrahamson
2200 Central Avenue NE

The north section of the building is in line with the adjacent store fronts; the south wing is set back and suggests public use. The interior of the building displays a fine relationship between the warm brick walls and the wood detailing.

7 **Hollywood Theatre,** 1937
Liebenberg and Kaplan
2815 Johnson Street NE

It is amazing how many variations this firm was able to come up with while working within the Streamline Moderne Style of the 1930s. This one is more sharp and angular than most.

M-1f Southeast

Through much of its history southeast Minneapolis has been divided into a number of separate areas: a milling and commercial district along much of the river, extending inland to 2nd Street Southeast; Nicollet Island, which has always been a mixture of industrial and residential developments; a very old residential area (parts of it going back to the 1850s) from 2nd Avenue Southeast to 15th Avenue Southeast with a commercial strip at the west side along Central Avenue and Hennepin Avenue; another residential area north of the Burlington Northern tracks; the University of Minnesota and its appendage of Dinkytown, centered around 4th Street Southeast and 14th Avenue Southeast; the residential area of Prospect Park; and an extensive commercial and industrial area to the east which forms the Minneapolis section of the Midway district. Since 1967 Highway 35W (parts of which are still under construction) has plunged through the heart of the residential area.

Although the district from 2nd Avenue Southeast to 15th Avenue Southeast was originally a residential area of single-family housing, it has always had a few multiple-family housing units. Some of its streets, such as 5th Street Southeast, were quite fashionable from the 1880s to the early 1900s, and they still contain a number of upper-middle-class houses of brick and wood. But for over fifty years this area has been going downhill, and many of the older dwellings have been torn down and replaced with multiple housing. Currently there is an interest in restoring what still remains of this pre-1900 past. With one high-rise structure, The Chateau on 13th Avenue Southeast, already in the area, however, it is likely that more high-density housing is on the way.

Milling district.

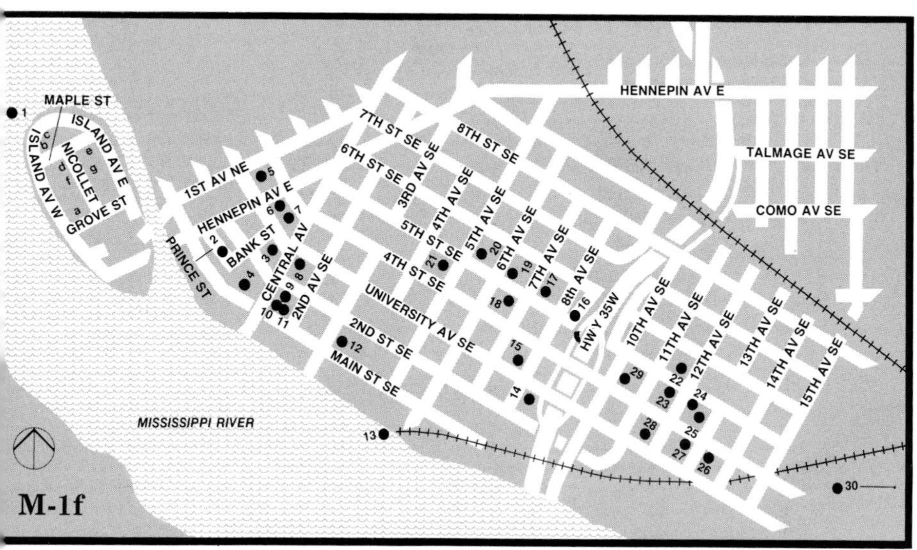

Nicollet Island
Off Hennepin Avenue E

In the nineteenth century the northern two-thirds of Nicollet Island was an important residential district of the city; by the early 1900s it had started to decay, and by the 1930s most of the single-family and multiple-family housing had fallen into disrepair. A proposal has been made to bring this section of the island back as a residential district by building new housing units there and by restoring many of the existing buildings.

Grove Street Flats.

(a) **Grove Street Flats,** 1870s
2–16 Grove Street
A three-story raised-basement building in the French Second Empire Style.

(b) **Griswold House #1,** 1891
Attrib. Frederick Corser
107-109 Island Avenue W
A Queen Anne dwelling.

(c) **Weinard House,** c. 1878
115 Island Avenue W
An Italianate house of the central-gable type.

(d) **Griswold House #2,** 1886
Attrib. Frederick Corser
11 Maple Place
A double house in the Queen Anne style.

(e) **House,** c. 1888
27 Maple Place
A plain dwelling with a mansard roof.

(f) **Mayell House,** c. 1874
93 Nicollet Avenue
A mixture of Greek and Italianate.

(g) **Barquist-Holmberg House,** 1881–82
167–169 Nicollet Avenue
A brick double house.

2 **First Universalist Church** (now Our Lady of Lourdes), 1857
21 Prince Street SE

This stone entrance-tower church was acquired by a French Catholic congregation in 1887 after the rear half of the building and the steeple had been added (1881). The present brick front entrance and niche were added in 1914.

3 **Godfrey House,** 1848
Chute Square: University Avenue SE between Bank Street and Central Avenue

A classic one-and-half-story Greek Revival cottage like those in New England and Ohio.

4 **Coca-Cola Bottling Company Building,** 1946
Ernest H. Schmidt and Company
124 Bank Street

The Streamline Moderne of the 1930s carried over into post–World War II years; horizontal bands of glass brick and rounded corners.

5 **Chute Building,** c. 1870s
301 Hennepin Avenue E

A three-story Ruskinian Gothic building; somewhat modernized in 1900.

5 Chute Building.

6 **Bank Building,** 1921
Long, Lamoreaux, and Thorshov
Southwest corner Hennepin Avenue E and 4th Street SE

A Beaux Arts bank building produced by the remodeling in 1921.

7 **White Castle Hamburger Shop,** 1936
Northwest corner Central Avenue and 4th Street SE

One of the few prefabricated White Cas-tles with white porcelain panels still exis ing in the Twin Cities. This one was orig inally located at 616 Washington Avenu Southeast; it was moved to this site in 1951.

8 **Pillsbury Branch, Minneapolis Publi Library** (now Doctors' Diagnostic Laboratories), 1904
Charles R. Aldrich
Southeast corner University Avenue SE and Central Avenue

The Beaux Arts in full glory — this building might have come directly from the 1893 Chicago fair or the 1904 St. Louis fair.

9 **"Main Place,"** 1974
Hammel, Green, and Abrahamson
120 2nd Street SE

A former service station restyled into a wood-sheathed box for retail sales.

10 **Pracna Building,** 1890
117 Main Street SE

A three-story brick Eastlake commercia building which carries over the Italiana in its rows of arched windows.

11 **Upton Block,** 1860
Northwest corner Main Street SE and 2nd Street SE

A three-story stone building now virtually in ruins.

12 **Pillsbury A Mill,** 1881
LeRoy S. Buffington
Main Street SE and 3rd Avenue SE

One of Minneapolis's major stone milli buildings. A walk along the river at th point affords a view of St. Anthony Fall other milling buildings on both sides of the river, and the raceways which used bring water in to power the mills. Unti World War I this area of the river was the industrial hub of Minneapolis.

3 **Great Northern Railway Stone Arch Bridge,** 1881–89
Charles C. Smith (engineer)
Southwest corner Main Street SE and 6th Avenue SE

The bridge, which can be seen from Main Street Southeast between 2nd and 5th Avenues Southeast, has long been one of the acknowledged landmarks of Minneapolis. The stone arch of the bridge crosses the Mississippi River in a gentle curve; it has been described romantically as Minnesota's updating of a Roman aqueduct.

3 Great Northern Railway Stone Arch Bridge.

4 **House,** c. 1860
814 University Avenue SE

A Greek Revival end-gable house has been made more "correct" with the addition of a bay window on the ground floor.

5 **Andrew-Riverside Presbyterian Church,** 1890
Charles S. Sedgwick
729 4th Street SE

English Gothic, with a crenelated tower and a picturesque turret. Supposedly the design is a replica of St. Giles's Church in Edinburgh, Scotland.

6 **First Congregational Church,** 1886
Warren H. Hayes
500 8th Avenue SE

An Akron-plan church; in style it is a little Gothic, a little Romanesque. The spire has been rebuilt since it was destroyed by a storm in 1967.

17 **Dudley House,** 1856–57
701 5th Street SE

A two-story dwelling, somewhere between the Greek and the Italianate.

18 **Lawrence-Nelson House,** c. 1872–73
622 5th Street SE

A brick Italianate house.

19 **Van Cleve House,** c. 1857–58
603 5th Street SE

A mixture of Greek and Italianate; sheathed in clapboard.

20 **Andrews House,** 1869
527 5th Street SE

Italianate, quite altered.

21 **Fisk House,** c. 1870
424 5th Street SE

A large two-story Italianate house in brick with an L-shaped plan.

21 Fisk House.

22 **Kappa Sigma Fraternity House,** 1968
Joseph E. Michels
1125 5th Street SE

A transformation of an older building into a warm, woodsy building of sticks.

23 **House,** 1892
Babb, Cook, and Willard
1126 5th Street SE

A Queen Anne dwelling surfaced in stone à la the Romanesque Revival.

24 **Frey House,** 1892
Warren H. Hayes
1206 5th Street SE

The Richardsonian Romanesque, classicized — almost Queen Anne/Colonial Revival.

25 "The Chateau" Apartment Building, 1973
Williams-O'Brien Associates
425 13th Avenue SE

The only real high-rise in Southeast Minneapolis west of the university. Several of the upper floors of this concrete building project out over the lower part of the building. Stylistically the structure is a reasonable exercise in the New Brutalism of the late 1960s and the early 1970s. It poses a real problem in community planning, however, for the residential area west and north of the university.

26 Varsity Theatre, 1938
Liebenberg and Kaplan
1308 4th Street SE

An excellent example of the Streamline Moderne theatres built by this prolific theatre-producing Minneapolis firm. What we see today is the late 1930s remodeling of a theatre that was built in 1915.

26 Varsity Theatre.

27 State Capitol Credit Union (now Southeast Branch, Minneapolis Public Library), 1962
Ralph Rapson and Associates
4th Street SE at 13th Avenue SE

A visually ponderous concrete canopy roof presses down on a glass box pavilion.

28 Phi Gamma Delta House, 1910–11
C. B. Stravs
1129 University Avenue SE

The Viennese Secessionist transported t the United States, almost but not quite Art Nouveau. Note the designs of the railings and the leaded glass.

29 Cutter House, 1856, 1874
Northwest corner 4th Street and 10th Avenue SE

A rare example of the Gothic Revival in the Twin Cities — a real gem. It is slowl losing its exterior wood ornamentation, however, and it has been stuccoed over.

29 Cutter House.

30 Archer, Daniels Midland Elevators, c. 1900
End of 29th Street SE, off 4th Street SE

This area of the Midway district is fille with cylindrical concrete and metal grai storage elevators of monumental size. From a distance the site is spectacular. The ADM elevators are of concrete.

M-1g Prospect Park

Prospect Park is composed of a pattern of irregular curved streets laid out around the well-known water tower. University Avenue defines the area to the north, the industrial zone to the east provides another boundary, and the railroad and the freeway (Highway 94) cut the wooded district off from the Mississippi River. The hilly terrain, the curving streets, the thick woods, and two parks (Tower Hill Park and Luxton Park) create a specific sense of place. As is the case with nearby St. Anthony Park, the area's central location, its nonurban quality, and its relative nearness to the university have helped it to survive over the years.

Most of the housing in Prospect Park is single-family residential, built between 1900 and the early 1920s. The most interesting of the early houses are the shingle and clapboard dwellings which represent the turn-of-the-century Colonial Revival, but by far the majority of the houses are stucco Craftsman dwellings — ample in size, functional, and nonassertive architecturally. Here and there among these houses are new (mostly woodsy) houses of the late 1950s and 1960s and a number of older houses that have been revamped. The major encroachment problem that faces Prospect Park today is not commercial/industrial developments nibbling away at its boundaries but noise pollution from the freeway. The new concrete sound barriers have helped, but the noise is still there, and in certain sections the barriers have destroyed one of the assets of the place — namely, its views of the two cities and the Mississippi River.

1 **Prospect Park Water Tower,** 1913
F. W. Cappelen
Seymour Avenue at Malcolm Street SE

The witch's-hat landmark of Prospect Park and the adjoining areas of Minneapolis and St. Paul. The image of the medieval tower was a popular one in the nineteenth century for such utilitarian structures as water towers. This one rises romantically from its wooded hillside — strongly enough to suggest that it is indeed a fragment of a medieval castle. Since 1953 it has not been used for the storage of water, but fortunately it has been preserved through the efforts of local citizens.

2 **St. Frances Cabrini Church,** 1947–48
Thorshov and Cerny
1500 Franklin Avenue SE

A modern (for the late 1940s) brick church which basically follows the tradition of the Saarinens.

3 **Willey House,** 1934
Frank Lloyd Wright
255 Bedford Street SE

This house, along with the later Johnson Wax Company Building (1936) in Racine, Wisconsin, and the famous "Falling Water" (1936), at Bear Run, Pennsylvania, marks the strong resurgence of Wright during the Depression years. The open plan for this house served as a prototype for Wright's Usonian houses of the late 1930s. In the Willey house he took the few elements — carport, kitchen, living/dining area, and bedroom wing — and placed them side by side in a single line. The house was once idyllically situated on a wooded knoll overlooking the river and the cities, but now a freeway roars only a short distance away; the high concrete sound barriers which were recently erected reduce the noise somewhat but also shut out the view.

4 **House,** 1938, 1940
Close and Scheu
252 Bedford Street SE

A Moderne house of the late 1930s; an arrangement of a group of rectangular flat-roofed boxes. This house is an interesting one to compare with Wright's house (#3) across the street. Wright's design, though more traditional in its use of hipped roofs, brick, and unpainted wood, represents a major departure, especially in its interior space. The house by Close and Scheu appears radical, but it is much milder in its effort to break with the past.

5 **Johnson House,** 1905; addition, 1969
Gerald S. Johnson
103 Seymour Avenue SE

An early cottage has been remodeled and enlarged beyond recognition (unless one looks closely at its sides and rear). A new studio above a garage has been added between the street and the house. Double shed roofs and diagonal wood sheathing have been used on the house and the studio.

5 Johnson House.

6 **Park Building, Luxton Park,** 1970
Hodne/Stageberg Partners
West corner Williams and St. Mary's Avenues SE

A mild New Brutalism design, in part built into the hillside.

7 **House,** c. 1950
Close Associates
90 Seymour Avenue SE

The informal, woodsy tradition of the post–World War II years kept closely in hand.

M-1h University of Minnesota Main Campus

The institution was established in 1851 and its first building, Old Main, was designed by Alden and Cutler and was constructed in 1857; in 1873 a new front wing designed by Alden and Long was added to it. By 1876 the campus had grown to occupy twenty-five acres. A number of buildings were constructed in the late 1880s and the 1890s, several of which still exist and are of major architectural importance. Among them are Pillsbury Hall (1889) and Nicholson Hall (1890), both designed by Harvey Ellis. These early buildings were sited along a gently curved avenue (now named Pillsbury Drive). The open areas between the avenue and University Avenue Southeast provided a parklike setting for the buildings.

On paper the site selected for the university on the high east bluffs of the Mississippi River looked fine, but in fact it was anything but ideal. It was bounded on the north by the Great Northern Railroad and on the south (above Washington Avenue Southeast) by the St. Paul and Northern Pacific. The regents of the university slowly acquired land south of the original campus and eventually extended the campus down to the river. In 1892 landscape architect Horace W. S. Cleveland submitted a proposal for a campus plan which envisioned the university as an English landscape park overlooking the river. Of his proposal Cleveland wrote, "For there will be nowhere any formal lines of division and the variety and unexpected changes of view and vistas thus afforded will tend to increase the apparent size of the area." His plans for the siting of buildings, the layout of roads and walkways, the installation of new plantings (especially evergreens), and the connection of the campus to the river by pathways were never carried out. In 1907 the regents (following the lead, it should be noted, of their counterparts at other universities across the country) reached the decision that a City Beautiful scheme should be drawn up for the orderly development of the campus. In the following year they appointed an advisory board to hold a competition for a plan for the university. The members of the board — Daniel H. Burnham, Walter Cook, and William M. Kenyon — selected Cass Gilbert. In 1910 Gilbert submitted his plan, which like other academic plans of the time was for an orderly Beaux Arts composition. The new campus was modeled in a general way on the plan of Columbia University, which in turn had been inspired by Thomas Jefferson's scheme for the University of Virginia. The buildings were to be arranged around a central mall with a large, domed auditorium at the north end, a campanile at the south end, and terraces and an outdoor garden leading down to the river. To the east were to be a series of quadrangles housing the engineering and medical schools. (Gilbert's plan called for tunneling the St. Paul and Northern Pacific tracks under the campus, but the tracks were removed by the company in 1924.)

Gilbert never had an opportunity to carry out his plans, for he was dismissed by the regents and replaced first by Edwin H. Hewitt and then by Clarence H. Johnston, Jr. Johnston, who ended up designing almost all the campus buildings from this point through the 1940s, gradually modified and changed Gilbert's plans so that the subtleties and the great breadth of his scheme vanished. The one change which did more than anything else to destroy Gilbert's plan was the decision contained in Morell and Nichols's campus plan of 1936 to locate the new student union at the south end of the mall, thus effectively eliminating the grand axial open space and the view of the river which Gilbert had envisioned. Cleveland's and Gilbert's proposals both sought to take advantage of the river location of the campus, but since 1939 the university's planners have ignored this natural asset. In the later development of the West Bank campus and its relationship to the East Bank campus one feels that the river and its deep channel were looked upon as an unfortunate affair — an affair that had to be overcome.

Since 1945 the campus planners have seemed bent on filling in as much of the remaining open space as possible, even to the point of building Peik Hall (1954) right on the edge of the old campus park — the only piece of greenery (except for the mall) that is still left. The recent decision to build the new bookstore and Admissions and Records facility underground (between Folwell Hall, Jones Hall, and the Nolte Center for Continuing Education) would appear to indicate an awareness that the remaining open space should be preserved, but a glance at the plans for the building (now under construction) reveals that the lawn which in part covers an underground parking garage will be eliminated to a large extent and replaced by concrete and sunken courts — the end result being anything but green.

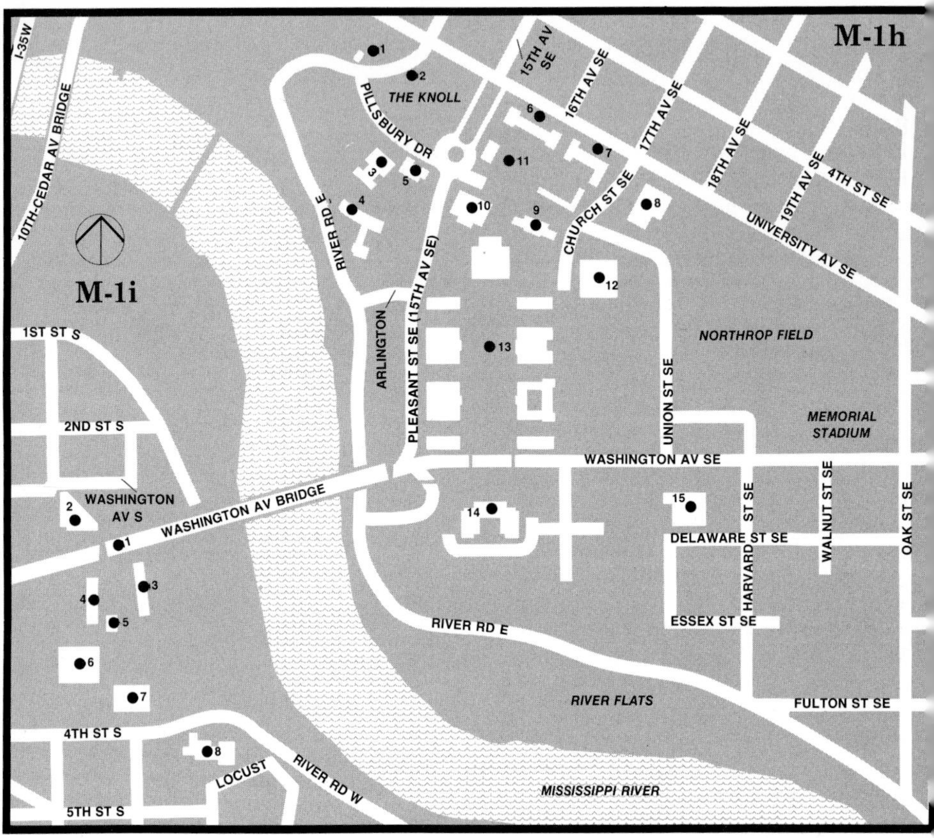

1 **Music Education Building,** 1888
Warren H. Hayes

A not-too-distinguished example of Richardsonian Romanesque.

2 **Peik Hall,** 1954
Magney, Tusler, and Setter

One of the first "modern" buildings on the campus, Peik Hall is a long, low brick box. The bands of windows have projecting fins. It is regrettable that the building takes up a section of the greenery in the old campus park.

3 **Burton Hall,** 1895
LeRoy S. Buffington (exterior); Charles S. Sedgwick (interior)

Buffington in a Greek mood. Without Harvey Ellis his designs never quite made it.

4 **Elliott Hall,** 1973–74
Parker, Klein Associates

4 Elliott Hall. Photo: Balthazar Korab.

This building and Griswold and Rauma's Auditorium Classroom Building (1972) on the West Bank are the most satisfactory buildings added to either of the campuses in recent years. The site for Elliott Hall is pressed, but the architects have made good use of it. The building works in well with the older adjoining building. The interior public space of Elliott Hall has character, but it is not openly dramatic.

Eddy Hall, 1886
LeRoy S. Buffington
Buffington before Ellis; a run-of-the-mill Eastlake college building.

Folwell Hall, 1905–1907
Clarence H. Johnston, Sr.
An imaginative version of central European late Renaissance/early Baroque architecture.

Bell Museum of Natural History, 1940
Clarence H. Johnston, Jr.
In 1940 this building, along with Coffman Memorial Union, was voted to be one of the best-liked new buildings in the Twin Cities. In style it is a tasteful and understanding version of PWA Moderne, both internally and externally. Note the sculptured relief panels and the metal light standards by the entrance. A new addition, which showed little sympathy with the original building, was added at the rear in 1967.

Armory, 1895–96
Charles R. Aldrich
The nineteenth-century Medieval can be a delight if a gifted designer and adequate funds are available. In the Armory, however, too many compromises were made and too little imagination was exercised.

9 **Pillsbury Hall,** 1887–89
LeRoy S. Buffington (Harvey Ellis)
Ellis's designs are almost always better on paper than in reality. Still, Pillsbury Hall is a classic example of Richardsonian Romanesque, and in terms of architectural history it is probably the most significant building on the campus.

10 **Nicholson Hall,** 1890
LeRoy S. Buffington (Harvey Ellis)
In this period Ellis was gradually moving toward the classical and away from the picturesque romanticism of Richardson.

11 **East Bank Bookstore/Admissions and Records Facility,** 1975
Myers and Bennett
Since Claude Nicolas Ledoux at the end of the eighteenth century, architects (along with science fiction writers) have been entranced with underground buildings. Cornell University has an underground bookshop — why not Minnesota? Unfortunately, this one did not leave the open and quiet lawn which once existed behind Folwell Hall — only a diagonal hole in the ground.

12 **Architecture Building,** 1960
Thorshov and Cerny
Nothing outstanding externally; the central court inside the building is pleasant, and that is about all. The building just does not have the character one would expect of an architecture building. It is too dainty and formal, and it demands an interior order of things never found in an architecture school.

13 **The Mall**
Cass Gilbert's Beaux Arts mall is defined by nine buildings. Of these, seven are committed to the classical, and two others straddle the fence between the classical and the modern. The oldest buildings are Smith Hall (1914), Walter Library (1925), Morrill Hall (1925), the Tate Laboratory of Physics (1928), Northrop Memorial Auditorium (1929), Vincent Hall (1938), and Johnston Hall (1951). All of these colonnaded red brick buildings were designed by Clarence H. Johnston, Jr. None of them is in any sense a distinguished example of architecture, although there are fragments of several that are quite good, including the three-story lobby of Northrop Memorial Auditorium and the stairs, lobby, and reading rooms of Walter Library. Nevertheless, the buildings do perform a visual function remarkably well when seen (among the rows of elms) as a backdrop to Gilbert's mall. In the other two buildings the designer's efforts to be both classical and modern are only marginally successful. Ford Hall (Magney, Tusler, and Setter,

1951) turns out to be a 1950s continuation of PWA Moderne. In Kolthoff Hall (Hammel, Green, and Abrahamson, 1971) the architects tried to solve the problem by posing a set of freestanding piers and an entablature in front of a brick cut-into box. (This approach might have worked if Charles Moore had designed the building.)

14 **Coffman Memorial Union,** 1940
Clarence H. Johnston, Jr.

In 1940 the editors of the *Architectural Record* canvassed representatives of the business and civic spheres in the Twin Cities, asking them to list the ten most distinguished buildings completed in Minneapolis and St. Paul in the 1930s. The only building which received all of the first votes was Coffman Memorial Union. The union reflects the PWA Moderne of the 1930s in a classical balanced composition, formal in plan yet Moderne in its detailing with curved walls, steel railings, glass brick, and the other hallmarks of the style. Although not by any means a great building, the union is still one of the few buildings on the campus to express anything approaching an architectural personality. In 1974 the decision was made to gut the public spaces of the building and to repackage parts of the exterior and the interior in the latest fashion — deep-cut apron windows, shed-roof and hipped-roof greenhouses, and the like — designed by Community Planning and Design. The architectural restyling is reasonably successful, but it is unfortunate that the campus has lost its major monument from the 1930s.

15 **Health Sciences Unit A,** 1973
The Architects Collaborative; Cerny Associates; Hammel, Green, and Abrahamson; Setter, Leach, and Lindstrom

Esthetically, this gigantic concrete pile can only be described as a visual disaster. It is overscaled (not necessarily oversized) for the site and this section of the university, and it is filled to overflowing with flamboyant design clichés. Even the entrance turns out to be fake: One approaches axially up the stairs, goes across the platform to enter the building, and then finds that there is no entrance there at all — it is off to the side. Within, the public spaces are compressed and parsimonious; the grandeur of it all lies entirely outside.

M-1i University of Minnesota West Bank Campus

By the 1930s the university already had its eye on the west bank of the Mississippi for possible expansion. In 1939 it proposed to build a new bridge to replace the old and crumbling Washington Avenue bridge and to erect two skyscraper pylons (for women's dormitories) on the west end of the new bridge. It was argued that the pylons would provide an impressive new entrance to the university.

Discussions became much more specific after 1945. In 1954 the acquisition of land began, and by 1970 sixty-five acres were available. In 1960 Pietro Belluschi, Lawrence Anderson, and Dan Kiley were engaged to work with the university's architect, Winston Close, and architects from three local firms — Hammel and Green, Cerny Associates, and Magney, Tusler, Setter, Leach, and Lindstrom — which had been given commissions for buildings.

In 1970 the Minneapolis firm of Hodne and Stageberg produced its "Phase One: Pilot Design Study" for the West Bank campus in which the firm sought to loosen up the rigidity of the 1960 plan. From the beginning it was felt that the new campus should be as compressed as possible and should utilize high-rise and megalithic structures. With sixty-five acres and an anticipated student population of 20,000 on the West Bank alone by 1980, all of this sounded very logical. Open space and greenery were to be gained by taking advantage of the landscaping of the adjoining freeways, and the eventual conversion of the West Bank industrial area on the river flats to a park. The scheme for the West Bank, like the plans for the adjoining Cedar-Riverside project, had all the earmarks of a modernistic City of the Future (in terms of 1925, however, not 1975) — an urban model which twentieth-century architects seem to return to again and again.

1 **Washington Avenue Bridge,** 1962
Sverdrup and Parcel
A dramatic missed opportunity. The basic functional proposal for the bridge, a two-deck structure with lanes for autos below and open and enclosed passageways for pedestrians above, was a good one, but the results are at best minimal. The approach to the bridge on the east side seems to be temporary; at the west end it simply peters out. The enclosed pedestrian passageway is just a long metal shed with no visual or utilitarian breaks. A bridge such as this could have been a thing of joy for those who use it, and as an object in space it could have been handled in a romantic fashion to unite visually the two banks of the river.

2 **Auditorium Classroom Building,** 1972
Griswold and Rauma
Although somewhat self-consciously fashionable, this building is the only one on the West Bank with interior spaces which are a pleasure to see and use.

2 Auditorium Classroom Building. Photo: Phillip MacMillan James.

3 **Anderson Hall,** 1967
Setter, Leach, and Lindstrom
Plain walls of brick with protruding glass bays.

4 **Blegen Hall,** 1964
Setter, Leach, and Lindstrom
Brick walls with rectangular boxed openings.

5 **Social Sciences Building,** 1963
Cerny Associates
Similar to Blegen Hall in the brick façade with protruding boxed windows, except that this building is in the form of a high tower.

6 **Wilson Library,** 1967
Cerny Associates
A four-story brick rectangle which like most of the other West Bank buildings has no real public space within.

7 **Rarig Center,** 1971
Ralph Rapson and Associates
Rapson's buildings always have character, if nothing else. Here he has rummaged through Le Corbusier's New Brutalism imagery of the 1960s to produce a theatrical piece of sculpture. As in all of Rapson's theatres the interior auditoriums work well.

8 **Middlebrook Hall Dormitory,** 1967
Griswold and Rauma
In 1965 Griswold and Rauma produced a plan for a group of dormitories on the West Bank campus. There were to have been four towers, but only one (of twelve stories) has been built. The tower is neutral in its external statement; the exterior and the interior are tastefully and simply detailed.

M-1j University of Minnesota St. Paul Campus

Because of its open space (provided in part by the state fairgrounds) the St. Paul campus of the University of Minnesota has not until recently conveyed the architectural self-consciousness which is found on the Minneapolis campuses. The first building constructed on what was to become the St. Paul campus (at first called the University Farm) was a plain farmhouse built in 1884. By the mid-1890s the St. Paul campus had six major buildings, all devoted to agriculture and home economics. By 1917 there were over thirty buildings, and the site was some 422 acres in size. Until the 1950s the St. Paul campus was directly and conveniently connected to the Minneapolis campus by the Inter-Campus Trolley Line (constructed in 1913), but this has now gone the way of all the street railroad lines in the Twin Cities.

The St. Paul campus never developed a grand overall plan comparable to Gilbert's 1910 plan for the Minneapolis campus. Much of the low-keyed planning of the campus was done by Morell and Nichols. Their plans divided the campus (in a not excessively imaginative way) into three sections: a northern area which followed the English landscape garden tradition; an axial central section which was quasi-Beaux Arts; and a southern section (for student housing) which was a mixture of Beaux Arts and the informality of the English.

In 1971 John Andrews Architects submitted a plan for the campus which more or less accepted things as they stood, but, as one might expect of the Andrews firm, they argued for the eventual building of several megalithic structures to be located between Buford and Commonwealth Avenues. While several of the post-1969 buildings are large (compared to the scale of the earlier buildings), none of the huge structures which Andrews had in mind have so far been built.

The playing field, the recreation area, and the large park with a pond (contained as late as 1952 in the Morell and Nichols plans) have been tastefully filled in with an irregular layout of student housing, and the central and northern sections of the campus are beginning to feel crowded.

1 **Kaufert Laboratory of Forest Products and Wood Science,** 1961, 1964
Magney, Tusler, Setter, Leach, and Lindstrom
Sited on the slope of a hill, the building is a series of three wood-sheathed boxes, one with a band of narrow horizontal windows which wraps around the building. The laboratory resembles a Finnish building of the late 1950s or the early 1960s.

2 **Entomology, Fisheries, and Wildlife Building,** 1969
Setter, Leach, and Lindstrom
Deep-cut vertical panels in brick establish the dominant note of this structure.

3 **Alderman Hall** (formerly Horticultural Sciences), 1971
Thorsen and Thorshov
A cut-into volume sheathed in brick.

4 **Stakman Hall of Plant Pathology,** 1941
Clarence H. Johnston, Jr.
A smooth-skinned box.

5 **Biological Science Center,** 1973
Setter, Leach, and Lindstrom
An eight-story brick volume punctured with small holes in a rectangular pattern.

6 Classroom–Office Building, 1972
Griswold and Rauma

6 Classroom–Office Building.
Photo: Phillip MacMillan James.

A large, low contemporary box of smooth brick in the greenhouse mode. Through its location and the nature of its uses (classrooms, offices, and public space) it functions effectively as the central core of the campus.

7 McNeal Hall, 1975
Hodne/Stageberg Partners

A handsome series of tightly related brick-sheathed volumes in the central part of the campus.

8 Thatcher Hall, 1939
Clarence H. Johnston, Jr.

PWA Moderne with two glass-brick stair towers. The building is axially sited at the south end of Eckles Avenue.

M-1k West Bank and Near South Side

The northern part of this area is one of the earliest occupied sections of the city. From the beginning it has been a mixed-use area with industrial, commercial, and institutional buildings and single-family and multiple-family housing. In the nineteenth century the railroad cut this section of the city into four parts, and the freeway system of the 1960s divided it even more. To the south Lake Street has always been strip commercial, and some industrial developments have occurred alongside the railroad tracks which run to the north parallel to Lake Street. North of Lake Street, mixed in with the housing, are several hospital complexes and (since the 1960s) high-rise towers with apartments for the elderly. The east side of the area is not replenished with parks, but it does have a strip of parks and open green spaces along the west bank of the Mississippi.

The blocks north of Highway 94 have long contained institutions — Augsburg College, Fairview Hospital, St. Mary's Hospital, and St. Mary's Junior College. The hospitals in particular have expanded over the past fifteen years, supplanting numerous blocks of lower-middle-class housing. Since 1960 these institutions have been joined by the University of Minnesota, which has reached across the river to establish its West Bank campus. The final note of newness is Cedar-Riverside, a new town-within-a-town. In this section of Minneapolis one is constantly aware of the freeways and their elaborate interchanges and the high-rise buildings. The single-family housing and the parks are still there, but they remain quite hidden.

M-1k

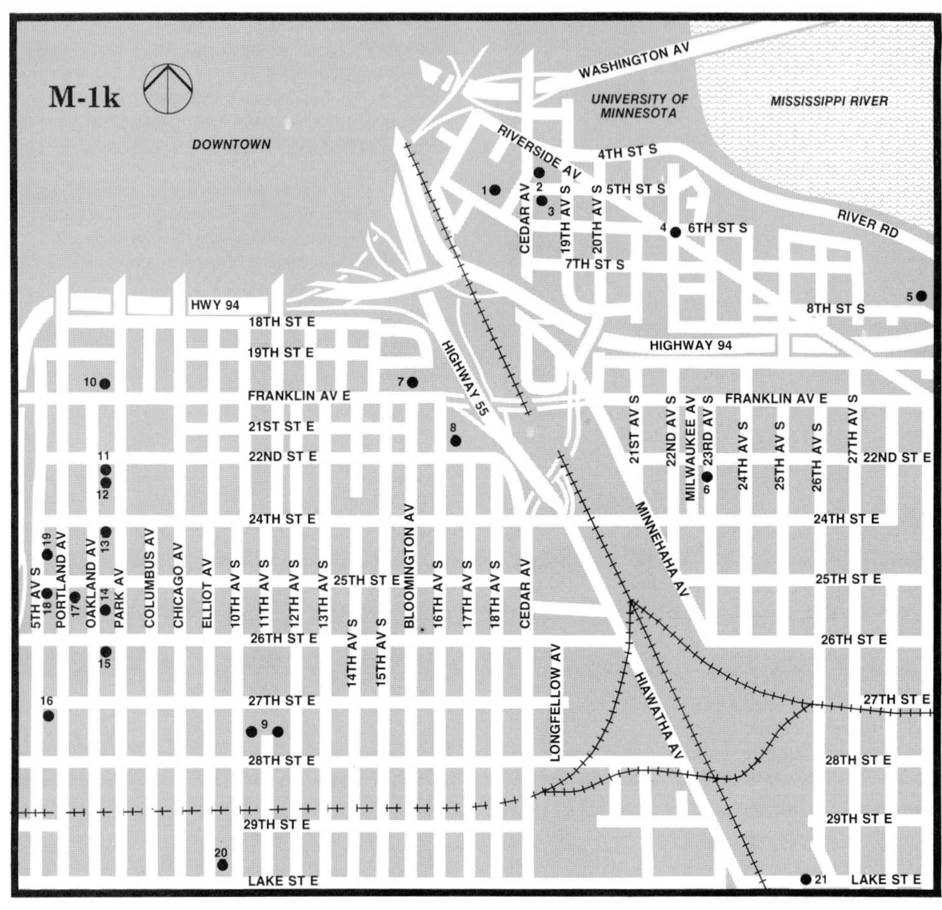

1 **Cedar-Riverside**
Cedar Avenue S between 3rd Street S and 6th Street S

Outside of the redevelopment of downtown Minneapolis, the Cedar-Riverside project is one of the most dramatic which the city has to offer. The locale would seem to have all the ingredients needed to invite redevelopment in an old, run-down urban area. By the end of the 1960s the area was surrounded by freeways on three sides; adjoining it to the north was the expanding West Bank campus of the university, and to the east were the Fairview Hospital and St. Mary's Hospital complexes. While most of the existing commercial, industrial, and residential structures were anonymous, there were a few buildings of architectural character which could add just that spice of history (as recollection) which architect/planners in the early 1970s felt was so needed on the urban scene.

With the freeways and their rapidly moving traffic as a backdrop (à la the futurism of the 1920s) a scheme was prepared involving skyscraper towers separated by lower buildings, parks, and parking garages. It was projected that by 1980 this city within a city would house thirty thousand people. The designers planned a variety of different types of housing — for the elderly, for families with children, and on down the line. Office space, shops, play areas, and theatres were integral to the scheme. The whole project smacked of human rationalism (as a symbol, not a fact), and it projected the atmosphere of a city of the future — more, it might be added, a city of the future of the 1920s than an image of what a city should be like, or would be like, in the 1970s and 1980s.

The harsh realities of finance and the normal governmental delays fortunately intervened, and just about everything was reduced in size; and the recent economic stringencies have virtually halted the project, at least for the moment. (The Riverbluff, Phase II of Cedar-Riverside, designed by Miller, Hanson, and Westerbeck was to be a group of narrow high towers and lower buildings which stepped down to the river; it has not been started, and in a way one hopes that it never will be). What we currently see in Cedar-Riverside are the five towers which make up Cedar Square West (designed by Ralph Rapson and Associates, 1968–73); the four units of housing for the elderly, including Griswold and Rauma's Cedar High, 1969; a partially revamped Cedar Avenue (between 7th and 3rd Streets South), which is slowly beginning to acquire the desired Walt Disney image of the past; and such functional and symbolic amenities as pedestrian bridges and parking garages. Rapson's high-rise units, each a beehive of boxlike drawers, are accented by bright colors — red, yellow, and blue — and the narrow, almost unusable balconies with their owners' bicycles stored on them add a light note to a project which is otherwise painfully serious. Even the attempt to lighten the affair with folksy murals does not do the trick. Perhaps when the plantings mature the project may become more amiable, although it should be noted that the buildings of Cedar Square West, like many "modern" buildings, are not aging very well.

1 Cedar-Riverside, Cedar Square West.

2 **Dania Hall,** 1886
Carl Struck
Northeast corner Cedar Avenue and 5th Street S

A four-story Ruskinian Gothic commercial block with a square corner tower. It is hoped that this building will be able to withstand the onslaught of the tasteful restoration.

3 **House,** c. 1870s
1819 5th Street S

A two-story brick Italianate dwelling of the central-pedimented pavilion type.

4 **Smiley's Point,** 1889–90
2200 Riverside Avenue

A two-story commercial block in brick, with great emphasis placed on a series of bulky pinnacles. Like many commercial buildings of the 1870s and 1880s it just does not fit into a convenient cubbyhole. It certainly isn't Queen Anne, but it isn't Eastlake either.

5 **Pavilion,** 1936
Riverside Park, northwest of 8th Street S and 29th Avenue S

A small, mildly Medieval park pavilion in stone. Produced during the PWA/WPA days of the 1930s.

6 **Workers' Housing,** c. 1885–1904
Milwaukee Avenue S between Franklin Avenue E and 24th Street E

A whole street of artisans' single-family dwellings. The typical one-and-a-half-story house on the street is of brick and has an end gable facing the street. Each has a front porch and a side-hall plan. All of the houses are rather plain, but occasionally in the wood detailing on the porches there is an indication of Eastlake or Queen Anne.

6 *Workers' Housing.*

7 **Urban American Indian Center** (now Minneapolis Regional Native American Center), 1974–75
Hodne/Stageberg Partners
North of junction Franklin Avenue E and Bloomington Avenue S

A complex and busy design in concrete and wood. The size of the site allows substantial planting, which eventually may be developed enough so that nature's greenery will somewhat soften the building's insistent forms. The outdoor and indoor spaces seem to work well.

7 *Urban American Indian Center (now Minneapolis Regional Native American Center).*

8 **Housing**
Around 16th Avenue S and 22nd Street E

The new fourteen-story Hiawatha Apartments for the elderly (1964) contrast dramatically with the surrounding one-and-a-half-story "mechanics' cottages" (c. 1890–1910).

9 **Hans Christian Andersen Elementary School,** 1975
Bissell, Belair, and Green
Southeast corner 10th Avenue S and 27th Street E

A concrete building with the sides arranged in sawtooth fashion. All of the earmarks of mid-1970s architecture are here — diagonals breaking through rectangles, shed roofs, and even circular openings — all put together in a convincing manner.

10 **Park Avenue Presbyterian Church** (now Park Avenue Covenant Church), 1888–89
Attrib. Charles S. Sedgwick
Franklin Avenue E at Park Avenue

A strong exercise in the Richardsonian Romanesque.

11 **House,** 1891–92
Arthur Bishop Chamberlain
2200 Park Avenue

The last of the Romanesque Revival residences still remaining on Park Avenue.

12 **Peavey House** (now an office building), 1903
William Channing Whitney
2214 Park Avenue

The Italian Renaissance Villa was a popular style for America's rich from the 1890s until World War I. As an image it worked very well (and still does): its classical form and reserve announce wealth, power, and institutional status.

13 **Lutheran Social Service Building,** 1957
Sovik, Mathre, and Associates
2414 Park Avenue

The fragileness of the 1950s at its best — Miesian in the center crowned by a folded roof with glass end gables.

14 **House,** 1915
2520 Park Avenue

The dignity of American Georgian, domestic but classical.

15 Turnblad House (now American Swedish Institute), 1903–1907
Christopher A. Boehme and Victor Cordella
2600 Park Avenue

With its surrounding high fence, turrets, and towers the Turnblad House comes close to resembling a child's version of what a medieval castle should be. In style the castle is Romanesque/Chateauesque; the interior is a comfortable mixture of the medieval, the classical, and the provincial of Sweden.

15 Turnblad House (now American-Swedish Institute).

16 House, 1887
2702 Portland Avenue

A Queen Anne/Colonial Revival dwelling in shingles and clapboard.

17 Ebenezer Tower, 1969–70
Thorsen and Thorshov
2523 Portland Avenue

A single fortresslike tower in ribbed concrete provides housing for the elderly.

18 House, c. 1890
2500 Portland Avenue

A rather plain clapboard house made exotic (Moorish) by an elaborate porch and two towers, each crowned with an onion dome. The house was moved to this site in 1898 from a location on Park Avenue.

19 Public Housing, 1971
Roger T. Johnson Associates
2419–33 5th Avenue S

Housing for the elderly (254 units) in two fourteen-story brick towers topped by a broken pattern of shed roofs.

20 Sears, Roebuck and Company Building, 1927
Nimmons, Carr, and Wright
Elliot Avenue at Lake Street E

This Chicago firm produced store buildings for Sears all over the United States. They were almost always of exposed concrete with an eye-catching tower and a rational, factorylike design. Nimmons had been a member of the Chicago Prairie School, but most of the Sears buildings his firm produced employed a light historic imagery — medieval, classical, and even pre-Columbian. The Minneapolis store is one of his classical products, somewhat reminiscent of the work of Goodhue.

21 Shop Fronts, 1940
2619 and 2621 Lake Street E

In the late 1930s and the early 1940s there was a rash of modernization of stores. The style most often used at the time was the Streamline Moderne, which can be seen, well preserved, in these two small retail store buildings.

22 El Lago Theatre (now Muntz TV), 1927
Eckman Holm Company
3500 Lake Street E

A 1920s interpretation of sixteenth-century Italian, used for the front of a motion picture theatre.

23 White Castle, 1963
3600 Lake Street E

The castle image of the White Castle hamburger shops worked best when it was miniaturized as in its buildings of the late 1920s and 1930s. Still this 1963 design is effective as an eye-catcher, and its large size proclaims that it has space within for a dining room as well as a lunch counter.

M-11 Longfellow, Powderhorn, Nokomis

This section of Minneapolis has not fared as well in its planning and growth as the southwestern part of the city. Its great drawback is the extensive swath cut diagonally through the area by the Chicago, Milwaukee, St. Paul, and Pacific Railroad and its accompanying industrial developments. With the exception of some pre-1900 housing and some dwellings on the east shore of Lake Nokomis and here and there on River Road West, the housing is almost exclusively single-family middle middle class and lower middle class (i.e., homes for "mechanics"). Although the older single-family housing (1900 to 1920) generally lies south of Lake Street, the dwellings in this section of the city represent quite a mixture of dates and styles. The most recent (post–World War II) single-family housing occurs around Lake Nokomis and toward the Crosstown freeway (Highway 62). Typical examples of single-family housing from the late 1920s and early 1930s can be seen around 48th and 49th Streets East and Chicago Avenue South. As far as parks are concerned the area is well off: Minnehaha Park and Minnehaha Parkway, Hiawatha Park, Lake Nokomis, Powderhorn Park, the West River Road, and nine recreational parks. Pockets of neighborhood commercial developments grew up at strategic points along the streetcar lines, and most of these have managed to survive, although in rather battered condition.

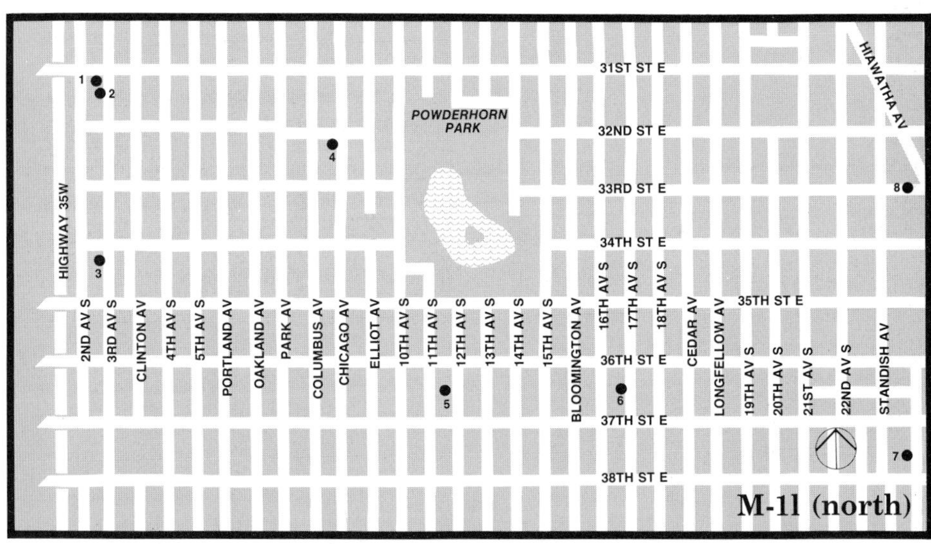

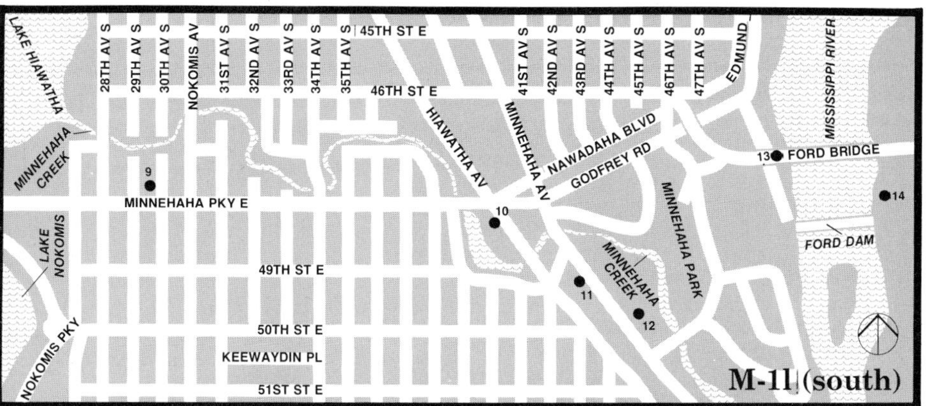

1 **Three Houses,** 1890–91
Southeast corner 2nd Avenue S and 31st Street E

Three Queen Anne houses, currently being restored, which still form an impressive group.

2 **Bennett-McBride House,** 1891
3116 3rd Avenue S

A good-sized Queen Anne clapboard house.

2 Bennett-McBride House.

3 **Central High School,** c. 1911
William B. Ittner
3416 4th Avenue S

Late English Gothic in brick — the Middle Ages as the fountainhead of academia.

4 **Modern Cleaners,** 1943–44
3200 Chicago Avenue

An anonymous 1909–13 building made "modern" in the 1940s with the transformation of its entire façade into a Streamline Moderne sign. The green and white surfaces carry on into the entrance.

4 Modern Cleaners.

5 **Holy Name Church,** 1961
Cerny Associates
3637 11th Avenue S

Brick, with a continuous clerestory under the overhanging roof.

6 **Carlson House,** 1916–17
Purcell and Elmslie
3612 17th Avenue S

An inexpensive variation of Purcell and Elmslie's two-story square-box houses, this one covered with a gable roof.

7 **Nile Theatre,** 1926, 1936, 1961
Liebenberg and Kaplan
3736 23rd Avenue S
A remodeled theatre with thin wiry forms, round balls, and other features reminiscent of the tail-fin decade.

•8 **Christ Lutheran Church,** 1949–50
Saarinen and Saarinen; Hills, Gilbertson, and Hayes
3244 34th Avenue S
The one church building in Minneapolis which is indeed a high art object. Everything about the design appears so simple and direct, and yet no one but the Saarinens could have done this so well. The church was designed at a high point in the careers of both father and son — a period which commenced just before World War II and continued on into the 1950s.

9 **House,** c. 1936
Larson and McLaren
2906 Minnehaha Parkway E
A group of large, similar boxes arranged to create a Streamline Moderne house.

10 **"The Longfellow House,"** 1906
Southwest corner Minnehaha Parkway E and Hiawatha Avenue S
A 1906 promotional brochure entitled *Longfellow Gardens, Minnehaha Falls* noted, "In the very center of the stretch along Minnehaha Parkway is a wonderful reproduction of the very house that was the lifelong home of Longfellow himself." The house is not an exact copy, but it is pretty close. It was originally one of a series of buildings that made up Longfellow Gardens, a public (but privately owned) zoological garden with lions, elephants, sea lions, exotic birds, and so on. The other buildings are now gone, and even the pony ride, which continued through the 1940s, is no longer there. In 1937 the house was converted into a branch library, but it is currently deserted and waiting for a new use.

11 **Minnehaha Railroad Depot,** 1875
Northwest corner Minnehaha Avenue S and 49th Street E (extension)
A charming and beautifully restored Eastlake Style suburban station.

11 Minnehaha Railroad Depot.

12 **Stevens House,** 1849
In Minnehaha Park, just east of Minnehaha Avenue and 50th Street E
A one-and-a-half-story Greek Revival house which was originally located in downtown Minneapolis and later (1896) moved to this site. For many years it was credited as being the first frame house built west of the Mississippi in Minneapolis, but recently this honor has been claimed for other dwellings. It has long presented a forlorn appearance, and it is hoped that it may resume a useful life someday.

13 **Ford Bridge,** 1927
N. W. Elsberg
46th Street and River Road W
An arched concrete bridge (1,521 feet long) over the Mississippi. The dam, the locks, and the hydroelectric plant lie below it and to the south.

14 **Hydroelectric Plant (Government Locks and Dam No. 1),** 1923
Stone and Webster (engineers)
South of Ford Bridge and west of Mississippi River Boulevard E
Probably as idyllic a picture as one could compose of an industrial complex — the bridge, the dam with its locks and hydroelectric plant, and then the Ford Motor Company plant situated amid landscaped grounds on the top of the east bank of the river. The dam and the bridge are heavy and monumental, although they have no outward historic detailing. The whole is similar to the stripped classical approach which Bertram Goodhue and others took toward architecture during the second and third decades of the century.

M-1m Lowry Hill and South

A few dwellings found their way onto Lowry Hill as early as the 1870s, but this section of the city did not come into its own until the late 1880s and on through the first two decades of this century. By the early 1900s it was a highly fashionable residential district. One of its enclaves extended from Oak Grove and Clifton Avenues south on Pillsbury and Blaisdell Avenues. Another was in the vicinity of 22nd Street and Stevens Avenue South. A block or two away from these enclaves in any direction were more modest upper-middle-class single-family dwellings and numerous multiple-family units ranging from duplexes and fourplexes to small apartment buildings; one of the more luxurious apartment buildings was Harry Jones's Romanesque Revival building (1892) on 24th Street East between Stevens Avenue and 1st Avenue South. Along some of the principal streets — especially the north/south ones — which go through the area were business blocks of one, two, and three stories. Since 1914 the center of the area has been the Minneapolis Institute of Arts and Fair Oaks Park, just across 24th Street East to the north.

The general impression which the neighborhood conveys is that of large turn-of-the-century houses placed on small lots. During the summer when the leaves of the elms create a green bower over the streets, the pressed nature of the buildings is not so apparent, but in the winter it is fully revealed.

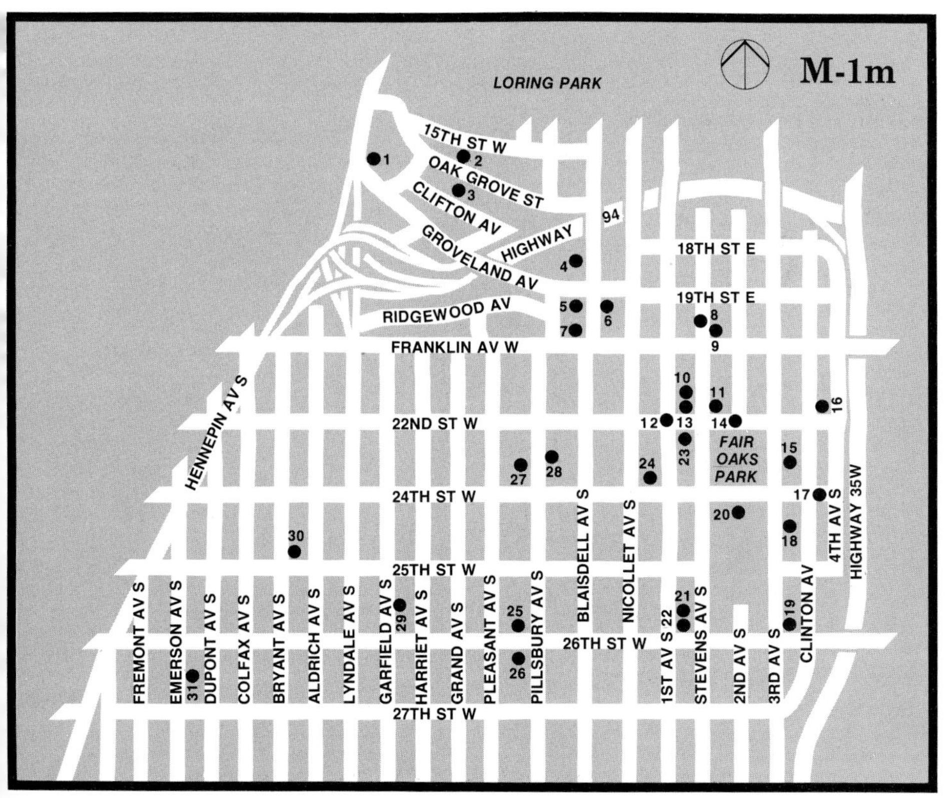

With the removal of the streetcar lines from Hennepin, Lyndale, and Nicollet Avenues, the function of the commercial strips has been greatly reduced. One of the freeways, Highway 94, runs through the northern part of the area and thus effectively cuts it off from Loring Park, The Parade, and downtown. The angular junction of Hennepin and Lyndale Avenues on Lowry Hill once provided a remarkable visual introduction to the parks below and to the downtown area; now the hapless confusion of Highway 94, which one moment is a freeway and another not, must make Loring, the father of the Minneapolis park system, wince. So far Lowry Hill has been able to ward off high-rise developments, being plagued only by three-story and four-story apartment buildings with fake mansard roofs, the looming pretentious bulk of the new addition to the Minneapolis Institute of Arts, and several moderate-sized high-rises at the base of the hill, parallel to Highway 94.

1 **Groveland Avenue Hotel,** 1927
Larson and McLaren
510 Groveland Avenue

Beaux Arts gentility, with great reserve.

2 **Woman's Club of Minneapolis,** 1926
Magney and Tusler
410 Oak Grove

The design of the building is adequate and competent; what brings it off is the site — a curved drive leading to the south front and a view from the terraces to the north side of the building overlooking downtown Minneapolis.

3 **Carpenter House,** 1906
William Channing Whitney
314 Clifton Avenue

The style of a three-story American Federal house reintroduced to the American scene.

4 **McKnight-Newell House,** 1888
Charles S. Sedgwick
1818 La Salle Avenue S

4 McKnight-Newell House.

The McKnight-Newell House is one of the last of the Romanesque Revival residences still standing in Minneapolis. An earlier, unrealized design for the project was done by Harvey Ellis while he was in the Buffington office.

5 **Van Dusen House,** 1892–93
Orff and Joralemon
1900 La Salle Avenue S

A romantic stone pile, part Richardsonian Romanesque, part Chateauesque. The stable connects with the house through an arched entrance, and it has its own twin towers.

6 **Plymouth Congregational Church,** 1907–1908
Shepley, Rutan, and Coolidge
1900 Nicollet Avenue

The Rural English Gothic in stone. The same Boston architectural firm built numerous Period Revival churches throughout the United States.

7 **House** (now Franklin National Bank), c. 1906
Marshall and Fox
100 Franklin Avenue W

The largest adaptation of the sixteenth-century or seventeenth-century Italian palace still standing in Minneapolis.

8 **Three Houses,** 1890, 1898, 1898
1920, 1924, and 1928 Stevens Avenue S

The Loring Park and Kenwood districts of Minneapolis are filled with examples of the Colonial Revival, the earliest of which are within the Queen Anne Revival of the late 1880s and 1890s. The post-1900 examples tend to be more "correct" and lean toward the eighteenth-century Georgian and Federal styles. The oldest of the three houses is Queen Anne/Colonial Revival and is sheathed in wood; the other two are Georgian and are built of brick.

9 **Hewitt House** (now a funeral home), 1906
Hewitt and Brown
126 Franklin Avenue E

The firm of Hewitt and Brown produced a number of houses after the turn of the century which loosely fit into the Craftsman tradition. Hewitt's own house nods to the English, but it is not really an example of the open use of historic images. The years in which these houses were produced mark the entrance of John Jager into the firm. Jager, who had studied with Otto Wagner in Vienna, could well have been involved with the designs of this and other houses.

10 **Farrington House,** 1906
William Channing Whitney
2100 Stevens Avenue S

One of Whitney's many versions of the American Georgian. This one is in red brick.

11 **Gale House,** c. 1912
Ernest Kennedy
2115 Stevens Avenue S

A suave version of the Italian palazzo.

12 **Charles Pillsbury House,** 1912
Hewitt and Brown
106 22nd Street E

Elizabethan Gothic with great reserve.

13 **Alfred Pillsbury House,** 1903
Ernest Kennedy
116 22nd Street E

13 Alfred Pillsbury House.

Gothic, but its rough stone exterior and its massing hark back to the Richardsonian Romanesque.

14 **Merrill House,** 1887
James C. Plant and William Channing Whitney
2116 2nd Avenue S

An early exercise (for Minneapolis) in the Chateauesque. The heavy rusticated stone makes it almost Romanesque.

15 **Christian House** (now Hennepin County Historical Society), 1919
Hewitt and Brown
2301–03 3rd Avenue S

The Renaissance and late English Gothic mixed together, as one might find in seventeenth-century England.

16 **Taylor Block,** 1886
E. S. Stebbins
Northwest corner 4th Avenue S and 22nd Street E

A three-story Queen Anne commercial block in red brick with a series of moongate windows.

17 **Morse House,** c. 1873–74
2402 4th Avenue S

A wood Italianate house with an overscaled cupola.

18 **Fair Oaks Apartments,** 1939
Perry Crosier
3rd Avenue S between 24th and 25th Streets E

The three-story garden apartments arranged around courts have been sensitively related to the older buildings nearby. In style there is a slight suggestion of the Colonial in the brick walls, the pattern of the windows, and the low overhanging roofs.

19 **House,** 1892
2542 Clinton Avenue S

Queen Anne/Colonial Revival with a suggestion of half-timbering in the high third-floor gables.

20 Minneapolis Institute of Arts, 1912–14
1973–74
McKim, Mead, and White
2400 3rd Avenue S

McKim, Mead, and White proposed a design with a series of large inner courts which would have included the whole block. Only the center frontispiece has been built, but it is a beautiful example of the Beaux Arts at its best in the great portico and stairs and the interior spaces. In 1973–74 Kenzo Tange, in association with Parker, Klein Associates, substantially enlarged the museum and added new buildings for the children's theatre, the art school, and a parking garage. The new additions are at best a disappointment. They are of immense scale, overwhelming not only the original Beaux Arts building of McKim, Mead, and White but the whole neighborhood and even the park to the north, and they are insistently formal, without any of the gentility conveyed by the original building. The new design also abandoned the old porticoed entrance in favor of a new ground-level entrance which leads into an awkward two-story sculpture court. Nevertheless, the interior of the new children's theatre works well, and the same can be said of the interior of the new art school building.

21 Donahue House, c. 1882
2536 Stevens Avenue S

A twice-moved Eastlake/Queen Anne house which recently has been meticulously restored.

22 Commercial Block, 1890
W. H. Dennis
Northwest corner Stevens Avenue S and 26th Street E

A relatively plain three-story brick building; if its style can be catalogued, it is Eastlake.

23 First Christian Church, 1954
Thorshov and Cerny
Southwest corner 22nd Street and Stevens Avenue S

The church, which has a low-pitched gable roof, is well related to its site and surroundings. The east end, with its end wall placed within the framework of the building, is articulated by rectangular squares with punctured round windows.

24 Christian Science Church
(now vacant), 1912–14
Solon S. Beman
4–10 24th Street E

The favored image of the Christian Science church was Beaux Arts Classical. Here we have it presented with a classical entablatured entrance porch and Ionic columns.

24 Former Christian Science Church.

25 Goosman House, 1909
Purcell and Feick
2532 Pillsbury Avenue S

A bungalow of a most unusual plan. Note at the rear of the house the built-in garage and the careful composition of the west wall.

26 Service Station, 1926
Southwest corner Pillsbury Avenue S and 26th Street E

There is still a scattering of old service stations to be found in Minneapolis. This one is of the double pier type; the pump area and the station are covered by a single low tiled hip roof.

27 House, c. 1910
2222 Pillsbury Avenue S

One of the paths taken by the Midwest Prairie architects was to the monumental and formal. This can be best seen in the work of the Chicago architect George W. Maher. This house is a variation on Maher's work and is similar to the Leslie House, at 2424 Lake Place in the Kenwood district, which was designed in 1914 by Louis Long.

28 House, 1903
2215 Pillsbury Avenue S
A richly detailed Colonial Revival house, with high-relief, engaged Ionic piers. The house was extensively remodeled in 1916 by Harry Jones.

29 Meyers House, 1908
Purcell and Feick
2513 Garfield Avenue S
A Prairie box. The entrance is at one side, with the living room across the front, the porch to the south, and the dining room and the kitchen to the rear. The current sheathing and colors are not original.

30 House, 1902
2447 Bryant Avenue S
A Queen Anne/Colonial Revival house of some size.

31 Goetzenberger House, 1909
Purcell and Feick
2621 Emerson Avenue S
Purcell's continued fondness for the dramatic gable-ended roof can be seen in this house. The plan is larger than that of the Meyers House (#29) but is otherwise similar to it.

M-1n Lake Harriet and Minnehaha Creek

For well over fifty years the areas around Lake Calhoun, Lake Harriet, and Minnehaha Creek have represented the ideal environment for the middle middle and upper middle classes. Horace W. S. Cleveland and Charles W. Loring both argued (as early as 1883) that the acquiring of land and the construction of parks and parkways not only would add to the beauty and the livability of the city but would be a sound investment for the city and for private speculators in that adjacent lands would tend to increase in value and would also become desirable places to live. The development of south Minneapolis beautifully illustrates how on occasion beauty, money, and public and private interests can be combined for everyone's benefit. Lakes Calhoun, Harriet, and Nokomis are linked together by wooded parks and boulevards. This extensive park system is supplemented by six neighborhood playgrounds, and as a result beaches and playgrounds are relatively close to all of the residential neighborhoods.

Although most of the streets are laid out on a gridiron pattern, the rows of tall elms along the streets provide a forest atmosphere in the area. This is supplemented by the occasional ups and downs in the terrain and in certain areas by curved streets which interrupt the north/south, east/west streets. Public transportation via the street railroad was close to perfect in this section of Minneapolis. The major lines extended out from the downtown area and connected with lines running east and west. The most pleasant of all the southwest Minneapolis lines was the one that ran on its own right-of-way along the east side of Lake Calhoun and Lakewood Cemetery and along Lake Harriet.

The housing in southwest Minneapolis is predominantly single-family dwellings, and well over 90 percent of it represents the design of builders rather than architects. The area just south of Lake Street contains some multiple dwellings and many single-family houses which were built between 1905

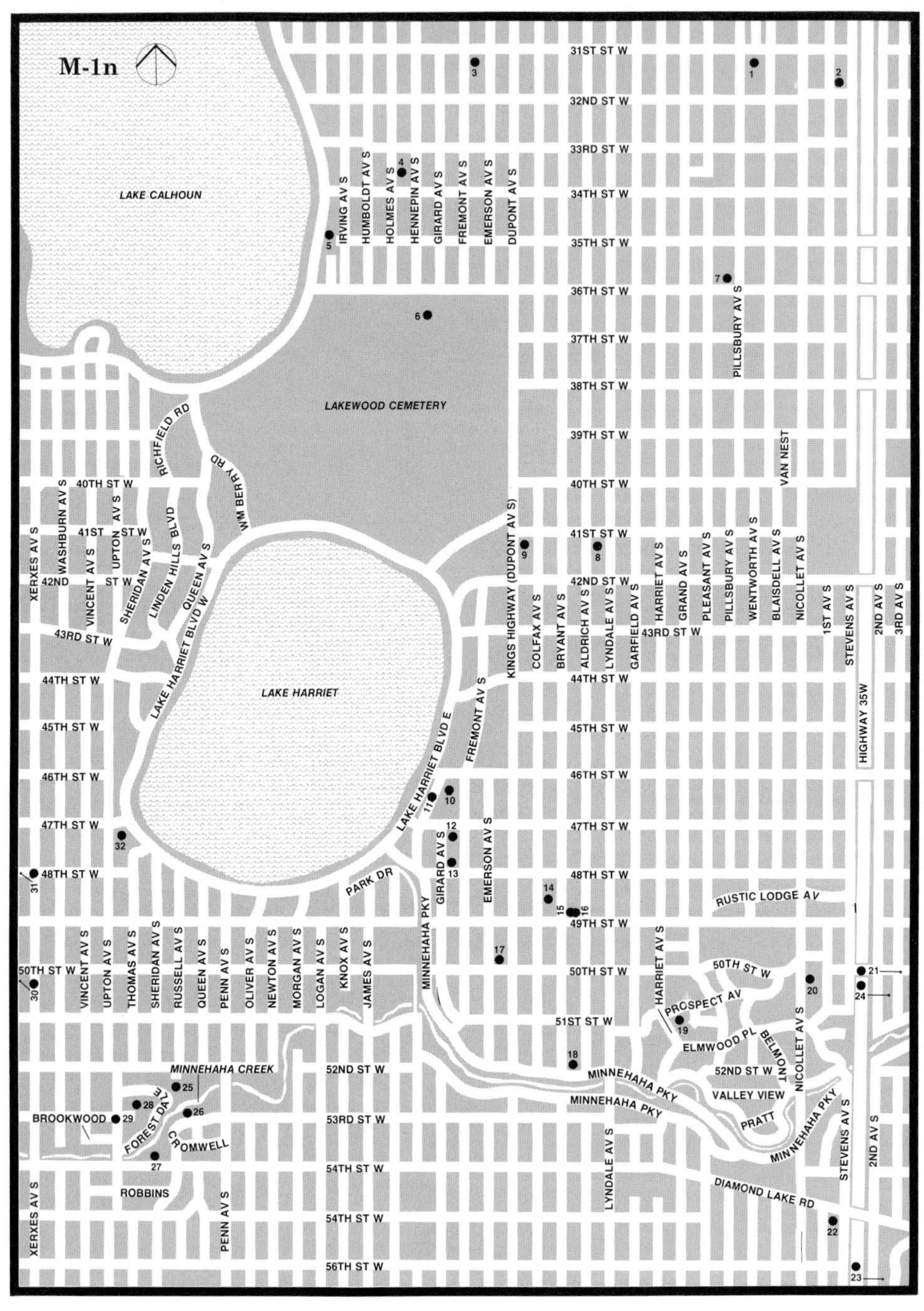
M-1n
LAKE CALHOUN
LAKEWOOD CEMETERY
LAKE HARRIET
MINNEHAHA CREEK
31ST ST W
32ND ST W
33RD ST W
34TH ST W
35TH ST W
36TH ST W
37TH ST W
38TH ST W
39TH ST W
40TH ST W
41ST ST W
42ND ST W
43RD ST W
44TH ST W
45TH ST W
46TH ST W
47TH ST W
48TH ST W
49TH ST W
50TH ST W
51ST ST W
52ND ST W
53RD ST W
54TH ST W
56TH ST W
IRVING AV S
HUMBOLDT AV S
HOLMES AV S
HENNEPIN AV S
GIRARD AV S
FREMONT AV S
EMERSON AV S
DUPONT AV S
PILLSBURY AV S
VAN NEST
RICHFIELD RD
WM BERRY RD
KINGS HIGHWAY (DUPONT AV S)
COLFAX AV S
BRYANT AV S
ALDRICH AV S
LYNDALE AV S
GARFIELD AV S
HARRIET AV S
GRAND AV S
PLEASANT AV S
WENTWORTH AV S
BLAISDELL AV S
NICOLLET AV S
1ST AV S
STEVENS AV S
2ND AV S
3RD AV S
HIGHWAY 35W
XERXES AV S
WASHBURN AV S
VINCENT AV S
UPTON AV S
SHERIDAN AV S
LINDEN HILLS BLVD
QUEEN AV S
LAKE HARRIET BLVD W
LAKE HARRIET BLVD E
PARK DR
MINNEHAHA PKY
THOMAS AV S
RUSSELL AV S
PENN AV S
OLIVER AV S
NEWTON AV S
MORGAN AV S
LOGAN AV S
KNOX AV S
JAMES AV S
RUSTIC LODGE AV
PROSPECT AV
ELMWOOD PL
BELMONT
VALLEY VIEW
PRATT
DIAMOND LAKE RD
BROOKWOOD
FOREST DALE
CROMWELL
ROBBINS

and 1925. Farther to the south, as one might expect, the housing is newer, much of it dating from the 1920s to the 1940s. There are pathways and islands of upper-middle-class housing along the shores of Lake Calhoun and Lake Harriet and the adjacent areas to the south and west, along parts of Dupont Avenue South (King's Highway), and overlooking Minnehaha Creek.

Commercial development within the area has been relatively well contained. Through the early 1930s the commercial developments occurred along the routes of the street railway; with the decline of this mode of transportation in the late 1930s shopping centers which were exclusively automobile-oriented grew up. Nicollet and Lyndale Avenues have occasional small neighborhood shopping centers, as does 47th Street and Cedar Avenue. The only large-scale shopping centers which grew up before World War II were on Lyndale Avenue South between 53rd Street and 54th Street (which included an early supermarket and a theatre) and another which represented a spill-over of the Edina shopping center at 50th Street West and France Avenue South.

The two greatest negative factors which affect the area are the freeway (Highway 35W), which slices right through the middle, and the presence of the metropolitan airport, which means that much of south Minneapolis is subjected to the incessant hum of jets. Still, the area provides one of the most agreeable places to live in the entire city.

1 **Charles Horn Towers,** 1971
S. C. Smiley and Associates
115 31st Street W

Three concrete towers, each twenty-two stories high, provide 501 units of housing for the elderly. As a high-rise complex it works well as long as low-density housing is maintained around it.

2 **Stewart Memorial Presbyterian Church,** 1908–1909
Purcell and Feick
116 32nd Street E

Purcell based the cruciform scheme of this church on Wright's Unity Temple (1906) in Oak Park, Illinois, but he made it more domestic and less monumental. Purcell and Feick's design for the church entailed a Sunday School wing to the west which would have added considerably to the total design of the building. The present wing was built later and is not their design.

3 **Joyce Memorial Methodist Church** (now Joyce United Methodist Southwest Parish Church), 1907
1219 31st Street W

The romance of the Mission Style had its heyday between 1900 and 1915, and even Minnesota could not escape its influence. Most of the Mission Revival buildings tend to be pretty thin as designs, but the design of this church has substance.

4 **Hennepin Aristocrat Apartments,** 1961
Liebenberg and Kaplan
3332 Hennepin Avenue

Here is the atmosphere of the 1950s and 1960s in all of its glory — a busy (almost Victorian) surface with grills and fancy lettering.

4 Hennepin Aristocrat Apartments.

5 **St. Mary's Greek Orthodox Church,** 1956–57
Thorshov and Cerny
3450 Irving Avenue S

A domed traditional Byzantine church made contemporary with a good dose of Mies. Best seen from the west shore of Lake Calhoun.

6 **Lakewood Cemetery Memorial Park,** estab. 1871
3600 Hennepin Avenue
Chapel and Entrance Gateway, 1890
Frank E. Read
Memorial Chapel, 1908
Harry Jones

A walk or drive through Lakewood Cemetery provides a lesson in architecture, especially historic period architecture. The classic predominates in the mausoleums of the rich, but here and there are examples of the Gothic. In a few instances the designer went even farther afield, as did LeRoy S. Buffington in his Egyptian-styled mausoleum (1923) for the Howe family. The entrance gates and the administration building are pristine Beaux Arts. Harry Jones's chapel is an exercise in the Byzantine, only it represents a kind of Byzantine building which never existed in the eastern Mediterranean. The narrow verticality of the typical Byzantine church has been made horizontal in this chapel as in Hagia Sophia.

6 Lakewood Cemetery Memorial Chapel.

7 **Bachus House,** 1915
Purcell and Elmslie
212 36th Street W

Purcell and Elmslie experimented with various ways of building Prairie houses very inexpensively. The square stucco form was much favored in Craftsman houses designed by builders and architects from 1900 through 1920. It was a form which Wright had employed successfully, especially in his $5,000 concrete *Ladies' Home Journal* house (1906). The Bachus House is essentially one ground-floor room divided up into entrance, living, dining, and cooking spaces. Two of the bedrooms upstairs were planned in such a way that they could be combined into one space.

8 **House,** 1915
Kirby T. Snyder
4101 Lyndale Avenue S

A very busy (in form and detail) Prairie house. In plan it is a fairly traditional dwelling which has been repackaged in the Prairie Style.

9 **Wolf House,** 1912–13
Purcell, Feick, and Elmslie
4109 Dupont Avenue S

The two-story Prairie box with the entrance on the north side, the living room across the front, and the dining room and the kitchen to the rear. The house was built without the architects' supervision, and the details of their planning were not fully carried out.

10 **Wiethoff House,** 1917
Purcell and Elmslie
4609 Humboldt Avenue S

Purcell was always fascinated with the traditional gable roof form, and here he presented the gable end toward the street. From 1915 on, the designs of the firm became increasingly lighter and more delicate, responding perhaps to the renewed interest in America's colonial past. In a way the Wiethoff house is Purcell and Elmslie's version of the American Colonial. The leaded windows and the other details of this house are especially fine. Note the design solution for the single-car garage.

11 McCosker House, 1909
Purcell and Feick
4615 Lake Harriet Boulevard

Although this house has been remodeled a number of times, one can still sense that it is a Purcell project. Like other pre-Elmslie designs (pre-1909) this house is more Craftsman than Prairie.

12 Wakefield House, 1911
Purcell, Feick, and Elmslie
4700 Fremont Avenue S

Whenever Elmslie put his hand to the Craftsman stucco box, he transformed it into an architectural high art object. Note the way the dormers sharply cut into and project out from the roof plane and the geometric surface pattern of wood, stucco, and glass of the stair-bay.

13 House, 1958
Benjamin Gingold
4745 Girard Avenue S

Although the house is insistently modern (it even has a two-story cylinder), its style is formal, almost Regency.

14 Parker House, 1912–13
Purcell, Feick, and Elmslie
4829 Colfax Avenue S

The high-pitched roof seems to pull the whole volume down to the ground. Note the sawed wood ornament over the entrance.

15 Mueller Studio, 1910–11
Purcell, Feick, and Elmslie
4845 Bryant Avenue S

This small, horizontal board-and-batten studio building was originally sited in a grove of pines which reached to 49th Street and eastward to the Mueller House on Aldrich. On the first floor there were two major rooms with an entrance/kitchen/bath section as the core. The garage was placed below the living room.

16 Mueller House, 1912–13
Paul Mueller
4844 Aldrich Avenue S

A Craftsman house designed by its owner, who was a landscape architect; impressive use of stone and wood. The studio (#15) was used as an office.

17 Hineline House, 1910
Purcell, Feick, and Elmslie
4920 Dupont Avenue S

Purcell and Elmslie's marriage of Craftsman and Prairie. The once-open screen porch to the south has now been enclosed, and the delicate sawed wood beams which projected from the corners of the entrance porch are gone.

18 House, 1927
Frederick C. Wilhelm
5140 Aldrich Avenue S

There are a few Spanish, Mediterranean, and Moorish buildings to be found in the northland of Minnesota. This one has a sumptuous entrance and an arcaded porch to the south.

19 Washburn Water Tower, 1931–32
Fellows and Huey; William S. Hewitt, engineer
Prospect Avenue

A concrete domed water tower in the Goodhue fashion of the 1920s. As a design it succeeds; the row of concrete ribs carried up to the crown of the dome reads well from a distance, and at closer range the series of oversized Teutonic knights and the row of eagles (all by John K. Daniels) give a needed richness to the structure.

19 Washburn Water Tower.

20 Lustron Prefabricated Metal Houses, 1948
Lustron Corporation
5015, 5021, and 5027 Nicollet Avenue

Three post–World War II metal (porcelain panel) bungalows, each of which has been personalized over the years. Another group of these houses can be found on Cedar Avenue (#24).

21 House, c. 1935
508 Minnehaha Parkway E

There are not many of these Streamline Moderne box dwellings in the Twin Cities. This one and its companion at 2906 Minnehaha Parkway East are among the few to be encountered in south Minneapolis.

22 Mayflower Community Congregational Church (now a funeral home), 1928–36
C. J. Bard
5500 Stevens Avenue S (at Diamond Lake Road)

A knowing essay in the Spanish Colonial Revival of the 1920s.

22 Mayflower Community Congregational Church (now funeral home).

23 Hope Lutheran Church, 1968
Ralph Rapson and Associates
5728 Cedar Avenue

Rapson's plunge into the West Coast Mine-Shaft School. Stucco with shed roofs.

24 Lustron Prefabricated Metal Houses, 1948
Lustron Corporation
4900 and 4916 Cedar Avenue

Perfectly preserved examples of Lustron's metal houses. (For others, see #20.)

24 Lustron Prefabricated Metal House.

25 Houses on Russell Court
Russell Avenue S and 52nd Street W
10 Russell Court (1950)
16 Russell Court (1950)
20 Russell Court (1964); Johnson and Nordbloom
30 Russell Court (1954); Benjamin Gingold

Four woodsy architect-designed houses of the 1950s and early 1960s.

26 House, 1920–21
5308 Russell Avenue S

An offshoot of both the Hispanic Mission Revival and the later Spanish Colonial Revival was the Pueblo Revival. The style began to surface in the early 1900s and continued on through the 1930s. This Minneapolis example has the usual stucco walls, parapeted roofs, and projecting vegas which became the hallmark of the style.

27 Houses on Cromwell Court
54th Street W (east of Upton Avenue S)
2602 Cromwell Court (1950)
2604 Cromwell Court (1951); Carl Graffunder
2606 Cromwell Court (1951); Carl Graffunder
2608 Cromwell Court (1961); Stowell D. Leach

Like the group of houses on Russell Court (#25), these post–World War II dwellings are low-keyed and seem to snuggle themselves into the wooded site.

28 Red Cedar Lane, 1904–50
John Jager
East of Upton Avenue S and 53rd Street W

The architect John Jager, a close friend of Purcell and Elmslie, laid out not only Red Cedar Lane, but the whole area running to Forest Dale Road and Minnehaha Creek. He planted red cedars along the lane and in the rest of the area he mixed deciduous and coniferous trees; as a result, the area is as green in the winter as it is in the summer. Jager's plain, rather puritanical house built of river boulders and clapboard is located at 6 Red Cedar Lane.

29 Speculative Housing, 1927–32
Purcell and Strauel

The architects worked closely with the developer-builder H. M. Peterson in the late 1920s and the early 1930s. They designed nine speculative houses in the area, plus a house for Peterson himself (3 Red Cedar Lane). The houses illustrate how these architects were able to mold the Period Revival imagery of the 1920s into compositions with a remarkable attention to function seldom found in run-of-the-mill architectural products of this decade.

Peterson House, 1927–28
William G. Purcell
3 Red Cedar Lane

A stucco, stone, and wood cottage; one story on the street, two stories to the south. Note the design of the leaded-glass windows and the sliding glass garage doors.

House, 1932
Purcell and Strauel
5309 Upton Avenue S

Somewhat English.

House, 1928
Frederick Strauel
5315 Upton Avenue S

English imagery.

House, 1928
Purcell and Strauel
5319 Upton Avenue S

House, 1929
Purcell and Strauel
5312 Upton Avenue S

The style may appear to be mildly English (or even Spanish, perhaps), but it is really late Craftsman.

• **House,** 1928
Purcell and Strauel
5312 Vincent Avenue S

In this house one can see how the architects created the image of a Colonial house, not by using correct detailing but by simplifying the whole so that it has the qualities we would expect to find in a house dating from the middle of the eighteenth century.

Bungalow, 1928
Purcell and Strauel
5217 Vincent Avenue S

A stuccoed late Craftsman bungalow.

House, 1929
Frederick Strauel
2825 Brookwood Terrace

English half-timbering; the most openly historical of the group.

30 Werness Brothers Funeral Chapel, 1963
Thorsen and Thorshov
3500 50th Street W

A brick building with a mansard roof, set formally on a podium.

31 Lutheran Church of the Good Shepherd, 1949–50
Hills, Gilbertson, and Hayes
4801 France Avenue S

A reasonable variation on the work of the Saarinens in the 1940s. The relationship of the rectangular volumes — the tall, narrow tower, the sanctuary, and the low Sunday School wing — is well handled. The force of the composition is compromised by the large relief sculpture on the west front and the patterning of the narrow slit windows of the Sunday School wing.

32 House, 1910
4700 Lake Harriet Boulevard W

A stuccoed Craftsman house with a hint of European Secessionist architecture from the turn of the century. Note the bold relief frieze on the second floor and the relief sculpture near the entrance. The house is now painted white; originally the exterior wood members and sculptures had a natural finish.

M-1o Kenwood and Lake of the Isles

The growth of the Kenwood and Lake of the Isles districts was closely tied to the development of the park system. In addition, the establishment in 1893 of The Parade provided an extensive greenbelt to the north which protected the area from commercial and industrial encroachment. To the west Kenwood Park, Kenwood Parkway, and Lake of the Isles (developed between 1886 and 1911) formed a lake and park district close to the downtown area. Hennepin Avenue, the eastern boundary, acquired a major streetcar line in 1891. Retail commercial strips began to develop along Hennepin Avenue. Eventually these joined with the commercial strip along Lake Street West, but the section of Lake Street near Lake Calhoun and Hennepin Avenue never became fully commercial. Apartment houses, small parks, and churches also occurred along these streets.

The area atop Kenwood Hill with its view to the north over the city early became a fashionable place to live. Between 1890 and 1915 large residences were built on Mount Curve Avenue and Groveland Terrace. Many of those on Mount Curve Avenue have survived, but almost all of those on Groveland Terrace are gone. The north/south grid of alphabetically named streets — Bryant through Logan — developed into a residential area similar to that in the Lowry Hill district to the east, with large turn-of-the-century houses on small lots. The houses toward the east (nearest Hennepin Avenue) were generally the oldest, and those near Kenwood Park and Lake of the Isles (with some exceptions) were built later.

Small apartment buildings (four or six units) were built near Hennepin Avenue from the beginning, but the rest of the housing was almost exclusively for single families. Although there are some late Queen Anne dwellings in the area (several are still standing on Kenwood Parkway), the Queen Anne/Colonial Revival is the style found in most of the earliest houses. After the turn of the century a wide range of styles was utilized. Lake of the Isles and much of the Kenwood Park area was built during the 1920s. Lake of the Isles Boulevard underwent two surges of building activity — the first between 1905 and 1915 on the eastern shores of the lake and the second in the 1920s on the north and west sides of the lake.

On the whole this district has survived: High-rise units have not yet intruded into the area, and commercial activity has not compromised its residential nature. Although many of the houses to the east began to fall into disrepair in the 1940s many have been sympathetically restored or remodeled; some have been divided into multiple-unit housing. The only area which has suffered as a result of post–World War II "improvement" is the lower part of Kenwood Hill. For instance, Kenwood Parkway from Morgan Avenue to Emerson Avenue was originally a secluded wooded glen with a number of Craftsman and Period houses built betwen 1910 and 1930, but the freeway (Highway 12), which bends toward the hill just west of The Parade, now contributes its fumes and noise to the sylvan scene.

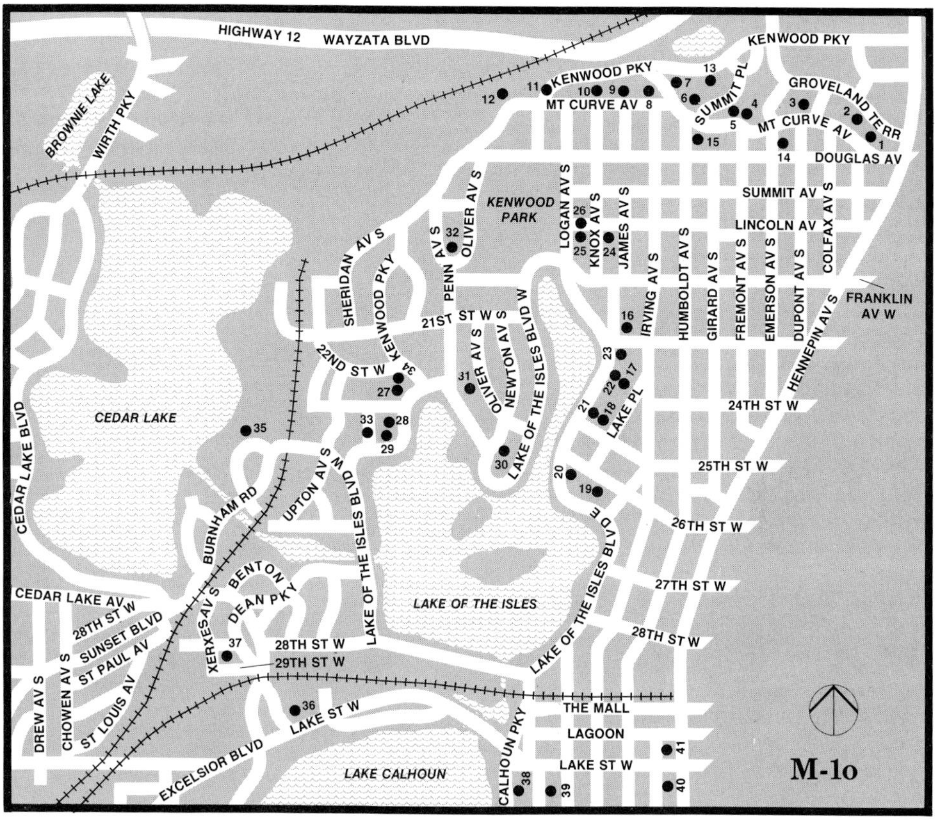

1 **Nott House,** 1892
Long and Kees
15 Groveland Terrace
Classicized Romanesque in rough-cut stone.

2 **Long House,** 1894
Long and Kees
25 Groveland Terrace
This house, a Richardsonian Shingle Style dwelling in stone, is the most impressive example of 1890s domestic design in the Twin Cities. The extensive tile roof is carried down almost to the ground. The entrance porch snuggles into one corner under the roof, and each of the gable ends is beautifully composed. The quality of the overall design is carried into the interior space and its detailing of stone, wood, and leaded glass.

2 Long House.

3 **Rood House,** 1948
Close Associates
1650 Dupont Avenue S

The entrance courtyard, framed by the stone wall from an earlier dwelling, and the wood-sheathed International Style house are highly successful.

4 **Martin House,** 1904
William Channing Whitney
1300 Mount Curve Avenue

The Renaissance palazzo in brick, placed far back from the street on a bluff overlooking downtown Minneapolis.

5 **Winton House,** 1910
George W. Maher
1324 Mount Curve Avenue

George W. Maher, who had worked with Wright in the Chicago office of James Lyman Silsbee in the late 1880s, developed a design which combined Sullivanesque, Wrightian, and Classical forms and details. This house is essentially an American version of an Italian palazzo (the low overhanging roof, the entrance centerpiece and terrace, and the detailing are all in the Prairie Style) — monumental, but modern for its time.

6 **House,** c. 1870s
46 Summit Place

A two-story white clapboard house with a T-plan; more rural than Greek.

7 **House,** 1969–70
Horty, Elving, and Associates
1520 Waverly Place

An International Style composition sheathed in wood. Vertical window units play off against the horizontal elements.

7 House.

8 **Thomas House,** 1905, 1915
Hewitt and Brown
1600 Mount Curve Avenue

A monumental Maheresque dwelling with Sullivanesque ornament. One wonders whether this house might have been designed by John Jager, who was in the Hewitt and Brown office at that time.

9 **House,** 1960
Bliss and Campbell
1700 Mount Curve Avenue

A post-and-beam house, reminiscent of the work of Neutra, with exposed wood beams and gray brick walls.

10 **Donaldson House,** 1906
1712 Mount Curve Avenue

A Maheresque house, more mellow than the Winton House (#5) and the Thomas House (#8). Note the Sullivanesque ornament.

11 **House,** 1964
Baker-Lange Associates
1916 Mount Curve Avenue

The wooded site and the woodsy house melt into one another.

12 **Water Tower** (now unused), 1919
Kenwood Parkway at Oliver Avenue

Medieval, with an indication of the Romanesque in the rows of narrow vertical panels.

13 **Miller House,** 1926
Liebenberg and Kaplan
735 Kenwood Parkway

An English cottage with a wraparound roof suggestive of thatching.

•14 **Quinlan House,** 1924
Frederick Ackerman
1711 Emerson Avenue S

A sophisticated and refined three-story Italian palazzo of late sixteenth-century design.

5 Johnson House, 1972
Roger F. Johnson
1717 Humboldt Avenue S

Two bays as boxes project toward the street from a central volume.

5 Johnson House.

6 House, 1911
1600 22nd Street W

A design based upon George W. Maher's designs for a number of small houses in and around Chicago. Most of these were rectangular volumes covered with wide overhanging hipped roofs and were formal in layout; they often had ornamentation in terra-cotta, wood, tile, and leaded glass.

7 Purcell House, 1913
Purcell and Elmslie
2328 Lake Place

The high point of the domestic designs of Purcell and Elmslie and one of the great Prairie houses of America. The dwelling has been set far back from the street on its narrow lot with a garden in front and open space in the adjoining gardens at the side. From the living and dining porch at the rear there is a view of Lake of the Isles. The main floor of the house is a dramatic single space composed of different levels with the living room lower than the entrance area and the dining room raised at the rear. The sunken pool and its fountain in front of the living room windows have been filled in.

8 Leslie House, 1914
Louis Long
2424 Lake Place

A Maheresque Prairie house.

19 Powers House, 1910
Purcell, Feick, and Elmslie
1635 26th Street W

A formal and slightly monumental Purcell and Elmslie house, indicating in part Elmslie's transition from the Sullivan office to that of Purcell. A terra-cotta ornamental panel occurs over the fireplace.

•20 House, 1930
Ernest Kennedy
2601 Lake of the Isles Boulevard E

A highly romantic English image in stone, half-timber, and stucco. A hexagonal tower faces onto 26th Street West.

21 House, 1910
2427 Lake of the Isles Boulevard E

A white Mediterranean villa perched on a podium and hidden behind a curved pergola. Stylistically the house represents an amalgamation of the Mission and Mediterranean styles with the Craftsman and Prairie styles. Houses of similar design were being built in California during this period.

21 House.

22 Gray House, 1907
Purcell and Feick
2409 Lake of the Isles Boulevard E

Purcell consulted with George Elmslie on the design of this house. In plan it is a variation on Wright's $5,000 concrete Prairie house, except that it is substantially larger. Originally there was a narrow screened passageway and a pavilion porch on the south side of the house (in the area now occupied by enclosed porches). The house once had light tan stucco, unpainted brick, and natural wood, all of which are now painted white.

23 House, 1911, 1922
2201 Lake of the Isles Boulevard E
A romantic assemblage of stone and stucco walls, a steep slate roof, gates, and terraces in Medieval English imagery. The present form of the house is the result of additions and remodeling which were done by Kenyon and Maine in 1922.

24 Gross House, 1921
1901 Knox Avenue S
A Prairie Maheresque house in brick with delicately detailed leaded glass windows.

25 House, 1941
1900 Knox Avenue S
Each decade has come up with its own interpretations of the historic styles of the past. Here the American Georgian is rendered with a delicacy and an attachment to the ground not found earlier.

26 House, 1913
A. R. Van Dyck
1901 Logan Avenue S
The Renaissance palazzo, more French than Italian. The house stands close to the street on the north with terraced gardens on the west and the south.

27 House, 1922
Liebenberg, Kaplan, and Martin
2388 Lake of the Isles Boulevard W
The image of the English cottage with a wraparound roof to suggest thatching and thick columns at the entrance.

28 House, 1920
Mark Frazer
2416 Lake of the Isles Boulevard W
Medieval via the turn-of-the-century English Arts and Crafts movement.

29 House, 1929
2424 Lake of the Isles Boulevard W
An English Medieval manor in stucco with stone trim.

30 Owre House, 1911–12
Purcell, Feick, and Elmslie
2625 Newton Avenue S
A Purcell and Elmslie classic. The two-story rectangular house is turned with its narrow side facing the street and its entrance (almost a secluded entrance court) facing north. This siting provided a view of the lake from the projecting glassed-i porch and the long living room/dining room window. To the rear is an early example of a detached garage by Purcell and Elmslie.

31 Tillotson House, 1912
Purcell, Feick, and Elmslie
2316 Oliver Avenue S
The plan is similar to that for the Owre House. The street façade of the Tillotsor House appears to be held in place by th high-pitched gable roof.

32 House, 1951–52
Close Associates
1941 Penn Avenue S
The non-urban image of the 1940s and the 1950s. The wood-sheathed house ha a low profile and stands amid a thick growth of shrubs and trees.

33 House, 1966–67
Hugh G. S. Peacock
2421 Russell Avenue S
The West Coast shed-roof tradition mad formal. Underneath the redesigning is the original 1907 house.

34 House, 1915
2405 22nd Street W
This is a rare example of a house type which was quite popular on the West Coast between 1905 and 1920. It consis of a one-and-a-half-story rectangular block, visually balanced by a low flat-roofed wing on each side. A broad terrac and entrance steps are situated in front of the central block. This Minneapolis example has Prairie styling in the treat ment of the surface and the ornamentation.

•35 Neils House, 1950–51
Frank Lloyd Wright
2801 Burnham Boulevard
The low-pitched roofs reach almost to th ground, covering the narrow, randomly laid marble walls below. The carport faces the street and a high angled window overlooks Cedar Lake. Both interio and exterior walls are of stone and woo

36 Calhoun Beach Club Apartments, 1927–29
Magney and Tusler
Northeast corner Lake Street W and Dean Boulevard

This high-rise apartment building was started just before the Depression of the 1930s and was not finished until the late 1940s. In style it is vaguely classical. The injection of a high-rise on the lake at this early date was regrettable because it opened the way for the construction of other high-rise units on the shore of Lake Calhoun during the 1950s and 1960s.

37 Two Duplexes, 1935–36
Perry Crosier
2801 and 2805 Xerxes Avenue S

Two duplex buildings which mix the Zigzag and Streamline phases of the Moderne.

37 Two Duplexes.

38 Apartments, 1973
Richard F. Zenisek
3033 Calhoun Boulevard E

The lakeshore side of the complex is laid out in a sawtooth manner so that each unit and its balcony faces the lake. The entire three-story structure is sheathed in wood.

38 Apartments.

39 Two Apartment Buildings, 1929
C. J. Bard
3021 and 3028 James Avenue S

The north/south avenues east of Lake Calhoun contain many apartment houses built during the 1920s. Because of their sites they are all long and narrow, and generally they differ only in their street elevations. These two examples give an indication of the variety of styles used (the house at 3021 James Avenue is Zigzag Moderne, and the house at 3028 James Avenue is Spanish/Moorish).

40 Granada Theatre (now Suburban World Theatre), 1927–28
Liebenberg and Kaplan
3022 Hennepin Avenue

A Spanish/Moorish motion picture palace that might seem more at home in California.

41 Uptown Theatre, 1941
Liebenberg and Kaplan
2906 Hennepin Avenue

An earlier theatre building (1913) was remodeled into the Streamline Moderne after a fire in 1939. The relief sculpture takes one back to the fashions of the New York World's Fair in 1939.

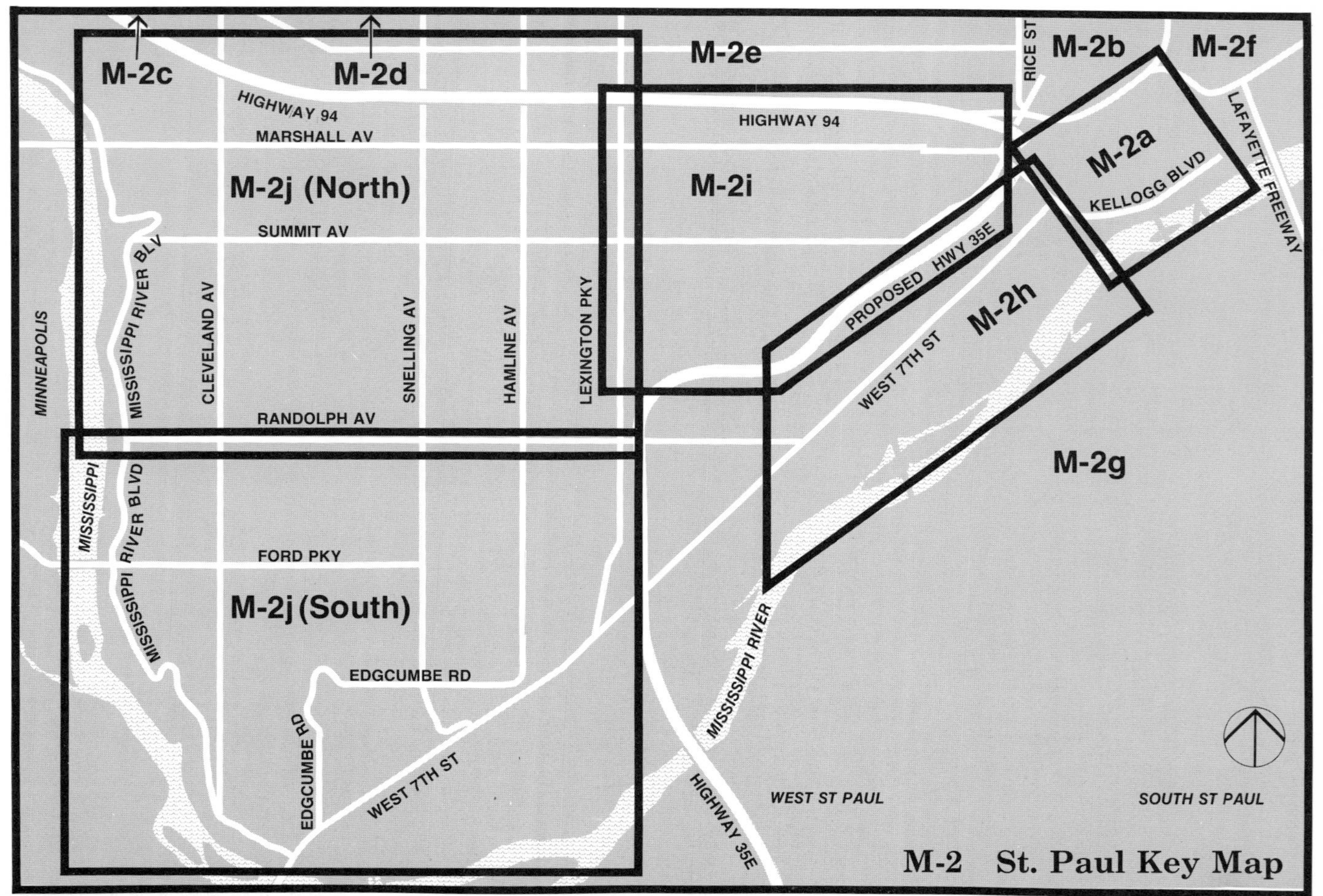
M-2 St. Paul Key Map
M-2a
M-2b
M-2c
M-2d
M-2e
M-2f
M-2g
M-2h
M-2i
M-2j (North)
M-2j (South)
LAFAYETTE FREEWAY
KELLOGG BLVD
RICE ST
HIGHWAY 94
PROPOSED HWY 35E
WEST 7TH ST
MISSISSIPPI RIVER
HIGHWAY 35E
SOUTH ST PAUL
WEST ST PAUL
LEXINGTON PKY
HAMLINE AV
SNELLING AV
EDGCUMBE RD
MARSHALL AV
SUMMIT AV
RANDOLPH AV
FORD PKY
CLEVELAND AV
MISSISSIPPI RIVER BLV
MISSISSIPPI RIVER BLVD
MISSISSIPPI
MINNEAPOLIS

M-2 St. Paul

The emergence of St. Paul as a major urban center in Minnesota was the outcome of three factors. First, the Mississippi River was easily navigable up to this point. Second, the city early emerged as the political capital of the state. Third, through the efforts of James J. Hill and others, the city became the major center for a railroad network which eventually reached to the Pacific coast.

The site selected for the city was on the bluff on the east bank of the river. The city had access to the river flats and the river, but it was high enough so that it was not threatened by floods; all in all it was a pleasant place to live and work. The bluff upon which the early city grew was adequate for a small river town, but it was hardly ideal for a large city. The terrain rose steeply behind the flat shelf of the bluff, so that the downtown area of St. Paul has always seemed constrained. As the city developed, it spread in all directions and very early it jumped across the river. Much of the land directly west of the downtown area is essentially flat, but the terrain to the northeast and across the river is composed of gently rolling hills.

The city began to be settled in 1840; it was designated the territorial capital in 1849 and the state capital in 1858. The first platting of St. Paul occurred in 1847; by 1851 the entire central core had been platted and maps had been drawn up for suburbs as far to the northeast as Dayton's Bluff and to the lowlands on the west side of the river by 1857. The 1870s and 1880s witnessed innumerable additions to the city: to the west, Summit Park (1871) and Macalester Park (1883–88); to the southwest, along West 7th Street (1873–91); and to the north and northwest, Arlington Hills (1873), Lake Como Villas, Como Park (1856 and 1857), and St. Anthony Park (1885).

M-2a Downtown

Downtown St. Paul has always conveyed the feeling of confinement, with the high bluffs of the river on one side of it and the steep hills behind it. This feeling of confinement has been accentuated since the construction in the 1960s of the freeways (Highways 56, 94 and parts of 35E). The freeway corridor along Highway 94 has effectively cut the downtown area off from the Capitol and its parks to the north, and the configuration of Highways 56 and 94 separates the northern downtown area from the Mounds Park and Lake Phalen areas. If the southwestern section of Highway 35E is completed, downtown St. Paul will be completely severed from its western and northern neighborhoods.

The character of downtown St. Paul is quite different from that of downtown Minneapolis. The Mississippi River looms as a much more important element here than it does in Minneapolis, and the wooded hills to the west (near Summit Avenue) bring suburbia close to the downtown area. The pattern of the downtown streets is bewildering and confusing, and this is compounded by the ups and downs of the terrain and by the recent designation of a maze of one-way streets. Through much of the 1950s downtown St. Paul was charming, conservative, and a bit (but not too much) run-down. By the end of the 1950s and on into the 1960s St. Paul plunged into urban renewal and, as in Minneapolis, the results have not always been good. The city has lost a number of architectural landmarks of real character — the Richardsonian Globe Building, the large and imposing Ryan Hotel (1885), the New York Life Insurance Company Building (1887–89), and many others. Nevertheless, the recent building activity has succeeded in creating a new image for the city through the introduction of the latest in high-rises, plazas, and skyways.

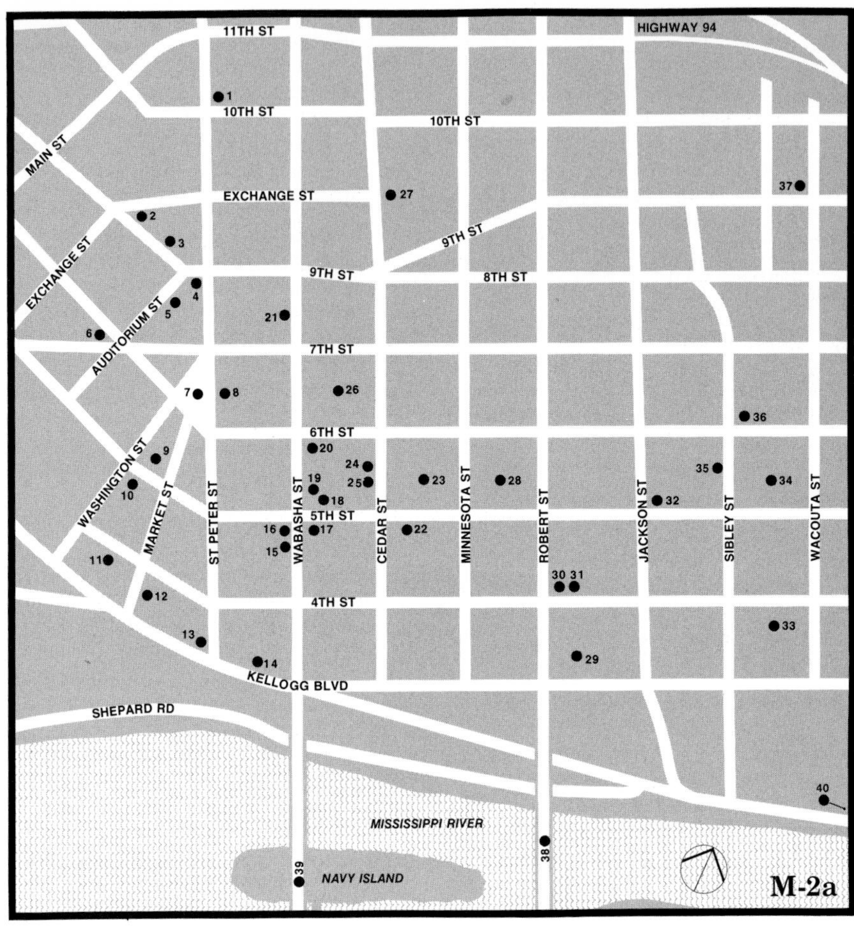

1 **Willard Apartments,** 1915
J. O. Eduberg
530–44 St. Peter Street

This brick building was remodeled in 1915 to expand it and to bring it up to date. The architect carried a classical loggia screen across part of the St. Peter Street façade; high balconies project from the façade on 10th Street West.

2 **Assumption Parochial School,** 1864
Northeast corner Exchange Street West and 9th Street West

A two-story ashlar block building in the Italianate Style. Its central cupola is gone.

3 **Assumption Church,** 1869–73
Joseph Reidl
51 9th Street W

The architect, who was the court architect to the King of Bavaria, loosely patterned this provincial church after the Ludwigs Kirche in Munich. In style it is a mixture of South German Romanesque and Baroque, neoclassical but lacking the richness of detail usually found in Bavarian and Austrian churches.

Mickey's Diner, c. 1935
Southwest corner St. Peter Street and 9th Street W
The railroad dining car lunch counter, still going strong.

Mickey's Diner.

Labor Temple
416–18 Auditorium Street
A 1931 remodeling which produced a Zigzag Moderne façade; over the entrance is a relief sculpture depicting the virtue of work.

White Castle Hamburger Shop, c. 1941
Southwest corner Auditorium Street and 6th Street W
A porcelainized-metal castle reminiscent of the 1930s and the five-cent hamburger.

Hamm Square, 1965
Joseph Michels, Michael McGuire, and Marion Frey
Southwest corner St. Peter Street and 7th Street W
The redesigning of this small triangular plot of ground included the addition of a fountain and three bunches of trees. Like many public squares and parks designed by architects and sculptors, Hamm Square ends up being too much architecture and too little nature — what is needed at this point in the city is a maximum of greenery, not more brick and concrete surfaces.

Hamm Building, 1919
Toltz, King, and Day
Southeast corner St. Peter Street and 7th Street W
A six-story commercial block sheathed in delicate terra-cotta and encrusted with classical motifs.

•9 **Old Federal Courts Building,** 1894–1904
J. Edbrooke Willowby
95 5th Street W
Cleaned-up Richardsonian Romanesque; beautifully sited for a public building, with a small park to the north (Hamm Park). The principal façade with its high tower overlooks Rice Park to the south. The building, which is currently undergoing renovation under the direction of Stahl/Bennett will be used by a variety of civic and public groups. The building originally housed the post office, the courthouse, and the customs house.

10 **Rice Park,** 1849
Southwest corner 5th Street W and Market Street
The park was redesigned in 1968 by Hammel, Green, and Abrahamson. Their major contribution was the new circular pool and the adjoining sloped concrete area. (The sculpture in the park is by Alonzo Hauser.) This is a fairly successful reorganizing of an existing park, but even here the amount of concrete surface by the pool seems excessive.

11 **Central Library,** 1916
Electus D. Litchfield
90 4th Street W
A high point in Beaux Arts architecture in Minnesota — both externally in the urban relationship of the building to Rice Park on the north and to Kellogg Boulevard on the south and internally in the series of beautifully conceived spaces from the entrance on to the Reading Rooms. Neither Cass Gilbert's Capitol Building nor McKim, Mead, and White's Minneapolis Institute of Arts can compare with the design quality of this building.

12 **Tri-State Telephone Building** (now Northwestern Bell Telephone Building), 1940
Clarence H. Johnston, Jr.
70 4th Street W
A continuation into the late 1930s of the Zigzag Moderne, plus the influence of Raymond Hood and Rockefeller Center. Like the Minneapolis Telephone Company Building, the St. Paul structure has been visually spoiled by new additions.

13 Women's City Club (now the Minnesota Museum of Art), 1931
Magnus Jemne
305 St. Peter Street

A highly refined example of the Moderne (Art Deco), stylistically somewhere between the Zigzag phase of the 1920s and the Streamline phase of the 1930s. The adaptation to its new use as an art gallery is highly successful.

13 Women's City Club (now Minnesota Museum of Art).

14 City Hall and Ramsey County Courthouse, 1931–32
Holabird and Root; Ellerbe Architects
15 Kellogg Boulevard W

A major monument of the late Zigzag Moderne — or, as it was labeled at the time, the American Perpendicular Style. Over the entrances facing Kellogg Boulevard and 4th Street are relief sculptures by Lee Lawrie (who also produced sculpture for Bertram Goodhue's Capitol Building in Nebraska and for the Rockefeller Center). The building also contains murals by John Norton (who in the teens worked with Purcell and Elmslie and with Wright on the Midway Gardens). The high point o the interior is the War Memorial Concourse — a public space measuring 85 fee by 24 feet and 41 feet high. In the middl of this darkened space is Carl Milles's onyx sculpture, "Peace Memorial" (completed in 1936). Here the bringing together of theatre and architecture charac teristic of the 1920s is fully realized.

14 City Hall and Ramsey County Courthouse.

15 Lowry Lounge, c. 1937
47 Wabasha Street

A 1930s Moderne façade with relief sculpture.

16 The St. Paul Building, 1888–89
J. Walter Stevens
6 5th Street W

An eight-story Richardsonian Romanesque office block; its decoration is in th combination of Romanesque and Byzantine often found in the Romanesque Reviv al. Much of the ground-level façade of the building has been remodeled insens tively.

17 Northern States Power Company Building, 1930
Ellerbe Architects
360 Wabasha Street

The Moderne or American Perpendicula skyscraper of the late 1920s, appropriately equipped with relief sculpture ove the entrance.

18 Osborn Building, 1968
Bergstedt, Wahlberg, and Wold
370 Wabasha Street

A tall box, clad in glass and stainless steel, with an emphasis on the vertical. On the east side of the building is "Above, Above," a sculpture by Alexande Liberman (1972).

19 Capitol Center Plaza, 1968
Hammel, Green, and Abrahamson
Northeast side Wabasha Street betweer 5th and 6th Streets E

One of several open plazas which break u the overpowering character of the adjoin ing high-rises and serve as important fea tures of St. Paul's pedestrian skyway sys tem. (At present, there are six skyway bridges which cross over major streets.)

20 Northern Federal Savings and Loan Association Building, 1972–73
Grover Dimond Associates
386 Wabasha Street

A reflective glass box.

21 Riviera Theatre, 1911
Mark Fitzpatrick
449 Wabasha Street

Beaux Arts Classical of the 1904 St. Louis Fair brought to a theatre.

22 First Federal Savings and Loan Association Building, 1971
Dykins and Handford
360 Cedar Street

Quite a bit going on for a small site — the building as a low angular piece of sculpture sits in front of a small reflective façade box. In the context of the high-rises nearby, its low scale is a visual relief.

23 Northwestern National Bank Building, 1969
Grover Dimond Associates
55 5th Street E

A play of boxes, one horizontal, the other set on end with a vertical articulation of its surfaces.

24 Blue Chip Restaurant, 1973–74
Team 70 Architects
369 Cedar Street

The latest — supergraphics via neon.

25 Green Lantern Restaurant, 1973–74
Team 70 Architects
365 Cedar Street

The nostalgic 1970s rage for the 1920s; the Zigzag Moderne (Art Deco) recreated in neon.

26 Dayton's Department Store Building, 1963
Victor Gruen and Associates
Southwest corner Cedar Street and 7th Street E

A characteristic Gruen retail commercial box which shuts off the outside world; a period piece from the 1960s. The brick façade features an element of interest in the short, narrow, vertical lines of raised brick. In the plaza of the building is Henry Moore's "Bone Woman" sculpture of 1964.

27 Central Presbyterian Church, 1889
Warren H. Hayes
500 Cedar Street

Romanesque Revival, not Richardsonian by any means but still a respectable building. The covering of the great rose window with a vertical and horizontal metal mullioned window has not helped the appearance of the building.

28 American National Bank Building, 1975
Kelly Marshall Associates
Northeast corner Minnesota Street and 5th Street E

Another stage in the evolution of the sheathing of the post-World War II skyscraper. Metal and light blue were the fashion in the 1950s and early 1960s, dark metal (black or brown) and reflective glass later in the 1960s, and brilliant white sheathing, often of concrete, in the 1970s.

29 Kellogg Square Apartments, 1972
Convention Center Architects and Engineers
111 Kellogg Boulevard

To bring people back to live in the downtown area has been a goal of urban renewal all over the country. This is St. Paul's contribution.

30 Pioneer Building, 1888–89
Solon S. Beman
Northeast corner Robert Street and 4th Street E

A Romanesque office block. The interior reveals an atrium open to the top, surrounded by a latticework of exposed metal elevators and stairways.

31 Endicott Building, 1889–90
Cass Gilbert and James Knox Taylor
141 4th Street E

The Northern Italian Renaissance palace reworked to accommodate a six-story office block. Severe, reserved, and slightly academic Beaux Arts.

32 Merchants National Bank Building (now McColl Building), 1890
Edward P. Bassford
366–68 Jackson Street

A four-story Richardsonian Romanesque building which has recently been renovated.

32 Merchants National Bank Building (now McColl Building).

33 St. Paul Union Depot, 1917–20
Charles S. Frost; Toltz Engineering Company
Southeast corner Sibley Street and 4th Street E

A somber gray sandstone structure with a front elevation of Doric columns. The City Beautiful Beaux Arts, in a somewhat grim mood.

34 Smith Park (now Mears Park), 1849
Northeast corner Sibley Street and 5th Street E

The third oldest park in the city — a public square of slightly more than two acres. In 1973 the park was replanned by St. Paul's Housing and Redevelopment Authority (William Sanders, designer). The new design provided a fountain and a pool, tables and sitting areas, and other amenities. As in Hamm Park, there is too much pavement and too many walls and raised planters; the architect should once again have let nature be the major element.

35 Commercial Block, 1888
J. Walter Stevens
379 Sibley Street

A five-story brick Romanesque Revival warehouse structure. The use of thin vertical clusters of engaged piers makes the building much more delicate than is usually the case in Romanesque Revival buildings.

36 Noyes Brothers and Cotler Wholesale Drug Building (now Park Square Court Building), 1886
J. Walter Stevens
Northeast corner Sibley Street and 6th Street E

A five-story Richardsonian Romanesque building of brick with stone trim.

37 First Baptist Church, 1875
William L. Boyington
Northwest corner Wacouta Street and 9th Street E

Ashlar block Gothic Revival church with a well-preserved interior. The stone spire, which was added at a later date, was removed in 1945.

38 Robert Street Bridge, 1926
West of corner of Robert Street and Kellogg Boulevard E

An arched concrete bridge which can be seen from below in Harriet Island Park. The pylons at each end are mildly Moderne.

39 Coca-Cola Bottling Plant, 1940–41
Ernest H. Schmidt and Company
84 Wabasha Street (southeast end of bridge)

Streamline Moderne with curved corners and glass brick — the packaging image for the Coca-Cola Company before and after World War II. The Schmidt firm also designed the bottling plants at Albert Lea (1941), Duluth (1946), Fergus Falls (1938), Mankato (1938), and Minneapolis (1946). Minnesota's Coca-Cola plants utilized a conservative image of the Moderne, especially when compared with the plants on the West Coast.

40 Holman Field
Lafayette Freeway (Highway 56), exit to Plato Boulevard, east to Airport Road

The airport was established at this site in 1926, and the mail service to Chicago commenced in the same year. The first hangar (City Hangar #1, designed by Frank Meirs) was built in 1926, but the Terminal Building was not started until 1938. The Terminal Building (designed by Charles A. Bassford) is a characteristic Minnesota PWA building in its conservative architectural style and its fine stone craftsmanship as well as in its funding. Like most PWA buildings it strove to be both traditional, with the authority of the Classic, and Moderne. As the *St. Paul Pioneer Press* noted when the building was opened, "Tasteful, modernistic appointments mark the passenger waiting room." Holman Field is no longer used by the major commercial airlines.

40 Holman Field Terminal Building.

M-2b State Capitol and Public Buildings

The State Capitol Building and its site were products of the City Beautiful movement at the turn of the century. Cass Gilbert's Capitol was to be the centerpiece of a reorganized and visually controlled stretch of St. Paul landscape — a wide, parklike boulevard was to penetrate straight as an arrow through the downtown area to the river and a bridge; other streets were to radiate to the southwest and the southeast. Like many of America's grand Beaux Arts schemes, the Gilbert plan was never fully realized, but one can obtain some idea of its breadth and scale by wandering around the grounds to the south of the Capitol and by viewing the building from various points on the east bank of the river. Perhaps economically and politically Gilbert's scheme was too ambitious, still today we can only regret that it was never carried out — it would have forcefully joined the river and its parks with the downtown area (providing open greenery), culminating in Gilbert's white marble pile. The design of the wide boulevard with its circles, monuments, and parks would not only have benefited the Capitol but would have substantially opened up the confining character of downtown St. Paul.

The post–World War II years have dealt harshly with Gilbert's vision. His long axial approach to the river (which was of course to be left open) has now been closed by the Veterans Service Building (1953–54). Dull gray public buildings have been constructed around the Capitol, and the freeways (Highways 35E and 94) have separated the Capitol from the downtown area and the river.

1 **State Capitol Building,** 1893–1904
Cass Gilbert
Aurora Avenue at the corner of Park Street

Gilbert's building was the third of Minnesota's nineteenth-century Capitols. The first, Greek Revival in style, was built in 1851 while Minnesota was still a territory. In 1872 and again in 1878 the building was remodeled and enlarged, and the new high drum and dome and other details transformed the 1851 building into the Italianate Style. In 1881 the building burned, and an entirely new structure was built (1882–83) from the designs of LeRoy S. Buffington. Buffington styled the building in the Romanesque, modeling it after the then-new New York State Capitol in Albany. This, too, proved to be inadequate functionally and as a symbolic image. In 1893 the legislature appointed a board to study the problem of a new site and also to select an architect on the basis of a competition. Cass Gilbert was selected in 1898, and the building was completed in 1904. The theme of the building is an old, rather tired one — a sixteenth-century Renaissance palace block with projecting wings and a colonnade drum surmounted by a dome (à la Michelangelo). Gilbert's version of this scheme added nothing really new, but his building was a success because of the quality of his design, his finesse in handling the proportions of the basic forms, and the relationship proportionately between the volumes below and the drum and the dome. If we look at other state capitol buildings of the late nineteenth and early twentieth centuries, we can sense how considerable Gilbert's talent was.

1 State Capitol Building.

As is fitting for a Beaux Arts pile, the building is loaded with "art," ranging from the gilded quadriga (by Daniel Chester French and Edward C. Potter), which adds much to the building, to the six "Virtues" above the loggia (by Daniel Chester French) and the murals (by Frank J. Millet, Edward Simmons, Kenyon Cox, and John LaFarge).

2 **State Administration Building,** 1966
Ellerbe Architects
50 Sherburne Avenue

A "modern" building made traditional by its sheathing of rough and polished granite.

3 **State Historical Society Building,** 1915–17
Clarence H. Johnston, Sr.
690 Cedar Street

Like most of the work of the Johnstons (father and son), pretty dry, but as a classical screen this building and the State Office Building across the mall suggest how it all might have looked if Gilbert's plan had been carried out.

4 **Centennial Office Building,** 1958
Thorshov and Cerny
658 Cedar Street

A horizontal box wrapped in vertical panels of granite alternating with panels of metal and glass.

5 **Veterans Service Building,** 1953–54; 1973
Brooks Cavin
20 Columbus Avenue

The only recent building that approaches Gilbert's talent. Here is a modern building which succeeds in being dignified and symbolically public. It is a shame that the only good contemporary building in this area had to be sited in such a way as to destroy Gilbert's axial vista.

6 **State Highway Building,** 1956
Ellerbe Architects
John Ireland Boulevard

The Corporate International Style of the 1950s made monumental.

7 **State Office Building,** 1932
Clarence H. Johnston, Sr.
425 Park Street

A classical screen, like the State Historical Society Building across the mall, to frame the Capitol.

M-2c St. Anthony Park

St. Anthony Park and nearby Prospect Park form isolated enclaves within an area which is primarily industrial and commercial. Of the two St. Anthony Park is the larger, and because it is adjacent to the St. Paul campus of the University of Minnesota it has been in a better position to ward off nonresidential inroads. It was laid out in 1873 by Horace W. S. Cleveland and was planned as a community of suburban estates, with the roads and streets winding around the hills and wooded glens of the area. With the development of the St. Paul campus in the 1880s the district slowly began to grow, although it never did develop into a place of large estates. In 1884 the St. Anthony Park Company was established, and it energetically advertised the community and pushed the sale of lots.

The characteristics of the place were well established by the end of the 1800s. The major railroad tracks and yards (Burlington Northern) divided the community into a northern area and a southern area. On its southern boundary the community adjoins the commercial district which came into existence around the railroads and along University Avenue. The eastern boundaries were formed by the state fairgrounds and the St. Paul campus of the university. Later the western boundary became Highway 280 and, farther north, University Grove and the University of Minnesota Golf Course.

The area was provided with many parks, the largest being College Park and Langford Park. The original growth of oaks and other trees has been liberally supplemented over the years so that the whole presents the feeling of a natural forest. Except for a small neighborhood shopping area around Como and Doswell Avenues, the northern area has remained residential. There are some older dwellings on Scudder Avenue and Raymond Avenue, but most of the houses were built between 1900 and 1920. In style they represent the Queen Anne/Colonial Revival and numerous variations on the turn-of-the-century Craftsman stucco box. With the proximity of University Grove there has been a slight spillover of modern single-family residences into St. Anthony Park.

1 **House,** c. 1895
2201 Scudder Avenue
A Queen Anne/Colonial Revival dwelling.

2 **McGill House,** 1888
2203 Scudder Avenue
A classic example of the Queen Anne Style. The wraparound porch and the carriage house are now gone.

3 **House,** c. 1887
2205 Scudder Avenue
On the border between late Eastlake and early Queen Anne.

4 **Muskego Church,** 1843–44
2375 Como Avenue (Luther Theological Seminary)
This log church was built at Muskego, Wisconsin, and was moved to its present site in 1904. The building is an example of the vernacular, but its interior space creates a strong sense of design. The image of nineteenth-century frontier puritanism pervades.

5 **House,** c. 1950
2230 Hoyt Avenue
The International Style as interpreted by the post–World War II Harvard School of Design.

6 **Gibbs Farm**
Northwest corner Cleveland and Larpenteur Avenues

A farm complex — even including animals and crops — maintained by the Ramsey County Historical Society. In addition to the farmhouse there is the one-room Steen School (1878), which was moved to the site in 1958, and the "Red Barn" designed in 1958 by Edwin Lundie. The farmhouse (1854–74) is a vernacular version of the Greek, plain and straightforward; the barn is Lundie's concept of how a properly designed barn should look — everything planned and nothing accidental.

7 **St. Anthony Park Drive-In Bank,** 1973–74
Joseph E. Michels
Southwest corner Como and Doswell Avenues

The building's low form and its landscaping fit the new complex into its site and relate it to the nearby commercial and residential buildings.

M-2d University Grove

University Grove provides an excellent overview of the styles, fashions, and history of single-family residential architecture in the Twin Cities from 1928 to the present. This area was set aside in late 1928 by the regents of the University of Minnesota as a housing area where tenured faculty and staff members could build their own houses within easy reach of the St. Paul and Minneapolis campuses. The university retains ownership of the land, which is leased to the faculty or staff member. The prospective homeowner is required to engage an architect, and the plans have to meet a number of specifications which have been laid down by the university. When the house is sold, it can be purchased only by another tenured faculty or staff member.

The first plan for University Grove was prepared in 1929 by Morell and Nichols, with Nichols, Mason, and Cornell as landscape architects and F. M. Mann as consulting architect. The planners applied the concept of super-blocks, which had come to the fore in Europe and (to a degree) in American planning circles from the early 1900s on. Open spaces (children's play courts) were provided in the center of each block, and pathways connected each resident with this common open space. The narrowness of the site plus the existing street patterns (two blocks wide) did not fully allow for the curvilinear natural layout of streets which is a hallmark of planned upper-middle-class communities throughout the United States, but still slight curves were introduced for the layout of Vincent, Northrop and Folwell Avenues.

University Grove originally extended from Fulham Street to the west side of Coffman Street to the east, Hoyt Avenue to the south, and to the north side of Folwell Avenue. A later addition (University Grove East) extended eastward toward Cleveland Avenue. The original complex provided for 76 houses, and the later addition raised this to 114. A glance through the list of architects who have designed houses in University Grove reveals virtually all the major practitioners of residential architecture in the Twin Cities. As one would expect, those architects who have been associated in one way or another with the university are well represented. The list includes such designers as Lundie, Cerny, Close, Graffunder, Nagle, Michels, Hammel, Green and Abrahamson, Rapson, and Progressive Design Associates.

In style the earliest houses utilized historic period imagery, mostly American Colonial and English; those of the late 1930s slowly became "Modern," and after World War II the Modern — usually of a woodsy type — predominated. The houses of the late 1940s and 1950s were relatively low-keyed. Since the early 1960s, however, the designs have tended toward the insistent imagery of high art, and the dwellings are no longer set back among the trees.

We have listed the houses which we judge to be the most interesting and also the most representative of the various periods. They are arranged in chronological order to enable the visitor who tours them systematically to observe the progression of architectural fashions through more than thirty-five years.

1 **House,** 1929
William M. Ingemann
2285 Folwell Avenue

2 **House,** 1930
Long and Thorshov; Roy Child Jones
1588 Vincent Avenue

3 **House,** 1931
Edwin H. Lundie
2273 Folwell Avenue

3 House.

4 **House,** 1931
R. C. Chapin
2267 Folwell Avenue

5 **House,** 1931
A. R. Van Dyck
2271 Hoyt Avenue

6 **House,** 1931
Edwin H. Lundie
1590 Vincent Avenue

7 **House,** 1931
Liebenberg and Kaplan
1576 Vincent Avenue

8 **House,** 1932
Edwin H. Lundie
2276 Folwell Avenue

9 **House,** 1932
Edwin H. Lundie
2292 Folwell Avenue

10 **House,** 1933
William M. Ingemann
2243 Hoyt Avenue

11 **House,** 1935
Jones and Robertson
1564 Vincent Avenue

12 **House,** 1936
R. C. Chapin
1583 Northrop Avenue

13 **House,** 1936
Wessel, Brunet, and Kline
2297 Folwell Avenue

14 **House,** 1937
Jones and Cerny
2279 Hoyt Avenue

15 **House,** 1939
Close Associates
1564 Fulham Street

16 **House,** 1940
H. H. Livingston
2261 Folwell Avenue

17 **House,** 1940
R. C. Chapin
2255 Folwell Avenue

18 **House,** 1941
Robertson, Jones, and Cerny
2231 Folwell Avenue

19 **House,** 1941
R. C. Chapin
2225 Hoyt Avenue

20 **House,** 1941
Jones, Robertson, and Cerny
1596 Northrop Avenue

21 **House,** 1949
Close Associates
1572 Northrop Avenue

22 **House,** 1949
Close Associates
1580 Northrop Avenue

23 **House,** 1950
Armstrong and Schlichting
1580 Fulham Street

24 **House,** 1950
McClure and Kerr
2216 Folwell Avenue

25 **House,** 1952
Larson and McLaren
2203 Hoyt Avenue

26 **House,** 1953
Close Associates
2202 Folwell Avenue

27 **House,** 1953
Close Associates
1588 Fulham Street

27 House.

28 **House,** 1955
Close Associates
1572 Fulham Street

29 **House,** 1954
Close Associates
2203 Folwell Avenue

30 **House,** 1954
Elving, Horty, and Associates
2189 Folwell Avenue

31 **House,** 1954
Robert G. Cerny
1589 Vincent Avenue

32 **House,** 1954
Graffunder and Nagle
2208 Folwell Avenue

33 **House,** 1954
McClure and Kerr
1571 Burton Lane

34 **House,** 1955
Close Associates
2286 Folwell Avenue

35 **House,** 1956
Frank K. Kerr
1579 Burton Lane

36 **House,** 1956
Frank K. Kerr
1587 Burton Lane

37 **House,** 1956
Close Associates
2225 Folwell Avenue

38 **House,** 1956
Ralph Rapson and Associates
2197 Folwell Avenue

39 **House,** 1957
Ralph Rapson and Associates
1564 Burton Lane

40 **House,** 1957
Close Associates
1578 Burton Lane

41 **House,** 1957
Close Associates
2190 Coffman Street

42 **House,** 1959
Ralph Rapson and Associates
1595 Vincent Avenue

43 **House,** 1960
Graffunder and Nagle
2291 Hoyt Avenue

44 **House,** 1962
Ralph Rapson and Associates
2140 Folwell Avenue

45 **House,** 1962
Tom Van Housen
2148 Folwell Avenue

46 **House,** 1964
Progressive Design Associates
2154 Folwell Avenue

47 **House,** 1964
Ralph Rapson and Associates
2160 Folwell Avenue

48 House, 1964
Joseph E. Michels
2123 Hoyt Avenue

49 House, 1964
Hammel, Green, and Abrahamson
2153 Hoyt Avenue

50 House, 1965
Cecil T. Griffith
2117 Hoyt Avenue

51 House, 1965
Close Associates
2124 Folwell Avenue

52 House, 1966
Ralph Rapson and Associates
2118 Folwell Avenue

53 House, 1967
Cecil T. Griffith
2132 Folwell Avenue

54 House, 1967
Close Associates
2170 Folwell Avenue

55 House, 1967
Graffunder Associates
2176 Folwell Avenue

56 House, 1967
McGuire Architects–Planners, Inc.
2111 Hoyt Avenue

57 House, 1968
Progressive Design Associates
2121 Folwell Avenue

58 House, 1968
Progressive Design Associates
2151 Folwell Avenue

59 House, 1968–69
Joseph E. Michels
2059 Folwell Avenue

60 House, 1968
Progressive Design Associates
2171 Folwell Avenue

61 House, 1969
Michael McGuire
2105 Folwell Avenue

62 House, 1970
Michael McGuire
2115 Folwell Avenue

63 House, 1970
Progressive Design Associates
2137 Folwell Avenue

64 House, 1970
Michael McGuire
2115 Folwell Avenue

M-2e University Avenue and Como Park

The University Avenue area from Snelling Avenue North across the Minneapolis city limits to 15th Avenue Southeast forms what has long been referred to as the Midway district. Around the extensive railroad yards has grown up a large industrial district composed of manufacturing concerns, grain elevators, wholesale houses, and so on. University Avenue itself has tended to attract business offices and even some retail establishments, and industrial complexes have developed on both sides of the avenue. Directly adjacent to the industrial zone are other land-use areas which range from parks to colleges and single-family and multiple-family housing.

The late nineteenth-century development of the area included several suburban residential parks: Prospect Park to the northwest in Minneapolis (1870s); Lake Iris Park, southwest of University Avenue at Lynnhurst Avenue (1883); Warrendale, northeast of Lexington Parkway and Jessamine Avenue West (1884); and others. All of these planned residential suburbs utilized the free-flowing English landscape garden tradition of curved streets, lakes, and parks.

From the 1870s on a concerted effort was made to acquire and develop parks and boulevards in this section of northern St. Paul. The major point of emphasis was of course Como Park, the acquisition of which began in 1873 (over, it should be noted, the objection of many members of the St. Paul community, who felt it was a waste of tax funds). The work of converting the area around Lake Como into a park had to wait until 1892 when Frederick Nussbaumer was appointed the superintendent of parks. In the early 1900s the land for Wheelock Parkway was purchased, thus providing a parkway link between Como Park and Lake Phalen Park to the east. The land for Lexington Parkway, extending from Summit Avenue to Como Park, and for the Como Avenue parkway was obtained piecemeal during the 1890s and the early 1900s.

Architecturally the housing in the University Avenue–Como Park district ranges from the Queen Anne of the late 1880s to the stucco Period Revival houses built after 1910 and during the 1920s. Toward the north there are a large number of post–World War II developer/builder houses (usually a version of the California ranch house). Examples of the earlier buildings exist throughout the area — for instance, the Ames House (1888 at 1285 Como Boulevard West and the Granger House (1890) at 1269 Como Boulevard West; both of these are in the Queen Anne Style.

Pockets of retail and commercial development emerged along the street railway lines. The most important of these lines were the Como Avenue line, which ran from downtown St. Paul to Como Park by 1891 and westward to Minneapolis by 1898; the Snelling Avenue line, which started in Highland Park to the south and brought its passengers to the doorstep of the state fairgrounds (1891); and the University Avenue line (1890). The architecture of the neighborhood shopping corners is generally plain and down to earth.

1 **H. J. Heinz Building** (now an office building), 1948
Skidmore, Owings, and Merrill
2583 University Avenue

Designed before the architects had imprisoned themselves in their characteristic version of the International Style. The functional projecting roof, the band of windows, the balance and arrangement on the ground level of the entrance, and the two small windows on each side go back to the firm's pre-1942 designs. Still a strong design today.

2 **M. Burg and Sons Building** (now a store and warehouse), 1917
W. R. Wilson
2402–14 University Avenue

The composition of the street elevation of this large building is taken directly from Sullivan's commercial designs of the 1890s; even the ornament is Sullivanesque.

3 **Montgomery Ward and Company Building,** 1920
Lockwood, Green, and Company
1400 University Avenue

The rectangular tower was used as an identifying device — a sign — to draw attention to this large concrete structure. The building is largely classical in style, but its fundamental image is utilitarian and factorylike. Originally the building was situated in an open park, almost all of which is now covered with acres of asphalt for parking. Brown and Bigelow's building at 1286 University Avenue (Kees and Colburn, 1913) retains much of its original landscaping and offers a better example of the park settings which were frequently developed around industrial and commercial buildings during this period.

4 **Knox Presbyterian Church,** 1914
1536 Minnehaha Avenue W

A Prairie-esque building in brick.

5 **Hamline University,** estab. 1880
Hewitt Avenue at Snelling Avenue North

Old Main (1883) is a classic example of Ruskinian Gothic architecture, although except for its pointed arches it is not really Gothic at all. Two recent buildings on the campus are of strong architectural character. These are Hammel, Green, and Abrahamson's Paul H. Giddens Alumni Learning Center (1972) and Bush Memorial Library (1974). The library plays a visual game of exposing, not exposing the horizontal members of its frame (the exposed concrete members being kept flush with the adjoining brick surfaces). The learning center is an example of Minnesota's cut-into brick box, cantilevered out here and there and topped at various locations with tile-roofed dormer monitors. The entrance of the 1907 library (now part of the learning center) is intact and forms an impressive piece of sculpture in the lobby.

6 **Hancock School,** 1974
Wold Associates
799 Snelling Avenue N

A modern fortress in the cut-into brick Box Style.

7 **Minnesota State Fairgrounds**
Como Avenue at Snelling Avenue N

On the fairgrounds there are a few examples of the PWA Moderne of the 1930s. The Poultry Building (1937) contains concrete relief panels designed by Samuel Sabean as part of the Federal Art Project of the Depression years.

•8 **St. Columba Church,** 1949–51
Barry Byrne
1305 Lafond Avenue

Barry Byrne was a young member of the Chicago Prairie School of architecture. During the 1920s and the years that followed, he turned to a highly personal version of Expressionism that was similar in certain ways to the early work of Bruce Goff. He built the St. Columba Church late in his career, but its character is still strongly expressionistic. He has employed an ordering of parts and details which conveys a sense of the unreal. This is a significant Twin Cities building, one often missed even by local residents.

8 St. Columba Church.

9 **Como Park Conservatory,** 1914–15
Frederick Nussbaumer; Toltz Engineering Company
Estabrook Drive at Aida Place

A metal and glass conservatory based upon nineteenth-century precedents. The Zoo Building behind it is a 1936 PWA Moderne stone structure.

10 **University Avenue Congregational Church,** 1911
Clarence H. Johnston, Sr.
868 Sherburne Avenue

A carpenter Gothic design made academically correct by the architect; the ornamentation is authentic.

11 **Grocery Store,** 1898
George J. Ries
Edmund Avenue at St. Albans

Here is a two-story brick building with a curved corner which anticipated the use of the curve in the 1930s and again today. The corner curve of the façade would normally have formed the base for a tower, but this has been eliminated and the result is a highly abstract composition.

12 **St. Agnes Catholic Church,** 1897–1904
George J. Ries
548 Lafond Avenue

The source was certainly central European — half Baroque and half Russian Orthodox.

13 **Minnesota Milk Company Building,** 1932
370 University Avenue

The remodeling of a 1912 building into the Moderne — Zigzag and Streamline. The symbolic association of the Moderne with science, hospitals, and cleanliness led to its use as an image by milk companies during the 1920s and 1930s.

M-2f Indian Mounds Park and Phalen Park

Sections of St. Paul's east side were platted as early as the 1850s. Dayton's Bluff, which lies northwest of Indian Mounds Park, was one of the earliest residential areas of St. Paul. Here one can still find examples of architecture from the late 1860s on, although many of the houses have been severely remodeled. To the north is a gently rolling and hilly area composed of middle-middle-class and "mechanics'" houses (1900–1915). To the north and west is street after street of post-World War II adaptations on a small scale of the single-floor California ranch house, each on a small lot.

The east St. Paul communities were connected to the downtown area by several major streetcar lines. The most important of these were the line on 7th Street East (1891), which eventually ran as far east as Hazel Street, and the Mississippi Street line (1890–91), which made its way north as far as Nebraska Avenue East. Residential and commercial developments occurred along these streets, along the streets which contained other branch lines, and elsewhere. Remnants of the nineteenth-century commercial buildings exist on Bates Avenue, Maria Avenue, Payne Avenue, and 7th Street East.

There are two major parks in the area: Phalen Park (acquired between 1894 and 1906) and Indian Mounds Park (1893 and later). Battle Creek Park (1922–25, 1945) forms the southern boundary. Two parkways cross the area — Wheelock Parkway, which connects Phalen Park and Como Park to the west, and Johnson Parkway (1913–32) which provides the landscaped link between Phalen Park and Indian Mounds Park. A large-scale freeway, Highway 35E (1961–65), cuts north/south through St. Paul's east side; since this freeway has been routed close to the existing railroad tracks, however, its negative impact has been minimal. On the other hand, Highways 12, 110, and 61 effectively cut this area off from Indian Mounds Park and the river.

1 **Muench House,** 1883
653 5th Street E

A transitional house, between the Eastlake and Queen Anne in style. Its angular, "sticky" quality is Eastlake, but its general massing and its corner octagonal tower are Queen Anne.

2 **Attached Row Houses,** c. 1895
234–38 Bates Avenue

A group of three-story townhouses with an arched entrance and windows on the ground level; above, each unit has a curved two-story bay. Close by at the corner of Burr Street and York Avenue is another unusual pair of brick townhouses. Both of these groups of townhouses are Romanesque/Queen Anne in style.

3 **Dayton's Bluff Elementary School,** 1974–75
Freerks, Sperl, and Flynn
262 Bates Avenue

An intense, pristine composition of purple brick volumes, cut into with pencil-thin horizontal windows. Its scale just might work as a place for children.

3 Dayton's Bluff Elementary School.

4 **House,** c. 1870
155 Urban Place
A side-hall Greek Revival house. The entablature entrance has a transom light above it.

5 **Eagon House,** c. 1860s
468 Hopkins Street
Another side-hall Greek Revival house; the entrance assemblage with its sidelights and recessed door is impressive.

6 **House,** c. 1890
686 Bradley Street
A very spindly Queen Anne design with a corner tower.

7 **St. Michael's Church and Grotto,** 1934
Gabriel Pizzuti
376 Rose Avenue E
St. Paul's own folk folly consisting of a river boulder grotto and a tiny church of river boulders and stucco. The church is almost, but not quite, Missionesque.

8 **House,** 1890
1750 Ames Place E
A Shingle Style house with a river boulder foundation, a band of clapboard, and shingles for the rest. The use of a gambrel roof, an oval window, and other elements indicates how deeply immersed the Shingle Style was in the Colonial Revival.

8 House.

M-2g Cherokee Heights

Cherokee Heights comprises the area on the east bank of the Mississippi opposite downtown St. Paul. There was some settlement in the area (which is commonly called the "West Side") in the 1850s, but this section of the city did not really begin to be developed until Robertson's Addition was laid out in the late 1860s. The southern part of the area was platted in 1874. On the river flats directly opposite downtown the grid ran northwest/southeast, but on the bluff it changed to the normal north/south, east/west arrangement. The two very distinct parts of the terrain — the flatlands and the bluff, with its superb view of St. Paul — were used for different purposes. The flatlands were commercial (including breweries and brick factories), while the heights were residential. Close to the top of the bluff were single-family houses for the upper-middle and middle-middle class, and farther inland to the south were "mechanics'" houses. Examples of the latter exist on King Street East between Gorman Avenue and Robert Street South and on Mount Hope between Page and Morton Streets East.

Cherokee Heights was connected to the main part of the city by the Smith Avenue high bridge and by the Wabasha Street bridge. The electric street railway was brought over the Wabasha Street bridge in 1890. This line, which extended to Smith Avenue, was supplanted in 1894 by a spur line which went south on Stryker Avenue South. Neighborhood commercial development occurred along the route of these lines and at several other locales.

Just after 1900 extensive areas of parkland were acquired for the West Side. Following along the top of the bluff was Cherokee Heights Park and Lookout Park (acquired between 1903 and 1906). Along the river the land for Harriet Island Park was acquired in 1900. The eastern area now includes two playground parks and a greenbelt which extends along Prospect.

1 **Service Station,** c. 1927
Southeast corner Smith Avenue W and Cherokee Avenue
An eye-catching layout for a mid-1920s service station. An L-shaped building contains the garage and the office. Within the L, placed diagonally, is a large double-pier pump structure with a hipped roof.

1 Service Station.

2 **Beal House,** 1891
23 Isabel Street W
A severe brick Queen Anne dwelling, situated in the woods, partway down the hillside.

3 **Minea House,** 1886
384 Winslow Avenue
Queen Anne in brick, with a variety of other stylistic ingredients. A round three-story tower with a conical roof terminates one side of the front; on the other side is a smaller open tower.

4 **Heimbach House,** 1880
64 Delos Street W
Eastlake/Queen Anne in style, with columns and exuberant sawed wood patterns on the porch.

5 **Row Houses,** 1889
46–52 Delos Street W
A series of Queen Anne (with a touch of Romanesque) brick townhouses.

6 **Rau-Strong House,** 1884–86
2 George Street E
A two-story French Second Empire house with a mansard roof and brush-hammered quoins at the corners. The house is of yellow limestone which has been stuccoed over. Note the carriage barn (behind the house) with its four-gabled cupola.

M-2h West 7th Street

The original link connecting downtown St. Paul and Fort Snelling was West 7th Street. The northeastern end of the street (near Irvine Park) was developed in the 1860s and later. Commercial usage occurred along various portions of the street and residential development took place on both sides of it. In 1890 the street railway extended out to Tuscarora Avenue, and by early 1891 the line went all the way to the Mississippi River opposite Fort Snelling. With the exception of upper-middle-class Irvine Park, most of the housing (by 1900) was lower-middle-class housing (single family), but there were apartment buildings and townhouses sprinkled here and there. Almost all of this housing was built before 1910. Since the railroad went in the same general direction, some industrial development also took place. If the currently proposed extension of Highway 35E occurs, then the flatlands of the West 7th Street area will be fully separated from the hills to the north.

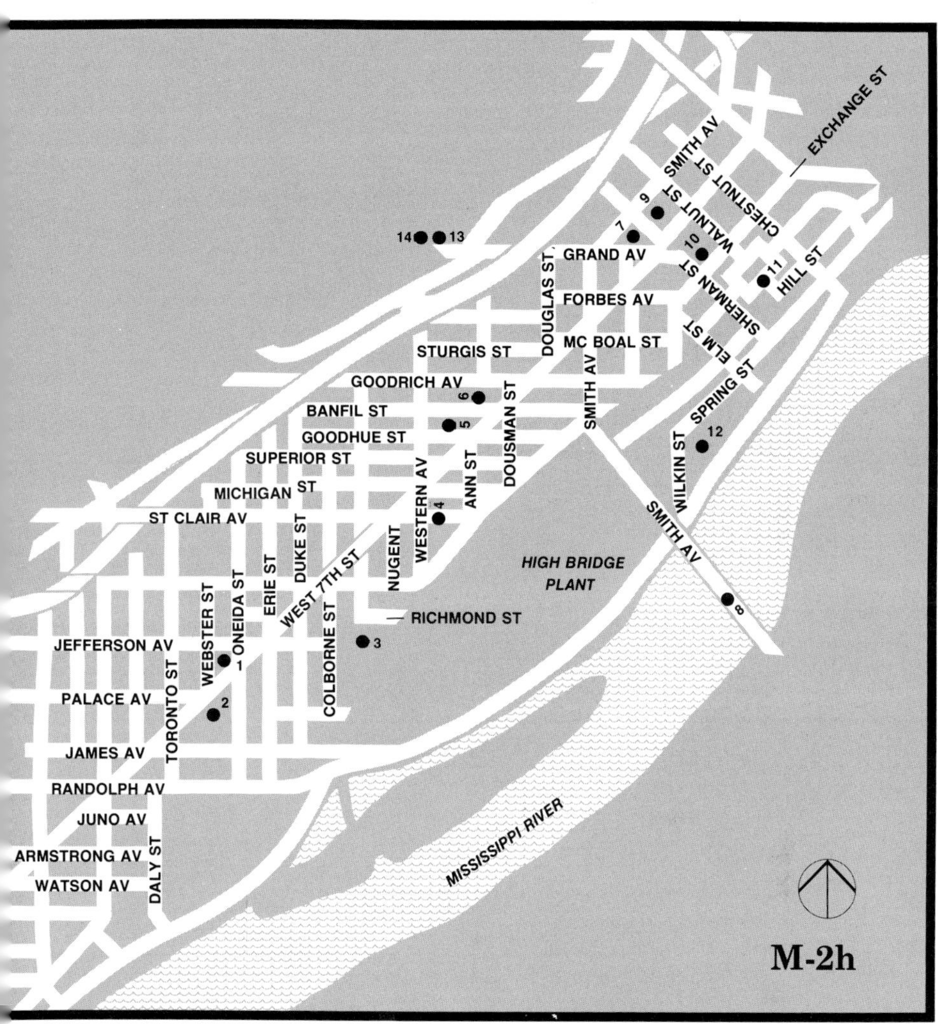

Marie Schmidt Bremer House, c. 1870s
Northwest corner W 7th Street and Oneida Street

A large stone Italianate dwelling; the present porch is a modification of the original one.

2 **Jacob Schmidt Brewing Company,** 1885; 1881
882 W 7th Street

The stone section of the building was constructed in 1855, the brick section in 1881. The later section conjures the aura of a castle with crenelated towers and arched-head windows. Note the wall painting (1971) by Donald Biebighauser and Earl Fahrendorff of Lawrence Signs, Inc. The painting is of a northern Minnesota landscape and is designed to blend into the pine forest planted in front of it.

3 Child Development Center and School Administration Center, 1972–73
Hammel, Green, and Abrahamson
360 Colborne Street

An elegantly detailed brick building. The metal window frames and the glass are kept close to the surface of the brick skin.

4 Lauer Flats, 1887
Henry Lauer and Charles Lauer
226 Western Avenue

A group of townhouses of stone, Greek Revival in character, and more English than American. One of the important treasures of nineteenth-century architecture in St. Paul.

4 Lauer Flats.

5 Apartment Building, 1889
351–53 Goodhue Street

A three-story Eastlake Style apartment house with leaded glass windows.

6 Double Townhouse, 1891
325–27 Banfil Street

The Queen Anne Style used in a pair of brick dwellings.

6 Double Townhouse.

7 Apitz House, c. 1860
314 Smith Avenue N

A small one-and-a-half-story house built of limestone. St. Paul once had scores of "mechanics'" houses similar to this. A quite similar house may be found at 202 McBoal Street (Weber House, c. 1856), and two-story examples may be seen at 445 Smith Avenue (Wildman House, c. 1860). A wood frame example exists at 403 Superior Street (c. 1870).

8 High Bridge, 1889
Smith Avenue

A 2,700-foot metal bridge, 150 feet above the Mississippi River. Its thin, spidery quality can best be seen from Harriet Island Park on the east bank of the river.

9 Louise Block, 1885
Asher Bassford
267–71 7th Street W

There are still a number of Eastlake/Queen Anne and Richardsonian business blocks along West 7th Street. The Louise Block, which is a three-story structure, is Queen Anne in style.

10 **Alexander Ramsey House,** 1868–72
Monroe Sheire
265 Exchange Street S

A mansion, including a carriage house and fenced grounds. The stone house is Italianate in style with a mansard roof.

11 **Irvine Park**

Irvine Park was laid out as an English square development. The park itself was given to the city in 1849 at the time the area was platted. Because of its proximity to the river and the downtown area it became a fashionable place to live. From the late 1860s through the 1890s houses were built near the park, but before the turn of the century it ceased to be a highly desirable residential area; by the 1950s many of the houses were in poor repair. Fortunately a plan has now been proposed to preserve and restore the existing dwellings and to construct new single and multiple dwellings which in design and scale will fit into and enhance the area.

Wood House, 1854
255 Sherman Street

A two-story Greek Revival dwelling in brick.

Forepaugh House, c. late 1870s
276 Exchange Street S

A two-story Italianate house.

Wright-Prendergast House, 1851; 1907
223 Walnut Street

A Greek Revival house made more Greek by the addition in 1907 of a two-story porch with Ionic columns.

11 Wright-Prendergast House.

Holcombe-Averill-Jaggard House, late 1870s
302 Exchange Street S

A three-story French Second Empire house with quoined corners and a concave mansard roof.

Minneheimer House, c. late 1870s
270 7th Street W

Although not in Irvine Park itself, this French Second Empire house was built when many of those in the park were constructed. The Minneheimer House is of stone, which is now stuccoed over.

12 **Farmers Union Grain Terminal Association Elevators,** 1915–30
266 Shepard Road (north of High Bridge)

A composition of concrete cylinders; best viewed from Harriet Island Park.

•13 **German Presbyterian Bethlehem Church** (no longer in use), 1890
Cass Gilbert
311 Ramsey Street

The most romantic and picturesque of all Gilbert's churches — right out of a fairy tale. In its small scale and the childlike romanticism of its design it resembles some of the West Coast churches of Ernest Coxhead in the 1890s. The church is threatened by the freeway (Highway 35E), and it is not in the best of repair.

14 **Townhouses,** c. 1890
333–49 Ramsey Street

A row of two-story Romanesque Revival townhouses climbs up the steep hillside.

M-2i Summit Avenue to Marshall Avenue

From the 1880s on Summit Avenue was a fashionable place to reside. Visitors to St. Paul in the 1880s and 1890s wrote in glowing terms of the magnificent and stately mansions which lined the avenue. Most of these dwellings were built during this period, although the Burbank House (#9) goes back to the 1860s and the Prairie House (#13) was not built until 1913. With the exception of the Italian Villa Burbank House, none of these dwellings is a singularly distinguished piece of architecture. What counts on the avenue is the overall effect of the great houses on each side, the extensive lawns, and the high arbor of trees. It is indeed a unique environment. Since the mid-1960s families have been moving back into the Summit Avenue area, and many of the houses and their grounds have been restored. The interest in reusing these dwellings of the past has slowly been spreading north to Portland and Holly Avenues and on toward Marshall Avenue and south to the edge of the bluff. If this trend continues and is sustained, St. Paul will possess an extensive historical district which is once again fulfilling the role envisioned in its original design.

As in many nineteenth-century American cities single-family housing and multiple-family housing here often occur side by side on the same avenue or street. The Summit–Marshall Avenue area contains a good number of nineteenth-century apartment buildings and townhouses, most of which were directed to the middle-middle and upper-middle classes. The whole of the area is almost exclusively residential, with limited commercial development on Grand Avenue to the south. There is also some commercial usage on Selby Avenue along the former route of street railway lines; the line which ran on Grand Avenue was established in 1890, and the Selby line was started in 1906.

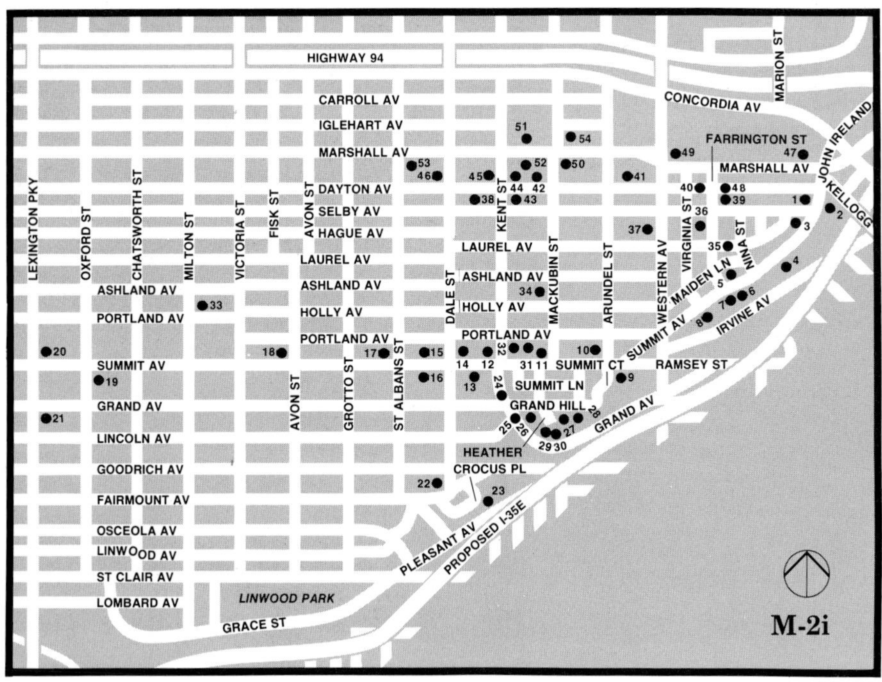

1 **Cathedral of St. Paul,** 1906–15
Emmanuel L. Masqueray
Summit Avenue just north of Selby Avenue

An early twentieth-century version of an Italian Mannerist/Baroque church. A 175-foot drum and dome have been awkwardly set on the high stubby building. Within there are windows designed by Charles Connick.

1 Cathedral of St. Paul.

2 **James J. Hill House,** 1889–91
Peabody and Stearns
240 Summit Avenue

A heavy-handed exercise in Richardsonian Romanesque with none of the subtleties of a genuine Richardson product. It is, though, ponderous and impressive in mass, size, and its picturesque hilltop location.

3 **Rugg House** (now Catholic Education Center), 1887
A. H. Stem
251 Summit Avenue

A Romanesque Revival dwelling, with luxurious relief sculptures of figures and floral patterns over the entrance of the front porch.

4 **Driscoll House** (now Epiphany House), 1884
William H. Willcox
266 Summit Avenue

Richardsonian Romanesque with a picturesque high tower (conical roof) on one side and an entrance from a later period with Tuscan columns and Art Nouveau metal railings.

5 **Gardner House,** c. 1908
Thomas G. Holyoke
301 Summit Avenue

A turn-of-the-century Colonial Revival house, in this case Georgian, in stone.

6 **Stuart House,** 1858–60
312 Summit Avenue

A large Italianate house which has been enlarged and simplified and stuccoed over.

7 **Lightner House,** 1896
Cass Gilbert
318 Summit Avenue

Richardsonian Romanesque made over into a Beaux Arts product with impressive results.

7 Lightner House.

8 **House** (converted from a carriage barn), 1969
Joseph Michels
360 Summit Avenue

All one can see from Summit Avenue are the chimneys; the house is on the far side of the hill, overlooking the river. A new entrance court has been provided and a radical revamping of the interior has taken place.

9 **James C. Burbank House,** 1865
Otis E. Wheelock
432 Summit Avenue

Minnesota's most impressive remaining Italian Villa dwelling. Three stories in height, with rough gray limestone walls, surrounded at the top by a grand belvedere. The interior, which has been remodeled several times over the years, reflects the changing world of architectural fashions.

10 **Harvey House,** 1884
445 Summit Avenue

A potpourri of the English Queen Anne Revival and Richardsonian Romanesque.

11 **House,** 1887
513 Summit Avenue

A wild interpretation of the Queen Anne Style, including parapeted gables.

12 **Apartment House,** 1896
579 Summit Avenue

In front of a plain three-story brick box the architect has placed an opulent Colonial Revival frontispiece of a three-story porch with large classical columns.

13 **House,** 1913
Ellerbe and Round
590 Summit Avenue

The Ellerbe firm employed a wide gamut of styles in the teens and twenties, one of which was the Prairie Style. Here it is used in a two-story stucco dwelling. Two other Prairie Style houses are nearby at 985 Portland Avenue West and 975 Osceola Avenue; both were built in about 1915.

14 **Summit Terrace,** 1889
587–601 Summit Avenue

Richardsonian Romanesque garb used for a series of row houses. Note the self-consciously modern addition to the rear of the house at 587 Summit Avenue.

15 **DuVander House,** 1878
649 Summit Avenue

French Second Empire in brick, with a tower.

16 **Nienaber House,** 1890s
W. F. Keefe
650 Summit Avenue

Queen Anne/Colonial Revival; the grand front porch has a central curved projection and a Palladian window.

14 Summit Terrace.

17 **Dittenhofer House,** 1898–99
Cass Gilbert
705 Summit Avenue

Essentially a classical house, but its details are Gothic.

18 **House of Hope Presbyterian Church,** 1912
Cram, Goodhue, and Ferguson
797 Summit Avenue

A characteristic Cram product, based upon English Perpendicular Gothic, accomplished here with fine stonework. A little dry, but as always with Cram, correct.

19 **Irvine House** (now Governor's Mansion), 1910–11
William Channing Whitney
1006 Summit Avenue

English Tudor (with a nod to northern Europe).

20 **St. Luke's Catholic Church,** c. 1919
John T. Comes
1079 Summit Avenue

The architect described this as an example of Italian Romanesque design.

21 **Lexington Restaurant,** 1953; 1969
Werner Wittkamp
1096 Grand Avenue

The Classical tradition brought up to date.

22 **Frank B. Kellogg House,** 1889
633 Fairmount Avenue

An extensive Romanesque Revival dwelling of masonry and shingle.

23 Rice House, c. 1887
4 Crocus Hill (now Crocus Place)

A brick Queen Anne dwelling, beautifully sited on the edge of the bluff.

24 Ingersoll House, c. 1894
535 Grand Avenue

A wood sheathed Queen Anne/Colonial Revival house.

25 House, c. 1890
A. H. Stem
532 Grand Avenue

Richardsonian Romanesque, but very stark.

26 House, c. 1890s
Cass Gilbert
520 Grand Avenue

Gilbert worked his way through the American and English Queen Anne and Shingle Styles to the Colonial Revival of the 1890s and on into turn-of-the-century Gothic and Classical designs. In this brick house he employed the Colonial Revival.

27 House, c. 1890s
Cass Gilbert
514 Grand Avenue

The Colonial Revival in clapboard.

28 House, c. 1900
Cass Gilbert
506 Grand Avenue

Here Gilbert combined the English Arts and Crafts mode of 1900 with the American Colonial Revival.

29 Gilbert House, c. 1890
Cass Gilbert
1 Heather Place

The English Queen Anne and Arts and Crafts movement form the basis for the design of Gilbert's own house. This house is one of his least academic designs and shares many similarities with the work then going on in the San Francisco Bay region by Ernest Coxhead and Willis Polk.

29 Gilbert House.

30 Goodkind Houses, 1910
Reed and Stem
5 and 7 Heather Place

The English Tudor Style used for two houses which are connected by a two-story passageway, enclosed above with an open porch below. The site of the houses and the outbuildings forms a romantic nonurban composition.

31 Two Townhouses, 1890
Clarence H. Johnston, Sr.
544–46 Portland Avenue

A composition of two three-story Richardsonian Romanesque townhouses.

32 Row Houses (Bookstaver House), 1888
Cass Gilbert
548–54 Portland Avenue

A stripped and simplified series of brick row houses, closely related to examples being built in England at the same time.

33 St. Clement's Episcopal Church, 1894
Cass Gilbert
901 Portland Avenue

A small-scaled stone church in the Gothic Revival Style of the 1880s and 1890s.

•**34 Three Row Houses,** c. 1890
Northwest corner Holly Avenue and Mackubin Street

Another example of a group of attached townhouses in the Richardsonian Romanesque Revival.

•35 **Laurel Terrace,** 1884
William H. Willcox and Clarence H. Johnston, Sr.
286–94 Laurel Avenue

A classic picture of a Victorian building. The two street façades terminate in the tall corner tower with its conical roof.

36 **Virginia Street Church,** 1886
Cass Gilbert
170 Virginia Street

A small Queen Anne composition which has much of the feeling of the American Shingle Style and the later Arts and Crafts movement. The church has river boulders on the lower part of the wall and shingles above them.

36 Virginia Street Church.

37 **Blair Apartment Building** (later the Angus Hotel), 1887
Hermann Kretz and William H. Thomas
165 Western Avenue N

An agitated five-story Queen Anne brick pile — really Victorian.

38 **Double House,** 1890
Hermann Kretz Company
579–81 Selby

A four-story brick building in lukewarm Romanesque.

39 **House,** 1888
Charles T. Mould and Robert McNichol
314 Dayton Avenue

A stone dwelling with classical details.

40 **House,** c. 1890
325 Dayton Avenue

A brick Queen Anne dwelling.

41 **House,** 1878
409 Dayton Avenue

An Italianate house with a side-entrance plan; a one-story porch across the front.

42 **Dayton Avenue Presbyterian Church,** 1885–86
Cass Gilbert and James Knox Taylor
Northwest corner Dayton Avenue and Mackubin Street

A Romanesque Revival Church, modeled loosely after Richardson's North Congregational Church in Springfield, Massachusetts (1868–73).

43 **Woodland Terrace,** 1888
Attrib. A. W. Barber
550–56 Dayton Avenue

Attached townhouses in the Richardsonian Romanesque Style.

44 **House,** c. 1890
557 Dayton Avenue

A two-story Queen Anne dwelling.

45 **House,** 1888
565 Dayton Avenue

A two-and-a-half-story clapboard house. The basic form is Italianate, but the detailing is Eastlake.

46 **House,** 1890
William Thomas
611 Dayton Avenue

Romanesque in brick and stone.

47 **Technical and Vocational Institute,** 1966–67
Ellerbe Architects
235 Marshall Avenue

A four-story box in brick and concrete with narrow band windows.

48 **House,** c. 1880
310 Marshall Avenue

A side-hall Italianate house with heavy wood details.

49 **St. Joseph's Academy**
Attrib. Edward P. Bassford
355 Marshall Avenue

The initial building (1863) was a three-story, central gable building in the Italianate Style. The first addition (1871) in basically the same style is on the west side of the building, the next addition (1877) is still farther to the west, and another addition in 1884 on the east matches the original building. Records indicate that Bassford did the 1877 and 1884 additions, and he probably did the original building and the 1871 addition as well.

50 **Two Houses,** 1891
492 and 496 Marshall Avenue

Adjoining dwellings in the Queen Anne Style.

Duplexes, 1907
233–35 and 237–39 Mackubin Street

These buildings and another duplex around the corner on Marshall Avenue are in the Mission Revival Style which enjoyed widespread popularity just after the turn of the century.

50 Two Houses and Duplex.

51 **Martin Luther King Center and Park,** 1971
Adkins-Jackels Associates
270 Kent Street

A complex concrete and brick building, partially sunk into the ground; it tends to be overly ponderous for a park structure.

52 **House,** 1890
546 Marshall Avenue

A brick Queen Anne dwelling with a corner tower.

53 **Wilder Foundation–Marshall Day Care Center,** 1973
David Runyan
666 Marshall Avenue

A warm and intimate brown brick and wood structure. It is a little on the formal side for its purpose, but still it comes closer than most recent buildings to meeting its real and symbolic needs.

54 **Luckert House,** c. 1858–59
480 Iglehart Avenue

An Italianate house (with some Greek Revival features) in stone. The front porch is now enclosed. It is reputed to be the oldest residence in this area of St. Paul.

M-2j Highland Park and Macalester Park

The southwestern section of St. Paul was late in becoming urbanized. The Macalester Park district, which lies around western Summit Avenue and Snelling Avenue South, was platted in 1881, but much of it was not built up until after 1900. Highland Park, which lies still farther west, did not begin to develop as a residential suburb until after 1910. These two sections of St. Paul were selected as sites for six private educational institutions: Concordia College, the College of St. Thomas, the St. Paul Seminary, Macalester College, the College of St. Catherine, and the St. Paul Academy. The injection of these campuses into the area meant that from the beginning there was an abundance of open green space. This was early supplemented by extensive additions to St. Paul's park system along the Mississippi River Boulevard, the Ford Parkway (1928), and Summit Avenue and later the areas of public land to the east which now comprise the Highland Park Golf Course and Highland Park (1923–27). Macalester Park and Highland Park were from the beginning free of industrial activities, with the exception of the Ford Motor Company assembly plant, which was designed to be set in its own park. Several of the east/west streets developed as partial commercial strips, and once again such development was in most instances the result of the location of the electric streetcar lines. Part of the Selby Avenue line ran on Marshall Avenue to the river (1906); the Grand Avenue line extended to Cretin Avenue South (1890), and the Randolph Avenue line was taken to the river in 1891. The Highland Village Shopping Center, at the corner of Ford Parkway and Cleveland Avenue, was developed at the end of the 1930s. The group of stores at the corner of Ford Parkway and Cleveland Avenue South (1939) was an auto-oriented shopping center, with parking provided in front and back. And an auto-oriented supermarket was built in 1940 on the north side of Ford Parkway below Cleveland Avenue. A glimpse of upper-middle-class Period Revival architecture of the 1920s and 1930s can be obtained along the Mississippi River Boulevard between Ford Parkway and Summit Avenue and in the Edgcumbe Road area from the fountain entrance into Highland Park (north of the junction of Edgcumbe and Montreal Avenue) to Randolph Avenue. The other end of Edgcumbe Road from Shelby Place to Fairview Avenue contains single-family, upper-middle-class housing, most of which was built after 1945. The district between Edgcumbe Road North and Ford Parkway was developed in single-family housing (with the exception of Ford Parkway) just before and after World War II.

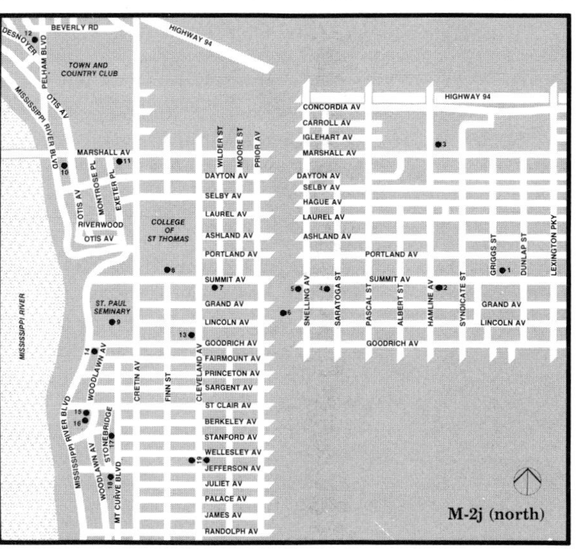

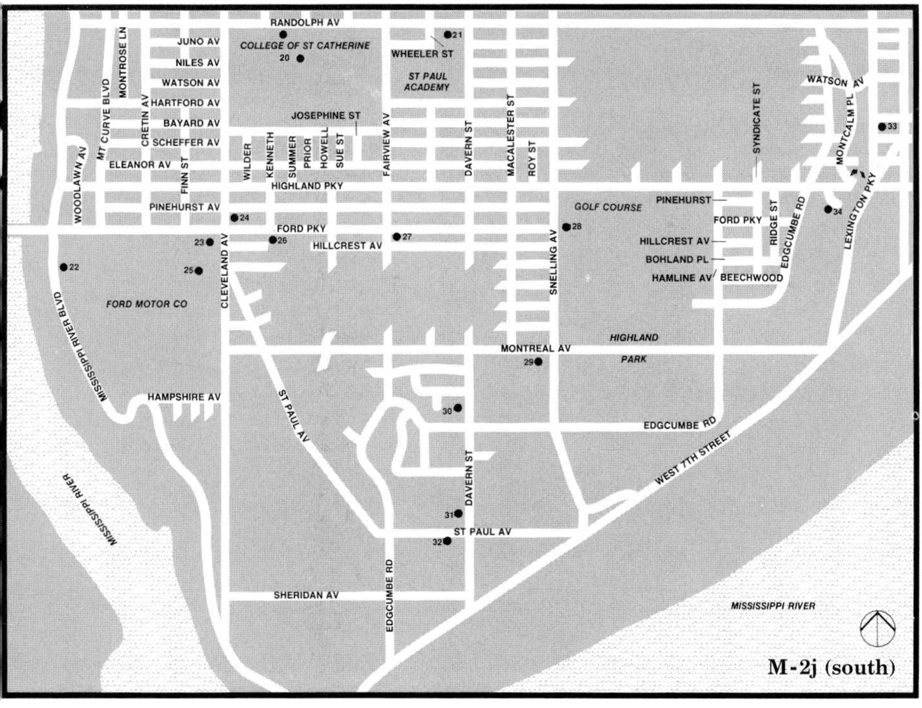

RANDOLPH AV
JUNO AV
NILES AV
WATSON AV
HARTFORD AV
BAYARD AV
SCHEFFER AV
ELEANOR AV
PINEHURST AV
COLLEGE OF ST CATHERINE
WHEELER ST
ST PAUL ACADEMY
JOSEPHINE ST
MONTROSE LN
MT CURVE BLVD
CRETIN AV
WOODLAWN AV
FINN ST
WILDER
KENNETH
SUMMER
PRIOR
HOWELL
SUE ST
FAIRVIEW AV
DAVERN ST
MACALESTER ST
ROY ST
HIGHLAND PKY
FORD PKY
HILLCREST AV
CLEVELAND AV
FORD MOTOR CO
MISSISSIPPI RIVER BLVD
GOLF COURSE
PINEHURST
FORD PKY
HILLCREST AV
BOHLAND PL
HAMLINE AV
BEECHWOOD
SNELLING AV
RIDGE ST
EDGCUMBE RD
SYNDICATE ST
WATSON AV
MONTCALM PL
LEXINGTON PKY
MONTREAL AV
HIGHLAND PARK
HAMPSHIRE AV
ST PAUL AV
EDGCUMBE RD
WEST 7TH STREET
DAVERN ST
ST PAUL AV
SHERIDAN AV
EDGCUMBE RD
MISSISSIPPI RIVER
MISSISSIPPI RIVER
M-2j (south)

1 **House,** c. 1914
1205 Summit Avenue
A Prairie Style house with strong emphasis placed on the geometric pattern of its wood casement windows.

1 House.

2 **Mount Zion Temple,** 1954–55
Eric Mendelsohn; Bergstedt and Hirsch
1300 Summit Avenue
Mendelsohn produced a number of important designs after World War II, several of which equaled the best of his work in the 1920s and 1930s. Mount Zion Temple is a fine piece of 1950s architecture, but it is not one of Mendelsohn's great designs.

2 Mount Zion Temple.

3 **Concordia College,** estab. 1893
Corner Marshall Avenue and Hamline Avenue S
The oldest of the original buildings was constructed in 1874 as a state reform school; later the buildings and the site were purchased by the Lutheran Church for the college. In 1971–72 Frederick Bentz–Milo Thompson and Associates designed a college union, an octagonal volume with vertical projecting shed roofs and deep cut-in openings in its walls.

4 **St. Paul's Church on the Hill,** 1912
Emmanuel L. Masqueray
1524 Summit Avenue
The architect of the Cathedral of St. Paul, at the head of Summit Avenue, shifted his course and produced an English Gothic design.

5 **Macalester College,** estab. 1885
Southwest corner Snelling Avenue S and Summit Avenue
The first building to be constructed at this site, Old Main, is still standing. The east wing of the building was constructed in 1884, and the major section of the structure was built in 1897. (Both parts were designed by Willcox and Smith.) Eventually American Georgian was chosen as the stylistic vocabulary of the college and a number of structures were built in this style. The best of these are Kirk Hall (Electus D. Litchfield and his associate Rogers; William M. Ingemann, 1926) and the Weyerhaeuser Library (William M. Ingemann, 1941). Of the buildings which have been built since 1960, the most important is the Weyerhaeuser Memorial Chapel, a six-sided glass box set down on the central mall (Cerny Associates, 1969).

6 **Grandview Theatre,** 1933
Myrtus A. Wright
1830 Grand Avenue
A 1933 theatre was remodeled into the Moderne in 1937 with a round window and glass bricks; it turned out to be a mixture of the earliest Zigzag Moderne and the later Streamline Moderne.

7 **Beebe House,** 1912
Purcell, Feick, and Elmslie
2022 Summit Avenue
One of the architects' roofy Prairie houses, with a high gable facing the street, an entrance on the east side of the house, and a summer porch and an upstairs sleeping porch on the west side. The present high contrast between the white stucco and the dark wood is not original — in the architects' design the colors of these two materials and the exterior stairway were kept very close in value.

8 **College of St. Thomas,** estab. 1888
2115 Summit Avenue

The first administration building (no longer standing) was the usual academic French Second Empire Style with a central tower (designed by E. P. Bassford in 1885). The prolific Emmanuel L. Masqueray entered the picture in the teens, and in 1917 he designed the chapel, which was "an adaptation to modern times and on suitable scale of Byzantine basilicas found in Ravenna, northern Italy." In the 1930s a number of stone buildings in Elizabethan Gothic followed, including Aquinas Hall (Maginnis and Walsh, 1931), O'Shaughnessy Hall (Rauenhorst, 1939), the Albert Magnus Science Hall (Richard C. Reieche, 1946), and others.

9 **St. Paul Seminary,** estab. 1892
2260 Summit Avenue

The original campus contained six buildings: an administration building, Cretin Residence, Loras Hall, a refectory, a classroom building (now gone), and a gymnasium (now converted into the central heating plant). These were all designed in 1892 by Cass Gilbert; according to the architect, they were built in an austere version of the Northern Italian Style, a mixture of Gothic and Renaissance. These buildings were later joined by the chapel (by Clarence H. Johnston, Sr., 1902–1905), which was "styled after the Church of St. Paul Outside The Walls, Rome."

10 **Prince of Peace Lutheran Church for the Deaf,** 1958
Ralph Rapson
205 Otis Avenue

The purity of the single-unit Palladian Villa made modern and — as is usual with Rapson — complex.

11 **Minnesota Dental Association Building,** 1956
Graffunder and Nagle
2236 Marshall Avenue W

The modularism of the 1950s Corporate International Style applied to a small office building.

10 Prince of Peace Lutheran Church for the Deaf.

12 **House,** 1941
Robert Cerny
375 Pelham Boulevard

The modernism of William Wurster's Second Bay Tradition in one of the best pre–World War II houses in the Twin Cities. The two-story house closes itself off from the street and opens up glass on the other side to a view of the river.

13 **Bungalow Court,** 1925
93–97 Cleveland Avenue S

The bungalow court was a popular housing form on the West Coast; it provided the sense of a single-family house but on a small scale. The first West Coast examples (from Pasadena) date from 1910. The form did not enter Minnesota in force until after World War I.

13 Bungalow Court.

•14 **Fridholm House,** 1923
Ellerbe and Round
151 Woodlawn Avenue

A Prairie Style house built as late as the 1920s.

15 **House,** 1953
David Gebhard; Norman C. Nagle
259 Woodlawn Avenue

A woodsy early 1950s house, tucked in among the trees and the older period houses. The columned walkway and the garage face the street; the living area opens to the enclosed courtyard and the garden.

16 **Metal Experimental House,** 1935
Raphael Heime; Eugene Lund; Walter J. MacLeith
265 Woodlawn Avenue

Following the Century of Progress Exposition in Chicago in 1933 experimental houses were built across the country. Most were not radical in their spaces and design, but they were radical in the new materials used and in the sophistication of their mechanical cores. This house is sheathed in porcelain metal panels; in style it is 1930s Regency.

17 **House,** 1955
Norman C. Nagle
244 Stonebridge S

House, 1952
Norman C. Nagle
250 Stonebridge S

House, 1953
Bergstedt and Hirsch
300 Stonebridge S

House, 1948
Harlan McClure
316 Stonebridge S

House, 1950
Norman C. Nagle
320 Stonebridge S

House, 1957
Bergstedt and Hirsch
324 Stonebridge S

The east side of Stonebridge between St. Clair and Jefferson Avenues is full of architect-designed "modern" houses from the 1950s. Some are boxes, but most are woodsy and self-consciously organic.

18 **Spangenberg House,** 1864–67
Attrib. Frederick Spangenberg
375 Mount Curve Boulevard

The Greek Revival in a two-story house constructed of limestone; it fits in well with neighboring Period Revival Style houses.

19 **Bungalow Courts,** 1925; 1927
333–35 and 336–38 Cleveland Avenue S

Two bungalow courts which utilize the Spanish Colonial Revival Style of the 1920s.

20 **College of St. Catherine,** estab. 1911
2004 Randolph Avenue

The chapel (designed by H. A. Sullwold) was built in 1924, modeled after the French Romanesque Style of the Cathedral of Saint-Trophime at Arles. The recent Fine Arts Center and O'Shaughness[y] Auditorium (Hammel, Green, and Abrahamson, 1968–70) are exposed concrete structures, one of which is angle[d] so that the windows on the north side obtain maximum light for the studios.

20 O'Shaughnessy Auditorium, College of St. Catherine.

21 **St. Paul Academy,** 1913
1712 Randolph Avenue

The first building for the academy was vaguely Elizabethan and medieval (designed by Thomas G. Holyoke, 1916; additions, 1932–35). In 1971 the Cambridge architectural firm of Benjamin Thompso[n] Associates designed a building complex consisting of a learning center, a living center, and a science/mathematics addition. The units are all modular structure[s] with exposed concrete frames and infillin[g] of white painted brick and glass.

1 Learning Center, St. Paul Academy.

Ford Motor Company Assembly Plant, 1923–24
Albert Kahn, Inc.; Stone and Webster
966 Mississippi River Boulevard S

An early industrial plant in a parklike setting. The building itself is an example of Kahn's stripped classicism of the 1920s.

Powers Department Store, 1959–60
Ellerbe Architects
Southwest corner Ford Parkway and Cleveland Avenue S

A suburban department store building well scaled to the other retail commercial buildings on both streets and compatible with adjoining Highland Village to the south. Of white brick with a strip window near the cornice and mosaics on the ground level.

4 **Highland Theatre,** 1939
Myrtus A. Wright
760 Cleveland Avenue S

The Streamline Moderne of the 1930s, only in this case angular and cubistic in the rotated rectangular surfaces and volumes.

5 **Highland Village Apartment Homes,** 1938–39
845 Cleveland Avenue S

The largest private housing project built in the Twin Cities before World War II. The two-story and three-story brick units are arranged around interconnected quads. The whole beautifully planted complex is today one of the most successful of the city's multiple-family housing projects. In style it is brick Colonial with small windows and shutters. The lack of garages is the only pronounced negative criticism which could be leveled at the project.

26 **Ford Parkway Branch Library,** 1970
Ellerbe Architects
1974 Ford Parkway

A thin-walled stucco building with vertical projecting monitor windows.

•27 **House,** 1939
1775 Hillcrest Avenue

The 1930s did not produce many Streamline Moderne houses anywhere in the United States. This house is a major monument in the style. The street elevation is dominated by a curved wall of glass brick, behind which stairs rise to the second floor.

28 **Water Tower,** 1927–28
Fox Towes
Ford Parkway at Snelling Avenue S

A visual landmark for the Highland Park area; in style it is lightly Medieval, with a Spanish Colonial Revival cast.

29 **Highland Park Junior and Senior High Schools**
Hammel, Green, and Abrahamson
975 and 1015 Snelling Avenue S

The junior high school (1958) is a Miesian product; the senior high school (1967) by the same firm is monumental. In front of the buildings on Snelling Avenue is the stone Mattocks School (1871), which was moved to this site in 1964; the schoolhouse is essentially a Greek Revival building with some Italianate details.

30 **House,** 1969
Parker, Klein Associates
1045 Davern Street

A low-profile composition of shingled boxes.

31 **Davern House,** late 1860s
1175 Davern Street

A central-hall Greek Revival house with Italianate detailing; situated on a wooded site overlooking the river.

32 Jewish Community Center, c. 1970
Parker, Klein Associates
1375 St. Paul Avenue

A return of the Streamline Moderne of the 1930s, only in this case in brick. A series of low volumes with rounded corners and a band of projecting brick going around the upper part of the building.

33 Ehlen House, 1912
Attrib. Marion Parker
648 Lexington Parkway S

A diminutive Prairie Style bungalow said to have been designed by Marion Parker, who was associated with the office of Purcell and Elmslie.

34 Ingemann House, 1927
William Ingemann
7 Montcalm Court

Ingemann explored the wide gamut of period architecture in the 1920s and 1930s. His own house is Medieval, more French than English.

M-3 Mendota and Eagan

The small community of Mendota (originally called St. Peter) is tucked along the bluff across the Minnesota River from Fort Snelling. It was established as an offshoot of Fort Snelling, and during its early days in the 1820s and 1830s it was a lively trading center. Today the town consists of a single short main street with a few stores, three historical houses, and a church. The stretch of land between Mendota and Hastings to the south remained agricultural until World War II, when one of the Twin Cities' large war arsenal plants was built at Rosemount. Some low-density residential development began in 1945, but it was not until the 1960s that suburbia moved in with full fervor. An industrial park was platted on Pilot Knob Road, other industries began to enter the area and condominium housing began to crop up here and there.

1 St. Peter's Catholic Church, 1853
Highway 13 just north of Mendota Bridge (east end)

A fieldstone Gothic Revival church of the central entrance-tower plan. Romantically situated on top of the bluff overlooking the confluence of the Mississippi and Minnesota rivers.

2 DePuis House (now Sibley Tea Room), 1854
Southwest corner D Street and Highway 13

A Federal/Greek Revival house in brick with a hipped roof. It has a central-hall plan and a balanced layout of rooms on each side. The construction brick was shipped from eastern Wisconsin.

3 Henry H. Sibley House, 1835
Willow Street southwest of D Street

A gable-roofed Federal/Greek Revival house of fieldstone. It is of the side-hall type with a small secondary wing off the northeast side. The house and its outbuilding were restored in 1909–10.

3 Henry H. Sibley House.

4 **Jean B. Faribault House,** 1834
Willow Street southwest of D Street
A fieldstone Federal/Greek Revival house with a central-hall plan .It was restored between 1935 and 1939.

5 **Trinity Lone Oak Lutheran Church,** 1902
Highway 55 northwest of junction with Highway 49 (Inver Grove)
A turn-of-the-century brick Gothic Revival church. Its interpretation of the Gothic harks back to the style prevalent in the early 1890s.

6 **Univac Park Office and Laboratory** (now Sperry-Univac), 1966–68, 1973–74
Cerny Associates; The Architectural Alliance
3333 Pilot Knob Road
The pristine International Style building is set down in an immaculate parklike lawn — stagey but well done.

7 **Blue Cross Building,** 1967–69, 1974–75
Cerny Associates; The Architectural Alliance
3535 Blue Cross Road (southwest of junction of Yankee Doodle Road and Highway 13)
Another corporate stage set, this one with its source in the late work of Eero Saarinen. On the river side are two drum towers, large and small, which seem put there to give added emphasis to this corporate palace.

M-4 Fort Snelling

Though sliced through by freeways since 1965–66, the older portion of the fort (now a somewhat beleaguered island) has been undergoing restoration under the guidance of Brooks Cavin. Among the major buildings (1820–22) to be seen are the often illustrated two-story round tower, the three-story hexagonal tower, the officers' quarters, and the commandant's house. Several new buildings were built on the grounds of Fort Snelling and the adjacent veterans' home during the 1960s. Of these the most interesting is the Veterans' Restoration Facility (1973) by S. C. Smiley and Associates. In front of the fort, spanning the Minnesota River, is the Mendota Bridge (designed between 1923 and 1926 by Walter S. Wheeler). At the time it was built, it was one of the longest concrete bridges (4,119 feet) in the United States.

M-5 Metropolitan Airport

An airport was established at what had been an automobile racing track in 1921, and in 1923 it was named Wold-Chamberlain Field. At first the field was a joint enterprise between the cities of Minneapolis and St. Paul, but St. Paul withdrew in 1926 and built its own Holman Field. In 1928 the airport property was taken over by the Minneapolis Park Board, and the following year the first terminal building (by Harold H. Eads) was started; the terminal was dedicated in 1930. In 1943 the Metropolitan Airports Commission was established. The commission eventually recommended that only one major airfield be developed for the Twin Cities. Consideration was given to the possibility of locating this new joint airport farther from the cities, but these proposals were rejected and major construction was begun at Wold-Chamberlain Field (now the Minneapolis-St. Paul International Airport). Though no one could deny that its present location is convenient, the problem of jet noise for the residents of South Minneapolis at times comes close to being unbearable — a heavy price to pay for convenience of location.

1 **Air Terminal Building,** 1961–62; 1974
Thorshov and Cerny; Cerny Associates
Highway 494/5, west of Highway 55

A glass box covered by a folded roof; approached by a ramped street. The passageways off two corners of the building are connected to long passenger loading arms. When built, the terminal had a court with a landscape park and a fountain in front; parking garages now occupy this space.

2 **United Airlines Hangar** (now International and Charter Terminal), 1968
Miller, Whitehead, and Dunwiddie Architects
34th Avenue S, ¼ mile north of Highway 494

A giant and workable hyperbolic paraboloid. Saarinen's TWA Building at Kennedy International Airport transformed from concrete into angular steel.

2 United Airlines Hangar (now International and Charter Terminal).
Photo: Dale Peterson/Warren Reynolds and Associates.

3 **Metropolitan Airports Commission Building,** 1966–67
Miller, Whitehead, and Dunwiddie Architects
6040 28th Avenue S

The Beaux Arts made modern; a dignified, formal building.

M-6 Burnsville

The horizontal spread of Minneapolis and St. Paul seems to continue unabated. In the late 1960s it started to spill across the Minnesota River Valley, and in the early 1970s new communities — especially of the planned variety — have been laid out hither and yon. Most of these occur around Highway 13, which runs parallel to the Minnesota River.

1 **The Embassy and Minotte's Restaurants** (now Corner House Restaurant), c. 1964
12020 Highway 35W, Embassy Road (use 122nd Street exit)

A Neo-Babylonian sight; Los Angeles carted out to the south Minneapolis suburbs. Originally it was painted in a wilder fashion than we presently see.

2 **Birnamwood,** 1969–75
Pemtom Design Group
Old Highway 13 (take Parkwood Drive to Birnamwood Drive)

Single-family attached townhouses (222 units) of wood and brick, laid out on forty-three acres. The adjoining Birnamwood Golf Course was also laid out by the Pemtom Design Group (1970).

1 The Embassy and Minotte's Restaurants (now Corner House Restaurant).

3 **Mary Mother of the Church (Catholic),** 1969
Hodne/Stageberg Partners
Cliff Road, ½ mile west of Cedar Avenue

Of brick, with a quarter of a cylinder profile.

3 Mary Mother of the Church.

M-7 Jonathan and Chanhassen

Jonathan
Benjamin H. Cunningham (planner); Masao Kinoshita, Sasaki, Dawson, and De May Associates (landscape architects); Bailey and Associates (landscape architects)

The community of Jonathan was in the planning stages from 1965 through 1967. It was not to be just another suburb, rather it was to be a "new town" which had its own industrial, commercial, and recreational activities as well as housing. Within its 8,142 acres was to be a town center for 15,000 people, three industrial parks, and a central commercial complex; each of the five villages (each with a population of 7,000) was to have a convenience service center. By 1990 the population was to be 50,000, and Jonathan was by then to be linked with the Twin Cities by some type of fixed-rail rapid transit system.

Major Twin Cities architects were invited in to design many of the first buildings. The Village Center, a Charles Moore-esque composition, was designed in 1970 by Hammel, Green, and Abrahamson; the Kallestad Laboratories Building came from the office of Miller, Hanson, and Westerbeck (1973), and the Vademecum Manufacturing Building was designed in 1967–68 by Hammel, Green, and Abrahamson. Ralph Rapson and Associates produced their "Red Cedar House" for *Better Homes and Gardens*, the dwellings making up Stockwood came from Progressive Design Associates (1970), the Hodne/Stageberg Partners produced sixty-four units of townhouses on the Center Green (1972), and Interdesign has produced some single-family special housing (1972). Everything seemed to argue for the good, but the events of recent years have been decidedly negative for Jonathan. (A similar fate, it should be noted, has befallen other American "new towns.") The negative economic aspects of the past few years have been compounded by the disappearance of most aid from the federal government. The principal backer of the project died, and factors such as the increasing cost of gasoline and changes in life-style have had their effect. Then too, there is the built-in blandness which any new community faces. Careful planning, as we all know, may more often than not lead to dullness — and Jonathan is visually dull — even though great efforts have been made to avoid it. Perhaps in the long run the slowdown in the development program will work to advantage, and meaningful variety will begin to emerge.

2 **Minnesota Landscape Arboretum, Educational and Research Building,** 1971–74
Edwin H. Lundie (completed by Bettenburg, Townsend, Stolte, and Comb)
3675 Arboretum Drive, Chanhassen
(Highway 5, ½ mile west of Highway 41)

Lundie's fondness for the medieval, expressed in a stone and steep-roofed building. Terraces at the front and rear help mold the building into its site; within, great timbers are used for the beamed ceilings and for vertical supports — all Medieval, but designed Medieval and not rustic. Those acquainted with Lundie's work will probably feel that the building would have been more successful had he been able to follow it through to completion.

2 Educational and Research Building, Minnesota Landscape Arboretum.

M-8 Bloomington

Bloomington is an extensive area reaching from Highway 494 south to the Minnesota River flats. Its northern boundary is heavily committed to commerce, ranging from the Metropolitan Sports Arena and Stadium (Cedar Avenue South at 79th Street) to the new commercial complex around the Radisson South hotel at the junction of Highways 494 and 100. Other medium-sized commercial nodules are found along Highway 35W as it proceeds south. Developer produced and designed housing, mostly from the 1960s, spreads out over the rolling countryside, and the most recent of these developments are of the condominium/apartment planned community type. The intensity of growth can be sensed by comparing the number of houses in existence in 1953 (3,600) with those existing in 1970 (22,538). Since much of the growth in this suburban area took place in the 1960s, the planning of parks and open spaces seems much better thought out than that usually found in suburbs developed between 1945 and 1960.

1 **One Appletree Square,** 1973
Ellerbe Architects
One Appletree Square, off Highway 494 at 34th Avenue S

A bronzed glass box. The project will eventually include two towers, one for offices and the other a condominium.

2 **Control Data Headquarters Building,** 1961, 1970–72
Community Planning and Design (1961); Henningson, Durham, and Richardson (1970–72)
8100 34th Avenue S

Corporate design over ten years. The most recent addition is made up of three boxes in reflective bronze glass.

3 **Pond House,** 1855
104th Street E (south end of Clinton Avenue S)

Barely visible through the trees (except in the winter) is a two-story brick Greek Revival dwelling. It is cubical in form with a hipped roof and has an elegant recessed doorway with sidelights.

4 **Donaldson Company Headquarters and Research Facility,** 1969
Hammel, Green, and Abrahamson
1400 94th Street W (west of Highway 35W)

In the middle and late 1960s there was a tendency to scale down the corporate palace. This example consists of low brick boxes, the center of each box covered by a shingled hipped roof with a skylight at its point.

5 **Planned Communities,** late 1960s
Near the corner of 102nd Street W and Normandale Boulevard (Scarborough)
Old Shakopee Road between Normandale Boulevard and Bush Lake Road (Woodstock)

The Scarborough community (63.7 acres) is a planned development by the Pemtom Design Group. The Woodstock development (38 acres) is a 323-unit condominium by Selvig, Stevenson, Peterson, and Flock. The architectural images vary: The Tarnhill units at 102nd Street West and Normandale Boulevard are white modified International Style buildings; the adjoining Lochmoor condominiums are of wood and brick with shed roofs.

6 **Normandale Office Park,** 1972
Setter, Leach, and Lindstrom
Normandale Boulevard at 82nd Street

A four-story bronze-skinned building.

7 **Radisson South Hotel,** 1968–70
Cerny Associates
7800 Normandale Boulevard

A twenty-two-story, 408-room hotel with a skylighted space forty feet high. The tall narrow slab of the building with the name "Radisson" across the top can be seen from afar. As an example of commercial speculation, the complex may well make sense. From the standpoint of planning one may wonder what this large-scale development and its satellites are doing here.

M-9 Richfield

While there were a few narrow strips of pre-1941 housing in Richfield along such streets as Lyndale and Nicollet, the remaining land was agricultural. In the post-1945 years the former farmlands have been overrun with developer-built housing, shopping centers, and the like. Freeways now penetrate and define the community — Highway 35W projects through it just west of Wood Lake; Highway 36 (Cedar Avenue) is on its eastern boundary, and Highway 494 with its intense commercialism runs along its southern limits.

1 **Naegele Building,** 1965
Peterson, Clark, and Griffith
1700 78th Street W

American Georgian raised to new heights.

2 **House,** c. 1856
7100 Oak Grove Boulevard

A two-story Greek Revival side-hall plan dwelling which fits in beautifully with all of the post-World War II period houses. New entrance porches — to make it more truly authentic — were added at a later date.

3 **Central Elementary School,** 1948
Long and Thorshov
7145 Harriet Avenue

A finger-plan school of one story in brick with modular infill panels. The low scale of the building is well related to its small occupants.

4 **Bartholomew House,** c. 1860s
6901 Lyndale Avenue S

A lukewarm Greek Revival house.

5 **Wood Lake Nature Interpretative Center,** 1971
Brauer and Associates (site architects); Robert Quanbeck (building architect)
735 Lake Shore Drive W

A woodsy group of high-pitched hipped-roof pavilions, set among the trees on the lakeshore. The whole is a little bit pressed for space, including the public land around the lake; still it has been carried out with sensitivity.

6 **Richfield Bank and Trust Company Building,** 1972
Setter, Leach, and Lindstrom
6625 Lyndale Avenue S

The usual monumental cut-into brick box — completely unrelated to the scale and usual visual confusion of a suburban retail/commercial shopping corner.

M-10 Edina

The Edina Mill on Minnehaha Creek was built in 1857; the village was incorporated in 1888. Nothing much happened to the small community until the 1920s. Slowly the section extending north and west of 50th Street West and France Avenue South began to emerge as an upper-middle-class, single-family housing area. Three golf courses were developed by the end of the 1920s — Edina Country Club, Interlachen Country Club, and Meadowbrook Golf Course. By 1930 the country club district of Edina was one of *the* places to live; it extended from France Avenue South to Minnehaha Creek, north to Sunnyside, and south to 50th Street West. The electric street railway line to Lake Minnetonka ran along the northern border (though it should be noted that by 1930 most of the families living in the country club district used the private automobile, not public transportation). The architecture which developed in the country club section of Edina was almost exclusively that of one or another of the Period Revivals — Colonial, English, and a few Mediterranean and French Provincial examples. Most of the houses were contractor-designed, and they differed from normal middle-class Minneapolis houses only in their increased size, larger lots, private driveways, and garages for more than one car. None of the houses could be thought of as an architectural monument, but the houses work well with one another and they establish a strong sense of place which is not often found in American cities. By 1941 a fashionable auto-oriented shopping area had emerged at France Avenue South and 50th Street West with the usual supermarkets and theatre dominating the scene.

After World War II equally fashionable upper-middle-class housing spread south to 56th Street and east and south of the Interlachen Country Club. The latest exclusive housing is to be found in the southwest corner of Edina by the recently laid out Braemar Golf Course. It all looks expensive, polished, and often correct. Although the low-density land use does not cry out for parks, Edina has laid out an abundant number of them — some left in their natural state, others manicured meticulously.

Edina is also the site of the Twin Cities' first large-scale planned shopping center, Southdale. The area around this shopping center now houses numerous commercial buildings, apartments, and (south of 70th Street West) planned condominium units.

•1 **Southdale Shopping Center,** 1954–56
Victor Gruen and Associates
Southeast corner 66th Street and France Avenue S

Gruen's first shopping center to be organized around an enclosed court. Nothing on the outside except neutral boxes and acres of cars. Inside the clerestory lighted court with its sculpture by Harry Bertoia is as pleasant as when it was built. The public passages leading to the court are on the dreary side, but what is indeed grim is the parking area, where not a tree, shrub, or flower raises its ugly head (except in a minor way along the public streets).

2 **Modern Medicine Building,** 1963
Thorsen and Thorshov
Southeast corner Highway 62 and Valley View Road

A composition of a wooded site, two small lakes, and a building with a curved façade. From a distance it comes off reasonably well, close up it is less impressive.

3 **Midwest Federal Savings and Loan Association Building,** 1964
Miller, Whitehead, and Dunwiddie Architects
3100 66th Street W

The circular pavilion of Edward Stone, made even more delicate and fragile. Eight other branch banks of this concern are of identical form — a real prefabricated product.

4 **Edina Municipal Liquor Store,** 1972–73
Cerny Associates
6801 York Avenue S

A wood-sheathed rectangular box and accompanying circular drum — the architectural idiom of the 1970s.

5 **Southdale Branch, Hennepin County Library,** 1974
Hodne/Stageberg Partners
7001 York Avenue S

The hovering-box school of architecture of the late 1960s and 1970s. Its cold concrete walls drop down into the asphalt parking area which serves the adjoining business. One has to look twice before it is apparent that this is a public building and not another office building or savings and loan establishment. Set in a surrounding of greenery, the building might well have come off.

6 **Edina Evangelical Free Church,** 1966
James E. Stageberg
5015 70th Street W

A low, quiet church of brick; its end wall is formed in a curve.

7 **House,** 1966
James E. Stageberg
6009 Dublin Circle

A two-story flat-roofed house, sheathed in wood, all seemingly rational and logical.

8 **House,** 1956
Bruce A. Abrahamson
7205 Shannon Drive

The Harvard version of the single-floor International Style box set on a wooded hillside.

8 House.
Photo: Warren Reynolds/Warren Reynolds and Associates.

9 **Braemar Golf Course Clubhouse,** 1963
Hammel, Green, and Abrahamson
Valley View Road just off Dewey Hill Road

A group of Ernest Kump-like boxes crowned with a double-pitched, broadly overhanging roof; picturesquely placed on a wooded hilltop.

10 **House,** 1966
Close Associates
6901 Dakota Trail

A butterfly-roofed, wood-sheathed dwelling perched over the woods and the lake.

11 **House,** 1967
Arthur Dickey Associates
6824 Valley View Road

Two tall shed-roof boxes, attached.

12 **Edina West High School,** 1972
Armstrong, Schlichting, Torseth, and Skold
6754 Valley View Road

The school as a monumental corporate factory; internally, the planning, especially that of circulation, is lighter in spirit.

13 **Calvary Lutheran Church,** 1959, 1969
Sovik, Mathre, and Madsen; Bergstedt, Wahlberg, and Bergquist
6817 Antrim Road

Perhaps a bit gadgety, but still fascinating as a design: a wedge-shaped form folds into a rectangular form, and at the point where they join is a U-shaped window.

14 **Alfred Erickson House,** 1950
Lloyd Wright
5408 Stauder Circle

A wood and stone post–World War II house which goes on and on. Beautifully sited on a wooded knoll.

15 **Arthur Erickson House,** 1950
Lloyd Wright
5501 Londonderry Road

A variation on the Alfred Erickson house (#14).

16 **Americana State Bank Building,** 1973
Grover Dimond Associates
Northwest corner France Avenue S and 51st Street W

The angled, cut-into box, only this time in white stucco.

17 **Edina Theatre,** 1936
Liebenberg and Kaplan
3911 50th Street W

A Streamline Moderne theatre; also note the small Streamline Moderne Edina Eye Clinic building next door (3939 50th Street West).

17 Edina Eye Clinic.

18 **St. Stephen's Episcopal Church,** 1938
Louis B. Bersback; Cram and Ferguson (consulting architects)
50th Street W at Wooddale Avenue

A 1930s interpretation of the English Gothic in stone with a low crenelated tower.

19 **Grange Hall,** 1879
Northeast corner Eden Avenue and Highway 100

An Eastlake Style building, later used as the Edina Town Hall.

20 **Cahill School,** 1864
Northeast corner Eden Avenue and Highway 100

Clapboard vernacular, with just a slight hint of the Eastlake Style in the detailing of the window frames.

21 **Westgate Theatre,** c. 1936
Perry Crosier
3903 Sunnyside Avenue

A modest Streamline Moderne theatre. Across the street with a vertical sign which reads "Restaurant/Soda" is a glass-brick Streamline Moderne building.

22 **Grimes House,** 1869
4200 44th Street W

A Gothic Revival cottage with Italianate details.

22 Grimes House.

M-11 St. Louis Park

Originally called Elmwood, then St. Louis Village, this suburban community is currently cut up in all directions by highways, freeways, railroads, and commercial strips. Housing still constitutes the predominant land use, and it ranges from upper middle class to middle middle class. Because of the patterns of highways and railroads the housing forms itself into strongly separate neighborhoods, each of which seems to have little relation to the whole. Visitors interested in early industrial architecture should note the Peavey Company grain elevators located south of the junction of Highways 7 and 100. These elevators were built in 1899–1900.

1 **Railroad Station,** 1870s
Jorvig Park, southwest corner Brunswick Avenue and 37th Street
An excellently restored Eastlake station.

2 **Recreation Center,** 1973
S. C. Smiley and Associates
5005 36th Street W
Concrete with a sloped and curved roof — a little grand and monumental for a building devoted to play.

3 **St. Louis Park Theatre,** c. 1938
Perry Crosier
4835 Minnetonka Boulevard
A Streamline Moderne theatre, not great but still worth a look.

4 **Lutheran Church of the Reformation,** 1958; 1968
Hammel, Green, and Abrahamson
2544 Highway 100 S
A wood-sheathed box has been sliced off at the corner (windows injected), and a small pointed tripod roof (one side open with glass) has been placed on top. Separate from it is the white bell tower, whose shape and color dramatically contrast with the wood box. An important church building of the 1960s.

4 Lutheran Church of the Reformation.

5 **Olfelt House,** 1958–59
Frank Lloyd Wright
2206 Parklands Lane
A modest brick bungalow with a low gable roof, designed near the end of Wright's life.

M-12 Hopkins

Hopkins was incorporated as a town in 1893. Both the Burlington Northern and the Milwaukee Road pass through the town, and very early it became a desirable place to locate industrial facilities. Through the 1930s the Hopkins area was a major truck farming locale. Suburbia has replaced all of this with housing and commercial developments.

1 **Hopkins Mall,** 1972
Gale and Mauk
Excelsior Avenue between 5th and 12th Avenues

Interest in urban renewal began in 1954, and the downtown mall was one aspect of that program.

2 **Hopkins Theatre,** 1941
Perry Crosier
429 Excelsior Avenue W

The theatre and the group of adjoining stores are designed in the Streamline Moderne style. The tower has recently received a coat of supergraphics which, while stylistically timely (a few years ago, at least), hardly helps.

3 **Blake School,** 1912
Hewitt and Brown
110 Blake Road S

English Collegiate Gothic in brick. The chapel was built in 1929.

4 **St. John the Evangelist Catholic Church,** 1968
Progressive Design Associates
6 Interlachen Road

The shapes of the buildings and the relationships of the forms have a Finnish, Aalto-esque quality to them. Certainly one of Minnesota's successful church designs of the 1960s.

4 St. John the Evangelist Catholic Church.

5 **Charles A. Lindbergh High School,** 1972
Hammel, Green, and Abrahamson
2400 Lindbergh Road

Somewhat formidable as an object in the landscape, but the interior with its complex vertical and horizontal space and the bright colors of the supergraphics provides a far less serious world.

M-13 Lake Minnetonka

In 1871 Lake Minnetonka was "the point for both pleasure-seekers and invalids who are well enough to 'rough it,' " according to Ledyard Bill in *Minnesota, Its Character and Climate.* The first settlements near the lake — Minnetonka Mills, Excelsior, and Wayzata — were agriculturally oriented rather than pleasure oriented. Minnetonka Mills was first settled in 1852 and was formally organized in 1858. By the early 1870s the town had become an important lumber milling and manufacturing center which utilized waterpower derived from Minnehaha Creek. Excelsior was colonized in 1853 by the Excelsior Pioneer Associates of New York. Wayzata was platted in 1854.

In 1860 Lake Minnetonka acquired the first of its steamboats, and by the late 1860s the settlements near the lake were connected to the Twin Cities by rail. Several resort hotels were built on the lake, including the Long View Hotel (1867), the Lake View Hotel (1869), the May House (1877) on St. Alban's Bay, the Hotel St. Louis (1879) at Deephaven, the Harrow House (1879) on Shady Island, and others. In the 1880s two of the largest resort hotels on Lake Minnetonka were built — the Lake Park Hotel (c. 1880s, later the Tonka Bay Hotel) on Gideon's Bay, with "every room on a veranda," and the Hotel LaFayette (1882), an Eastlake/Queen Anne extravaganza. By this time one could travel along the northern shore via the Great Northern railway or along the southern shore via the Chicago and Northwestern.

A major advance in rapid rail transportation to Lake Minnetonka was begun in 1905 with the introduction of electric streetcars which ran from the Twin Cities to Excelsior. The Twin Cities Rapid Transit Company's routes were rapidly expanded, and eventually two lines served the southern route with stations at Excelsior, Wildhurst, and Tonka Bay, and a central route along the eastern shore to Groveland, Maplewood, Northome, and Deephaven. In the 1900s the company opened its amusement park on Big Island, one-half mile north of Excelsior. The buildings in the park were Mission Revival in style.

Beginning in the 1890s some elaborate summer homes were built on the lake, and the Colonial Revival/Shingle Style LaFayette Club (designed by William Channing Whitney) was opened at the end of the decade. In the early 1900s large and small lakeshore cottages began to appear, and the hotels began to recede in importance. By 1919 only six hotels were still operating, and by the late 1950s all had disappeared along with the large lake steamers. The amusement park on Big Island was dismantled, and a new park was opened after World War I right on the waterfront of Excelsior.

Private residence, Lake Minnetonka. Ralph Rapson.

Private residence, Lake Minnetonka. I. W. Colburn.

The electric streetcars continued to run during the 1930s, but increasingly the automobile became the preferred mode of transportation. After 1945 the expansion of Highways 12 and 7 into freeways led to increased suburbanization, especially on the east shore of the lake from Excelsior to Wayzata. With the construction of new major shopping centers such as Ridgedale, and the moving of corporate headquarters of company's such as General Mills to the west of the Twin Cities, the whole area is slowly emerging as a western suburb of Minneapolis. Many of the modest lakeshore cabins have either been transformed into year-round residences or have been replaced by new houses.

The Lake Minnetonka area has been the site of the most outstanding examples of domestic architecture and residential design in the state over the past fifty years. It is unfortunate that very few of these architectural monuments are accessible and visible to the public. The majority of them are ensconced in their own private fiefdoms. Among the most widely known are the Gallaher House (1909–10) by Purcell and Elmslie and the Sexton House, which was remodeled in 1910 by the same firm. Hewitt and Shaw, • Frank Joseph Forster, McEnary and Krafft, • Edwin Lundie, and others produced large-scaled Romantic Period Revival lake residences from the 1920s into the 1940s. After World War II Norman Nagle, Elizabeth and Winston Close, and Robert G. Cerny designed some of their most interesting buildings on and around the lake. In 1950–52 Philip C. Johnson designed a courtyard-oriented Miesian house for Richard Davis. The list is equally impressive in more recent years: Several houses by Ralph Rapson, including • a major Wayzata residence (1964) that has become a classic example of the agitated forms associated with the Minnesota School of the mid-1960s; a half dozen Wrightian residences by John H. Howe, the earliest built in 1961; a 1960s Romanesque Revival castle (1963–65) by I. W. Colburn; • a knowing revival of Le Corbusier's work of the 1920s in a Deephaven house completed in 1973 by Frederick Bentz–Milo Thompson Associates; a simple but elegant private tennis pavilion for the Woodhill Country Club (1973) by the Hodne/Stageberg Partners; and even a sophisticated "East Coast Whites" design by Mitchell-Giurgola Associates.

Although these additions to the area's architectural heritage are impressive, there have also been a number of major losses, especially the tearing down of Purcell and Elmslie's Decker House (1912–13) in Northome in the late 1940s and the bulldozing in 1972 of the Little House (1913), also in Northome, Frank Lloyd Wright's major work in Minnesota. These famous landmarks have been replaced by bland, undistinguished dwellings. Fortunately, in the case of the Decker dwelling the original two-story service building and the connecting passageway are still intact.

House. John H. Howe.

1 **Cowles House** (now Spring Hill Conference Center), 1961–63, 1972
Edward Larrabee Barnes
County Road 6, 2 miles west of Highway 101 (Wayzata)

The center was initially built as a private residence for John and Sage Cowles in 1961–63. In 1972 Barnes added to the complex and transformed it into a conference center. Along with the Walker Art Center the Spring Hill Conference Center is one of the most important high art monuments in Minnesota. Note the pristine Barnes forms and the play of shed-roofed and flat-roofed volumes.

1 Cowles House (now Spring Hill Conference Center).

2 **Hennepin County Park Reserve District Building,** 1972
Douglas A. Baird Architects
Morris T. Baker Park Reserve at County Roads 24 and 19 (Maple Plain)

The transformation of a gable-roofed barn and silo into an office space has been well handled. Its only drawback is that perhaps it has all been done too seriously.

3 **"Skyway Plaza" Office Building,** 1965, 1974–75
Kilstofte and Vosejpka; Richard B. Vosejpka
1415 Wayzata Boulevard E (Wayzata)

The first of these office units is quite Wrightian, the second less so. The newer units concentrate on the visual qualities and potentials of the stucco box.

•4 **Wayzata Theatre,** 1932
Liebenberg and Kaplan
619 Lake Street E (Wayzata)

The most important feature of the theatre is the cantilevered Zigzag Moderne (Art Deco) marquee, which is best seen at night. The ticket booth and entry area below it have been remodeled.

5 **Bank Building** (now Wayzata Insurance Agency), c. 1910
305 Lake Street E (Wayzata)

The building is a classical screen. Four large-scale Corinthian columns, each on its own brick base, support a classical entablature; behind these on the front façade of the building circular windows are placed above each of the lower pedimented openings.

5 Bank Building (now Wayzata Insurance Agency).

6 **Highcroft Campus of the Blake Schools,** 1963
James E. Stageberg
301 Peavey Lane (Wayzata)

Brick pavilions with a pattern of exposed structure and vertical window units.

7 **Old Hill School** (now Minnetonka Art Center), 1892
County Road 51 at Briar Street, 1 block west of County Road 146 (Orono)

Queen Anne/Colonial Revival, with an open bell tower on the ridge of the roof.

8 Camp Memorial Chapel (now St. Martin's by the Lake Episcopal Church), 1887
Cass Gilbert
County Road 15 at Lafayette Bay (Minnetonka Beach)

A small, dainty Shingle Style building, part Queen Anne and part early Craftsman. The open entrance porch has now been enclosed, and other changes have been made in the building.

8 Camp Memorial Chapel (now St. Martin's by the Lake Episcopal Church).

9 Bungalow, c. 1905
County Road 15, ½ mile east of junction with County Road 19 (Minnetonka Beach)

A one-and-a-half-story Colonial Revival shingle bungalow.

10 Fresh Water Biological Institute, 1974
Close Associates
East corner of County Roads 15 and 19 (Navarre)

Projecting wood-sheathed volumes contrast with the adjoining brick surfaces.

11 Trinity Episcopal Church, 1862
322 2nd Street (Excelsior)

A remarkably early use of concrete (lime and gravel) for the walls of a building in Minnesota. The church was moved to its present site and was restored in 1907.

12 Wyer-Pearce House, c. 1880s
201 Mill Street (Excelsior)

An Eastlake/Queen Anne clapboard house, picturesquely situated on a knoll overlooking the lake.

13 Bayshore Manor Townhouses, 1965–66
Cerny Associates
423 Lake Street E (Excelsior)

Picturesque shingled forms best seen from across the bay after a snowstorm.

14 Minnetonka Municipal Building, 1971
Thorsen and Thorshov
14600 Minnetonka Boulevard (Minnetonka)

The cut-into brick vocabulary of the late 1960s and 1970s. In this instance the play of the gentle sloping roof against the vertical brick utility volume is Scandinavian in feeling.

14 Minnetonka Municipal Building.

15 Minnetonka Fire Station, 1974
Liebenberg, Smiley, and Glotter
Northeast corner Minnetonka Boulevard (County Road 5) and Williston Road (Minnetonka)

A second increment in the Minnetonka Civic Center.

16 Village Hall, c. 1900
13231 Minnetonka Boulevard (Minnetonka Mills)

Colonial Revival which comes close to being Greek Revival.

17 Burwell House, 1883
Northwest corner McGinty Road and Minnetonka Boulevard (Minnetonka Mills)

An Eastlake villa directly influenced by a design (plate 14) in Palliser's *American Cottage Homes* (1878). A three-story gable-roofed tower rises from the L of the house. Originally there were also twelve workers' cottages (mildly Gothic Revival) associated with the main house.

M-14 Golden Valley, Crystal, and Plymouth

Golden Valley and Crystal are already well developed; Plymouth, Maple Grove, and the other communities farther west are poised on the brink. Like St. Louis Park, Golden Valley seems more of a vague geographic district than anything approaching a community with a sense of specific place. The rolling hills just west of Theodore Wirth Park (on Minneapolis's western boundary) were developed as Tyrol Hills and South Tyrol Hills, and along their wooded and winding streets is an array of single-family (and in many cases architect-designed) houses which were built in the late 1930s and thereafter. The rest of the area seems to be a developer's paradise.

Within Golden Valley, Crystal, and Plymouth are a number of structures from the 1950s and later (not listed) which are well worth a visit: Hammel, Green, and Abrahamson's 1968 Minneapolis Clinic of Psychiatry and Neurology (4225 Golden Valley Road); the Architectural Alliance's 1973 Valley Square Professional Building (7500 Golden Valley Road); and Ellerbe Inc.'s 1970 Honeywell Solid State Electronic Center (12001 Highway 55 in Plymouth).

1 **McClure House,** 1951
Harlan McClure and Frank Kerr
1323 June Avenue S

White House, 1957
Norman C. Nagle
1400 June Avenue S

The McClure House is a small International Style box with a structural steel skeleton and extensive glass. The White House is a box hovering over its indented concrete base. Both houses have been modified and are no longer as "pure" as they once were.

2 **General Mills Headquarters Buildings**
Skidmore, Owings, and Merrill
9200 Wayzata Boulevard

A palatial industrial estate designed by the firm which was (and still is) the master of American Corporate architecture. The main building was designed during 1957–58, and the west wing was finished in 1966. The interior of the Betty Crocker Kitchen was designed by Walter Dorwin Teague. The most recent addition, the east wing, was designed by A. Epstein in 1969–70. As is fitting for an estate, the grounds abound with large-scale works of sculpture — a large metal construction by Charles Huntington, "Flight" by Robert Engman, and others.

3 **Rockford Road Branch, Hennepin County Library,** 1973
Parker, Klein Associates
6401 42nd Avenue N

A rectangular box, cut diagonally, beautifully fitted to its needs and site.

3 Rockford Road Branch, Hennepin County Library.

4 **Neil A. Armstrong Senior High School,** 1971
Bissell, Belair, and Green
10635 36th Avenue N

A meant-to-be impressive concrete and brick pile, set on a fifty-four-acre site; planned to accommodate 2,400 students. Why must these new school complexes appear so monumental and factorylike? To whom are they really addressing themselves?

5 **Driver's License Examination Station,** 1972–73
Frederick Bentz-Milo Thompson and Associates
2455 Fernbrook Lane N

A pristine white box with a Kahn-like pattern of windows. (Do not visit on weekends. The chain-link gates are closed then, and the mounded landscape hides the buildings.)

5 Driver's License Examination Station. Photo: Ken Smith.

6 **Ridgedale Shopping Center,** 1974–75
Gruen Associates, Frederick Bentz-Milo Thompson and Associates, and others
Wayzata Boulevard at Plymouth Road

The newest of the large shopping centers in the Twin Cities area. It is quite successful as a picturesque object seen from the freeway (its forms are bold enough to capture attention), and it also works out well internally with the orientation around the central court.

6 Ridgedale Shopping Center.

M-15 Minneapolis and St. Paul: North Suburbs

Though some housing had pressed north of Minneapolis and St. Paul before the 1950s, most of the land remained agricultural. The first appreciable inroad was made in 1941–42 with the construction of the extensive army ammunition plant at New Brighton by Smith, Hinchman, and Grylls and Toltz, King, and Day. The major opening up of the countryside awaited the arrival of the freeway (1961), and from that moment on new housing tracts, apartments, and condominiums began to be developed along with major shopping centers such as Rosedale. At present the area is a hodgepodge of the good, the bad, and the indifferent (more of the last than anything else). Whether it can be saved through coordinated metropolitan planning remains to be seen. Some interesting buildings (not described) are the Brooklyn Center Civic Center (including the firehouse) designed by Cerny Associates (1968–71) located at 6301 Shingle Creek Parkway in Brooklyn Center; Parker, Klein Associates' Salem Baptist Church (1966) at 1995 Silver Lake Road in New Brighton; and Ellerbe Architects' Medtronic, Inc. Building (1973) at 3055 Highway 8 in St. Anthony Village.

1 **Rosedale Shopping Center,** 1968–69
Victor Gruen and Associates
Northwest corner Highway 36 and Fairview Avenue N (Roseville)

An enclosed-mall shopping center; it does not seem to come off as well as the earlier Southdale Shopping Center in Edina, or the later Ridgedale Shopping Center in Minnetonka.

2 **House,** 1966
Joseph Michels
3301 32nd Avenue N (St. Anthony)

This architect seems often to be able to manage that delicate balance between an assertion of modesty and real character. Here is another of his successful wood-detailed houses.

3 **Foss House,** 1890
Corner Silver Lake Road near County Road E (New Brighton)

A Queen Anne brick dwelling now painted white.

4 **Home of the Good Shepherd,** 1968
Hammel, Green, and Abrahamson
5100 Hodgson Road (North Oaks)

Brick boxes with a cut-in pattern of vertical and horizontal window bands.

4 Home of the Good Shepherd.

5 **Locke House,** 1847
Locke Park (Fridley)
1½ miles north of Highway 694 on East River Road

Essentially a simplified Greek Revival house.

6 **House,** c. 1938
1800 Shore Drive E (Maplewood)

The Streamline Moderne — in this case a curved stairway bay, partially in glass bricks, attached to strong rectangular volumes.

M-16 White Bear Lake

In 1871 Ledyard Bill noted in *Minnesota, Its Character and Climate* that "White Bear Lake is a favorite place with all classes" and that "it is second in interest only to . . . Minnetonka Lake for both invalids and pleasure-seekers during the summer and fall months." By 1870 one could travel to the lake from St. Paul or Stillwater on the St. Paul and Duluth Railroad, and by 1879 one could reach it from Minneapolis on the Minneapolis and St. Louis Railway. By the mid-1870s the west shore had been marked off into village lots, and a number of cottages had already sprung up. Visitors from the cities were accommodated in summerhouses, in tent cities, or in the hotels which developed on the lake —

Archer Log Cabin, White Bear Lake.

the Leip House, the Williams House, and the Southshore House. The Williams House and its separate cottages, which were built in 1871, had facilities for over one hundred guests. The town of White Bear Lake was incorporated in 1881, but other communities around the lake have remained unincorporated.

In 1892 the St. Paul and White Bear Railroad introduced electric train service to the area and established an amusement park at Wildwood on the south shore of the lake. This park offered orchestral concerts, bowling, a carousel, a roller coaster, a water chute, and restaurants. By 1899 the railway line was extended from White Bear Lake to Stillwater, and in 1904 the town of White Bear Lake was provided with streetcar service to other communities on the lake.

By the end of the 1880s some fairly extensive summer residences had been built on Manitou Island and in Dellwood (on the east shore), and by 1930 modest lakeshore cabins had been built in Mahtomedi, Birchwood, and Cottage Park. With the steady expansion of the freeway system (Highways 35E and 694) much of the White Bear Lake area is now suburban, and the housing is occupied the year around.

Like Lake Minnetonka (only on a much smaller scale), White Bear Lake has a number of highly important architectural monuments which are not open to the public. The fifty-four-acre Manitou Island, which is connected to the mainland by a causeway, holds several significant dwellings: Cass Gilbert's Dean House (1893), Edwin Lundie's Weyerhaeuser House (1930) and Westin House (1942), and others. In the Dellwood area are the Archer "log cabin" (1920s) and other houses.

1 **House,** c. 1894
Cass Gilbert
4320 Cottage Park Road (Cottage Park)
The Shingle Style (in this instance a combination of Queen Anne, Colonial Revival, and Craftsman). The horizontal band of the bracketed eaves has been carried across the gable end to form a wide triangle which ties the window into a single horizontal band.

1 House.

2 **"The Red Chalet,"** 1879
303 Lake Avenue (White Bear Lake)
An Eastlake cottage with a Swiss flavor — about as close to Vincent Scully's Stick Style as one will find in Minnesota.

2 "The Red Chalet."

3 **Erd-Geist Gazebo,** 1883
Matoska Park; east side of Lake Avenue at east end of 5th Street
A private Eastlake gazebo which has recently been moved to Matoska Park. It is said that the lower level was originally a honeymoon cottage.

•4 **Bank Building** (now Bankers Building), c. 1915
316 Washington Avenue (White Bear Lake)
The classical vocabulary used to create the picturesque. Somewhat Georgian, but more like a child's cast-iron penny bank.

5 **Shields House,** 1941–42
Edwin H. Lundie
Dellwood
Medieval — but not really Norman or English Tudor — in stone, brick, stucco, and half-timbering. The gabled volumes seem to wander in all directions across the wooded hillside.

5 Shields House.

6 **House,** c. 1910
Southwest side Highway 244, south of White Bear Yacht Club (Dellwood)
A two-story stucco Craftsman house emerges from the ordinary via an elaborate columned pergola which connects the two principal wings.

M-17 St. Paul Suburbs: East and South

St. Paul's eastern expansion is still to come; eventually, if the prevailing laissez-faire view of land use continues in the 1970s and into the 1980s suburbia will extend east to the St. Croix River and beyond. The ring road freeway west of St. Paul is now poised and ready, as are Highways 12 and 36, which reach directly over to the St. Croix River. In the southern area Highway 10/61 runs along the northeastern side of the Mississippi to Hastings, and Highway 52 goes past Hastings to the west.

Within the southern territory are some well-developed communities: West St. Paul, South St. Paul, and (on the east side of the river) St. Paul Park. The Gopher Ordnance Works at Rosemount (1942–45) was the first despoiler of the idyllic open farmland of the Inver Grove area, but now new commercial establishments and housing are beginning to fill in between Rosemount and South St. Paul.

1 **Minnesota Mining and Manufacturing Company Center,** 1955
Ellerbe Architects
Corner Highway 94 and McKnight Road (Maplewood)

A Miesian complex placed on a 417-acre site.

2 **Kacmarcik House,** 1962
Marcel Breuer
2065 Wildview Avenue (St. Paul)

Breuer (along with Gropius) has developed a set formula for the private dwelling. A major element of this formula is the open contradiction of twentieth-century machine forms and products with traditional materials such as masonry (brick and stone) and wood. The Kacmarcik House plays hard (and well) on this theme.

3 **St. Thomas Aquinas Church,** c. 1964
Ralph Rapson and Associates
1021 10th Avenue (St. Paul Park)

An immense horizontal roof, thick in profile, hovers over a continuous glass band and battered concrete walls below — all very theatrical.

4 **Severance House,** 1888; 1917
Cass Gilbert
Southwest corner County Roads 20 and 19 (Cottage Grove)

What we see today is a handsome Colonial/Revival mansion, colonnaded and pedimented porches and all. Underneath all of this is Gilbert's original Queen Anne Style dwelling.

5 **Congregational Church** (now Acacia Lodge No. 51), 1858
North of junction County Road 20 (70th Street) and Lamar Avenue N (Cottage Grove)

An important example of the Greek Revival in Minnesota. The gabled façade has arched windows with a delicate pattern of dentils and a richly decorated, pedimented entrance which encloses a set of double doors. Somewhere along the line the original front windows were partially filled in and square window units were inserted.

6 **Wentworth House,** 1887
1575 Oakdale Avenue (West St. Paul)

Queen Anne in brick with its front gable-end presented in half-timbering.

7 **Exchange Building,** c. 1889
Northeast corner Concord Street and Grand Avenue (South St. Paul)

A Romanesque pile with romantic conical roof towers at each corner.

8 **Inver Hills Community College,** 1970–72
Bergstedt, Wahlberg, Bergquist, and Rohkohl
8445 College Trail E

These brick shed-roof buildings are carefully molded into the hills which make up the campus. The result is that the campus conveys a sense of modesty and scale too often lacking in other recent educational complexes.

8 Inver Hills Community College.
Photo: Bergstedt, Wahlberg, Bergquist, and Rohkohl.

9 **Gopher Ordnance Works,** 1942–45
E. I. duPont deNemours Company
145th Street E and Akron Avenue (Rosemount)

This World War II complex included over two hundred buildings, among which were an administration building, a hospital, a fire station, a steam plant, and twenty-five residences. With a few exceptions the buildings were of wood. The complex was never completed, nor did it ever produce powder as expected. It is now occupied by the University of Minnesota Experimental Area. An experimental solar house (1973–75) built by architecture students of the university stands within the area. Its esthetic and functional image is mixed — a marriage of the do-it-yourself wood butcher's art and the utilitarian (sod roof, shingles, and solar collectors). The Dakota County Area Vocational Technical Institute (1969) at 145th Street East and Akron Road was designed by Haarstick and Lundgren.

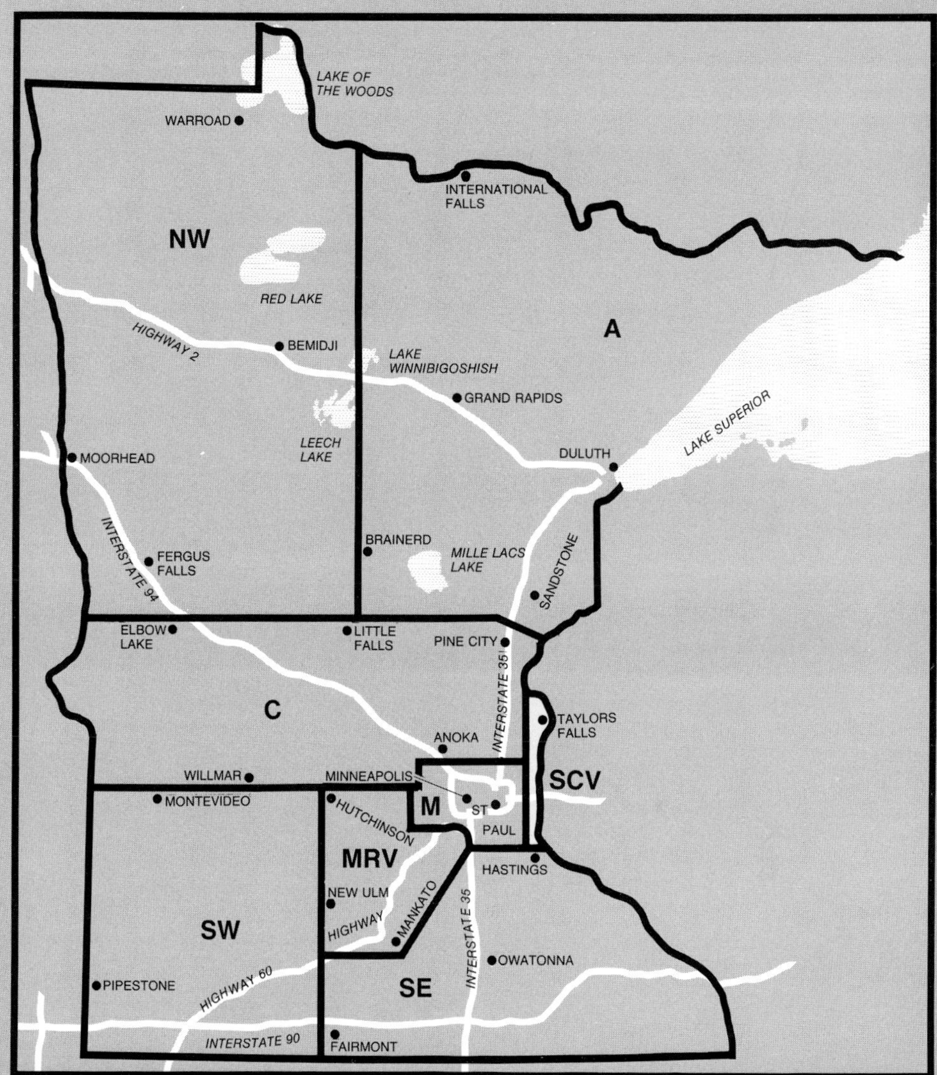

LAKE OF THE WOODS
WARROAD
INTERNATIONAL FALLS
NW
RED LAKE
A
HIGHWAY 2
BEMIDJI
LAKE WINNIBIGOSHISH
GRAND RAPIDS
LAKE SUPERIOR
LEECH LAKE
MOORHEAD
DULUTH
INTERSTATE 94
BRAINERD
MILLE LACS LAKE
SANDSTONE
FERGUS FALLS
ELBOW LAKE
LITTLE FALLS
PINE CITY
INTERSTATE 35
C
TAYLORS FALLS
ANOKA
SCV
WILLMAR
MINNEAPOLIS
MONTEVIDEO
M
ST PAUL
HUTCHINSON
MRV
HASTINGS
NEW ULM
MANKATO
HIGHWAY
SW
INTERSTATE 35
OWATONNA
PIPESTONE
HIGHWAY 60
SE
INTERSTATE 90
FAIRMONT

SCV-1 Afton, Valley Creek, and Lakeland

Afton, on Lake St. Croix, was first settled in 1837 and was platted in 1855. In its early days it contained several lumber mills which processed logs that were floated down the St. Croix River to the site. It is now a quiet village primarily oriented to the summer visitors who own vacation homes along the river and the lake.

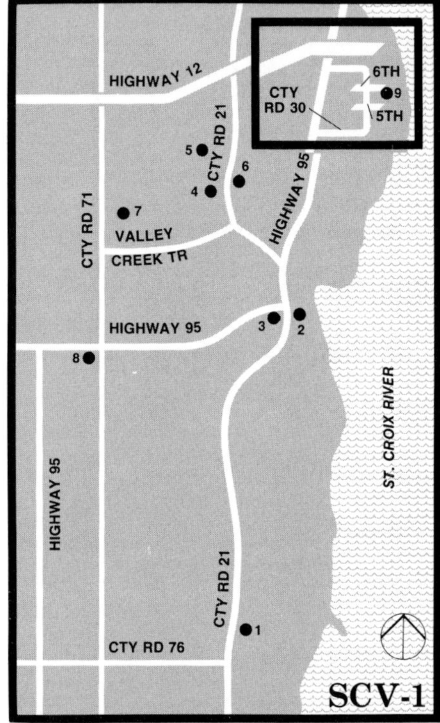

1 **St. Mary's of Basswood Grove Episcopal Church,** 1864
4½ miles south of Afton on County Road 21
An early board-and-batten Gothic Revival church.

2 **Octagon House,** c. 1860
In town on County Road 21
A two-story frame house sheathed in vertical board-and-batten. There is a small cupola in the center of the roof.

3 **Mackey House,** 1855
14026-15th Street S
A single-story Greek Revival house. The long porch was added later.

4 **Geer House,** 1874
West side County Road 21, 2¼ miles south of Highway 12 (Valley Creek)
A Greek dwelling, remarkably late for the style.

5 **Gilbert House,** 1861
Southwest corner County Road 21 and 15th Street, 2 miles south of Highway 12 (Valley Creek)
A side-hall Greek Revival dwelling with end gables and a piered porch on two sides of the lower floor.

6 **Bolles House,** 1857
East side County Road 21, 2¼ miles south of Highway 12 (Valley Creek)
A tiny one-and-a-half-story Greek Revival cottage with end gables; side-hall plan. The Greek Revival doorway is one of the few to be found in Minnesota. The entrance composition of the door and its sidelights is covered by a thin but wide pediment.

7 *Afton Mill (Bahnemann Barn).*

7 **Afton Mill** (now Bahnemann Barn)
¾ mile east of Highway 71, 2½ miles south of Highway 12 (between Valley Creek and County Road 71)

The two-story board-and-batten mill was moved to this site and converted into a barn in 1872. The foundation is stone. A cantilevered boxlike volume projects from the side of the building; this element and the location of the windows and doors provide an abstract composition any professional designer could be proud of.

8 **Octagonal Barn,** c. 1910
Southwest corner County Road 71 and Highway 95

A metal-sheathed octagonal barn with a small vented octagonal cupola on top.

9 **Cyphers House,** 1857
661 Quinnell, Washington County Road 30, east of Highway 95 (Lakeland)

A one-story stone "grout house." The balanced façade has a central door with a lunette window above it and pairs of windows on each side. This all adds up to an essentially Greek design, but the bargeboards on the end gable are Gothic.

9 Cyphers House.

SCV-2 Arcola

The sawmill village of Arcola on the St. Croix was established in 1846-47. • The Mower House (c. 1850) is a large two-story Greek Revival house with a central hall. Paneled engaged piers define the corners of the building, and the cornice and the plain entablature are both classic features of the Greek Revival. Arcola is located about five miles north of Stillwater on Highway 95, one-half mile south of the junction with County Road 59.

SCV-3 Franconia

Franconia, which is located south of Taylor's Falls on the St. Croix River, was one of the earliest lumbering towns in the state. The town was first settled in 1852 and was platted in 1858. Because of the height and the abruptness of the hills behind the town, the railroads bypassed it. At present only a dozen or so buildings are left. The Paul Munch House (c. 1856) is a handsome Greek Revival structure that was originally built as a store; in the 1860s it was moved to its present site. Much of its current form is the result of remodeling in the early 1870s. The Munch House is located at fire marker N907 (east of the creek). Farther down the

Paul Munch House, Franconia.

street at fire marker N913 is the white clapboard Ingemann House (c. 1870). This house exhibits a Greek Revival element in the pedimented window headers, but the high pitch of the gable roof is not typical of the style. Across the street from the Ingemann House is a nineteenth-century log cabin, now equipped with a screened porch. South of Franconia on Highway 95 (one-half mile north of County Road 86) is the Old Rochel School (c. 1900), which now serves as the Franconia Township Hall. On the front roof plane of the building rests a low but substantial tower, its belfry area articulated by paired arched openings.

SCV-4 Lindstrom

Lindstrom is situated on the north shore of South Lindstrom Lake. It was platted in 1880, and at first its primary economic orientation was agricultural. After the turn of the century, however, it began to develop as a spot for lakeside summer homes.

1 **Trinity Lutheran Church,** c. 1905
Southeast corner Newell Avenue and Elm Street
The English Gothic (in clapboard) with Craftsman overtones. The "modern" addition at the side detracts from the effectiveness of the building.

2 **House,** c. 1890
411 Newell Avenue
Queen Anne with some Eastlake details and a square Eastlake tower. The front porch was probably added after 1900.

3 **House,** c. 1910
404 Newell Avenue
A square house of concrete blocks with an arched and parapeted Mission Revival porch. The small arched and parapeted dormer on the roof is another Mission Revival touch.

4 **Cottage,** c. 1890
61 Newell Avenue
A one-and-a-half-story Queen Anne cottage. Its thin, spindly quality is close to the earlier Eastlake.

SCV-5 Marine on St. Croix

This community was first called Marine Mills; it was settled in 1838–39 and was platted in 1853. As it now exists, one can drive through it and be unaware of passing anything but a small commercial junction. To the east of the junction of Highway 95 and Gustander Trail (County Road 4) is the commercial section of the town dominated by a general store, a library, and a bank building. Hidden away to the south on Main Street are a few houses dating from the nineteenth century onward. North of Main Street and toward the river are a few more residences. On the hill west of Highway 95 are several distinguished Greek Revival dwellings and the old stone building which once housed the meeting hall and the jail (#6). Two nineteenth-century log cabins have been moved into the town; one is now situated next to the meeting hall, and the other is next to the Shell service station off Highway 95.

Security State Bank, c. 1915
East of Highway 95, southwest of Main Street

A small box of a building which has received a metal face in the form of a classical distyle-in-antis temple. Delicate, almost Adamesque wreaths and medallions decorate the entablature and the gable. A duplicate of this façade is to be found on the old bank building in Frontenac (#1).

General Store, 1870
East side Main Street

Flat pedimented windows plus paired brackets for the roof place the building midway between the Greek and the Italianate.

Village Hall (now a library), 1888
East side Main Street

A miniature balustraded balcony above the entrance symbolically provides a location from which the city officials can address the multitudes. The detailing of this false-fronted building is Italianate.

*illage hall (now library) and Security State Bank, Marine
n St. Croix.*

4 **"Sun Wood" House,** 1848
North on Main Street, 1st Street to river

A Greek Revival dwelling with later additions.

5 **House,** c. 1850s
Highway 95, opposite Security State Bank

A two-story Greek Revival house of the central-hall type with single balanced windows on each side of the entrance and three windows above it.

6 **Meeting Hall and Jail** (now a museum), 1872
West on Gustander Trail to 1st Street

Precisely carved stone blocks form the quoining of this ashlar block building. The gabled front has a central segmented arched entrance with a transom light and two segmented arched windows, one on each side. The sense of the building is more Georgian than Greek.

7 **Parker House,** 1855
1st Street (north of Meeting Hall)

The most elegant of the town's Greek Revival houses. A two-columned Ionic porch with a balcony forms the centerpiece of the front. A wide entablature is carried down to the headers of the second-floor windows.

SCV-6 Scandia

The village of Scandia is located on County Road 3, south of Highway 97. The detailing and the vertical siding of the Mattson-Berglund Store (c. 1880) are Eastlake. Also Eastlake in its form and fragileness is the community's water tower (c. 1890). South of the water tower, at the northeast corner of County Roads 3 and 52, is the two-story Scandia Mercantile Company. The clapboard section of the store was built in 1879 and is mildly Italianate; the bric section was built in about 1900 and is somewhat classical. One and one-half miles south of town on County Road 3 i the Hay Lake School (1879), a gable-roofed brick volume with an Eastlake porch and a small open belfry tower. A gambrel-roofed log barn has recently been moved to a site directly behind th school.

Mattson-Berglund Store, Scandia.

Hay Lake School, Scandia.

SCV-7 Stillwater

Stillwater is a museum of commercial and residential architecture from the second half of the nineteenth century. The town was founded in 1843 and was formally organized in 1854. For many years it was a major lumber and logging center with mills and other industries. By 1870 it was connected by rail to St. Paul. The commercial part of town is situated on the river flats; behind it the steep hill ascends to a relatively flat plateau upon which the town's residences have been built. In 1918 Morell and Nichols proposed a modest City Beautiful plan for the city. Chestnut Street was to be an axis which connected a circle and a bridge with a civic center located north of 3rd Street. Although several modest Beaux Arts public buildings were built, this scheme was never realized.

In the downtown area there are a number of late nineteenth-century bric commercial blocks including the John Karst Building (1891) at 125 Main Street South; the Staples Block (c. 189(at 119 Main Street South, which is a three-story Romanesque Revival building; and the two-story Excelsior Block (1882) at 120 Main Street North, whic is Eastlake in style. But the real joy o Stillwater is in the residential streets on the hill. Here one finds not one or two but many examples of the Greek Revival, the Italianate, and many othe nineteenth-century architectural style West of Stillwater but unfortunately n accessible to the public is the Lovness House (1954) designed by Frank Lloyd Wright and a cottage designed by Wright (completed in 1975).

The warden's house (c. 1850s) of the old state prison at 602 Main Street North is now the Washington County Historical Museum. Information about the city and its buildings can be obtained at the museum.

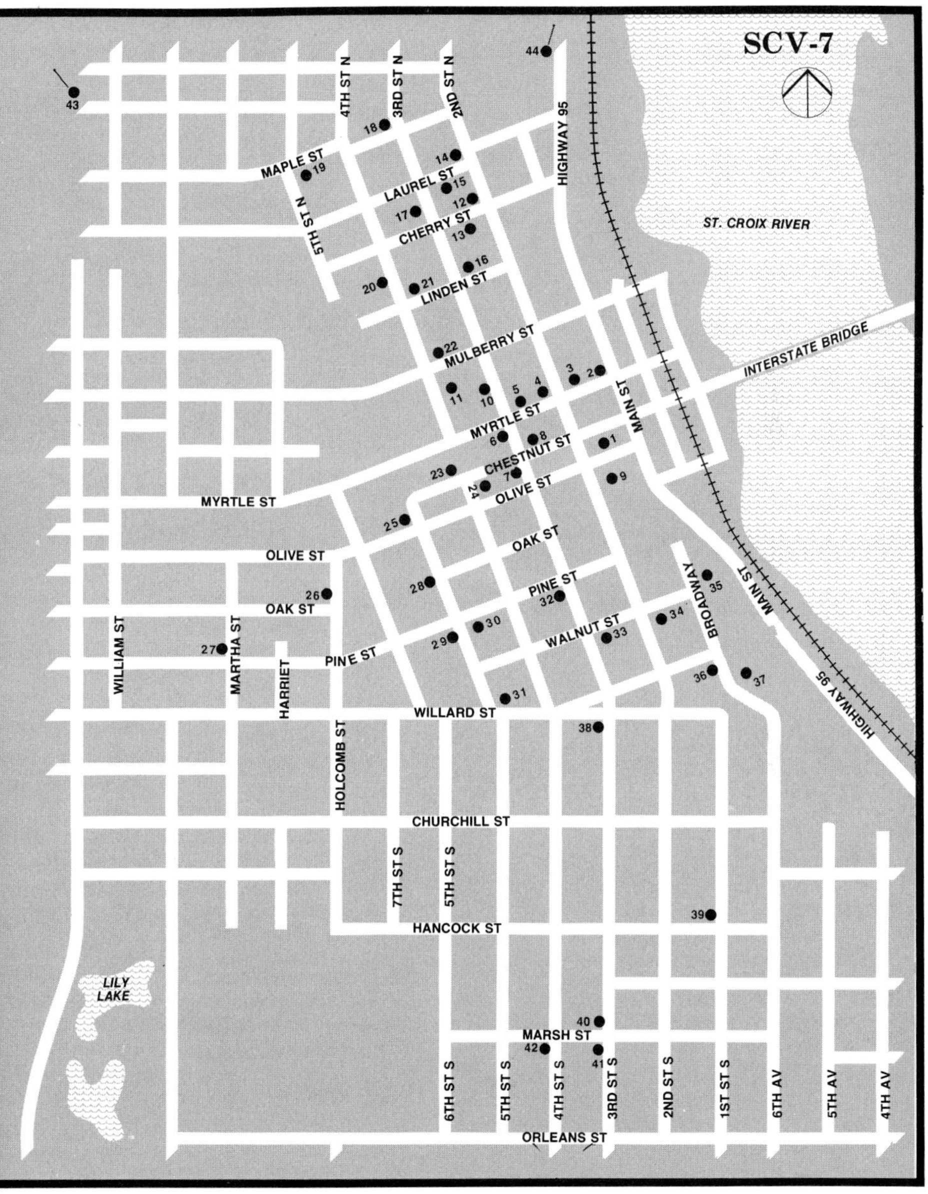

1 **First National Bank Building,** c. 1912
213-15 Chestnut Street E
A Beaux Arts bank building equipped with an Ionic-columned façade.

2 **House** (now office and residence), c. 1860
226 Myrtle Street E
A side-hall Italianate house in brick with a belvedere on top.

3 **Post Office** (now gift shop), c. 1900s
Northeast corner Myrtle Street E and 2nd Street S
The Beaux Arts in a Neo-Baroque mood.

4 **Lowell Inn,** 1936
William M. Ingemann
102 2nd Street N
The present Lowell Inn is clothed in the 1930s version of the Colonial Revival (more Federal than Georgian). It replaced the 1855 Sawyer Hotel, which was a distinguished example of the Greek Revival in Minnesota.

5 **Cottage,** c. late 1860s
110 Myrtle Street E
A one-and-a-half-story Greek Revival cottage (side-hall plan) with sidelights and a transom light in the recessed entrance.

6 **Presbyterian Church** (now unused), late 1870s
Southwest corner Myrtle Street W and 3rd Street S
Ruskinian Gothic with wood Eastlake details — the open belfry tower is especially effective.

7 **Jason Block,** 1886
200 3rd Street S
The Queen Anne Style applied to a three-story commercial block. A high, thin pediment projects above the cornice and proclaims the name of the building and its date.

• 8 **House,** late 1860s
106 Chestnut Street E
An elegant Italianate townhouse. A pair of double doors stand within a recessed pedimented entrance; the windows of the principal rooms on the lower level extend to the floor.

9 **Auditorium/Theatre,** c. 1905
215 2nd Street S
Another of Stillwater's turn-of-the-century Beaux Arts buildings, this one three stories high and in brick.

10 **Ascension Episcopal Church,** c. 188
214 3rd Street N
Gothic, as interpreted by a disciple of Eastlake, with a crenelated tower and ornamentation in pressed brick.

11 **Carnegie Public Library,** 1902
223 4th Street N
A small Beaux Arts library building se in a park, well back from the street.

• 12 **McKusick House,** 1868
504 2nd Street N
A French Second Empire cottage with semicircular dormers and a hooded entrance. A very full and complete expres sion of the style.

13 **House,** c. 1890
113 Cherry Street E
Queen Anne in style with a profusion o spindle work.

14 **House,** late 1920s
118 Laurel Street E
A Colonial Revival Period house of the late 1920s, sheathed in shingles.

15 **House,** 1875
107 Laurel Street E
A blend of Greek and Italianate in a house with end gables and a side-hall plan.

16 **House,** c. 1860s
401 3rd Street N
A Greek Revival house with end gables and a side-hall plan.

17 **House,** 1870s
510 3rd Street N
Another house which mixes the Greek and the Italianate.

18 **Cottage,** 1860s
Northwest corner School Street W and 3rd Street N
A one-and-a-half-story Gothic Revival cottage in clapboard.

9 **Musser-Sauntry Recreational Hall,** 1902
625 5th Street N

Stillwater is not exactly the place where one would expect to encounter an Islamic Revival building, but here it is, right out of southern California, with horseshoe windows and a bracketed overhanging roof.

9 Musser-Sauntry Recreational Hall.

0 **House,** c. 1870
410 4th Street N

A Greek and Italianate house with end gables and a side-hall plan.

1 **House,** 1856
122 Linden Street W

A hipped-roof Greek Revival house with Italianate details.

2 **House,** c. 1890s
East side 4th Street N between Mulberry and Linden Streets E

A voluminous Queen Anne Revival design, slanting toward the Colonial Revival.

3 **Nichols House,** 1857
208 Chestnut Street W

A clapboard house made Gothic by high-pitched gables and bargeboards.

4 **House,** c. 1890
Off east end of 200 block on Chestnut Street W

Arches with thin spindles and columns define the first-floor porch. A three-story tower with a curved roof commands a view of downtown Stillwater.

5 **House,** late 1870s
318 Olive Street W

An Eastlake version of an Italianate house.

26 **House,** c. 1860s
320 Holcombe Street S

The often-repeated side-hall Italianate house, this one in brick.

27 **House,** late 1890s
704 Pine Street W

The turn-of-the-century return to the Colonial Revival, here impressively stated in a two-story entrance porch with four columns.

28 **Hershey House,** 1878
416 5th Street S

A Queen Anne design with a square tower and a belvedere on top of the house. The top floor was damaged in a fire in 1926.

29 **Jenks House,** 1871
504 5th Street S

An Eastlake brick house with a tower.

30 **Cottage,** c. 1860
223 Pine Street W

A brick Gothic cottage.

31 **House,** c. 1860s
Northeast corner 5th Street S and Willard Street E

A brick Italianate house with a side-hall plan.

32 **Washington County Courthouse,** 1869–70
Augustus F. Knight
Pine Street E, corner 3rd Street S

An Italianate courthouse on a cruciform plan with a tall, narrow drum topped by a dome.

33 **St. Michael's Catholic Church,** 1873
611 3rd Street S

Gothic Revival in stone. The tall spire and the hilltop location give the church great prominence.

34 **Magee House,** 1865
205 Walnut Street E

A small Gothic cottage tucked among the trees.

35 **Webster House,** 1866
435 Broadway S

A graceful Italianate house with a side-hall plan. A belvedere with arched eaves (and arched windows below) surmounts the center of the house.

36 House, 1867
610 Broadway S

A Greek Revival house with end gables and a side-hall plan.

37 House, c. 1870s
657 Broadway S

An assertive French Second Empire house.

38 Tozer House, 1870
704 3rd Street S

A brick Italianate house, now painted. Note the cast-iron fence.

39 Nelson Public School, 1895
Southwest corner 1st Street S and Hancock Street E

Classical gentility at an early date.

40 "Gramma Bean's Playhouse"
1224 3rd Street S

An Eastlake pavilion with a strong emphasis on the vertical.

41 Lammers House, c. 1889
1306 3rd Street S

The Queen Anne at its fullest with a seashell balcony and horseshoe arches.

41 Lammers House.

42 House, c. 1895
1312 4th Street S

A Queen Anne dwelling with a round bay-tower on the left, a recessed porch on the second floor, and an unusual cut-in corner staircase window enclosed in lacy ornamentation of sawed wood.

43 Stuccy House, c. late 1870s
West of town on Highway 96 (north side) before Mendel Road

The Eastlake Style employed in a towered Italianate house.

44 Lyman House, pre-1850
North of Stillwater on Highway 95 to Arcola Trail, northeast to Arcola Lane, and southeast to house

A white clapboard Greek Revival house.

SCV-8 Taylor's Falls

Taylor's Falls, platted in 1850–51 and incorporated in 1858, was another of the early sawmill and logging towns on the St. Croix. Near the river on Riverside Drive are residences dating from the 1850s to the present. The commercial district along Highway 95 is now quite small. On a shelf of the hillside overlooking the lower town is Angel's Hill, a handsomely preserved mid-nineteenth-century community. A church, a schoolhouse and meeting hall, and an array of clapboard dwellings are grouped around a central green. Almost all of these buildings are in the Greek Revival mode, although some have been so extensively remodeled that one has to look twice to find the recessed entrance with sidelights or the end gable which reveals what the building once was. Several of the houses have been beautifully restored, and the visual effect is that of a Vermont village.

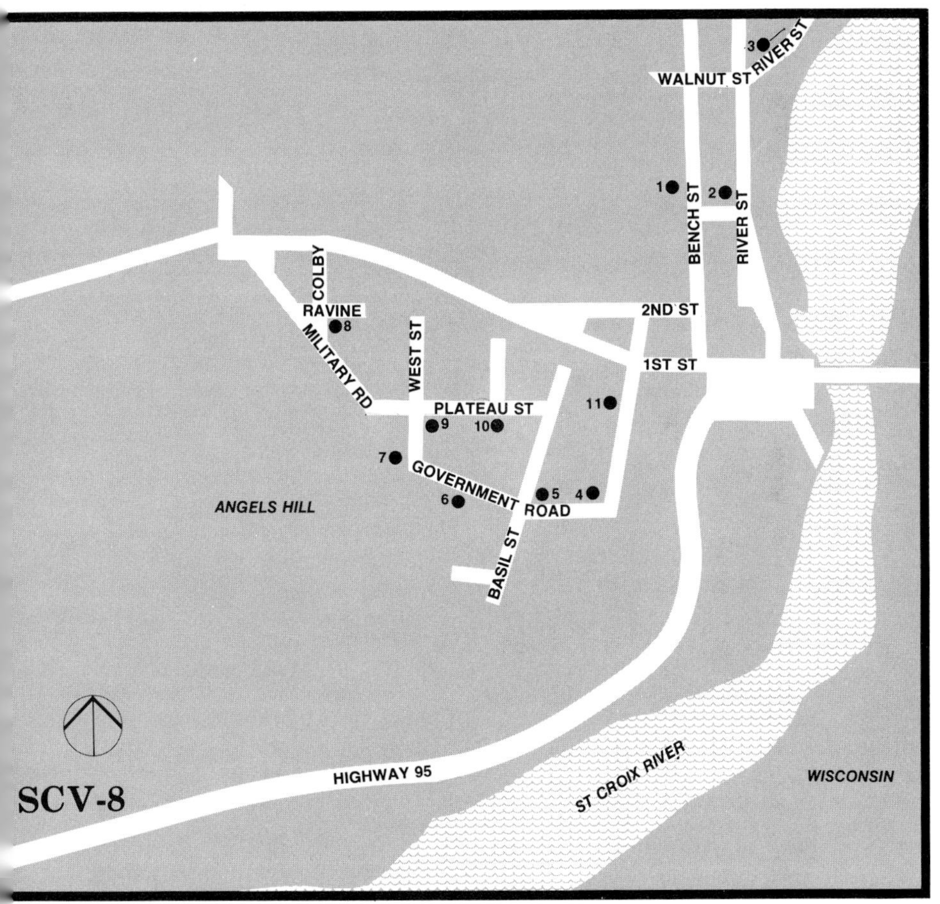

• 1 **Public Library Building,** 1854, 1887
Bench Street between 2nd and Walnut Streets

This small single-story clapboard structure was originally built as a combined residence and tailoring shop. In 1887 it was purchased by the local library board. It was remodeled at this time, and the front elevation was clothed in the latest Eastlake sawed and turned work with fish-scale shingles on the gable end.

2 **Munch-Roos House,** c. 1853
Northwest corner 2nd Street and River Street

A side-hall, end-gable Greek Revival dwelling. The pediment exhibits a vented lunette device.

3 **House,** c. 1900
River Street between Linden and Oak Streets

This one-and-a-half-story Colonial Revival house displays an unusual Palladian window in the front gable.

4 **Folsom House,** 1854–55
Bend of Government Road (east of Basil Street)

An L-shaped two-story Greek Revival house. A porch with a balcony runs along the east side of the house, and the entrance is on the gable end.

4 Folsom House.

5 **First Methodist Church,** 1860
Northeast corner Government Road and Basil Street

Greek Revival. Below the front pediment are entrances to each side with a pair of tall narrow windows between them. A square belfry surmounts the stubby square tower.

5 First Methodist Church.

• 6 **Winslow-Scott House,** c. 1853
Near southwest corner Government Road and Basil Street

A side-hall Greek Revival cottage with end gables. The deeply recessed front door has sidelights and a transom light. A one-and-a-half-story rear wing was added at a somewhat later date.

7 **Fox-Dobney House,** 1852
Government Road and West Street

A Greek Revival Cape Cod cottage with a central entrance and porch.

8 **House,** c. 1850s
Junction Ravine Street, Colby Street, and Military Road

A one-and-a-half-story Greek Revival house, now covered with shingles.

9 **Gray House,** c. 1864
Southeast corner West and Plateau Streets

This gabled and dormered Gothic cottage was remodeled in the 1880s, and an Eastlake porch was added.

10 **House** (known as McKusick House), c. 1850s
Plateau Street opposite Centre Street

A two-story Greek Revival house.

11 **First Schoolhouse and Village Center** ("Town House"), 1852
Third building south of Government Road and 1st Street

A simple clapboard Greek Revival building with a gable roof.

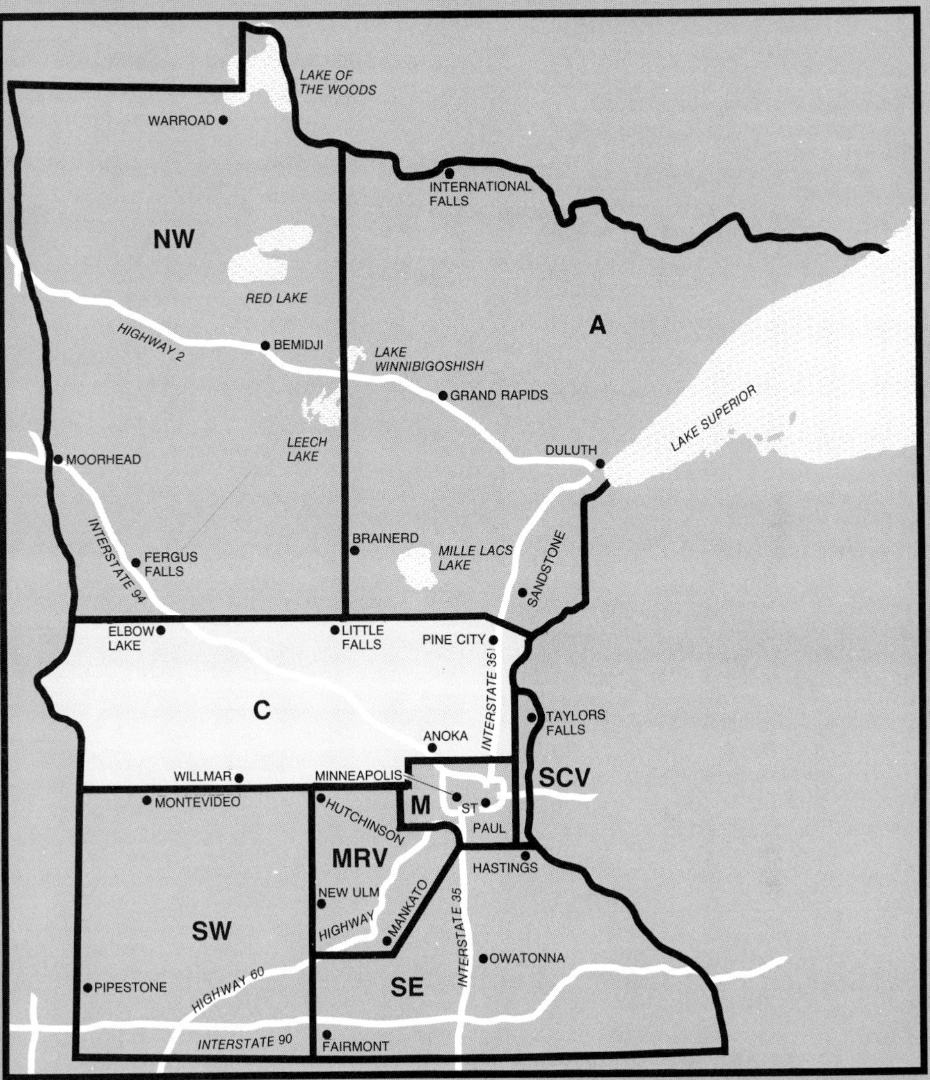
LAKE OF THE WOODS
WARROAD
INTERNATIONAL FALLS
NW
RED LAKE
HIGHWAY 2
BEMIDJI
LAKE WINNIBIGOSHISH
GRAND RAPIDS
A
LAKE SUPERIOR
DULUTH
LEECH LAKE
MOORHEAD
INTERSTATE 94
FERGUS FALLS
BRAINERD
MILLE LACS LAKE
SANDSTONE
ELBOW LAKE
LITTLE FALLS
PINE CITY
INTERSTATE 35
C
TAYLORS FALLS
ANOKA
WILLMAR
MINNEAPOLIS
SCV
MONTEVIDEO
HUTCHINSON
M
ST PAUL
MRV
HASTINGS
NEW ULM
HIGHWAY
MANKATO
SW
OWATONNA
PIPESTONE
HIGHWAY 60
SE
INTERSTATE 90
FAIRMONT

C-1 Albany and Freeport

Adam Winter Building.

The railroad village of Albany was incorporated in 1890. On its main street is the Adam Winter Building (1913), which was formerly a theatre and a saloon. The second-floor street façade of this building presents a composition of four small Ionic columns with three recessed arches above the columns. The central arch (the largest) is inlaid with a wonderfully inventive pattern of brightly colored pieces of glass. A more subtle architectural gem is the city hall/library, situated just east of the Adam Winter Building on Main Street. This is a one-story building (c. 1900) of concrete block in imitation of stone with four grand but entirely flat arches along its major façade (the openings within the arches are now partially filled in with glass bricks). On 2nd Street is the Catholic Church of Seven Dolors (1899), a late nineteenth-century brick Gothic Revival church.

At Freeport are a nineteenth-century roller mill and the brick Gothic Revival Sacred Heart Roman Catholic Church (1905). The Germanic design of the church is similar to that of St. Paul's Catholic Church in Sauk Center.

City hall and library.

C-2 Alexandria

Since the 1920s (and even before) Alexandria's reputation has been that of a resort community. Beautiful lakes abound in all directions: Bordering the city to the north and the west are two lakes, Lake Agnes and Lake Winona, and within a few miles are half a dozen or so other lakes, some of considerable size. By the 1920s resort hotels dotted the lakeshores, but today the largest of these — the Geneva Beach Hotel, the Hotel Blake, the Dickenson Inn, and others — no longer exist. The city's early economy was agricultural, and the completion of the railroad in 1873 (although the first passenger train did not arrive until late in 1878) meant that the city became a transportation center for the region.

1 **First National Bank Building,** 1970
701 Broadway

A suburban image, placed at the edge of the downtown area. The cornice is treated as an extended horizontal box placed over the recessed walls below. A large central monitor window projects above the roof.

2 **Post Office,** 1910
Earl and Aiton
623 Broadway

A somewhat stodgy brick and stone building; more English Georgian than English Renaissance. The entrance, with its recessed doors, Tuscan columns, a window above, and two classical light standards, is a learned composition, if nothing else.

3 **Farmers National Bank Building** (now Herberger's Department Store), 1912
522 Broadway

A cast-iron penny bank blown up in scale to a full-size building. It is dignified and restrained and beautifully conveys the feeling of solidity and safety for its contents.

•4 **Bank Building** (now Bob's Clothes Shop), 1919–20
Peter Linhoff
520 Broadway

Beaux Arts; classical façade with six engaged Corinthian piers; pedimented entrance and open balustrade on the roof.

5 **Olson's Supermarket Sign,** late 1950s
West side Broadway between 4th and 5th Avenues

5• *Olson's Supermarket Sign.*

The design of the supermarket itself is not remarkable, but the sign is a classic of the late 1950s and early 1960s. The row of round holes, the distinct separation of the parts, and the thin, pipelike quality of the whole assemblage suggest the stylistic period of automobile tail fins and bulbous fenders expressed in a sign.

6 **Viking Figure,** 1965
End of Broadway at 3rd Avenue

If the rune stone doesn't convince us, this large-scaled statue of a helmeted Viking should, that America was "discovered" by the Scandinavians, not the Spanish, English, or French. The shield of the warrior makes the message plain: "Alexandria, Birthplace of America."

6 *Viking Figure.*

7 **Van Hoesen House,** 1883
421 7th Avenue W

A large Queen Anne brick house. The two-story bays on each side of the house are its strongest design feature. The light, woodsy quality of the bays contrasts with the plain brick wall adjacent to them.

8 **Ward House,** 1903
422 7th Avenue W

A two-and-a-half-story Craftsman house. There is a suggestion of half-timbering on some wall surfaces. The other walls are shingle and narrow clapboard.

9 Douglas County Courthouse, 1894, 1972
Foss, Engelstad, and Foss
Southwest corner Elm Street and 7th Avenue W

Romanesque Revival in brick, with a high square tower. The building has been altered and added to, and in general the changes have hardly helped either the building or its parklike setting. The 1972 addition (Foss, Engelstad, and Foss), with its deeply cut horizontal windows and curved walls, manages to be entirely contemporary à la the early 1970s and at the same time to fit in well with the original building.

10 Williams Brothers Pipeline Company Building, c. 1938
Highway 82 northwest of town, across from the Douglas County Fairgrounds

Not an exciting example of Streamline Moderne, but all the major elements of the style are here — curved walls, glass brick, porthole windows, and covered metal canopies.

11 Arrowwood Resort, 1968–70
Bergstedt, Wahlberg, Bergquist, and Rohkohl
Northwest shore of Lake Darling; northwest of town on Highway 22, north on Lake Louise Road

Mildly unbelievable: A five-story building block composition just like those in the latest architectural journals. Each unit has a balcony, separated from the adjacent balconies by projecting and layered shingled shed-roof boxes.

11 Arrowwood Resort.
Photo: Bergstedt, Wahlberg, Bergquist, and Rohkohl.

C-3 Annandale

This railroad village was platted in 1886, and the former Soo Line passenger depot, a log house, and a blacksmith shop are now located in the Minnesota Pioneer Travel Park one-half mile east of town on Highway 55 (south side). The proportions of the station are Eastlake, although the wood-frame building is devoid of any sawed or turned work. In town at the corner of Highway 55 and Maple Avenue is the three-story Annandale Hotel (c. 1888) with its three layers of open porches.

C-4 Anoka

Anoka was established at the confluence of the Mississippi and Rum rivers in 1853. The city straddles the Rum River, with commercial and residential areas lying on both sides of it. A large area along the river provides an attractive park. With the gradual spread of the Twin Cities Anoka is slowly being drawn into the metropolitan orbit.

1 Public Library.

1 **Public Library,** 1965
Griswold and Rauma
2135 3rd Avenue
A rhythmic series of clerestory boxes project out of the main volume of this brick building.

2 **St. Stephen's Catholic Church,** 1970
Voigt and Fourre
Southeast corner 5th Avenue N at Jackson Street
Shed-roof volumes covered with shingles project out over the brick sections below. The open bell screen with a Greek cross on top houses four bells.

3 **Open Air Theatre,** 1914
Purcell and Elmslie
East side Ferry Street, 1½ blocks south of Main Street (on west side of Rum River)
The protective wall, the ticket booths, and the projection box are now gone, but the curved seating which works its way down the hill, the sunken orchestra pit, and the raised grass "stage" are still in place.

4 **Woodbury House,** 1854
1632 Ferry Street S
A clapboard Greek Revival dwelling with many additions.

3 Open Air Theatre.

5 **De Graff House,** c. 1860
302 Fremont Avenue S
A two-story Greek Revival house with a one-and-a-half-story wing at the side. The sawed wood capitals of the porch columns are Eastlake in design.

6 **Green House,** c. late 1860s
Northeast corner Fremont Avenue S and Franklin Lane
A two-story Italianate house of large scale.

C-5 Appleton

The town of Appleton, four miles northeast of the junction of the Minnesota and Pomme de Terre rivers, was founded in 1871–72. The railroad reached the community in 1879.

1 **Appleton Flour Mill and Grain Elevators**
North end Miles Street
The tall rectangular mill and storage buildings were built before 1900, and the cylindrical elevators were built somewhat later. The mill buildings are of wood and have gable roofs, and the elevators are of concrete block (molded in imitation of stone).

1 Appleton Flour Mill and Grain Elevators.

2 **Reno Theatre,** c. 1938
Miles Street N between Thielke and Sorenson Streets
A low-keyed but stylistically successful Streamline Moderne theatre.

3 **City Hall,** 1896
Southwest corner Miles and Schlieman Streets
A two-story brick Romanesque building with a tower. The style of this building is similar to the form of Romanesque used by Louis Sullivan in the early 1890s.

4 **Gethsemane Episcopal Church,** 1879
Southeast corner Snelling Avenue and Hering Street
An early (particularly for this section of Minnesota) Gothic Revival church similar to those built in central Minnesota by Bishop Whipple. The building is now stuccoed, but one assumes that the exterior was originally board-and-batten.

5 **Benson House,** c. 1890–91
Southeast corner Mrozek and Rooney Streets
A two-story brick house with steep gable roofs and Queen Anne sawed work. The end gables are sheathed in patterns of shingles.

C-6 Atwater

At the southwest corner of Highway 12 and 3rd Street is • the First Baptist Church (c. 1890), an example of Carpenter's Gothic with Queen Anne detailing — clapboard, shingles, and sawed work. A block south on 3rd Avenue between Minnesota and Atlantic Avenues on the west side of the street is a turn-of-the-century building of pressed metal (formerly the Atwater State Bank). Pressed metal has been used for everything — the imitation ashlar blocks, the engaged paneled piers, the entablature, and the projecting cornice and pediment. The building is now used as an upholstery shop.

C-7 Beardsley

In the small railroad village of Beardsley (platted in 1880) is St. Mary's Catholic Church (1904), which seems to represent a mixture of the Romanesque and the American Colonial Revival (late eighteenth-century Georgian). Three doors with half-circle lunette windows lead into the vestibule of the church.

C-8 Bellingham

This Great Northern railway town was platted in 1887 on the flat prairie between the Minnesota River and the Yellow Bank River to the west. As one approaches Bellingham from the south on Highway 75, one finds an Eastlake Style dwelling (c. 1890) on the northwest corner of the first major cross street. The simple rectangular form of the house and its brackets point to the Italianate, but the swayed roof, the iron balustrade at the top, and above all the spindle work on the porch are Eastlake. One block north on Highway 75 and one block west (on the southwest corner) is a much remodeled Eastlake dwelling (c. 1890) with a gable-roofed tower. East on the same cross street (two blocks beyond Highway 75) is the Zion Church of the Evangelical Association of Bellingham (1911), a Carpenter's Gothic building with quite interesting windows of stained glass.

C-9 Benson

Benson was platted by the Great Northern Railroad in 1870, and its original grid was laid out perpendicular to the railroad. The community lies west of the Chippewa River and is separated from it by the extensive Benson Park. The Swift County Courthouse (1897), at the northeast corner of Idaho Avenue and 14th Street, was designed by Buechner and Jacobson. It is a vigorous Richardsonian Romanesque pile with a tall corner tower, a secondary tower, gables, dormers, and a triple-arched entrance. At the southwest corner of Idaho Avenue and 13th Street is the Gothic Revival board-and-batten Christ Episcopal Church (c. 1875). An entrance tower with a tall spire has been placed at the corner on one side of the building, and dormers spring from the roof cornice of the spire.

East of Benson is the Bethesda Swedish Lutheran Church (1874). This church, an example of Carpenter's Gothic, is a clapboard building with a central entrance tower and spire. The building has been positioned on a new raised-basement foundation, and all of the old windows have been replaced with glass brick. The church is located four and one-half miles north of the town of Murdock on County Road 33 and one-half mile west on County Road 16.

C-10 Brown's Valley

The town of Brown's Valley is on the east bank of Big Stone Lake, which forms part of the boundary between Minnesota and South Dakota.

1 **Carnegie Public Library,** 1915
Southeast corner Highway 7 and first cross street (approaching town from the southeast)
A raised-basement Beaux Arts building. The classical detailing is carried out almost completely in the pattern of raised brick in different colors. Two large plate-glass windows light the reading rooms.

2 **Valley Theatre,** c. 1950
Southwest side Highway 7 between second and third cross streets (approaching town from the southeast)
The sign as the building: the overscaled letters of the word "Valley" work into the horizontal pattern of the cornice of the low-scaled theatre entrance.

3 **Union State Bank,** c. 1895
Southwest side Highway 7 between second and third cross streets (approaching town from the southeast)
A one-story Romanesque Revival vault improved by metal-framed windows, doors, and glass brick.

4 **House,** c. 1880s
Northwest of town, off Highway 7 extension, on road leading to Sam Brown House (marked)
An Eastlake cottage. The jigsaw arches of the porch are cut into a flower-and-stem pattern. Elaborate sawed and turned work occurs on the gable ends of the house and on the dormers.

4 House.

5 **Sam Brown House,** c. 1863
Northwest of town, off Highway 7 extension, on marked road
This one-and-a-half-story log cabin was built forty miles west of Brown's Valley and later was moved to a site in town in 1871.

C-11, C-12, C-13

C-11 Buffalo

The village of Buffalo was platted between Buffalo Lake and Lake Pulaski in 1856. The Wright County Courthouse is located one-half block west of the junction of Central Avenue and 2nd Street. This 1950s courthouse was designed by Patch and Erikson. The second floor, sheathed in metal and glass, is placed on a stone-veneered base — not great architecture, but sensitively scaled and related to the residential setting. On the east side of Central Avenue at the northeast corner of 1st Street Northeast and 1st Avenue Northeast is the Old Swedish Mission Church (1890s), a brick and shingle building in the Romanesque Revival Style.

C-12 Cambridge

The village of Cambridge was incorporated in 1876. The Cambridge Lutheran Church, at 621 North Main, was designed by Jonas Norell in 1879–84. In plan it is of the central entrance tower type. The brick building has some Eastlake detailing, but its basic character is classical, close to the Greek Revival. The original clapboard sheathing has been bricked over.

C-13 Clearwater

The village of Clearwater is situated on the Mississippi River southeast of St. Cloud. Its buildings represent a variety of architectural styles dating from the 1860s on.

1 **Stevens House,** 1857
Northwest of junction of Highway 24 and County Road 75.
A much remodeled octagonal house, picturesquely situated in a grove of cedar trees.

2 **Congregational Church** (now Assembly of God), 1861
2 blocks east of County 75, 4 blocks north of Highway 24
A classic Greek Revival church with a tower entrance and end gables.

3 **Tollington House,** c. 1870
1 block north of church, 1 block east, ½ block north (on east side)
A two-story wood Italianate house.

4 **Webster House,** c. 1860s
½ block north of Tollington House (on west side)
An end-gable Greek Revival house sheathed in blue clapboard.

4 Webster House.

5 **Masonic/GAR Hall,** 1888
Northwest corner Main Street and Old Ferry Landing Road
A two-story brick commercial building with arched windows, lightly Romanesque in style.

6 **Salinger Cottage,** c. 1870s
East side Main Street, ½ block south of Masonic Hall
A Gothic Revival cottage with walls of vertical board-and-batten.

C-14 Cokato

Cokato was established in 1869 when the St. Paul and Pacific Railroad reached the site. Three miles north of town at the southwest corner of County Roads 3 and 100 is a pre-1900 Finnish cabin of hand-hewn logs; it measures only about six feet by ten feet. In Cokato itself, on 6th Street west of Broadway, is a somewhat larger log cabin. The dwelling at 505 South Broadway has the appearance of an 1870 Italianate house; between the two major wings is a two-story Queen Anne Colonial Revival tower with a concave domed roof. To the west at 385 5th Street is a two-story brick Queen Anne dwelling with double bays.

C-15 Cold Spring

During a major invasion of locusts in this area in the nineteenth century, according to local tradition, a group of farmers vowed to build a chapel to the Virgin if she would rid their fields of the locusts. Miraculously the locusts did disappear, and the wood-frame Gothic Revival Locust Chapel was built in 1877. The original building was destroyed by a tornado in 1894, and the granite Assumption Chapel we see today was built in 1951. The interior presents an array of surfaces in polished stone. The front and rear walls are battered out to form buttresses, and pairs of buttresses intervene on the lateral walls. The chapel can be reached by driving east of Cold Spring on Highway 23 to Chapel Street, then south to Pilgrimage Road, and east and north to the chapel.

Assumption Chapel.

C-16 Collegeville

The Benedictine monastic establishment of St. John's was chartered in 1857. The first Abbey Church (similar in design to the Assumption Church in St. Paul) was built during the years 1879–80. The main quadrangle of plain brick buildings (classrooms, dining facilities, conference rooms, and offices) was built in 1880. Architecturally, St. John's did not appear on the regional or national scene until the administrators engaged Marcel Breuer in 1954 to prepare a new master plan for the campus and to begin his studies for the designing of the church. The basic element in Breuer's master plan was the creation of a quadrangle in the southern part of the campus — a quadrangle, partially open to the north, which would be dominated by the new church. Other features of his plan were the placement of dormitories to the west overlooking Stump Lake and the later location of an ecumenical center across the lake from the dormitories. Although buildings by Breuer and others have been added to the campus since the completion of the church, it is the church which asserts itself — as Breuer had planned — over the whole of the campus.

1 **Abbey/University Church,** 1954–61
Marcel Breuer

The church structure is composed of three elements: the famous Banner Bell Tower, which like an Italian campanile stands out in front of the church proper; the sanctuary, with its side walls angling toward the rear; and a rectangular block (on an axis perpendicular to the church) which houses the monastery. The church is an example of Le Corbusier's New Brutalism of the post–World War II years, in which concrete is used and exposed to create monumental sculpture, this is also the case in Breuer's bell tower. Since the tower's major function is the highly important one of symbolism, Breuer insisted that "it will be a strong statement before you come into the church," and indeed it is; it is a sort of gigantic Alexander Calder stabile in poured concrete.

1 Abbey Church.

2 **Alcuin Library,** 1967
Marcel Breuer and Hamilton Smith

This low rectangular building encloses the north side of the quadrangle in front of the church. Although the building is low-keyed externally, Breuer's sculptured structural gymnastics occur within. A pair of dramatic concrete trees help support the roof, and between the trees is a freestanding concrete stairway.

2 Alcuin Library.

3 **Science Hall,** 1968
Marcel Breuer and Hamilton Smith

Another low rectangular block of concrete with projecting tile sunscreens. A small trapezoidal auditorium sheathed in granite projects off the main block. In the interior of the auditorium Breuer has returned to the use of structure (in concrete) for the purposes of drama.

4 **Dormitories,** 1959, 1968
Marcel Breuer and Hamilton Smith

The St. Thomas dormitory — an L-shaped structure — was the first of the new dormitories. This was followed by • the dormitories named for St. Bernard, St. Boniface, and St. Patrick, which were built in 1968. Of the group the St. Thomas dormitory is the most successful; it is a simple rectangular box composed of a repeated pattern of smaller boxes. The later dormitories are more self-consciously sculptured with heavy cut-out exterior panels of concrete which seem overscaled for such modest buildings.

4 Dormitories.

5 **Ecumenical Center,** 1968
Marcel Breuer and Hamilton Smith
A low-keyed collection of granite boxes across the lake (to the west) from the campus.

6 **Warner Palestra,** 1973–75
Traynor, Hermanson, and Hahn
A physical education complex in brick, situated at the north edge of the campus.

7 **St. John's Prep School and Dormitory,** 1961–62
Hanson and Michelson
The barrel-vaulted classroom building steps down the hillside. • The forceful dormitory next door is completely open inside — a single large room.

7 Classroom Building, St. John's Prep School.

C-17 Darwin

One-half mile east of Darwin on Highway 12 is the Old Things Curiosity Corner. The title describes it all — hundreds of utilitarian farm objects from plows to wagons and other farm implements have been arranged by type.

C-18 Dassel

Located at the northwest corner of Parker Avenue East (Highway 12) and 1st Street North is the office of Danielson Auto Sales. The building, probably constructed as a service station in the late 1920s, has an octagonal form and a high-pitched segmented octagonal dome for a roof. A small semicircular hood projects over the entrance.

Danielson Auto Sales.

C-19 Delano

The St. Peter's Catholic Church (1912) at the southwest corner of Rockford and 2nd Streets carries out the nineteenth-century Neo-Baroque with a complicated columned drum supporting an onion dome similar to those on Bavarian and Austrian churches. In town on Bridge Street is the diminutive State Bank of Delano (c. 1910). Its street elevation consists of two arched openings — one for a large window, the other for the entrance — which one guesses adds up to a Classical statement.

C-20 Elbow Lake

The town of Elbow Lake lies southeast of the large lake of the same name. The site for the town was selected in 1874 as the seat for the Grant County Courthouse, but the town itself was not platted until 1886. The courthouse (1906), set in a wide and expansive park along Highway 79, has remained to the present day as the major visual focus of the community. In style the building is classical, a mixture of very late nineteenth-century classicism and early Beaux Arts. The pronounced and strong movement of its surfaces and its open central tower with a segmented dome tend to be a rather free interpretation of the Baroque. The building was designed by Bell and Detweiler.

C-21 Elk River

The first settlement at the site of Elk River was established in 1848. The village of Orono was platted in 1855, and the village of Elk River was platted the following year. By 1881 the two villages were united and incorporated under the name Elk River. In the 1860s the town was connected by the St. Paul and Pacific Railroad to the Twin Cities and St. Cloud.

The Sherburne County Courthouse is situated just off Highway 10 at Lowell Avenue. This building, designed by W. C. Warner, dates from 1877 and is one of the earliest county courthouses still standing in the state. It is scaled and designed almost as an Italianate Style dwelling. The building has been stuccoed over, an incongruous entrance has been added, and the interior has been remodeled. Next door is a single-story brick annex (Weimlinger-Remley, 1971), which has cut-in openings articulated by projecting piers. The Nu-Elk Theatre (c. 1936), located on Main Street at Jackson, is styled in the Streamline Moderne (although it is not too "streamlined"). The white stucco section with glass-brick corners and a curved vertical sign projects out over the entrance below.

East of town at the junction of Highways 10 and 169 is the often-illustrated United Power Association generating plant (originally the Rural Cooperative Power Association), which was designed in 1949–50 by Thorshov and Cerny. The series of stepped volumes works its way up the hillside and terminates in a group of three large metal stacks. Two and a half miles southeast of Elk River on Highway 169 (on Kelley Farm Road) is the Oliver H. Kelley House. This house, the dwelling of the founder of the National Grange, was built in 1869. It is styled in the Italianate, although its two-story clapboard volumes are quite puritanical and plain.

C-22 Fairhaven

On the Clearwater River one finds the Fairhaven mill and dam (1867). The mill building, which is slowly falling into ruin, is a two-and-a-half-story wood structure sheathed in shingles. Nearby are other abandoned wood buildings which were part of the mill complex.

C-23 Foley

This town was established in 1882–84, when the Great Northern Railroad was extended through Benton County. In 1901 the county seat was moved to Foley and a courthouse designed by S. H. Hass in a lukewarm Romanesque Revival Style was built. The new concrete frame addition (1974) designed by Traynor, Hermanson, and Hahn does not attempt to destroy or overpower the older building. The courthouse is located at 531 Dewey Street. Down the street at 621 Dewey Street is the St. John's Catholic Church (1909), a brick Romanesque Revival building with two corner towers, the taller of which functions as a separate campanile. The Romanesque employed in the building combines some Richardsonian elements with more "correct" Italianate Romanesque details.

C-24 Glenwood

The town, situated on the northeast shore of Lake Minnewaska was platted in 1866. Both the Burlington Northern and the Soo Line pass close by it. The Pope County Courthouse (1919), at the southeast corner of Minnesota Avenue (Highway 28) and 1st Street Northeast, is a classical three-part composition. Its central pavilion boasts engaged piers, entablatures, and decorated panels. In Barsness Park (in the southeastern part of town off Highway 104) is the Pope County Historical Society Museum, which consists of three historic buildings: a tiny log cabin (pre-1866) which was the first county courthouse; a gable-roofed clapboard schoolhouse (1896); and a Carpenter's Gothic church (1896). Northeast of town is the wooden roundhouse (pre-1900) of the Soo Line. It can be reached by traveling east on Highway 28 past the railroad viaduct, then northwest on the first road. East of Glenwood at Grove Lake is a small romantic Congregational chapel. The original Congregational Church was built in about 1886, and the present stone chapel was built to replace it in about 1966. The bell tower on the center of the ridge appears to be the one from the earlier church or a copy of it. The chapel can be reached by driving southeast of Glenwood on Highway 55 seven miles to the small community of Sedan, north one mile on County Road 29 to County Road 20, east four miles to County Road 39, and north one and a half miles.

Soo Line Roundhouse

C-25 Herman

Herman, on the Burlington Northern Railroad, was platted in 1875. Like many railroad towns, its grid follows the alignment of the tracks rather than the cardinal points of the compass. Southwest of Highway 27 and the railroad tracks stand the large-scaled concrete grain storage elevators which have just been completed (1975). The northeast side of the elevators forms a series of gently undulating curves. On the north corner of Highways 27 and 9, on the first perpendicular street northeast of the railroad, is a single-story Beaux Arts bank building (c. 1912) which now houses a drugstore. A small entrance with classical pediments and columns leads into the building. On the northeast side of Berlin Avenue (north of 2nd Street) is a complex of single-story houses in brick with vertical siding. The complex was developed by the Federal Farmers Home Administration to provide housing for farm workers. The gable-roofed buildings are arranged around a partially enclosed open space. The housing was designed in 1968 by Robert F. Ackerman and Associates.

C-26 Howard Lake

This railroad town was platted below Howard Lake in 1869. Its village hall (1904) is at the northeast corner of 6th Street (Highway 12) and 8th Avenue. The building has an open octagonal corner tower highly reminiscent of those found on nineteenth-century Shingle Style buildings. On 1st Street opposite the fairgrounds at 13th Avenue is an 1876 schoolhouse with bracketed eaves and a small open bell tower.

C-27 Kandiyohi

St. Patrick's Catholic Church was built in 1876 and was expanded and remodeled in 1894 and again in 1948. The two most interesting details of the clapboard building are the tower, which consists of a stepped pattern of blocks terminating in the octagonal belfry and spire, and the windows on the two flanks of the building. The windows are round arches, with each arch contained within a flat pediment. The church is located two blocks north of Highway 12 on 3rd Street. On the northwest corner of 6th Street and Atlantic Avenue is a carpenter's pattern-book Gothic church, the Ebenezer Lutheran Church (c. late 1890s).

C-28 Litchfield

The community was initially established in 1858 and was named Ness. In 1869, when the St. Paul and Pacific Railroad reached the site, it was platted and renamed Litchfield. It has its economic base in the dairy industry and in the processing and shipping of agricultural products. With its location in the midst of the lake country, the resort and tourist trade has become increasingly important to its economy. The community possesses buildings representing a wide array of architectural styles from the 1870s to the present. The Trinity Episcopal Church, attributed to Richard Upjohn, ranks as one of Minnesota's most important nineteenth-century buildings, and the new Meeker County Courthouse demonstrates how well Minnesota's contemporary architects handle present-day forms.

1 **Hotel,** 1880
Northwest corner Sibley Avenue N and Depot Street W
A three-story-plus mansard-roofed hotel of brick now painted white. The thin square tower and the entrance door form a forty-five-degree angle at the corner.

2 **Hollywood Theatre,** c. 1936
Liebenberg and Kaplan
East side Sibley Avenue N between 2nd and 3rd Streets E
The Moderne restrained by Classical considerations. The design includes both the theatre and an adjacent store. The marquee, the tall vertical sign, and the entrance areas below are Streamline.

3 **Bandstand,** 1913
City Park, bounded by Sibley and Marshall Avenues N and 3rd and 4th Streets E
A bandstand design competition was held in 1913. One of the entries was by Purcell, Feick, and Elmslie; their design was a treelike structure with a single support and a cantilevered roof. The winning design is seen in the present bandstand — a dignified classical pavilion with twelve Tuscan columns supporting a low-pitched hipped roof.

4 **Meeker County Courthouse,** 1973–74
Genesis Architects
Southwest corner Sibley Avenue N and 4th Street W
The 1885 Italianate courthouse was recently replaced by this two-story white stucco structure with deep cut-in horizontal band windows and apron glass on the ground level.

•5 **Trinity Episcopal Church,** 1871–72, 1879
Attrib. Richard Upjohn and Company
Northeast corner Sibley Avenue N and 4th Street E
If this handsome board-and-batten church was not designed by Upjohn, it certainly may have been derived from his published drawings. The tower is at the side of the gabled front; a doorway with a long, pointed arch dominates the entrance façade, and small dormers with quatrefoil windows peer out of the roof.

6 **GAR Hall** (now Meeker County Historical Society), 1885
East side Marshall Avenue N between 3rd and 4th Streets E
Medieval with a half-octagon tower projecting from the front and a suggestion of square turrets at each corner. The round-arched windows are suggestive of the Italianate.

7 **House,** c. 1890s
307 Holcombe Avenue N
The visual sense of this large house is Chateauesque, although the placement of the tower and other details point to the Queen Anne.

8 **First Presbyterian Church,** 1905
Southwest corner Holcombe Avenue N and 3rd Street E
The late nineteenth-century Carpenter's Gothic and the Craftsman combined. The church has a crenelated tower and small square windows arranged in a Greek cross.

9 **Northwestern National Bank of Litchfield,** 1968
Kilstofte and Vosejpka
Northeast corner Marshall Avenue N and Depot Street E
Wrightian with battered concrete and stone walls à la Taliesen West.

10 **House,** c. 1890s
215 Sibley Avenue S
A frame clapboard house with extensive sawed and turned work on the porch.

11 **House,** late 1890s
216 Sibley Avenue S
Queen Anne/Colonial Revival with a round corner tower topped by a bulbous onion dome.

12 **Hotel,** c. 1870s
Southwest corner Marshall Avenue S and Commerce Street E
A two-story clapboard hotel with a two-story porch, the upper section of which boasts a delicate pattern of Eastlake sawed designs. The front entrance is pedimented with a transom and sidelights.

C-29 Little Falls

The community was platted in 1855 on the east and west banks of the Mississippi River. The fall of water in the rapids, augmented by a dam that was constructed in 1890, provided a power source for several lumber, flour, and paper mills along the river. The major highways formerly went directly through town on 1st Street and on Broadway, but the new bypass of Highways 10 and 371 now goes east and north of the town.

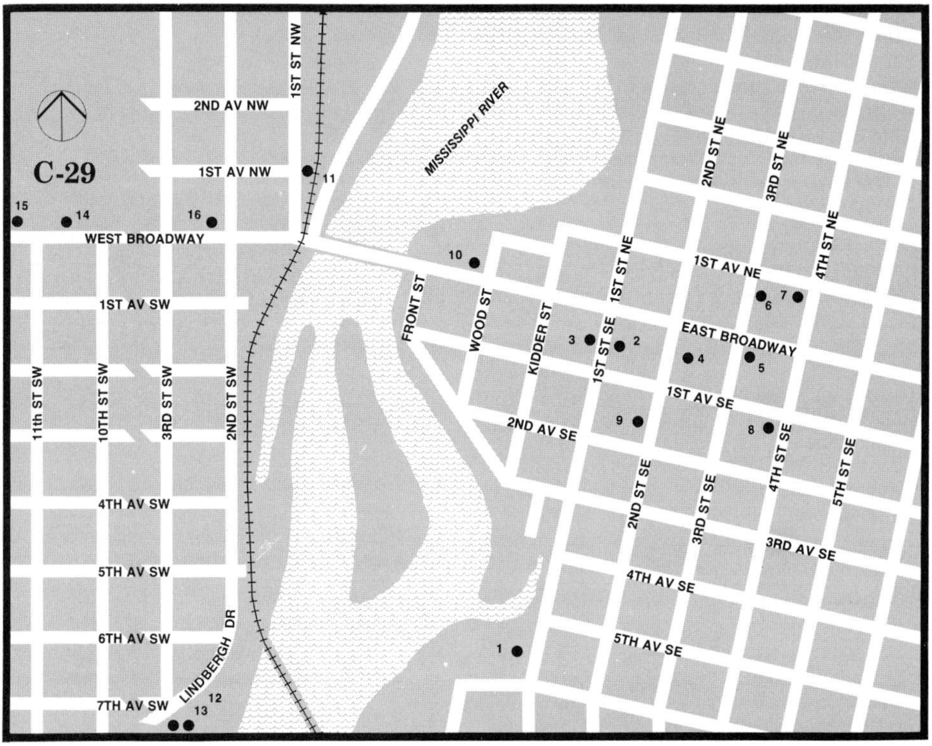

1 **Rosenmeier House,** c. 1898
606 1st Street SE
The Colonial Revival with real spirit. A two-story central porch is balanced on each side by single-story curved pavilion porches.

2 **Falls Theatre,** c. 1934
115 1st Street SE
Zigzag Moderne. Angled rays form the side of the marquee.

1 Rosenmeier House.

3 **Black and White Hamburger Shop,** c. 1934
114 1st Street SE
A rare find — a small hamburger shop in glazed white brick with a suggestion of the Medieval.

4 **Morrison County Courthouse,** 1891
Foster and Smith
Southeast corner Broadway E and 2nd Street E
A turreted and gabled Romanesque Revival building in brick with stone trim. The picturesque tower holds a clock. A bland office addition (1950s) with vertical ribbon windows and a more recent concrete projecting-drawer box have been added in the same block.

5 **Assembly of God Church,** 1946
300 Broadway E
The 1930s Moderne carried over into the post–World War II years in a brick building with stepped window headers and glass brick.

6 **Carnegie City Library,** 1905
Fremont D. Orff
108 3rd Street NE
A Craftsman house of river boulders, brick, and shingles as a library.

7 **Episcopal Church of Our Savior,** c. 1903
John Lutcliff
113 4th Street NE
Craftsman imagery through and through. The lower walls and the tower are of river boulders with half-timbering above; the whole is scaled to the domestic.

8 **Randall House,** c. late 1870s
200 4th Avenue SE
A rather large French Second Empire building in brick.

9 **House,** c. 1936
210 2nd Street SE
The flat-roofed Moderne (not very streamlined in this case) used in a white stucco dwelling.

10 **Post Office,** 1916
James A. Wetmore
27 Broadway E (at Wood Street)
A one-and-a-half-story portico with six columns. The scale and the cornice and other detailing make this building almost Georgian.

11 **Northern Pacific Railroad Depot** (now Burlington Northern), 1899
Cass Gilbert
200 1st Street NW
The heavy triangular forms of the gable roofs seem to press the building onto the site suggesting shelter in the extreme. Its imagery, which one occasionally encounters in the less pretentious examples of Gilbert's work, is late Queen Anne (Shingle Style) and Craftsman.

11 Depot.

12 **Lindbergh Interpretive Center,** 1972
West side Mississippi River, about 2 miles south of Broadway W
The house in which Charles A. Lindbergh grew up is a pleasant Craftsman bungalow (1906) by Carl Bolander; it is set on a raised stone basement. The center as a whole, beautifully sited on a wooded hillside overlooking the river, was designed by Myers and Bennett. It combines an odd arrangement of volumes (including a hyperbolic paraboloid roof) and an agitated form.

13 **Weyerhaeuser Museum,** 1975
Miller-Dunwiddie Architects
West side Mississippi River about 2½ miles south of Broadway W
A very quiet traditional clapboard building, almost Greek Revival in feeling.

14 **House,** c. 1890
1016 Broadway W (Pine Grove Park)
The three-and-a-half-story square tower fits into the L of this brick house. The detailing is Queen Anne.

•15 **Williams Barn,** c. 1890s
Northwest of town on Broadway W to County Roads 214/234, then north ½ mile
A clapboard barn with a pointed hooped roof on the main section of the structure and also over the main entrance and on the tiny cupola.

16 **Our Lady of Lourdes Catholic Church,** c. 1905
208 Broadway W
A central European image in the pair of onion-domed towers and Baroque detailing.

15 Williams Barn.

C-30 Long Prairie

Although a Federal Indian Agency was established at this site as early as 1848, the town as such did not begin to develop until the late 1870s. It was incorporated in 1883. Central and 2nd Avenues, between 1st and 4th Streets, present a remarkably well preserved group of one-story and two-story commercial buildings from the turn of the century.

1 **Commercial Building,** c. 1905
Northeast corner Central Avenue and 3rd Street
Each of the two façades has a central pediment, but each is quite different at ground level. On one side there is a centerpiece of six arches; three of the arches and their columns form a loggia. The other side of the building has a composition of four engaged columns and an entablature.

2 **Bank Building,** 1903
North side Central Avenue between 2nd and 3rd Streets
A two-story brick building with a bold handling of stone trim, especially in the two nonsymmetrical arches over the ground floor. The off-balance nature of the design is restated in the upper part of the building.

3 **Village Hall,** 1909
239 Central Avenue
A free interpretation of the classical order. The two engaged Ionic columns and pediment are surmounted by a small centrally placed pediment.

2 Bank Building.

4 **Post Office,** 1937
Louis A. Simon
350 Central Avenue
PWA, more Moderne than classical; with two delicate metal Greek lampstands at each side of the entrance.

5 **Todd County Courthouse,** 1883
T. J. Pauley; Charles H. Sparks
2nd Avenue between 2nd and 3rd Streets
Impressively situated high on a hill. In style it is thinned-down Romanesque with a central hipped-roof tower.

6 **House,** c. mid-1880s
Northeast corner 2nd Avenue and 8th Street
Though Queen Anne in style, its thin vertical quality is decidedly Eastlake. Note also the Gothic house farther to the west on 2nd Avenue (south side of street).

C-31 Louisburg

The town, one of a series which was platted by the Great Northern Railway in the late 1880s, houses the Lac qui Parle Public School (1911). This two-story schoolhouse with its strong vertical accent has the overall feeling of a building designed in the late 1880s, but it exhibits little in the way of ornamentation. The front entrance has a Romanesque arch with a half-round lunette windows; the sidelighted door below it is Colonial Revival.

C-32 Luxemburg

A short side trip south of St. Cloud on Highway 15 brings one to Luxemburg — population, one hundred. Its monument, St. Wendelin's Catholic Church (c. 1880s), is an entrance-tower church with buttressed side walls. There are two miniature stone lean-tos on each side of the tower. The low, pressed-down quality of the church, its rough stone walls, and its site amid open lawns and trees fully capture the nineteenth-century prairie feeling of central Minnesota.

C-33 Milaca

Milaca began as a lumbering town which was owned by James J. Hill. With the deforestation of the area the community became an agricultural center. The Mille Lacs County Courthouse (1923), located at 635 2nd Street Southeast, is a City Beautiful building, only the image in this case is more Georgian than Roman. The central entrance pavilion boasts a second-story balcony supported by a console, a pair of fine engaged and fluted corner piers, and a garland motif in the parapet. In strong contrast is Louis Pinault's PWA city hall (1936), located at 145 Central Avenue South. The city hall comes close to being an Arts and Crafts product with its rough stone exterior; when it was first built, it was described as an example of "rustic architecture." Above the door, as a stone lunette, is a relief sculpture by Samuel Sabean depicting Native Americans, English traders, and a stylized eagle.

City hall.

C-34 Monticello

The town of Monticello was platted in 1854 on the southwest bank of the Mississippi River. Formerly the major highway between the Twin Cities and St. Cloud ran directly through town, but now the freeway, Highway 94, skirts the town to the southwest. At the north corner of Broadway and Minnesota Street is the Sherwin House (c. 1905). The two-story columned porch forms an impressive façade for the very modest one-and two-story dwelling. Farther to the east, at 318 Broadway, is a Queen Anne/Colonial Revival cottage. Its main gable, which faces the street, is penetrated by an open porch defined by a broad, thin arch.

C-35 Mora

Mora was platted in 1882 and was named for a Swedish city. The Kanabec County Courthouse, located at the southeast corner of Maple and Vine Streets, is a Richardsonian Romanesque (1894) building with brick and stone trim. An insensitive addition has been attached to the side, and the interior has been modernized. South of Mora on Highway 65 one passes a giant horse (an enlarged toy), which stands in the Kanabec County fairgrounds. The horse is said to be a copy of one at Mora in Sweden. Farther south on Highway 65 (one-half mile south of its junction with County Road 14) is a picturesque gambrel-roofed barn with an attached wood silo.

Statue of horse, Mora.

C-36 Morris

The community was laid out on the northeast shore of Crystal Lake in 1869. It is the seat of Stevens County and the site of the University of Minnesota at Morris (the former West Central Agricultural College). Two lines of the Burlington Northern Railroad bisect the town.

1 **Morris Theatre,** c. 1937
6th Street, northeast of Atlantic Avenue (Highway 9)
A large Streamline Moderne theatre. The curved vertical sign and the projection of the second-story parapet bring emphasis to the marquee and the entrance below.

2 **Morris State Bank,** c. 1958
Northwest corner Atlantic Avenue and 7th Street
The formal entrance of polished stone contrasts with the metal sheathing of the rest of the building. The bank's name carried on a thin horizontal band is the main visual statement on the 7th Street side of the building.

3 **Stevens County Courthouse,** 1956
Foss and Company
Colorado Avenue between 4th and 5th Streets

A two-story Corporate International box with a strong emphasis on the horizontal. Only the stone wall which juts out perpendicular to the front of the building hints (along with the flagpole) that the building may be public and civic.

4 **Stanton House,** c. 1900?
907 Park Avenue

Impossible to catalogue. The house has a hipped-roof tower on one side, half-timber paneling on the surface, and small-paned lights in the upper sections of the double-hung windows.

5 **University of Minnesota at Morris**

The most dramatic building on the campus is the power plant (1970) by Cerny Associates, a simple equilateral triangle of brick with its roof touching the ground at one end. As a design it looks to the Danish styling of Arne Jacobson. The same firm has also designed the Food Center Service Building (1971), another Danish building but more domestic in scale and less concerned with pure form than the power plant. Ralph Rapson and Associates designed the Humanities Building (1969–71) and the Fine Arts Center (1972). Like much of the work of the Rapson firm, the design of the Fine Arts Center may have looked simple and direct on paper, but it turns out to be highly agitated; there is a strong contradiction between the series of rectangular boxes with the band windows at the top and the steep form of the projecting shed-roof enclosures.

5 *University of Minnesota Power Plant.*

C-37 Ortonville

At the southeast end of Big Stone Lake Reservoir (on the Minnesota River) is the town of Ortonville, which was platted in 1872. During the 1920s and 1930s the town developed as an important canning center and also as a source of red granite. The town is strung in a narrow band along the southeastern shore of the lake with the commercial area to the south and the residential section to the north.

1 **Big Stone County Courthouse,** 1901–1902
Fremont D. Orff
Northeast side 2nd Street between Jackson and Lincoln Avenues

Romanesque with a classical prejudice. The brick building has stone trim.

2 **Geier Brothers Building,** 1886
124 2nd Street NW

A tiny single-floor building with rusticated masonry and above it a brick panel surrounded by stone. The effect is mildly Romanesque.

3 **Columbian Hotel,** 1892
Northwest corner of 2nd Avenue and Jefferson Street

A three-story brick hotel combining the Queen Anne and the Romanesque. The front sidewalk is sheltered by the upper two floors, which are cantilevered out and supported on columns.

4 **Bungalow,** c. 1908
Southeast corner Dassell Avenue and 4th Street NW

A large Craftsman bungalow sheathed in river boulders.

5 **Artichoke Town Hall,** c. 1890
13 miles east of town on Highway 12 and 4 miles north on County Road 25 (west side of road)

The roof of the octagonal building sweeps up to a small central belfry, strongly suggesting an artichoke and its stem. The trim is appropriately painted in artichoke green.

•6 **Larson Round Barn,** c. 1900
10 miles north of town on Highway 75, 4 miles east on County Road 6, and 3 miles north on County Road 69

Probably the largest round barn in Minnesota. The walls of the lower floor are of stone. The upper floor, the gable dormer, and the silo top are sheathed in wood.

5 Artichoke Town Hall.

C-38 Osakis

Osakis, situated in the lake resort area of northwestern Minnesota (off Highway 94), is not teeming with great buildings, but it does contain one structure — Hurricane House — which is well worth a visit. The town is located on the south shore of Lake Osakis. Its main thoroughfares — Lake Street, Main Street, and Nokomis Avenue (formerly Highway 52) — and the railroad run parallel to the lakeshore. A park separates part of the shore from Lake Street, on which there are two interesting turn-of-the-century carpenter-designed houses: a clapboard house at 610 Lake Street and an Eastlake house at 209 Lake Street.

1 **Hurricane House,** c. 1900
107 Nokomis Avenue

Minnesota is not blessed with an abundance of idiosyncratic buildings, but the few which have been built are rare delights and this is certainly one of them. A self-conscious Expressionist of the twenties could not have arrived at a more peculiar roof pattern than that of Hurricane House: the essentially flat roof is cut into on the four corners by four valleys, thus making the upper floor a sort of cruciform. Corner windows occur throughout both floors of the house, and each is treated as a bay with a cornice. On the upper floor the corner bay windows are V-shaped; below they are rectangular. The wall surfaces below each of the deeply cut roof valleys are sheathed diagonally, while elsewhere there is horizontal sheathing. The play of diagonals against the vertical and horizontal design of the house is matched by the form of a V-trunked dead birch tree, the stumps of which are now surmounted by two birdhouses.

1 Hurricane House.

2 **Service Station,** c. 1924
Southeast corner Lake Street and 1st Avenue E

For those fascinated with the commercial vernacular, here is a gable-roofed Colonial Revival station, its colonial front porch serving as one of the drive-through bays at the gasoline pumps.

C-39 Paynesville

Among the one-story and two-story "modernized" buildings of plain brick on Paynesville's main commercial street (Washburn Avenue) is the First National Bank Building (c. 1915). This classical building with four elegant polished Ionic columns possesses a civic dignity completely lacking in the other buildings. The bank is situated near the northwest corner of Washburn Avenue and James Street.

C-40 Pierz

Pierz was platted on the west bank of the Skunk River in 1891. Its visual landmark is the St. Joseph's Catholic Church (1888), a brick structure with a central tower. The styling is Gothic, although the body of the tower is rather heavily proportioned. The church is situated at the southeast corner of Main Street (Highway 25) and 1st Avenue Northeast. Farther south on Main Street, at the southwest corner of Main Street and 1st Avenue Southwest, is the Star Theatre, a strong statement in the Streamline Moderne of the 1930s. The white stucco theatre and the adjoining stores form a single horizontal composition, topped by a nautical railing at the edge of the roof. On the northeast corner of Main Street and 2nd Avenue Southeast is a bank building (1914) which is now a restaurant. This little-known Prairie Style bank is devoid of ornament and relies exclusively on the placement of its rectilinear piers to establish its character. Still farther south on Main Street one finds several brick dwellings from the 1890s, the most interesting of which are located at 322 and 331 Main Street and on the southwest corner of Main Street and 4th Avenue Southwest.

C-41 Pine City

This railroad village was platted in 1869. A well-preserved nineteenth-century store building, the Lahodney Millinery Shop (c. 1880s), is situated at 615 3rd Avenue. It is a small false-fronted store building which still has its small-paned windows and wood and glass double doors. Northwest of town is a replica of the nineteenth-century Connor's Fur Trading Post. This log complex, which was reconstructed in 1969, is situated on County Road 7 (Hillside Avenue), one and a half miles west of Highway 35.

Lahodney Millinery Shop

C-42 Princeton

Princeton was first settled in 1854, and its street pattern was platted in 1856. The Burlington Northern station at the southwest corner of 1st Street and 10th Avenue is a brick building (stone trim) which was originally described as Jacobean in style. At 907 1st Street is a small PWA power plant (1938); its entrance is emphasized by smooth stone trim and a pair of Moderne lights. Set quite far back from the street at 202 5th Avenue South is the new Princeton State Bank (1971) by Charles Dykins. The bank's rectangular forms, partially sheathed in wood, ease themselves around the landscaped corner.

C-43 Richmond

Long before the small town of Richmond (platted in 1856) can be seen from the highway, the tall pointed spire of the Catholic Church of Sts. Peter and Paul (1884) becomes visible. This brick church well illustrates how the Gothic was frequently combined with the Romanesque. The entrance tower with its stepped arch, the round-arched windows, and the arched corbel table are Romanesque. The church is located in the town, one-half mile north of Highway 23.

C-44 Rockville

As its name implies, the town sits on a mountain of granite. For most of the twentieth century the town's economy has been based on its granite, and to a degree this is reflected in its architecture.

1 **John Clark School,** 1935–36
Southeast corner Highway 23 and County Road 8
A finely fitted granite-faced school building in the PWA Moderne of the 1930s but with decided leanings toward Fascist classicism.

2 **Bank Building** (now unused), c. 1911
South side Highway 23
A brick box made classical by pasting on a classical (Roman) cornice and entablature and placing a small pedimented porch on one side. The columns are polished granite, but the rest is cast stone.

3 **Village Hall and Fire Department,** 1908
South side Highway 23
The often encountered two-story commercial building with a false front. If we read the signs carefully, we discover that it is indeed a public building, not the local hardware store. The fire department now occupies the whole front of the building, and a new addition (also in stone) has been built at the side. There are several other stone buildings in town, among these a stone house situated just south of Highway 23 at the east end of town.

C-45 St. Cloud

A small community was established at this site in 1854. With its location at the headwaters of the Mississippi (as far as navigation is concerned) the community early became a significant river trading post. The first town plat, laid out in 1854, ran parallel to the Mississippi River, which at this point is oriented northwest/southeast. The platting of streets with reference to the river continued on both sides of the river for some time, but later additions to the west, north, and south were oriented to the cardinal points of the compass.

In 1866 the St. Paul and Pacific Railroad reached the town, and two years later the community was officially incorporated. Other important events which decidedly helped to shape the

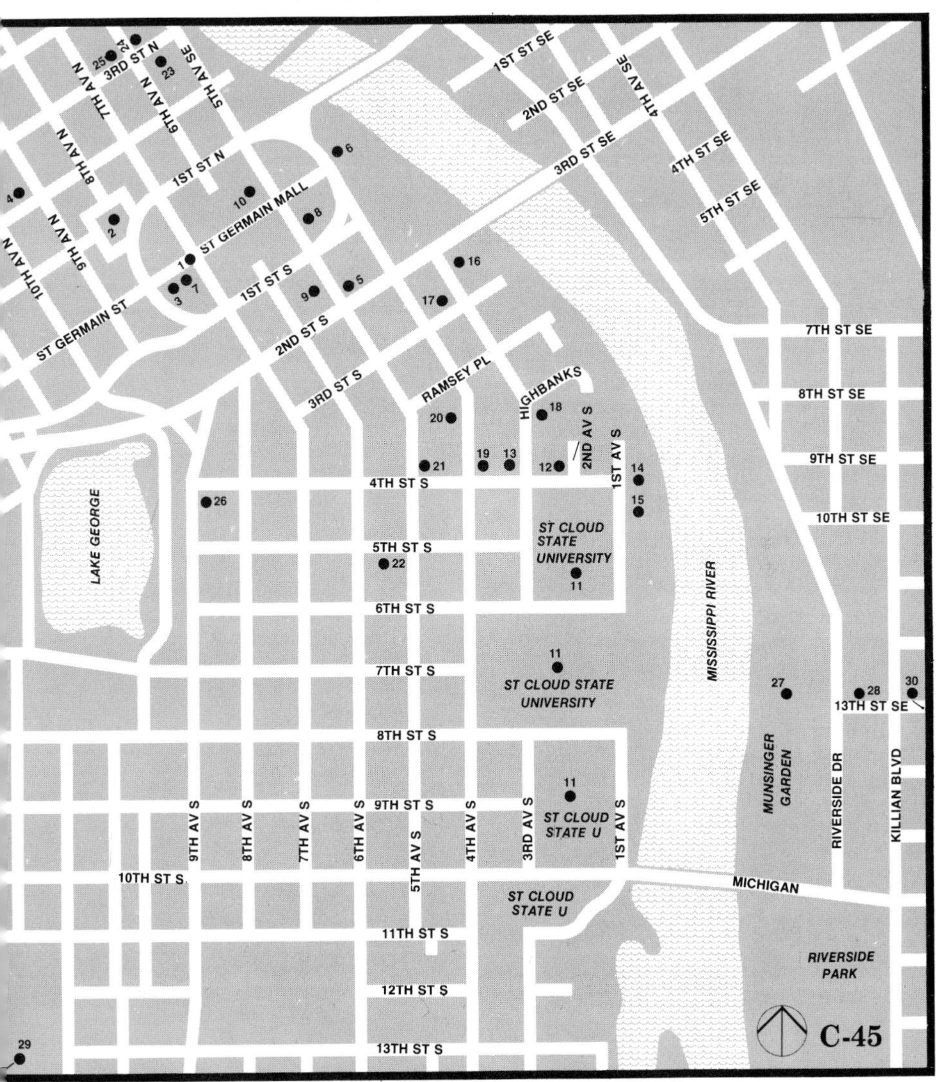

physical pattern of the community were the opening up of granite quarries in 1868, the construction of a dam across the river in the 1880s, and the building of the state reformatory, just east of town, in 1889. Through much of its existence St. Cloud's economy has been based on the city's role as a service center for the surrounding agricultural area, on its function as a shipping point, and on its quarrying and stone carving industries. There have been flurries in other directions, an example being the brief production of an automobile, the Pan Car, in 1917 and the establishment of Pan Town (in the vicinity of 2919 8th Street North), north and west of downtown. Currently the agricultural orientation of the city is supplemented by a number of manufacturing concerns of moderate size.

St. Cloud has on the whole made an effort to take advantage of its riverside location. On the east bank of the Mississippi are Munsinger Park and Wilson Park, and on the west bank is the campus of St. Cloud State University. Within the gridiron of the city are several large parks — Eastman Park, City Park, and Centennial Park — and to the north on the banks of the Sauk River is Alice Whitney Park. The new downtown mall (#1) and urban planning now going on argue well for the city's future.

1 **St. Germain Mall,** 1972–73
Hodne/Stageberg Partners
St. Germain Street between 4th and 8th Avenues, west of river

The plantings and the material used for the walkways and other street furniture indicate an awareness of what will survive in the Minnesota climate. The organic forms of Anthony Caponi's 1973 "Granite Trio" really do contribute to the mall — something that does not always happen when "art" is used in the downtown areas of our cities.

2 **Stearns County Courthouse,** 1921–22
Toltz, King, and Day
8th Avenue N (north of St. Germain Mall)

Situated — as a City Beautiful courthouse should be — in a square (no greenery to speak of) with four major city streets terminating at the courthouse block. The porticoed building is topped by a low drum and yellow-tiled dome, and within there are murals by Elsa Jemne.

2 Stearns County Courthouse.

3 **Federal Building,** 1936
R. Stanley Brown
720 St. Germain Mall

PWA Moderne, leaning toward the "Fascist." Note the Classical/Moderne stone and metal lamp standards to the side of the main entrance.

4 **Post Office,** 1937–38
9th Avenue and 2nd Street N

The visitor who has difficulty in pinpointing this design may be interested to know that it was described when built (by the PWA) as Modern Gothic. Within is a Federal Art Project mural by David Granahan.

5 **Public Library,** 1902
124 5th Avenue S

A not very distinguished City Beautiful library in brick and stone.

6 **City Hall,** 1903
314 St. Germain Street

Another of St. Cloud's classical structures, this one with Roman arches and walls of smooth granite blocks. It was built originally as the Federal Building, and in 1937 it was moved to its present site and converted for its present functions.

7 **Stearns County Service Building,** 1951
700-702 St. Germain Mall
In style it is 1941 PWA Moderne, built just ten years too late. A fine "Fascist" eagle over the entrance.

8 **McClure-Searle Building,** 1883; 1886
14 5th Avenue S
Searle Building, 1886
18 5th Avenue S
BPOE Building, 1913
22 5th Avenue S
Petters Building, c. 1890s
26 5th Avenue S

Here is a group of commercial buildings which should be revamped for new uses. In style they range from the McClure-Searle Building, which is pure Victorian Eastlake, to the mild Classicism of the BPOE Building. As a group and individually these buildings have character, and it would be difficult to argue that they do not add appreciably to the visual/historical atmosphere of St. Cloud.

9 **Commercial Block,** 1880
109–13 5th Avenue S
A highly original interpretation of the Romanesque. The suggestion of a pavilion projects from the center of the building, and a one-and-a-half-story arched opening leads into the building. Note the handsome rough granite block walls of this building, as in many of St. Cloud's buildings.

9 Commercial Block.

10 **First National Bank Building,** 1889
501 St. Germain Mall
What we see today is a remodeled and added-to building. The structure was built in 1876 and then was made "modern" in 1889 by conversion to the Queen Anne Style.

11 **St. Cloud State University**
1st to 3rd Avenues, south of 4th Street
The school opened in 1869 as a state normal school; it later became a state teachers' college, then a state college, and now a state university. Its original seven-acre site has long been outgrown, and the campus now spreads as far east as 1st Avenue South. Its old buildings are puritanically plain and nondescript. Its new ones are of real architectural interest: the Newman Center (Freerks, Sperl, and Flynn, 1965); the Performing Arts Center (Haarstick and Lundgren, 1965); Halenbeck Hall (Traynor and Hermanson, 1965); the Learning Resource Center (S. C. Smiley and Associates, 1969); and the new Mathematics and Science Building (S. C. Smiley and Associates, 1974). All of these buildings are, to one degree or another, examples of the New Brutalism of the 1960s and the early 1970s — exposed concrete frames and sculptured concrete shapes played off against brick walls and brick infills. The most imposing and monumental is • the Mathematics and Science Building. A fascinating visual game occurs at the side of this building where a glass greenhouse and conservatory are played off against the solid block form of the main building.

12 **House** (now part of university campus), c. 1908
201 4th Street
A flat-roofed and parapeted stucco box — straight off the streets of Los Angeles.

13 **Foley House,** c. 1890
385 3rd Avenue S
An institutional version of the Richardsonian Romanesque used for a residence. Note the small group of colonnettes beside the front door.

14 Brower House (now part of Newman Center), c. 1923
Clarence Johnston, Jr.
396 1st Avenue S

The versatile Johnstons, this time in an English Elizabethan mold; now appropriately vine-clad from top to bottom.

15 House, c. 1912
412 1st Avenue S

A Craftsman/Prairie house with wide overhanging gable roofs, tile inserts in the stucco walls, geometric patterned windows, and battered walls. To the street it presents its entrance and garage; toward the river it has two stories.

16 House, c. 1906
214 3rd Avenue S

The Beaux Arts in the manner of a late eighteenth-century French villa; quoined corners and mansard roof with arched roof dormers.

16 House.

17 Abeles House, c. 1900
223 3rd Avenue S

Queen Anne/Colonial Revival. An extensive curved porch with Ionic columns follows the corner bay around the house.

18 Clarke House, c. 1890
356 3rd Avenue S

Richardsonian Romanesque in brick.

•**19 St. John's Episcopal Church,** 1971
Hammel, Green, and Abrahamson
390 4th Avenue S

A thinly delineated series of shed-roof stuccoed forms reminiscent of designs by Arne Jacobson and Charles Moore.

20 First Presbyterian Church, 1917
373 4th Avenue S

Rural English Gothic with fine-pointed stonework.

21 Double House, 1894
398 5th Avenue S

A classic Queen Anne house with a round three-story tower at one corner.

22 Dickinson House, 1871
503 5th Avenue S

A Gothic Revival cottage with a central gable, verge boards on the gable overhangs, and a front porch with a cusped arch.

23 House, c. 1890
251 6th Avenue N

Queen Anne Revival in brick and shingles.

24 House, c. 1904
302 6th Avenue N

A one-and-a-half-story Queen Anne/Colonial Revival house; the contour-gabled dormer contains a Palladian window.

25 Holy Angels Church, 1883
William Schickel
Northwest corner 3rd Street N and 6th Avenue N

A low, rather squat church in brick; Romanesque, but certainly not Richardsonian Romanesque. Two small drum towers terminate each of the front corners; in the center is a low entrance tower with a double arched window and a circular window above, near the top.

26 Majerus House, 1891
Theodore Kerenhoerster
404 9th Avenue S

French Second Empire in brick with a mansard roof and tower.

27 Rosenberger Log House, c. 1855
Munsinger Park off Riverside Drive

Reputed to be one of the oldest log houses in central Minnesota.

28 TenVoorde House, c. 1935
Foss and Company
1228 Riverside Drive

An example of the Streamline Moderne of the 1930s. White stucco walls, flat roof, band and corner windows, curved corners, and a large porthole window.

29 Radio Station KFAM Building, 1937
South of town on Highway 152
Certain building types of the 1930s were expected to be "advanced" and modern, and radio stations were in this category. Here the glories of radio and the 1930s are preserved in a one-story structure with curved walls and glass brick.

30 Minnesota State Reformatory, estab. 1889
On Reformatory Drive, northwest of junction Highway 10/52 and Minnesota Boulevard
The penal institution as a Romanesque fortress; grim and forbidding — a convincing marriage of fact and image.

C-46 St. Joseph

West of St. Cloud, south of Highway 52, is the community of St. Joseph, where St. Benedict's College is located. Like St. John's University, St. Benedict's houses a full range of architectural styles from the Gothic Revival of the 1880s to the latest New Brutalism in brick and concrete. The college's main building, constructed in the 1880s, is a characteristic Collegiate Second Empire building in brick, three stories high. Behind it to the west is the Sacred Heart Chapel (c. 1890), a drum and dome classical pile which is more French than Italian. North of these two structures are a stone rectory and another church building (c. 1880s), connected by a low single-story wing which repeats the central gable of the rectory. The church is English Gothic in style, although the belfry and the spire are Norman. In the center of the campus is Mary Commons, with Mary Hall (designed by Hammel and Green in 1954). In design this three-story brick structure is part 1950s International Style and part New Brutalism. Farther south on the campus is the Benedicta Arts Center (Hammel, Green, and Abrahamson, 1963), which seems to go off in a number of directions historically — the PWA Moderne of the 1930s, the Dutch brick vernacular of Willem Dudok, and the agitated forms of Ralph Rapson.

Another building in St. Joseph which is worth note is the First State Bank Building (c. 1917) on the north side of County Road 2. Its street façade is highly reminiscent of the work in the teens of Purcell and Elmslie, only here the flavor is Egyptian rather than Sullivanesque. All in all, it is a successful quasi-Prairie School design.

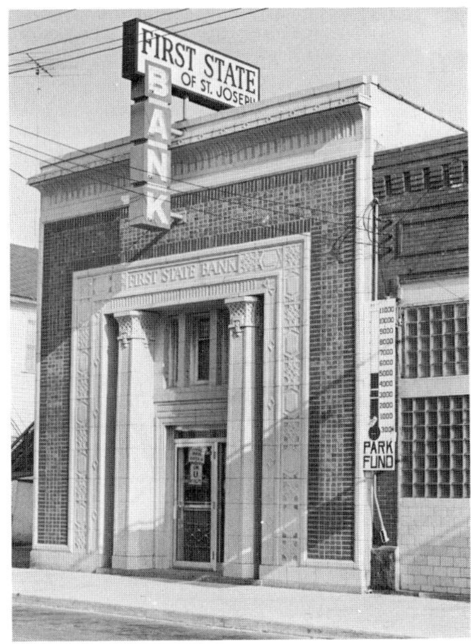

First State Bank Building.

C-47 Sauk Center

Sauk Center was established as early as 1856, but it was not until 1863 that the town was platted and a gristmill was built adjacent to the rebuilt dam across the Sauk River. In the late 1870s the railroad arrived, and the town later became a meeting terminal for the Northern Pacific and the Great Northern rail lines. The city's fame rests on Sinclair Lewis's boyhood life in the place, and his home (#4) is a well-preserved historic landmark.

1 **House** (now Anderson Florist Shop), late 1880s
605 Main Street S
A brick two-story Queen Anne house, which is far closer to the late nineteenth-century English Queen Anne Style than to the American Queen Anne. The only point of Victorian exuberance is the stone-trimmed keyhole window of the living room.

2 **Church of the Good Samaritan (Episcopal),** c. 1870s
529 Main Street S
Gothic Revival, with roofs reaching down to the ground. The St. Paul's Catholic Church (1904) at 304 Sinclair Lewis Avenue utilizes a German Gothic image.

3 **First Congregational Church** (now United Church of Christ), c. 1905
Northwest corner Oak and 5th Streets
A low-lying brick Craftsman version of the Gothic. Note how the angled entrance bay on the 5th Street façade has been fitted into the design so that it projects between the rear gable section and the side walls of the sanctuary.

4 **Sinclair Lewis's Boyhood Home,** c. 1880
812 Sinclair Avenue
A restrained Eastlake one-and-a-half-story cottage.

5 **Sarepta House,** late 1890s
Southwest corner Walnut and 2nd Streets
A brick Queen Anne house on its way toward the Colonial Revival.

4 Sinclair Lewis's Boyhood Home.

6 **Minnesota Home School** (Department of Corrections), 1911–24
Clarence H. Johnston, Sr.
Main Street N (north of Highway 71)
Most of the buildings were designed between 1911 and 1924 by Clarence H. Johnston, Sr., when he held the position of state architect. Of these the most interesting is Morse Hall (the administration building), which he designed in 1912. In style it is a correct American version of the Georgian — a red brick entrance with white columns, parapeted end walls with paired chimneys, and gable dormer windows. Freer in design and in the use of classical elements are the nearby Sinclair Lewis Hall (1913) and the group of four cottages to the west (Sullivan, Richard, Alcott, and Stowe).

C-48 Sauk Rapids

The "molehill" at 601 3rd Avenue North is one of Minnesota's contributions to America's small number of folk follies. The elements of the folly — towers, temples, pools, bridges, and grottoes which conjure up an improbable world — were created over a period of twenty-five years (1948–73) by Louis C. Wippich out of scrap granite which he obtained from nearby quarries and stoneworking concerns. The design of the largest of the towers (forty-five feet high) comes remarkably close to several designs by Bruce Goff.

C-49 Terrace

The 1871 village of Terrace on the east branch of the Chippewa River is the site of the early Enterprise Mill. The original three-story wood mill building was built in 1868; it was destroyed the following year and then was rebuilt in 1870. The gable sides of the building are sheathed in clapboard, and the other two sides are covered with shingles.

Enterprise Mill.

C-50 Wheaton

Wheaton, on the southeast bank of the Mustinka River, became the seat of Traverse County in 1886. Its main monument is the high Farmer's Co-op elevator complex, located south of Highway 27 and west of 10th Street. At 911 Broadway is the Streamline Moderne Gopher Theatre (c. 1939).

C-51 Willmar

The city was laid out by the St. Paul and Pacific Railroad company on the southern shores of Foot Lake and Willmar Lake. The lakeshore and the peninsulas have been well utilized as parks. Over the years the city has lost several of its architectural monuments including Cass Gilbert's Railroad Passenger Depot (1891–92) and the Central Hotel and Stella Opera House (1891) with its façade of cast iron and sheet metal.

1 **Commercial Building,** 1913
Southeast corner Litchfield Avenue and 5th Street W
A delicate and refined classical design, almost Rococo in feeling. The surface is sheathed in glazed yellow brick, and the classical frosting is in white terra-cotta. The building lacks the usual terminating cornice, a fact which appreciably modifies the classical image. The second-story addition was built in 1941.

1 Commercial Building.

2 **Cinema Theatre,** c. 1936
West side 4th Street W between Litchfield and Becker Avenues
The Moderne in a classical vein. The building has a smooth stone veneer and a conservative marquee.

3 **War Memorial Auditorium,** 1935–36
William M. Ingemann
East side 6th Street W between Litchfield and Becker Avenues
PWA Moderne realized primarily through a pattern of contrasting stone inlaid in the brick walls. Over the entrance are three relief panels in stone depicting the glories of agriculture, government, and transportation.

4 **Kandiyohi County Courthouse,** 1964
Gauger and Associates
Southeast corner Becker Avenue and 6th Street W
Agitated Moderne of the 1950s. Two-story triangular piers support a projecting roof with a sawtooth edge.

5 **Jorgenson House,** c. 1890
601 Becker Avenue W
A square box of brick. The basic form and the details such as the segmented arched windows with projecting brick hoods are Italianate, although certainly late examples of this style.

6 **Jenness House,** c. late 1880s
Northwest corner Gorton Avenue and 7th Street NW
Eastlake, one would guess.

7 **House,** c. 1900
924 Ella Avenue
Queen Anne/Colonial Revival with a central tower and Palladian and oval windows.

8 **Sperry House,** c. 1895
228 Porto Rico Street
A brick Queen Anne house. The major emphasis is placed on the front central gable with its arches and paired columns.

9 **Long Lake Lutheran Church,** c. 1890
North of town on Highway 71 and west on County Road 27 about 3 miles
Carpenter's Gothic with a small rose window in the tower and round-headed windows elsewhere.

10 **Endersen Cabin,** pre-1863
North of town on Highway 71, west on County Road 25 to County Road 5, north ½ mile, and west 2 miles
A one-and-a-half-story cabin of hand-hewn logs. The gable ends and the roof are covered with board-and-batten.

11 **Mamrelund Swedish Lutheran Church,** 1880, 1900
Northwest of town on Highway 12, north on County Road 116 about 4 miles
Carpenter's Gothic sheathed in clapboard with an entrance tower and pointed windows.

Arrowhead and Iron Range A

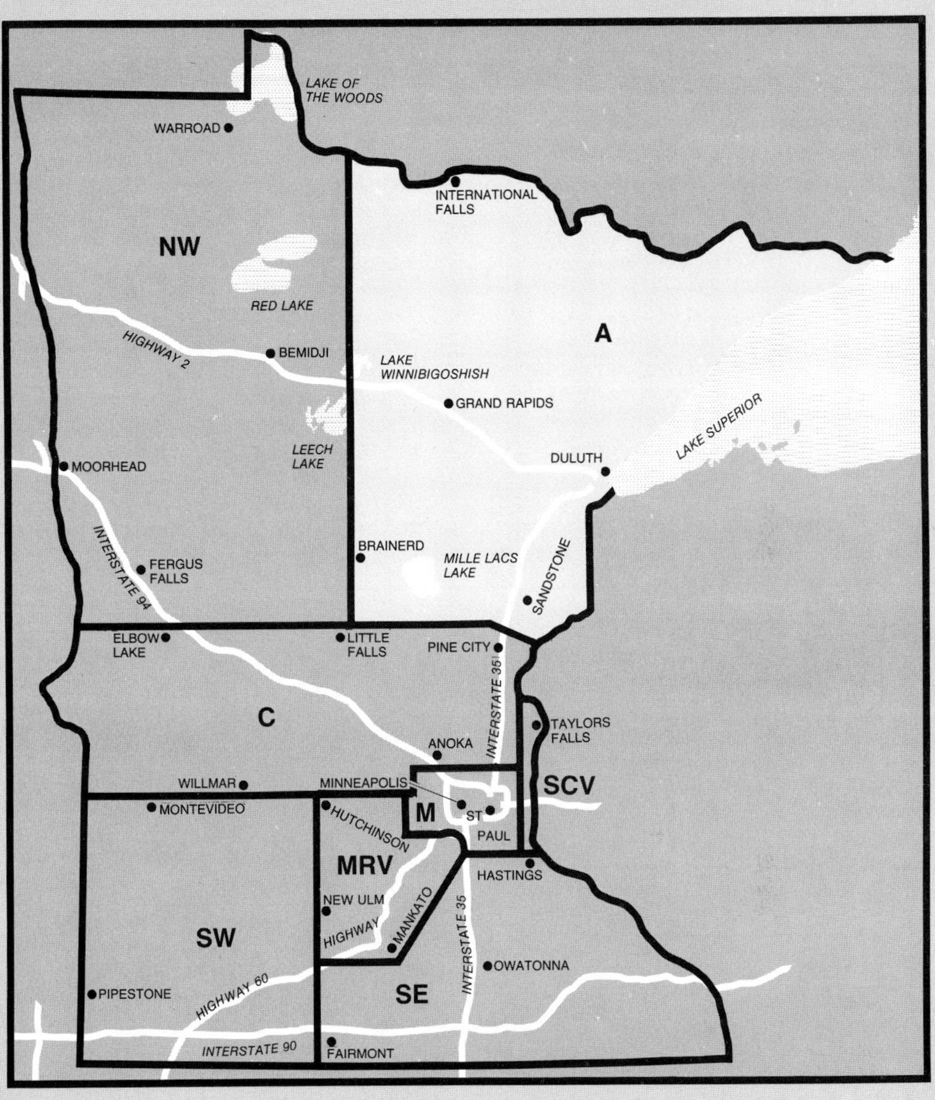

A-1 Aitkin

The town of Aitkin was established in 1870 by the Northern Pacific Railroad. The Aitkin County Courthouse (designed by Toltz, King, and Day, 1929) at 209 2nd Street Northwest (Highway 210) is a flat, boxy brick building with classical Beaux Arts attributes which are defined by very flat stone elements. The community library (1911) at 121 2nd Street Northwest is also classical, but it is much more sculptural with its recessed entrance portico and columns. In the commercial section of town, on the northwest corner of 2nd Street Northwest and Minnesota Avenue Northwest, is a two-story brick store and office building (c. 1914). Its element of distinction is the glossy violet blue and green terra-cotta ornament, whose patterns were derived from the work of Sullivan or Elmslie. At 220 Minnesota Avenue Northwest is the Rialto Theatre (c. 1935) in which Zigzag Moderne is casually applied to the building and its marquee. South on Minnesota Avenue (Highway 169) across the railroad tracks and to the west one discovers a Mission Revival Railroad Station (c. 1912) in brick with scalloped end gables and a tile roof. South of Aitkin are the Ak Sar Ben Gardens (Ak Sar Ben is Nebraska spelled backward), a 1920s folk folly with miniature stone castles and bridges. The Ak Sar Ben Gardens can be reached by driving west of Aitkin on Highway 210 to Highway 6, then south to Crow Wing County Road 14 (three miles east of Bay Lake).

A-2 Big Fork

This small railway village on the Big Fork River has a distinctly styled village hall (1936) located on Highway 38. The PWA composition of river stone houses the village offices, a meeting room, and the fire department. A sculpture of a lumberjack shouldering an ax stands at the entrance.

Village hall.

A-3 Brainerd

The town of Brainerd was platted in 1871 when it became apparent that the Northern Pacific Railroad was going to build its bridge over the Mississippi River at this site. Later in the same year the first train rolled into the newly established community. Brainerd's early economy was based first on the existence of the railroad and its shops, then on lumber and paper mills, and in the twentieth century on mining. Since the 1940s the resort trade has become an important factor in the economy of the city.

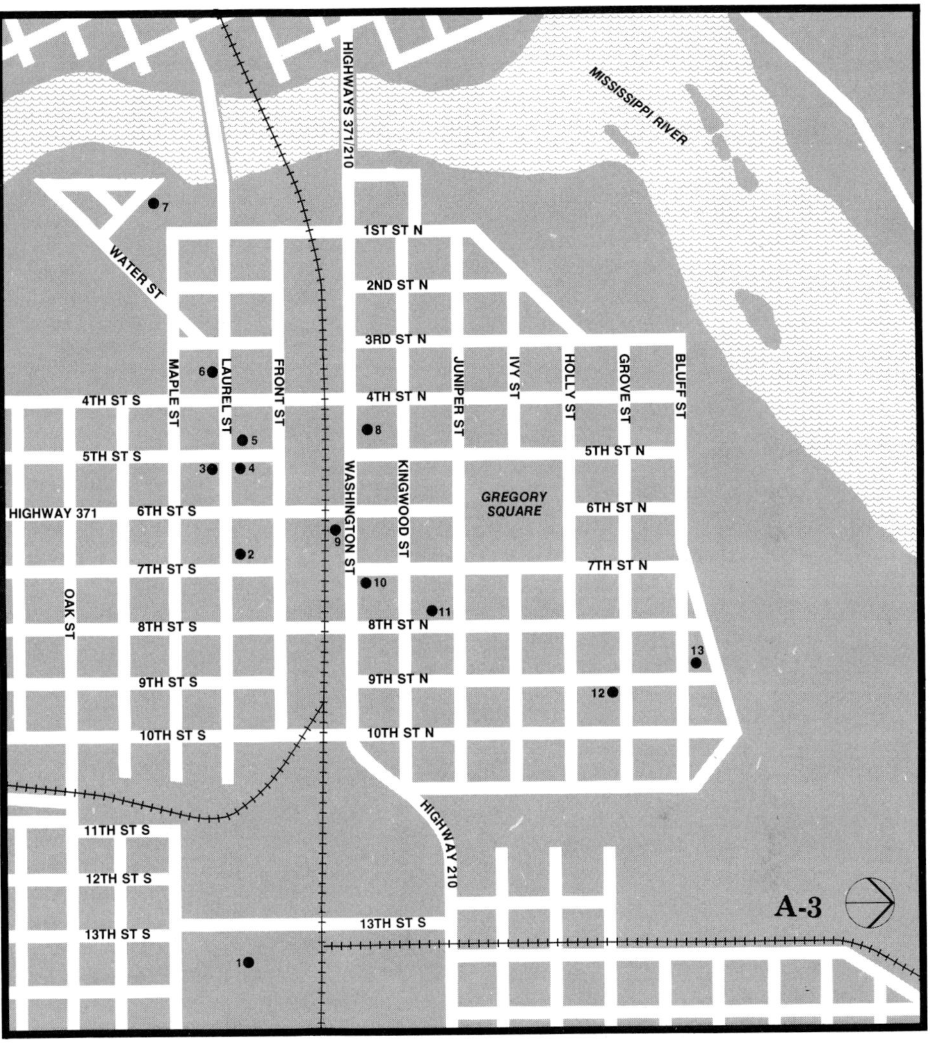

1 **Northern Pacific Headquarters Building and Shops,** 1871
East of 13th and Laurel Streets

A long two-story brick structure with a tower placed centrally at one end. Mildly Eastlake in design.

2 **Commercial Block,** c. 1900
Northwest corner 7th and Laurel Streets

A three-story brick block with a rounded corner. The theme is Romanesque, all smoothed out with turn-of-the-century classicism.

2 *Commercial Block.*

• 3 **Greyhound Bus Depot,** 1945
Stuart W. Leck, Sr., designer
506 Laurel Street

The Streamline Moderne at its most sophisticated. The building has long horizontal windows with rounded ends and a curved corner entrance, all beautifully proportioned.

4 **City Hall,** 1914
Alden and Harris
Northeast corner 5th and Laurel Streets

City Beautiful classical imagery used sparingly.

5 **Armory,** 1936
P. C. Bettenburg
Northwest corner 5th and Laurel Streets

PWA Moderne in the hoop-roofed auditorium and the adjacent two-story office block.

6 **Crow Wing County Courthouse,** 1919–20
Alden and Harris
320 Laurel Street

The usual City Beautiful scheme for a courthouse, with a rusticated basement (actually the first floor) and a two-story order of piers and columns above it — all well handled in this design with touches of sixteenth-century Italianate.

7 **North Star Apartments,** 1970
Miller and Melby
Southwest corner 1st and Maple Streets

A thin eleven-story International Style slab situated on the west bank of the Mississippi River. Perhaps vegetation will eventually help this complex for the elderly fit into its surroundings.

8 **City Jail** (now unused), 1871
North side Washington Street, east of 4th Street

A small Italianate building in brick (now painted). Note the roof brackets rendered in brick.

9 **Water Tower,** 1918–21
L. P. Wolff, engineer
Southeast corner Washington and 6th Streets (Highway 371)

This 141-foot tower represents an early use of reinforced concrete in a water storage facility. The tower was to be torn down in 1975, but it has been saved as a major landmark of the city.

10 **Carnegie Public Library,** 1904
206 7th Street N at Washington

As many small turn-of-the-century library buildings in Minnesota attest, Grecian styling was preferred for these citadels of culture. Here an Ionic-columned portico leads into a central domed space.

11 **House,** c. 1889
311 8th Street N

Queen Anne. The curved two-story corner projecting brick headers over the windows.

12 **House,** c. 1870s
624 9th Street N

A brick side-hall Italianate house with projecting brick headers over the windows.

13 **House,** late 1880s
811 Fir Street N

The Eastlake moving into the Queen Anne. A second-story rectangular bay emerges above as a tower.

A-4 Calumet

Another early twentieth-century village founded with the expansion of mining activities in the area. Calumet was laid out by the Powers Improvement Company in 1909. The business district consists mainly of simple clapboard buildings with false fronts. The brick village hall (1937) by J. C. Taylor is at the corner of Main Street and 2nd Avenue. The best part of its PWA Moderne design is in the lettering above the front door. One block south and one block east of the village hall is the clapboard, gable-roofed Duluth, Missabe, and Iron Range Depot (c. 1910).

A-5 Carlton

The village was first named Northern Pacific Junction because of its location at the junction of the Northern Pacific Railroad and the Lake Superior and Mississippi line. At the northeast corner of Chestnut Avenue and 2nd Street is the Carlton Auto Company Building, the original part of which was built in 1926. In the late 1930s it was remodeled and now the two piers are enclosed in glass brick. The parapet of the original building has a pattern of two automobile wheels worked into its design. The Carlton County Courthouse (designed by Clyde W. Kelly, 1922) situated at the northeast corner of 3rd Street and Walnut Avenue, is a very correct Beaux Arts building. A slightly recessed Ionic column formalizes the entrance elevation of the building.

Carlton County Courthouse.

A-6 Chisholm

In Chisholm (established in 1901) is a stone-walled school bus garage designed in 1940 by Elwin Berg (at 2nd Avenue Southwest between 4th and 5th Streets Southwest). This PWA building is much more traditional than many of the federally funded buildings of the 1930s. The center section of the building has a high-pitched gable roof, and there are flat-roofed wings on each side. On the street side deeply cut-in windows are organized into horizontal bands. One-half mile south of Chisholm on Highway 169 (just east of the highway) at the now-abandoned Glenn open-pit iron mine is the new Iron Range Interpretative Center. This building, designed by Architectural Resources, Inc., in 1975–76, consists of a cut-into concrete box and a Miesian cantilevered glassed-in observation bridge.

School bus garage.

A-7 Cloquet

Cloquet is the only American community that can boast of having a service station designed by Frank Lloyd Wright. The station (1956–57) is located at the southeast corner of Highways 33 and 45. Its hovering witch's-hat roof is reminiscent of Wright's much earlier designs at Lake Tahoe (1920s) and Broadacre City (1930s). The busy complexity of the building and its details is set against an equally busy background of pumps, oil products, soft-drink machines, and automobiles. Just off the corner of Highway 33 and Stanley Avenue is Wright's Lindholm House, "Mäntylä" (1952), in which dramatically cantilevered gable roofs are set upon walls of concrete block.

Service station.

A-8 Coleraine

Coleraine was planned as a model village for the employees of the Oliver Iron Mining Company and was platted in 1905. The following year the Duluth, Missabe, and Northern Railroad reached the town. At the northwest corner of Cole and Olcott Streets is the Episcopal Church of the Good Shepherd (1908). Its walls up to the eaves are of logs, and the high-pitched gable ends are shingled. In design it is Craftsman with Gothic overtones. Farther down Cole Street at its intersection with Gayley Street (northwest corner) is the First Methodist Episcopal Church (also 1908). The lower body of this church is of stone, and the gable ends are shingled. At the northeast corner of Cole Street and Clemsen Street is the Beaux Arts Carnegie Public Library (1909), which has an octagonal drum with clerestory lighting and an angled corner entrance.

Episcopal Church of the Good Shepherd.

A-9 Duluth

Duluth, the third largest city in Minnesota, enjoys the most romantic and picturesque location of any city in the state. The ruggedness of its hillside location, the sheer granite cliffs dropping precipitously to the cold blue lake, the coniferous forests and sharp rock outcrops — represent perfectly what the eighteenth-century English landscape architects referred to as "the horrid and the sublime."

The central section of Duluth was platted in 1856, and after several schemes were considered and rejected the gridiron was finally laid out parallel to the lakeshore. East Duluth was eventually platted in 1870, and slowly the residential streetcar suburbs pushed their way up the lakeshore — (Congdon Park, Lakeside, and Lester Park) — and also somewhat inland forming the suburbs of Kenwood, Glen Avon, Hunter's Park, Morley Heights, and Woodland. To the southwest the city eventually absorbed a number of originally independent communities located along the west bank of the St. Louis River. These included Fond du Lac (1856), New Duluth (1890), Gary (1916), Morgan Park (1914–16), Ironton (1889–93), Oneota (1856), Rice's Point (1858), and Riverside (1916). These communities were oriented to industry and shipping and also provided housing for workers. The area up the shore to the northeast has always been a middle-middle-class and upper-middle-class suburbia.

Duluth, much more than the Twin Cities, has been a city of economic booms and busts. Its first boom was during the years 1870–73, when the Lake Superior and Mississippi Railroad (now the Burlington Northern) was built to Duluth, and when the canal was dug through Minnesota Point (1871), thereby opening up St. Louis Bay as a major harbor. The bust of Jay Cooke's financial empire in 1873 sent Duluth downhill, and the city did not make a comeback until the late 1880s. The years from 1886 through 1920 were buoyant and highly optimistic ones for the community. In the mid-1920s, for example, it was forecast that by 1950 the city would have a population of half-a-million (a forecast somewhat off the mark, for by the mid-1970s the city's population was only about 100,000).

Like the Twin Cities, Duluth has developed an extensive system of parks and boulevards over the years. When the city was initially laid out in 1856, two small public squares were created. As subsequent additions were made to the city, parks of various sizes were acquired. The major period of acquisition occurred during the City Beautiful years, 1900–10; during this period Chester Park (1905), Lake Front Park (1907), and Congdon Park (1908) were obtained. Other important parks were planned and developed in the years that followed; these included Kitchi Gammi Park, Lincoln Park, Enger Park, and others. (Several of these parks are now joined together by the twenty-nine-mile Skyline Parkway.)

Along with the State Capitol complex in St. Paul Duluth presents the fullest realization of the turn-of-the-century City Beautiful movement in Minnesota. The Duluth Civic Center, comprising the St. Louis County Courthouse (1908–1909), the Duluth City Hall (1928), and the Federal Building (1920), is one of the most impressive Classical civic centers in the country. The Duluth Civic Center and its counterpart in San Francisco also mark a high point in the work of the master of the City Beautiful movement, Daniel H. Burnham.

Because of its economic connections with Chicago and cities in the east, Duluth has kept up with the latest in architectural styles much more than Minneapolis and St. Paul have. A number of America's major designers — ranging from Daniel Burnham to Marcel Breuer — have designed business blocks, civic buildings, churches, clubs, and private dwellings in Duluth. This is especially true in its residential architecture in the eastern suburban area, which contains more architecturally impressive dwellings than any similar area in the Twin Cities.

For a much richer view of Duluth's architecture, the reader is referred to one of the best city guides yet published, *Duluth's Legacy: Volume 1, Architecture*, by James Allen Scott. The guide was published in 1974 by Duluth's Department of Research and Planning.

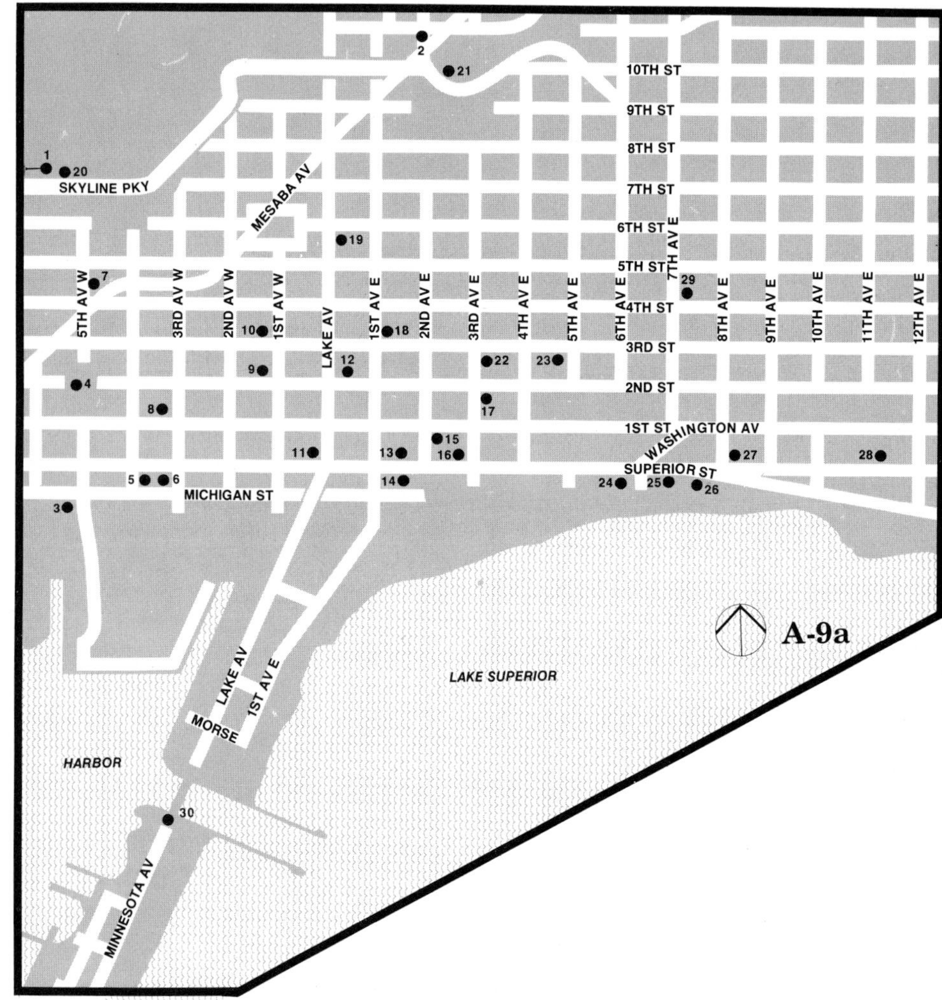

A-9a Central Duluth

The core area of the city contains the civic center, the major business blocks, and on the hillside the old residential district with its early churches and schools. At the west end of the central district there are docks along the Duluth Harbor basin, a band of railroad yards, business buildings between Michigan Street and Fourth Street, and another area of old residences, churches, and schools to the north. The projected northeastern extension of the freeway (Highway 35) now threatens much of the waterfront area along Lake Superior itself.

1 **Enger Tower,** 1939
A. Reinhold Melander
Enger Park, off Skyline Parkway and 18th Avenue W

A five-story stone tower and observation platform. The forty-foot blue granite tower is a landmark for the entire downtown area. In style PWA — back to the primitive.

2 **Airport Terminal,** 1974
Architectural Resources
North of Highway 53, 5 miles north of downtown Duluth

A large-scale shed-roofed structure within an earth berm. There is underground parking in the berm.

2 Airport Terminal.

3 **Union Depot,** 1892
Peabody and Stearns
South corner Michigan Street and 5th Avenue W

Medieval, early Renaissance/ Chateauesque styling for a railroad passenger depot, mildly picturesque.

4 **Civic Center,** 1908–30
Daniel H. Burnham and Company
1st Street W between 4th and 6th Avenues W

The scheme for the public square, closed in on three sides by public buildings and open toward the lake, came from the Burnham office. This office also produced the Beaux Arts St. Louis County Courthouse (1908–1909), which forms the center of the horseshoe. In the square facing the courthouse is the Soldiers' and Sailors' monument designed by Cass Gilbert (c. 1921) with a sculpture by Paul Bartlett. The city hall next door was built in 1928 (Thomas J. Shefchik), and the Federal Building across the street was completed in 1930 (United States General Services Administration). All three are rather ponderous examples of the Beaux Arts — each has a rusticated ground floor with a mezzanine and a large-scale order of columns — but the total effect of the three buildings and the park is impressive. Individually the three buildings are not the best advertisements for the City Beautiful movement.

5 **Medical Arts Office Building,** 1932–33
Ernest R. Erickson and Company
324 Superior Street W

The American Perpendicular Style of the early 1930s via Raymond Hood's *New York Daily News* Building (1930). Stylized sculptured heads of Native Americans make the building Minnesotan.

6 **Alworth Building,** 1910
Daniel H. Burnham and Company
306 Superior Street W

A narrow sixteen-story skyscraper with Sullivanesque emphasis on the vertical and classical detailing to make it respectable. The lower floors have been modernized.

7 **Munger Terrace,** 1891–92
Traphagen and Fitzpatrick
405 Mesaba Avenue

Eight adjoining townhouses (of sixteen rooms each) treated as a single Romanesque Revival pile.

8 **Board of Trade Building,** 1894–95
Traphagen and Fitzpatrick
301 1st Street W

A formidable Richardsonian Romanesque pile in brick and stone. The building seems even more severe since the removal of its original entablature and cornice.

9 **Carnegie Public Library,** 1902
Adolf F. Rudolph
Southwest corner 1st Avenue W and 2nd Street

A Beaux Arts library building with a central Ionic-columned portico and a low dome.

10 **Marvin House,** c. 1882
123 3rd Street W

Exuberant Queen Anne with a tower, moon-gate openings onto the porches, and other ingredients of the style.

11 **Wirth Building,** 1886
Attrib. Oliver G. Traphagen
13 Superior Street W

A three-story stone commercial building which plays with both the Gothic and Romanesque.

12 **Old Duluth Central High School,** 1891–92
Emmet S. Palmer and Lucien P. Hall
Northwest corner Lake Avenue and 2nd Street

The tower of the high school, like the tower of the Minneapolis Courthouse, was based on Henry H. Richardson's much publicized tower for the Allegheny County Courthouse in Pittsburgh (1884–87). The high school boasts extensive sculptures, some of which are representational, others based on vegetation. Another Romanesque school building in Duluth is the Liberty Public High School (1887) at 226 North 1st Avenue East.

13 **Oppel Block,** c. 1885
Attrib. Oliver G. Traphagen
115 Superior Street E

Richardsonian Romanesque employed in a three-story commercial block.

14 **City Hall and Jail** (now office building), 1889
Oliver G. Traphagen
126 and 132 Superior Street E

Here the Richardsonian Romanesque has been appreciably modified by a sixteenth-century French bay window unit.

15 **Orpheum Theatre,** 1910
J. E. O. Pridmore
East side 2nd Avenue E, north of Superior Street E

The purity of the Greek made unreal in the hands of a Beaux Arts enthusiast.

16 **Hotel Duluth,** 1925
Martin Tullgren and Sons
227 Superior Street E

A 1920s version of the Beaux Arts for a 500-room hotel. Renaissance classical details richly displayed on the ground level and in the entablature and the cornice.

17 **First Presbyterian Church,** 1891
Traphagen and Fitzpatrick
300 2nd Street E
Richardsonian Romanesque with a massive corner tower.

18 **Firehouse No. 1** (not in use), c. 1890
Traphagen and Fitzpatrick
Northwest corner 1st Avenue E and 3rd Street

The fire engines were housed behind the large Romanesque arched openings at each side of the entrance.

19 **House,** c. 1887
520 Lake Avenue N

Queen Anne with a thin, fragile Eastlake quality.

20 **Cook House,** 1900
I. Vernon Hill
501 Skyline Parkway W

Duluth's gifted turn-of-the-century architect used the Shingle Style (Queen Anne/Colonial Revival) in this hillside residence. The wide triangular gable displays a single Palladian window. The walls, stairs, terraces of native stone and the stone sheathing of the lower floor relate the building to its site.

20 *Cook House.*

21 First United Methodist Church, 1965–66
Pietro Belluschi; Melander, Fugelso, and Associates
230 Skyline Parkway E

Four stone corner volumes appear to support a copper pyramid with folded gables along its eave. The building is thinly sheathed in granite. As a design the building is midway between the quiet of the elder Saarinen's designs and the usual agitated jazz of post-World War II church architecture.

21 *First United Methodist Church.*

22 Adas Israel Synagogue, 1902
302 3rd Street E

Two low square towerlike forms hug the somewhat stubby gabled central volume. Two tiny minarets at the corner of each of the low towers suggest the mysteries of the eastern Mediterranean.

23 Duluth Clinic, 1974
Setter, Leach, and Lindstrom
400 3rd Street E

A five-story cut-into box. The cut-in windows are arranged in repeated horizontal bands (International Style).

24 Fitger's Brewery, 1890
Traphagen and Fitzpatrick
600 Superior Street E

The spirit is Medieval, conveyed by the rusticated masonry surface, the strong corner quoining, and the arched windows.

25 Northwest Oil Company Service Station, 1921
706 Superior Street E

A City Beautiful service station which has lost its dramatic cantilevered canopy.

25 *Northwest Oil Company Station.*

26 Hartley Office Building, 1914
Bertram G. Goodhue
740 Superior Street E

An example of the work of Goodhue in the period when he began to strip historic forms of their many details and to return to the basics. In this instance the historical form is Elizabethan Tudor in brick.

26 *Hartley Office Building.*

27 **Kitchi Gammi Club,** 1912
Cram, Goodhue, and Ferguson
831 Superior Street E

English Tudor in brick, with a classical Georgian tinge but not as much of it as in Goodhue's Hartley Office Building (1914).

28 **Loeb House,** 1900–1901
John T. Wangenstein
1123 Superior Street E

Turn-of-the-century Colonial Revival. It states its classical pedigree strongly in the two-story porch with Corinthian columns. At the side an angled bay with lunette windows and engaged piers projects into the garden.

29 **Halkman Store and Apartments,** 1889
701–705 4th Street E

A two-story Queen Anne/Richardsonian Romanesque building in brick.

30 **Aerial Lift Bridge,** 1905, 1929–30
Southeast end Lake Avenue at canal

The first aerial lift bridge was built by the Modern Structural Steel Company from a design by the engineer C. P. Turner (and Thomas F. McGilvray). The bridge was rebuilt in 1929–30 by the Kansas City Bridge Company from designs by the engineering firm of Harrington, Howard, and Ash.

A-9b West Duluth and the West End

The docks and other industrial development are concentrated within the first five or six blocks adjacent to the St. Louis River, and the residential developments are laid out above Grand Avenue. Much of the housing was built for workers in the adjacent industrial/shipping area. The freeway (Highway 35) now plows its way through the industrial section.

1 **Denfeld High School,** 1925–26
Holstead and Sullivan
West corner 44th Avenue W and 4th Street

A highly original version of English Collegiate Gothic, especially in the central tower with its pyramid roof.

2 **Duluth, Missabe, and Iron Range Railroad Ore Docks,** 1915
Southeast end 35th Avenue W

The docks (2,304 feet long) are not only impressive engineering works, but the contrast of their solid and open forms creates a highly abstract sculptural pattern jutting into the lake.

3 **Park Shelter, Lincoln Park,** c. 1934
25th Avenue W at 3rd Street W

A stone PWA building with twin towers, early Romanesque in spirit.

A-9c Fond du Lac, Morgan Park, and Riverside

Although many of the communities along the St. Louis River were platted as early as the 1850s, the industrial and commercial buildings and workers' housing date from the 1890s and later. One of the most interesting of these communities is the company town of Morgan Park (1914–16), which was laid out by the Minneapolis planning firm of Morell and Nichols, with Owen Brainard as the consulting engineer, and the Chicago architectural firm of George S. Dean and Arthur Dean. The housing and other facilities were for workers employed at the nearby United States Steel Corporation plant. The overall plan of Morgan Park is a combination of Beaux Arts axialism, the grid scheme, and the irregular curvilinear patterns of an English landscape garden. Civic amenities — parks, schools, recreational buildings, playgrounds, general stores, and garages — were provided. Many of the dwellings were laid out in parallel rows with a band of individual garden plots between them. Northeast of Morgan Park the company communities of Gary and Riverside provided similar amenities but not in such profusion.

1 **Peter J. Peterson House,** 1867
13328 3rd Street W (Fond du Lac)

A two-story, mildly Greek Revival dwelling. The ground-floor porch and other elements were added at a later date. The Peterson House is the oldest dwelling in the Duluth area.

2 **Atlas Iron and Brass Works,** c. 1880
South end Commonwealth Avenue, south of Highway 23 (New Duluth)

A three-story brick building covered with a mansard roof.

3 **Smith House,** 1892
218 94th Avenue W (New Duluth)

Standard Queen Anne with an imaginative octagonal bay-tower.

4 **United Protestant Church,** 1915–17
Dean and Dean
88th Avenue W and Arbor Street (Morgan Park)

English Gothic in concrete block (in imitation of smooth stone). The design is stripped of all but the stylistically essential details.

5 **Workers' Housing,** 1915–17
Dean and Dean
Morgan Park

A variety of housing for workers, ranging from boarding houses to single-family dwellings, is offered here. All of the houses are built of concrete block. As designs they are adequate but certainly not inspired. Dean and Dean did design in the Prairie Style, and there are occasional suggestions of this style in their buildings in Morgan Park. The best examples of the types of housing available in Morgan Park can be found on 88th Avenue West and along the 1400 block of 90th Avenue West.

6 **St. Mary-Margaret Catholic Church,** 1915–17
Dean and Dean
1467 88th Avenue W (Morgan Park)

A change of pace for these architects. The church is Mission Revival in white stucco. The parsonage combines the Mission Revival Style with the vertical fenestration and the gabled parapets which we associate with the work of George W. Maher.

6 St. Mary-Margaret Catholic Church.

7 **Workers' Housing,** 1917–18
Cato Avenue (Riverside)

The McDougall-Duluth Shipping Company utilized the Craftsman bungalow image for workers' housing. Most of the houses have been altered over the years.

A-9d East End to Congdon Park

The east side of Duluth, along the lake, was platted in 1870, and in the years that followed additions were made along the lake shore to and including Lester Park; inland this section of the city proceeds north producing such suburbs as Glen Avon, Hunter's Park, Morley Heights, and Woodland. All of these middle-class and upper-middle-class districts were connected to the downtown area by an electric streetcar system by 1920. Close to the lake (through 26th Avenue East) a large number of the houses and their grounds are upper middle class and extensive; beyond 26th Avenue East, on and around Branch Street, are numerous middle-middle-class Period houses of the 1920s and a few from the late 1930s. This area of Duluth has, as one would expect of such a district, many parks and much vegetation, and the irregularity of the terrain tends to dominate the houses.

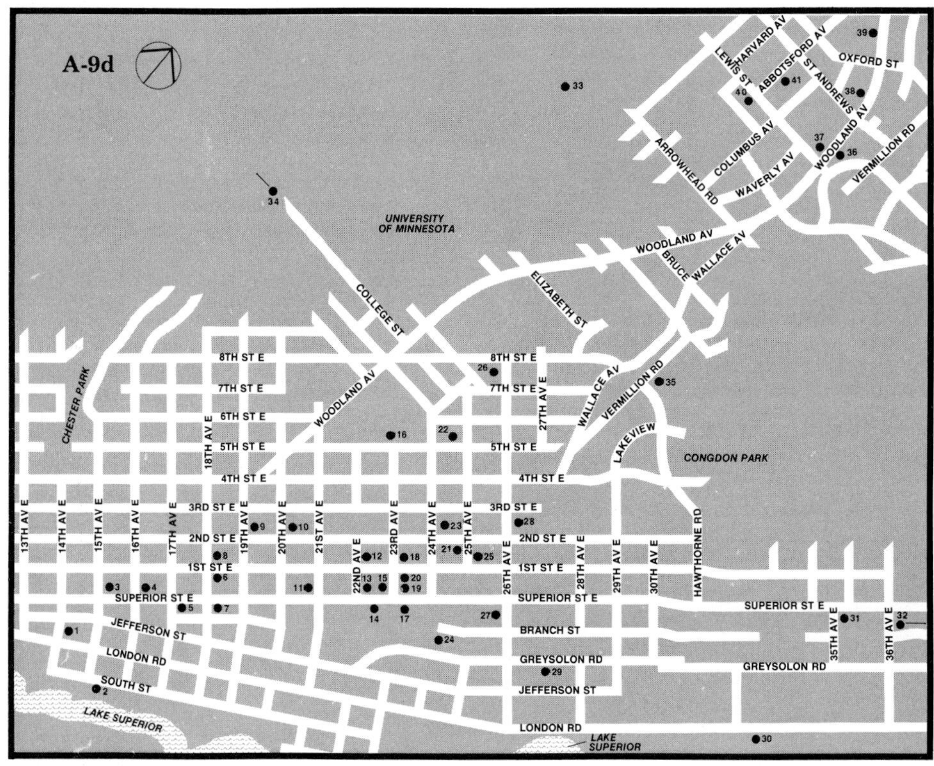

1 **Cottage,** 1891
1424 Jefferson Street

A narrow one-and-a-half-story cottage in shingle and clapboard with voussoired windows.

2 **Endion Passenger Depot,** 1899
Gearhard A. Tenbusch and I. Vernon Hill
South side of South Street at end of 15th Avenue E

A small, picturesque suburban station in stone and brick; Romanesque in flavor.

• 3 **Traphagen (Double) House,** 1892
Traphagen and Fitzpatrick
1511 Superior Street E

Richardsonian Romanesque in appropriately correct red sandstone.

4 **Elston House,** 1893
1609 Superior Street E

Queen Anne/Colonial Revival in shingle, clapboard, and stone with a Palladian window in the gable bay-tower and paired classical columns.

5 **St. Paul's Episcopal Church,** 1912
Cram, Goodhue, and Ferguson
1710 Superior Street E

English Rural Gothic in finely cut stone. A crenelated tower occurs over the crossing of the nave and the transept.

6 **First Unitarian Universalist Church,** 1910
1802 1st Street E

A tiny, almost domestic Craftsman Medieval church in stone and half-timbering.

7 **Joseph Sellwood House,** 1902
Palmer, Hall, and Hunt
16 South 18th Avenue E

A romantic and picturesque combination of images in stone — Colonial Revival, Chateauesque, and Craftsman.

7 Joseph Sellwood House.

8 **Endion School,** 1890
Adolf F. Rudolph
1803 1st Street E

A severe essay in the Richardsonian Romanesque. It is saved from being pedestrian by its entrace and tower and its grouping of thin dormers.

9 **Richard M. Sellwood House,** 1903
Kees and Colburn
1931 2nd Street E

The Colonial Revival as a Georgian mansion.

10 **Burgess House,** 1904
W. T. Bray or I. Vernon Hill
2019 2nd Street E

A run-of-the mill two-story gabled Colonial Revival dwelling which becomes exotic in the almost Art Nouveau balustrade of sawed wood on the porch and the balcony.

11 **Crosby House,** 1902
I. Vernon Hill
2029 Superior Street E

A two-story stone house with a low-pitched hipped shingle roof. An exotic overtone is contributed by the elaborately carved stone balcony-entrance. The ornament itself is Richardsonian/Sullivanesque, but the overall effect is reminiscent of Viennese Art Nouveau.

11 Crosby House.

12 **McDougall House,** 1910
Bray and Nystrom
2201 1st Street E

Somewhat Colonial Revival, but the central dormer and the thin engaged piers that project into it point to the work of George W. Maher and others.

13 **Brewer House,** 1902
2215 Superior Street E

The Colonial Revival via late eighteenth-century American Georgian and the Federal Style of about 1800.

14 **Hill House,** 1902
I. Vernon Hill
2220 Superior Street E

A peculiar grouping of details and volumes derived from the English half-timber tradition. Some of the maneuvering of elements in this house designed for Hill's own use is similar to the work of the West Coast architect Bernard Maybeck.

• 15 **House,** 1903
2219 Superior Street E

The late Queen Anne Shingle Style. The central staircase tower with its pattern of small-scaled square windows is remarkably close to the San Francisco designs of Ernest Coxhead.

16 **Duluth Normal School,** 1898
Palmer, Hall, and Hunt
North side 5th Street E and 23rd Avenue E

Beaux Arts (Renaissance) but still within a Romanesque framework.

17 **Patrick House,** 1901
I. Vernon Hill
2306 Superior Street E

A double-gable composition hovers over a tower bay and rough stone walls; in style, Medieval mixed with Craftsman. One of Duluth's most exciting buildings.

17 Patrick House.

18 **Cotton House,** 1906
Kees and Colburn
2309 1st Street E

The image of a Renaissance palace — eminently respectable, authentic, and dry.

19 **Ordean House,** 1905
Palmer and Hunt
2307 Superior Street E

Colonial Revival in brick on a large scale. The image is more English Georgian than American.

20 **Olcott House,** 1904
W. T. Bray
2316 1st Street E

Colonial Revival via the Georgian with a semicircular two-story entrance porch and a grand entrance with leaded sidelights and a curved leaded transom.

21 **Heimbach House,** 1923
2432 2nd Street E

A stone English Cottage Style house with a rolled roof in imitation of thatching.

22 **Loeb House,** 1923
2407 5th Street E

Spanish Colonial Revival (really Mediterranean).

23 **Clark House,** 1910
Bray and Nystrom
2423 2nd Street E

This version of Frank Lloyd Wright's 1906 *Ladies Home Journal* house is in stucco with wood trim and low-pitched hipped roofs.

24 **Pattison House,** 1914
William A. Hunt
2429 Greysolon Road

American Colonial in the brick Georgian image with a two-story semicircular entrance porch and a gambrel roof.

25 **Meyers House,** 1909–10
Bray and Nystrom
2505 1st Street E

The Chateauesque rendered in rough stone.

26 **Tweed House** (now residence of the Provost, University of Minnesota, Duluth)
Frederick W. Perkins
2531 7th Street E

The sense of this two-story brick house is Mediterranean.

27 **Barnes House,** 1906
William A. Hunt
25 South 26th Avenue E

Southern California's Mission Revival with a long segmented arched porch and porte cochere.

28 Williams House (now home of Dominican Sisters), 1912
Frederick W. Perkins
2601 2nd Street E
English Tudor in brick.

• **29 Starkey House,** 1955
Marcel Breuer; Herbert Beckhard
2620 Greysolon Road E
The post-World War II International Style in a group of attached boxes suspended over a masonry base. The house is impressively detailed and beautifully maintained.

30 Congdon House, 1907–1908
Clarence H. Johnston, Sr.
3300 London Road E
A brick Elizabethan manor, appropriately set in its own wooded park.

31 Thompson House, 1924–25
Howard VanDoren Shaw
3500 Superior Street E
A Tudor house in stone, radiating art and sophistication. The historic parts tend to exist as fragments attached to the simplified and rationalized series of picturesque volumes.

32 Hartley House, 1915
Bertram G. Goodhue
3800 Superior Street E
This English Medieval dwelling has a hint of the work of Charles F. A. Voysey and Edwin Lutyens about it.

33 Student Housing Facility, University of Minnesota, 1974
Architectural Alliance
Northwest corner Woodland Avenue and College Avenue E
A well-disciplined exercise in brick with horizontal ribbon windows. The four-story units are somewhat cold and impersonal for Duluth. Also on the campus note the bronze sculpture "Sieur Duluth" by Jacques Lipchitz and the new athletic facility in weathering steel (Parker, Klein Associates, 1975).

33 Student Housing Facility, University of Minnesota.

34 College of St. Scholastica, 1928, 1937–38
O'Meara and Hills; G. E. Quick
College Avenue and Kenwood Avenue
English Tudor in stone. Visually most successful from a distance.

35 Ames House, 1912
Frederick G. German
1618 Vermilion Road
A wonderfully loose Medieval English composition with a corner bay-tower in brick, half-timbering, stone, and leaded glass windows.

36 Glen Avon Passenger Station (now a residence), 1892
2102 Woodland Avenue
A playful and happy Queen Anne cottage, designed originally as a small suburban waiting station for the street railway.

36 Glen Avon Passenger Station.

37 Glen Avon Presbyterian Church, 1905
German and Lignell
2105 Woodland Avenue

English rural Gothic as a Craftsman product in stone with a crenelated tower at one side.

38 Morterud House, 1909
John Wangenstein
2216 Woodland Avenue

Colonial Revival in clapboard with an order of giant Corinthian columns supporting the front entrance porch and the balcony.

39 Hunter House, 1892
Ronald M. Hunter
2317 Woodland Avenue

A stone cottage which is Medieval in image, although not specifically Gothic or Romanesque.

40 House, 1911
Bray and Nystrom
236 Lewis Street

A Prairie house based on Frank Lloyd Wright's *Ladies Home Journal* scheme (1906).

41 Kreager House, 1916
2114 Abbotsford Avenue

A Prairie design. The slightly curved and upturned dormer and the hooded entrance roof suggest the personal style of George W. Maher.

A-9e Lakeside to Lester Park

Along the shore of the lake, London Road follows the east line of the lake; but inland a north/south, east/west grid pattern was imposed. At the southwest corner of the area the Northland Country Club provides extensive greenery, and at the northeast side Lester Park serves a similar function along the Lester River. As in Congdon Park and the East End the natural setting with its trees and the lake forms the dominant note.

1 C. W. Peterson House, 1910
Peter Olsen
4131 Superior Street E

A one-and-a-half-story Craftsman bungalow with an extensive glass area on the ground floor. Note the small V-shaped dormer in the second-floor gable.

2 Russell House, c. 1910
W. T. Bray
4440 London Road

In the design of this house (as in several others) Bray seems to have been inspired by George W. Maher.

3 House, 1938
Hugo W. Wold
4631 London Road

Streamline Moderne in rough stucco with rounded corners, corner windows, and a flat parapeted roof.

4 Wells House, c. 1890
4811 McCulloch Street at London Road

The two corner-bay towers — one with a bulbous mushroom roof, the other in the form of a segmented cone — introduce the variety and the movement which were always considered essential in the Queen Anne Style.

5 Two Residences, 1890
4840 and 4842 London Road

Two adjoining Queen Anne houses built by the Lakeside Land Company (the developers of this area of the lakeshore). The plans of the two houses have been reversed, and the builder has introduced minor variations in the two street façades.

6 House, 1938
Hugo W. Wold
4901 London Road

At the end of the 1930s designers often combined the Moderne and the Colonial as in this two-story residence. The result is the best of the past and the near-future.

7 House, 1950
Otto M. Olsen
4920 London Road

A clean and hygienic essay in the Streamline Moderne.

8 House, c. 1914
5718 London Road

A very individual example of the Prairie Style. Two pierlike forms narrowly close in the entrance and the window above it and then penetrate through the gable roof.

9 Lester River Fish Hatchery, 1885–87
South side London Road at 60th Avenue E

A two-story Eastlake design. Note especially the exposed frame of the street entrance with its horizontal, vertical, and diagonal patterns.

A-10 Ely

Ely, situated in the heart of the Superior National Forest, was platted in 1887. In the following year the Duluth and Iron Range Railroad connected the city with the rest of the state. Mining and tourism have over the years provided the community's economic basis. The city hall (1928) was designed by William M. Ingemann. This small but monumental PWA Moderne structure at 2nd Street East and Chapman houses the city offices and the fire department. On Highway 169 between 2nd and 3rd Streets East is a run-of-the-mill Streamline theatre building (the State Theatre, c. 1936), and close by, on the corner of 2nd Street East and Highway 169, is an impressive service station (c. 1930). Two Zigzag Moderne (Art Deco) towers draw attention to this double-pier station.

A-11 Eveleth

The mining town of Eveleth was founded in 1894, but six years later iron ore was found under the town and so the town was moved to a new location. • The manual training school (1914) designed by Bray and Nystrom is a fine example of a Prairie Style building. Its façades are articulated with banks of square engaged piers which have horizontal bands for the capitals. The school is on the east side of Roosevelt Avenue (northeast corner) between Jones and Jackson Streets. Downtown at 311 Grant Avenue is an excellent example of the Streamline Moderne in Connie's Bar and Lounge (early 1940s) with its circular window, curved glass-brick wall, and original neon lettering. Two miles south of the Highway 37 turnoff to Eveleth (on the west side of Highway 53) is the new Iron Range Resources and Rehabilitation Commission Headquarters (1975). This building, designed by Damberg and Peck, is a single-story structure sheathed in wood with a striking large-scale circular window on the left; on the right offices with horizontal windows are arranged in a sawtooth fashion.

Connie's Bar and Lounge.

A-12 Finlayson

The Finlayson railroad station, situated south of Highway 18, was built in 1870, and the simple board-and-batten building, together with its wood platform, wood railings, and signals, presents a rare remaining image of the nineteenth century. Other nineteenth-century buildings are to be found on the street which runs parallel to and one block south of Highway 18. These include a hotel with a two-story front porch (c. 1890) and a clapboard commercial building with a well-preserved storefront facing the street (c. 1890). On a street perpendicular to Highway 18 and one block west of the railroad station is a store (1912) with a two-story front of pressed metal and a small one-story commercial building with a simple gable-roofed structure hidden behind the false front (c. 1890). North of Highway 18 on the same street is the brick St. Joseph's Catholic Church (1894), which in its design makes a mild nod to the Gothic. The one element of modernity in the town is the combined village hall, fire hall, and bar (c. 1940) located between the railroad station and the hotel. This little brick building with its horizontal and porthole windows applies the Streamline Moderne to its packaging needs.

Commercial building.

A-13 Grand Marais

In 1927 the Brule Land and Outing Company developed the Naniboujou Club as an exclusive private resort fifteen miles east of Grand Marais. The company obtained three thousand acres, including one mile of frontage on Lake Superior, and options on an additional eight thousand acres. The club had facilities to serve a thousand members, and Jack Dempsey, Ring Lardner, and Babe Ruth were among its charter members. With the coming of the Depression the grandiose scheme was abandoned. • The main clubhouse (1928–29) was designed by the Duluth firm of Holstead and Sullivan. The interior of the rustic shingled lodge is brightly painted in red, orange, yellow, green, and blue. Some of the painted patterns are Art Deco (Moderne), others are a sort of Alice-in-Wonderland rendition of stylized animals and birds.

On Highway 61 just east of Grand Marais is the St. Francis Xavier Church (1895), a remarkable carpenter's composition of gabled volumes on a single axis.

A-14 Grand Portage

The Northwest Fur Company established an important post here in the late 1700s. By 1798 the post included sixteen log buildings surrounded by a high wood stockade. The complex is now the Grand Portage National Monument, and the main hall (which may have been built as early as 1778) and several other buildings have been reconstructed. The main hall is a one-and-a-half-story log structure which conveys a sense of French Canadian architecture, especially in its broad front porch and its small gabled dormers.

Main hall, Grand Portage National Monument.

A-15 Grand Rapids

The village of Grand Rapids was incorporated in 1891, a year after the Duluth and Winnipeg Railroad reached the community. Timber and specifically the production of paper are its prime economic base. A dam on the Mississippi River provides power for the paper mill and other energy needs. The central and major portion of the town is located north of the river, and several lakes (Forest Lake, Hale Lake, and Crystal Lake) form the northern boundaries of the town. Fourteen miles southeast of town on County Road 3 (along the river) is the 1897 Splithand School (1897), one of the few log schoolhouses still surviving. Twenty miles west of Grand Rapids on Highway 2 at Ball Club is the Big Fish Supper Club, which advertises its wares with a gigantic sculpture of a fish; the building is a simple clapboard structure with a false front.

1 **Itasca County Courthouse,** 1950
Jyring and Jurenes
Northwest corner 4th Street E and 2nd Avenue E

Post–World War II Moderne with band windows and a framed entrance with glass inside; the entrance canopy is separated from the building. The words "Itasca County Courthouse" are worked into the entrance railing.

2 **Great Northern Passenger Depot,** 1928–29?
Southwest corner 4th Street W and Pokegama Avenue N

According to histories of Grand Rapids the original depot (1891–92) designed by Cass Gilbert was destroyed by fire in 1893. The existing station, probably built in 1928–29, is of very late Craftsman design and has wide overhanging gable ends with bracketed struts. The gable ends are half-timbered, and the lower part of the building is sheathed in clapboard.

3 **Standard Oil Service Station,** c. 1930
Northeast corner 4th Street E and Pokegama Avenue N

The Spanish Colonial Revival image was frequently employed in Standard Oil stations at the end of the 1920s. Glazed brick, false tile roofs, and scalloped parapets characterized the style. This station is one of the few still around which remains unaltered.

3 *Standard Oil Service Station.*

4 **Old Central High School,** 1895
Northwest corner 4th Street W and Pokegama Avenue N

Richardsonian Romanesque in brick with minimal stone trim.

5 **Village Hall,** 1928–29
Holstead and Sullivan
Southeast corner Pokegama Avenue N and 5th Street E

Almost, but not quite, an example of American Expressionism. The clustered engaged piers are characterized by sharp angles, and their capitals with highly three-dimensional shields give the design an agitated feeling. The eagle in the entrance parapet is a Zigzag Moderne detail.

6 **Post Office,** 1937
Louis A. Simon
Northwest corner 5th Street W and 1st Avenue W

A rather bland building, but it contains a 1939 Federal Arts Project mural by James Watrous.

7 **Itasca County Fairgrounds**
Northeast corner 3rd Avenue NE and Ridgewood Road

There are several log buildings of interest on the fairgrounds. As a design the most impressive of these is the WPA Conservation Building (1937).

8 **House,** c. 1936
1111 4th Avenue NW

A two-story Classic Moderne house of the 1930s. The profile of the flat-roofed volume is brought to the ground by the low wing on one side and the garage on the other.

9 **Grand Rapids High School,** 1973
Ellerbe Architects
West of 3rd Avenue NW on 16th Street W

The building is sited on thirty-eight acres overlooking Hale Lake. The structure is hidden from view (even from the lake) by the surrounding forest. The building is of concrete, realized in an exposed frame, with infilling of ribbed concrete and concrete blocks.

5 *Village Hall.*

9 *Grand Rapids High School.*

A-16 Hibbing

The first village of Hibbing was platted in 1893, approximately one mile north of its present location. By the early 1900s it was apparent that the town was situated on a deposit of rich iron ore, and part of the town was moved south in 1919. Life in the older part of town continued for a number of years, and a bus service was established between the two sections; out of this small bus company grew the nationwide Greyhound Bus system. Howard Street, Hibbing's main commercial street, is much more homogeneous than most small-town main streets because most of it was developed at the same time. Many of the two-story commercial buildings have a slightly Gothic image, and some have a trace of Prairie styling. One of the remarkable features of the town is the number of Moderne houses from the 1930s. There are twelve or more of them grouped around Minnesota Street and on 9th Avenue, 11th Avenue, and Howard Street.

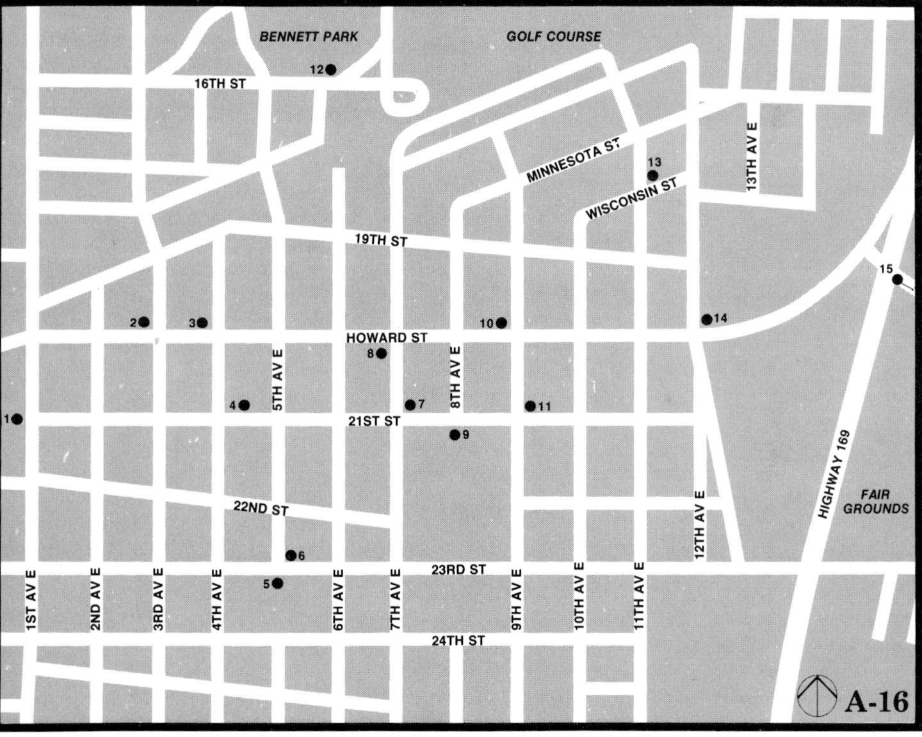

1 **H. B. Reed Building,** 1939
2121 1st Avenue
A rather formal Streamline Moderne building of three stories.

2 **First National Bank Building,** 1920
A. Moorman and Company
219 Howard Street E
A Classical Beaux Arts bank, more delicate in detail than most pre-1920s banks. A stylized eagle occupies the central spandrel. On the parapet of the roof is a garlanded base for a flagpole.

3 **State Theatre,** c. 1925
Liebenberg and Kaplan
North side Howard Street between 3rd and 4th Avenues E

A garlanded classical building with engaged Corinthian piers. A Streamline Moderne marquee and a vertical sign were added to the front in the 1930s.

4 **Village Hall,** 1921
Holstead and Sullivan
North side 21st Street between 4th and 5th Avenues E

A twentieth-century Georgian building, supposedly modeled after Faneuil Hall in Boston. A high tower overlooks the Ionic-columned entrance.

5 **Hibbing Memorial Building,** 1935
Erickson and Company
23rd Street, south of 5th Avenue E

An immense PWA structure which contains an auditorium, a memorial hall, a service club, a theatre, a curling rink, and other community facilities. In style, lukewarm Streamline Moderne.

6 **Our Savior's Lutheran Church,** 1952
Hills, Gilbertson, and Hayes
Northeast corner 5th Avenue E and 23rd Street

This firm designed several churches which have as their source Saarinen and Saarinen's Christ Lutheran Church (1949) in Minneapolis. These designs all work reasonably well as long as they closely follow the detailing and massing of the original — when they depart from the original, they are much less successful.

7 **St. James Episcopal Church,** 1927
J. C. Taylor
Northeast corner 7th Avenue and 21st Street

The exoticism of the Mission Revival in northern Minnesota. The parapeted entrance screen is worked out especially well in this church.

8 **Mesaba Transportation Building,** c. 1940
Southwest corner Howard Street and 7th Avenue E

The Streamline Moderne at its best. A curved second floor hovers over the bus shelter below. The brick surface, glass bricks, and windows are kept on the same plane.

9 **Hibbing High School,** 1920–23
W. T. Bray
South side 21st Street between 7th and 9th Avenues E

An odd but effective mixture of the Medieval and the Classical. A classical screen poses in front of an Elizabethan Tudor brick building with octagonal corner towers. The auditorium is supposedly patterned after the Capitol Theatre in New York. In the school's library is a mural by David Workman, and in the entrance are six panels by David Ericson.

10 **House,** c. 1936
Northwest corner 9th Avenue E and Howard Street

In this Streamline Moderne house the two-story corners are rounded. A pattern of three projecting bands ties the second-floor windows and doors together.

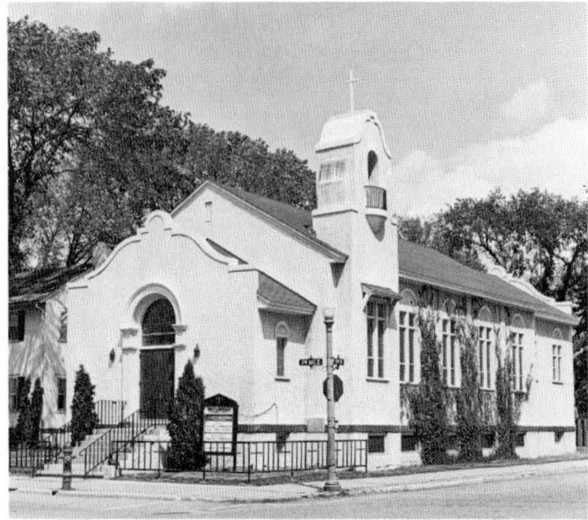

7 St. James Episcopal Church.

10 House.

11 **House,** c. 1927
Northeast corner 21st Street and 9th Avenue E
An English cottage with a composition shingle roof which wraps itself around the eaves of the building and lifts up its edges shyly to reveal dormer windows.

12 **Park School,** 1935
J. C. Taylor
505 16th Street E
The Moderne (not Streamline) with a profusion of glass bricks. When it was new, it was called the "glass school."

13 **House,** c. 1927
1101 Wisconsin Street
A two-story Colonial Revival house with dormers. The porch with arched and paired columns is Georgian. An appropriate white picket fence sets it all off.

• 14 **St. Louis County Courthouse,** 1954
Jyring and Jurenes
Northeast corner Howard Street and 12th Avenue E
Post–World War II Moderne, carefully restrained by Classical precedent. The main section effectively declares its public intent through a long two-story porch with piers.

15 **Municipal Sewage Treatment Plant,** 1938–39
J. C. Taylor; Roberts and Schaefer, engineers
East of intersection of Howard Street and Highway 169 (behind the fairgrounds)
A PWA composition of two domed filtration buildings and several other concrete buildings — somewhat like a fragment of the Maginot Line.

A-17 International Falls

This community on the Canadian border was incorporated as a village in 1901. Its economy is based on the existence of paper mills, which utilize the falls of the Rainy River for power. Since the late 1930s summer recreational activities have provided another source of income. Surprisingly, the most interesting buildings in International Falls are Moderne structures of the late 1930s.

1 **Sports Stadium,** 1941
Highway 71, north of 13th Avenue
The back of the grandstand has been formally treated with the windows arranged horizontally. A decorative band goes around the parapet, and a large relief sculpture depicts the virtue of sports.

2 **Three Moderne Houses,** c. 1936
1000, 1006, and 1025 2nd Street
The house at 1006 2nd Street is the most elaborate of the three. All have flat roofs, corner windows, and other attributes of the Streamline Moderne of the 1930s.

3 **House,** c. 1910
901 2nd Street
Shingles, river stones, and bricks sheathe this one-and-a-half-story Craftsman bungalow. Extended triangular brackets support the projecting roof on the gable ends.

4 **"Smokey the Bear" Sculpture,** 1954
North of Highway 71 at 6th Avenue
A grown-up Smokey (twenty-six feet high) is accompanied by two cubs.

4 "Smokey the Bear" Sculpture.

5 Band Shell, c. 1941
North of Highway 71 at 8th Avenue
A Moderne composition of semicircles, squares, and rectangles.

5 Band Shell.

6 Municipal Building, 1939
A. Reinhold Melander
South side Highway 71 at 6th Avenue
A characteristic PWA Moderne composition with a high central pavilion of two stories and a pair of low matched wings, one on each side. The three-part division of the façade of the central pavilion suggests a piered entrance.

7 Public Library, 1938
A. Reinhold Melander
South side Highway 71 at 8th Avenue
PWA Moderne with restraint and dignity.

8 Library Building (now Boise Cascade offices), c. 1910
2nd Street, north end of 4th Avenue
A tasteful reuse of an older building. The signing and the new doors of the entrance to this classical building enhance the original design.

9 Koochiching County Courthouse, 1910
C. E. Bell
Southwest corner 4th Street and 7th Avenue
Beaux Arts Classical, but much more nineteenth century than twentieth century. A new addition (1975) by Thomas and Vecchi has closely followed the original design.

A-18 Ironton

In the mining and railroad village of Ironton, at the northwest corner of Curtiss Avenue and 4th Street, is the two-story Spina Hotel (c. 1900). Its one element of architectural distinction is its angled corner balcony with two Tuscan columns; the rest of the building tends toward the classical.

A-19 Lutsen

The well-known Lutsen Resort on the north shore of Lake Superior (Highway 61), one of the earliest resorts in Minnesota, was built in 1887. The present lodge and other buildings were designed by Edwin Lundie in 1949. The image of these wood buildings is Scandinavian — gabled roofs, many dormers, clapboard and diagonal siding, stone foundations, and heavily ornamented detailing in wood. On the whole the details, such as the wood and stone entrance posts and the office porch, are the more impressive parts of the buildings. Nearby are the Lutsen Sea Villas (1968) and several cabins (1967–68) designed by Sovik, Mathre, and Madsen.

Lodge, Lutsen Resort.

A-20 Mountain Iron

Mountain Iron was settled in 1892. The village hall and the public library, both built in 1915, are two examples of Minnesota's essays in the Beaux Arts. Both buildings are of yellow brick with classical detailing in white terra-cotta. The village hall is on the northeast corner of Mountain Avenue and Main Street, and the library is across the street at 456–57 Mountain Avenue.

A-21 Sandstone and Hinckley

The village was platted in 1887, and it was named for the quarries of sandstone found on the bluffs of the Kettle River. Between Main Street and Old Highway 61 is the Great Northern Railroad Roundhouse (c. 1900), beautifully crafted in sandstone. Another building of the same sandstone is the former Sandstone State Bank at the northeast corner of Main and 4th Streets. Though the ashlar blocks give a sense of the Romanesque, the bank's design with its Palladian window is actually classical. At the northeast corner of 5th Street and Commercial Avenue is the 1901 public school, also in red sandstone. With its towers and arches its imagery is Medieval. The miniature white

Great Northern Railroad roundhouse, Sandstone.

Classical building near the northeast corner of Main Street and Highway 123 was once the Quarryman's Bank (now a law office). The lunette of its front window still spells "Bank" in leaded glass; below it glass bricks have replaced the plate-glass window.

Eight miles south of Sandstone in Hinckley is the Burlington Northern Railroad Depot (corner of Old Highway 61 and 1st Street Southeast). In style the station is simplified Eastlake, although it was built after the town was leveled in 1894 by a forest fire.

Quarryman's Bank (now law office).

A-22 Tower

Tower, on the south shore of Lake Vermilion, was platted in 1882. The Duluth and Iron Range Railroad arrived at the community in 1884. Lumbering, then mining, and finally the resort trade have formed the town's economic base. On the south side of Main Street (Highway 169) is the former city hall and fire department (c. 1884). This single-story brick building presents a remarkable façade with arched openings of various sizes and an entablature-cornice of projecting bricks arranged to suggest a corbeled table. One block west of it is the new municipal building, a PWA project designed by William M. Ingemann and built in 1939. The design of this white stucco building is Streamline Moderne, with a nod to the past in the strongly accentuated Greek-key pattern carried as a horizontal band around the building. Another Streamline Moderne building (c. 1940) is situated on Main Street, just east of Spruce Street. This small brick • commercial building (now a residence) originally had a central entrance with a large circular window on one side and a stepped glass-brick window on the other side.

Municipal building.

A-23 Two Harbors

The town was originally platted in 1857 as Burlington Bay, and the present community did not come into being until the railroad and the ore docks were built in 1884. It was incorporated as the village of Two Harbors in 1888. • The Lake County Courthouse (1905), located at the northwest corner of 3rd Avenue and 6th Street, is James Allen MacLeod's sophisticated version of a City Beautiful courthouse. The low dome, covered with stamped metal in a fish-scale pattern, is silver with touches of blue and gold around the cornice. Across the street is the 1906 First Presbyterian Church (now the United Church). This low stone church with its parapeted corner tower employs the rural English Gothic image as interpreted through the Craftsman esthetic. The Harbor Theatre (c. 1950), which is located at 616 2nd Avenue, has an angled cut-in marquee and bold lowercase lettering. Almost twenty miles up the North Shore on Highway 61 is the dramatically situated Split Rock Lighthouse (1909), which was designed by Ralph R. Tinkham. Farther up the North Shore are several cabins and • lakeshore houses designed by Edwin Lundie (including his own cabin) during the late 1930s and on into the early 1950s. There are also a scattering of cabins from the late 1960s and early 1970s including • one designed in 1971 by Times Annex Architects. These private vacation dwellings are not visible from the highway.

Cabin of Edwin Lundie, 1941.

A-24 Virginia

Virginia sits in what was once a virgin pine forest but now is an area dotted with iron ore mineshafts, mine dumps, and tailings ponds. The city was platted in 1892 after the discovery of the nearby Missabe Mountain Mine. In 1893 and again in 1900 the city was destroyed by forest fires. Each time that it was rebuilt it was improved upon, although the original gridiron street plan remained intact. The second rebuilding took place during the period when the City Beautiful movement was very popular, and this is strongly reflected in the civic architecture. Fifth Avenue, one of the principal north/south streets, has been given a formal touch in the double row of five-branched cast-iron lampposts, creating the effect of a Beaux Arts boulevard. The Masonic Hall, the city hall, the post office, the public library, the St. Louis County District Court Building, and Roosevelt High School are all Classical designs.

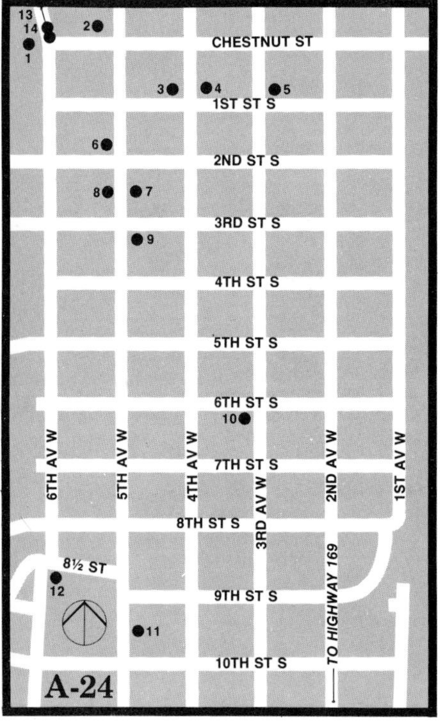

1 **Duluth, Winnipeg, and Pacific Railroad Depot** (now Northern State Bank), 1913
West end Chestnut Street at 6th Avenue W

A Chateauesque Style railroad station in brick with stone trim has been remodeled into a bank by Augar, Jyring, Whiteman, and Moser (1966).

• 2 **Maco Theatre,** c. 1940
Liebenberg and Kaplan
Chestnut Street near 5th Street W

The Streamline motion picture theatre at its best. The sign, with vertical fins, is attached to a curved glass-brick volume which works its way into the building. The marquee and the stepped design in its signing are most impressive.

3 **Masonic Hall,** c. 1916
1st Street S between 4th and 5th Avenues W

Red brick Georgian with a bowed central projection.

4 **City Hall,** 1923–24
Elwin H. Berg
Northeast corner 1st Street S and 4th Avenue W

A brick volume with a classical portico. The main floor has large-scale arched windows.

5 **Post Office,** 1912
James Knox Taylor
Northeast corner 1st Street S and 3rd Avenue W

The classical Beaux Arts tradition via Palladio and Jefferson.

6 **Public Library,** 1912
Jackson and Stone
Northwest corner 5th Avenue W and 2nd Street S

A severe classical design reminiscent of the eighteenth-century designs of Peter Harrison.

7 **St. Louis County District Court Building,** 1910
Bray and Nystrom
East side 5th Avenue W between 2nd and 3rd Streets S

A classical screen of four paired Ionic columns poses in front of a classical brick box.

7 St. Louis County District Court Building.

8 **Roosevelt High School,** 1928–30
J. Albert Codding
West side 5th Avenue W between 2nd and 3rd Streets S

The classical brought into the late 1920s. The deep porch has Ionic columns.

• 9 **House** (now a funeral home and chapel), c. 1910
402 5th Avenue W

A commodious turn-of-the-century Craftsman (Arts and Crafts) house with shingles on the upper walls and clapboard below. Note the late 1920s "Sunset Chapel" sign on the side entrance.

10 **House,** c. 1910
304 6th Street S

A one-and-a-half-story Craftsman house.

11 **Horace Mann School,** 1914, 1924
Bray and Nystrom
5th Avenue W between 9th and 10th Streets S

A mildly Prairie design which is quite similar to the work of Purcell and Elmslie in about 1914. See also Bray and Nystrom's Prairie Style manual training school in Eveleth.

11 Horace Mann School.

• 12 **House,** c. 1908
520 8½ Street S

The stone walls of this Craftsman bungalow have a tactile quality seldom found in turn-of-the-century bungalows.

• 13 **Musakka House,** c. 1910
Fourteen miles north of Highway 53 bypass, north of town

A cross-gable house of hand-hewn logs, one and a half stories high. The log walls create three main rooms on the first floor.

14 Russian Orthodox Church of Sts. Peter and Paul, 1918
North of town on Highway 53 to Cook, west on Highway 1 to Highway 65, then north 6 miles to Bramble

In front of a dark coniferous forest stands this white clapboard church with a central tower. The church is made exotic by the onion dome on top of the tower. An excellent example of folk architecture.

14 Russian Orthodox Church of Sts. Peter and Paul.

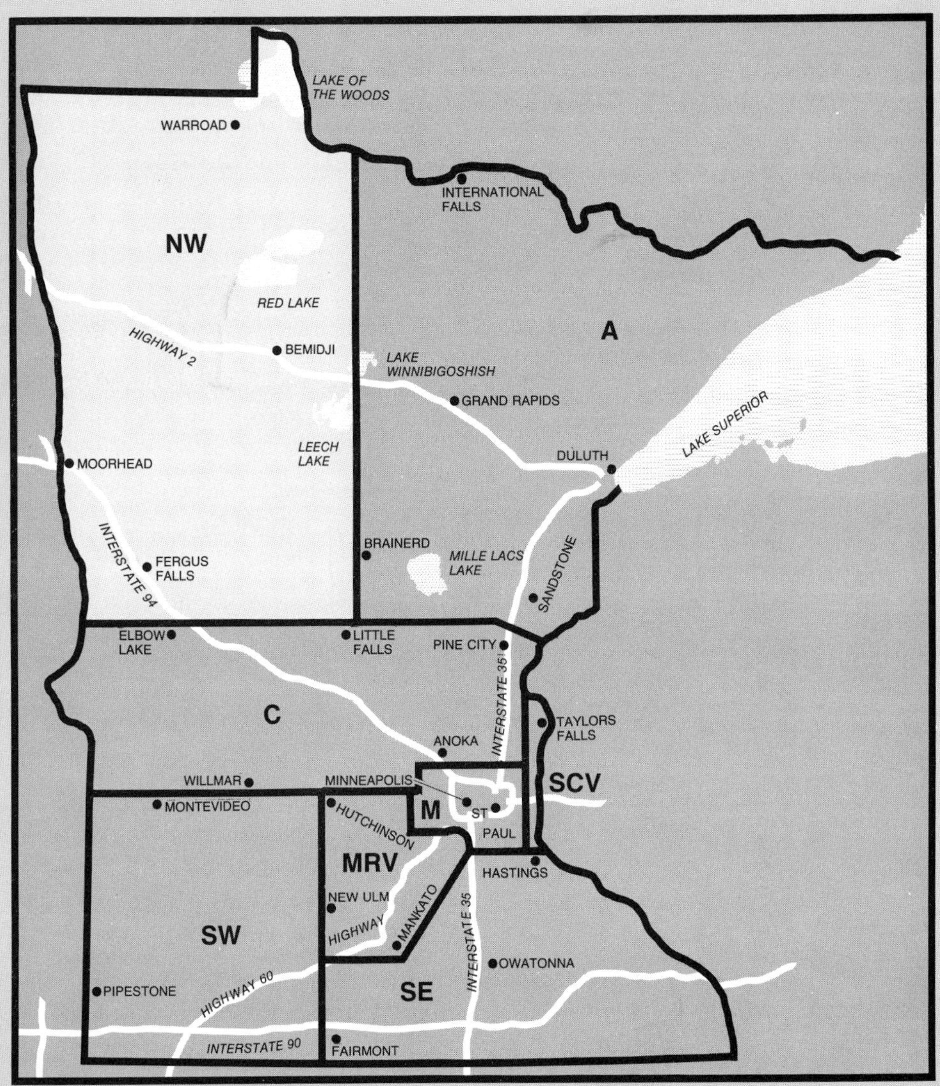

LAKE OF THE WOODS
WARROAD
INTERNATIONAL FALLS
NW
RED LAKE
HIGHWAY 2
BEMIDJI
A
LAKE WINNIBIGOSHISH
GRAND RAPIDS
LAKE SUPERIOR
LEECH LAKE
MOORHEAD
DULUTH
INTERSTATE 94
BRAINERD
MILLE LACS LAKE
SANDSTONE
FERGUS FALLS
ELBOW LAKE
LITTLE FALLS
PINE CITY
INTERSTATE 35
C
TAYLORS FALLS
ANOKA
WILLMAR
MINNEAPOLIS
SCV
M
ST PAUL
MONTEVIDEO
HUTCHINSON
MRV
HASTINGS
NEW ULM
MANKATO
HIGHWAY
SW
INTERSTATE 35
OWATONNA
PIPESTONE
HIGHWAY 60
SE
INTERSTATE 90
FAIRMONT

NW-1 Ada

Ada, the Norman County seat, is situated on the Marsh River, twenty miles southeast of its confluence with the Red River. The town's plan is almost a stereotype of many prairie towns — a railroad right through the center and two parallel main streets, one on each side of the tracks.

1 **Norman County Courthouse,** 1903
Meyer and Thori
Southwest corner 3rd Avenue E and 1st Street E
It is amazing how stylistically late are many of Minnesota's courthouses. Here is a Richardsonian Romanesque Revival building, tower and all, which one might assume was built at least a decade earlier. This version of the Romanesque has all the expected elements: a corner pavilion, a central gabled wing, and a central tower. Later remodelings of the interior and the windows have certainly not improved the building.

2 **Congregational Church of Ada** (now Memorial Educational Museum of Norman County), 1900
200 1st Street E
An overscaled, stout crenelated tower surmounted by a small Queen Anne belfry presses down onto a turn-of-the-century shingle and brick Craftsman sanctuary. Another church, also now a historic building, is located at the southwest corner of Thorpe Avenue and 2nd Street West. Behind this building is a clapboard schoolhouse which was moved to the site.

3 **House,** c. 1895
208 2nd Street E
A two-story late Queen Anne house with a spindly front porch and a narrow octagonal tower at one side.

4 **House,** c. 1895
501 2nd Street W
Queen Anne with a few hints of the Colonial Revival. The U-shaped spindled porch has two pedimented entrances, one at each side.

NW-2 Bagley

This section of north central Minnesota was once heavily forested in spruce and pine, but it now has hardly any large stands of trees. Much of the land has been turned to agricultural production, and Bagley, the Clearwater county seat, has been replanted with spruce and pine. For the visitor the three obvious landmarks in town are the metal-tripod-supported water tower, the railroad with its station and adjacent storage facilities, and the county courthouse.

1 **Clearwater County Courthouse,** 1937–38
Foss and Company
Northwest corner Highway 92 and 5th Street W
One of those marginally interesting but respectable PWA public buildings of the 1930s — this one just makes it, for in a lighthearted manner it is modern (in its glass entrance and other details), and correctly monumental (in its visual heaviness and its Beaux Arts plan and façades).

2 **Railroad Passenger Depot,** c. 1937
North of railroad tracks, west of Highway 92
A Colonial Revival clapboard station made Moderne by the use of glass bricks.

3 **Gran Lutheran Church,** 1897
Clearwater County Fairgrounds (originally situated in Popple Township, Itasca County)
A gable-roofed building of hewn logs.

NW-3 Barnesville

The dominant visual note in Barnesville, as in many other towns on the prairie, is the futuristic complex of grain elevators (the Barnesville Farmers Elevators) located on the northwest corner of Main Street and Front Street Southwest. The complex is composed of high cylinders and tall volumetric boxes accompanied by low structures below, some of which are metal prefabricated buildings.

●The town's other architectural monument is its "Old Stone House" (c. 1895), situated at the southwest corner of Main Street and 4th Street Southwest. This house certainly came from the hands of a highly sophisticated designer. It is essentially a raised-basement cottage which is sheathed in stone on the lower level; its high-pitched gables are covered with fish-scale shingles. The front is organized around an off-center circular tower, and one flank of the building boasts a broad stone chimney with windows. The tower element is somewhat Chateauesque, although other details are Queen Anne/Colonial Revival.

Barnesville Farmers Elevators.

Old Stone House, Barnesville.

NW-4 Battle Lake

A resort community on the southwestern shores of West Battle Lake. The street layout is the usual gridiron in a north/south, east/west pattern. There are no street signs; the locations described in the accompanying paragraphs are based on the assumption that one enters the community from the south on Highway 78.

1 **First National Bank Building,** c. 1890s
Southeast corner Highway 78 and first major cross street

The picture of a small-town bank: raised basement, arched windows on the street elevation and along the flank of the building, and flower boxes with real flowers. It was brought up to date by glass bricks as sidelights of the entry and, on the side wall, the addition of a drop-in deposit box which is approached by its own short walk and a single step to make it accessible.

2 First Baptist Church.

2 **First Baptist Church,** 1893
Southwest corner Highway 78 and second major cross street

A shingle and clapboard church; Gothic with a suggestion of Colonial Revival. The tower, with its pointed roof, has been treated as a dormer projection from the main roof; in terms of design the church's most interesting feature is its rear, where a shed-roof/gable wing tucks itself under the arch of the main body of the building.

3 **House,** c. late 1880s
Southwest corner, 1 block west of Highway 78 and second major cross street

Late Eastlake, almost Queen Anne.

4 **House,** c. 1889
Two blocks west of Highway 78, north of second major cross street; west side of block

A comfortable example of a small-town Queen Anne house. A porch runs around three sides of the projecting street wing of the house. Note the delicate sawed and turned work and especially the well-preserved screen door with its pattern of diagonals and quarter circles.

NW-5 Bemidji

The town occupies the west shore of Lake Bemidji and extends southward to Lake Irving. The gridiron plan is adhered to except near the lakes, where the streets (especially Birchmont Avenue) follow the contour of the shore. Much of the lakeshore, from Cameron Park south, is planned for public recreation.

1 **"Paul and Babe,"** 1937
East of corner Bemidji Avenue and 2nd Street

The figures of Paul Bunyan and Babe, the Blue Ox, in reinforced concrete, the come-on image for commercial Bemidji. This is folk art transformed into a programmatic sign.

1 "Paul and Babe."

2 **Chief Theatre,** 1937
Liebenberg and Kaplan
314 Beltrami Avenue

A Streamline Moderne example with red, yellow, blue, and green ribbons. In this case the marquee, with its curved corner projections (lighted by neon), seems to have been designed independently of the building.

3 **Commercial Building,** c. 1910
304 3rd Street

A successful Prairie Style solution for a single-floor building. The façade consists of a large arch which springs almost from the ground. The impression is that the designers boldly took one of the large arched windows of Sullivan's Owatonna Bank Building and used it as the façade of this structure.

3 Commercial Building.

4 **Post Office** (now Bemidji Public Library), 1917
James A. Wetmore
Northeast corner Beltrami Avenue and 6th Street

Red brick; small-paned double-hung windows; columns, pediments, and open balustrades; a full and knowing exercise in Colonial Revival. The current use of the building as a public library is a good example of the recycling of a structure for a new use.

5 **Beltrami County Courthouse,** 1902
Kinney and Detweiler
Northwest corner Beltrami Avenue and 6th Street

A classical end-pavilion building. The central tower is surmounted by a dome with a sculptured figure on top; the dome and its figure are visually distinct from the rest of the building. A new brick and glass addition to the front openly ignores the older structure.

6 **Cottage,** c. 1895
1001 Minnesota Avenue
A Queen Anne cottage with a spindlework porch.

7 **House,** c. 1936
1403 Bemidji Avenue
The Streamline Moderne as a box with corner windows. The upper and lower rows of windows are attached by moldings to convey the effect of a horizontal band. The house is even equipped with a porthole window.

8 **Two Moderne Houses,** c. 1937
1505 and 1509 Birchmont Avenue
Two Streamline Moderne classics, one with a semicircular glass projection.

9 **High School,** c. 1920
Northwest corner Bemidji Avenue and 16th Street
Between 1910 and 1930 hundreds of schools were built similar to the main building of the Bemidji High School. In plan, two bands of classrooms are arranged around an axial hall. Almost all of these buildings were sheathed in brick, and in style they referred either to the classical tradition, as in the Bemidji High School, or to the medieval tradition. The Bemidji High School's auditorium (c. 1939), which is east of the main building, is of more interest; it is PWA Moderne, with a slightly curved front, a porch with piers, and a Greek-key motif on the upper part of the façade.

9 High School Auditorium.

NW-6 Breckenridge

One of the early Red River Valley towns. Breckenridge was settled in 1857, before the Civil War, but its period of growth did not occur until the 1870s when the railroad came through (1871). As in other towns of northwestern Minnesota the buildings are set in wide-open spaces of lawn and trees; nothing seems pressed in, even in the downtown area.

1 **Wilkin County Courthouse,** 1928–29
Buechner and Orth
East side 5th Street S between Dakōta and Oregon Avenues
A vigorous classical pile with a projecting pavilion on all four corners, a second-floor columned loggia, and a domed tower, open at the base. It all has the feeling of John Vanbrugh's work as it might have been interpreted by Edwin Lutyens in the early 1900s.

2 **Post Office,** 1936
Louis A. Simon
224 5th Street N
A PWA rectangular box of brick with a slightly projecting stone frontispiece. Murals inside by Robert Alloway.

3 **Ridge Theatre,** c. 1938
516 Minnesota Avenue
Not a great Streamline Moderne theatre, but still quite good. Its marquee and the vertical sign above are original, as are the ticket booth and the adjacent storefronts.

4 **House,** c. 1939
430 6th Street N
A white, stuccoed Moderne box.

5 **Schoolhouse,** c. 1890s
Wilkin County Fairgrounds, 4 blocks west of 5th Street N on Nebraska Avenue
The roofs make this building: a normal gable roof turns into two shed roofs at front and back, and the low bell tower is set on three recessed building blocks.

NW-7 Browerville

The small community of Browerville on the Long Prairie River holds two monuments well worth a visit: the Browerville Village Hall and St. Joseph's Catholic Church with its accompanying sculpture garden. At first glance the Village Hall seems unremarkable — it is a two-story brick box from the turn of the century. What distinguishes the building is its black and white entrance, which is amazingly reminiscent of Vienna during the same period and of the work there of Otto Wagner, Joseph Hoffmann, and others. The town's other monument is St. Joseph's Church (c. 1895), a classic pile with nineteenth-century Neo-Baroque overtones. Its crowning glory, though, is its elongated drum surmounted by columns and its onion dome. To the right and left of the church are what appear to be an eighteenth-century English folly and grotto, only in this case the intent is religious — a depiction of Christ in the garden of Gethsemane. The boulder composition on the right, with its sculptured figure, and the cascade on the left were created in the early twentieth century by Joseph Kieselewski.

Village hall, Browerville.

Sculpture garden, St. Joseph's Church, Browerville.

NW-8 Crookston

The city, situated on the Burlington Northern Railroad line, was settled in 1872 and incorporated in 1879. The winds and twists of the Red Lake River divide the community into a number of distinct areas. The original town plan was laid out parallel and perpendicular to the railroad tracks, which did not run north/south. Later additions to the town were oriented north/south, east/west, with the result that irregularity of street patterns is a characteristic of the place.

1 **Kiewel Building,** c. 1900
West side Broadway, southwest of 2nd Street

The second floor of the building is orange brick and has two oval bay windows with leaded stained-glass transoms. The lower floor has been modernized beyond recognition.

2 **Bank Building** (now offices), c. 1890
Northwest corner Broadway and 2nd Street

A two-story Richardsonian Romanesque Revival building which in its formal qualities is closer to the Beaux Arts than to the medieval. There is an eye-catching corner entrance with a single stubby Romanesque column.

3 *Retail Building (now Pantorium Cleaners).*

3 **Retail Building** (now Pantorium Cleaners), c. 1900
104 2nd Street W

A delicate, almost fragile, temple-fronted building of white brick.

4 *Presbyterian Church.*

4 **Presbyterian Church,** c. 1914
510 Broadway N

Church, sanctuary, Sunday School room, and other facilities are housed in a flat-roofed rectangular block. Its esthetic and religious programmatic intent is conveyed almost exclusively in a two-dimensional way through the use of arched openings of various sizes and a horizontal band of crosses carried across the upper part of the building. Each of the two principal façades ends up being a sophisticated independent composition.

5 **Polk County Courthouse,** 1968
Ellerbe Architects
Southwest corner Broadway and 7th Street

If the "message" of this neutral two-story rectangular box is that government has become anonymous, then the building has succeeded.

6 **Winter Sports Arena,** c. 1938
Robert Street, corner Bridge Street

A white stucco PWA sports arena with a curved front and a band of Broadway-face letters.

6 *Winter Sports Arena.*

7 **Kiehle Learning Resources Center, University of Minnesota**
Frederick Bentz-Milo Thompson and Associates
North on University Avenue (Highways 2 and 75), just before Grand Forks Road

A brick box was added to the earlier building in 1971–72, and the window units have been placed within low-relief segmented arched recesses. The addition has its own strong personality, but because of its scale and the neutral expanses of its brick surfaces it fits in well with the older structure.

7 *Kiehle Learning Resources Center, University of Minnesota.*

NW-9 Detroit Lakes

A town generally oriented to the summer tourist. To the south is Detroit Lake with its public beaches, parks, trailer courts, and fairgrounds. Two railroads, the Burlington Northern and Soo lines, converge on the city. The northwest/southeast diagonal of the Burlington Northern and the irregularities of the Pelican River, plus the usual oddities of land division, continually interrupt the logic of the gridiron scheme.

1 **Commercial Buildings,** c. 1890s
Corner Washington Avenue and Holmes Street W

On and around this corner are several two-story commercial buildings which have individual elements of interest.

2 **Becker County Courthouse,** 1942
Foss and Company
East side Lake Avenue between Holmes and Frazee Streets W

PWA Moderne set down on a treeless block.

3 **Carnegie Public Library,** 1913
Claude and Starke
1000 Washington Avenue

Wright's 1892 Winslow House reworked into a public library. A band of Sullivanesque terra-cotta ornamentation goes around the building directly under the wide overhanging roof soffit. The building was designed by a Madison, Wisconsin, firm which worked in a number of styles including Prairie and Beaux Arts.

3 Carnegie Public Library.

4 **Public School,** 1895
Southwest corner Summit Avenue and Front Street W

An extensive two-story raised-basement structure with impressive walls of stone. Random-cut stone has been used for the raised-basement and first-floor walls, and small rough river stones have been employed in the second-floor walls.

•5 **House,** c. 1940
1219 Washington Avenue

The Streamline Moderne as a cabin cruiser. A curved glass-brick prow juts out toward the street, and a wood railing surmounts the edges of the flat roof. This is a real classic of the Moderne in Minnesota.

6 **Fairyland Cabins,** late 1920s
410 West Lake Drive

These small units are lined up in a row, but they are all slightly angled and therefore end up being read as a group. The cabins are white with red trim and have large white columns.

NW-10 Fergus Falls

The height of the falls of the Otter Tail River at this point (110 feet) made the location a natural one for a town. The area was explored in the 1850s, and the town site was platted in 1870. It was incorporated as a village in 1870 and as a city in 1881. The young city's growth was assured by its designation as the Otter Tail county seat and by the arrival of the Great Northern Railroad in the late 1870s. By the 1920s the community had supplemented its milling activities with small-scale manufacturing and the development of extensive cooperative creameries. In its growth Fergus Falls has taken advantage of its riverside location. Parks and public and private buildings adjoin and overlook the river. The city has been park-conscious for many years, and it now has twenty-two parks (totaling 17.3 acres), plus the nearby Pebble Lake recreation area. The river, various lakes, and other irregularities of the terrain have introduced numerous modifications in the usual gridiron scheme. The sense of the city is that of a gently rolling, lake-oriented hill town. A walk or a drive through town will reveal a number of late nineteenth-century commercial buildings on Lincoln Avenue. The city hall, which is supposedly a variation on Independence Hall in Philadelphia, is on Washington Avenue. The Beaux Arts classical revival post office is on South Mill Street. Also note the programmatic sculpture of an otter (the Otter Tail Empire Monument).

1 **Lincoln J. Mills Building,** c. 1890
101 Lincoln Avenue E
A two-story Victorian Eastlake building in brick, relatively plain except for the tall, narrow, pedimented entrance with its two columns and the arched and pedimented false front projecting above the roof parapet.

2 **Lower Newman Block,** early 1890s
216–20 Lincoln Avenue W
A nondescript brick commercial block suddenly emerges as something of interest with a centrally placed projecting chimney that seems to rise out of the entrance door below.

3 **Otter Tail County Courthouse,** 1920–21
Buechner and Orth
Southeast corner Junius Avenue and Court Street
The ample lawns and trees save a dry textbook version of the Beaux Arts tradition from being completely boring. Everything is "correct," including the interior murals.

4 **Adams Elementary School,** 1939
301 Bancroft Avenue W
A respectable single-floor PWA Moderne brick school. A similar design, also of 1939, is represented by the Jefferson Elementary School (1001 Mt. Faith Avenue East).

5 **Hillcrest Lutheran Academy,** 1901
West end Vernon Avenue W
Classicized Romanesque Revival, with a pencil-point belfry.

6 **Fergus Falls State Hospital,** 1895
W. B. Dunnell
Northwest corner Fir Avenue W and Union Street N
An eight-story tower topped by a witch's-hat roof seems at first glance to be Romanesque, but it turns out, as is true of the rest of the building, to be Beaux Arts classical of a sort. Recent additions and remodelings have at best been an embarrassment to the original brick building.

7 **House,** c. 1900
506 Lincoln Avenue W
Queen Anne kept in hand by the classical discipline of turn-of-the-century Colonial Revival.

8 **Hunt House,** c. 1890
627 Cavour Avenue W
Queen Anne Style with a corner round tower.

9 **House,** c. 1912
226 Summit Avenue W
A Craftsman/Prairie volumetric box covered with a low-hipped roof.

10 Page House, c. 1875
219 Whitford Street N
The Federal/Greek mode made fashionable by Italianate overtones. The symmetry of the street façade has been broken by a first-floor bay on the left and the service wing, with its porch, on the right.

11 Clement House, late 1870s
604 Burlington Street
An Eastlake villa with a projecting three-story tower in front; shed-roof hoods, supported by angled struts which continue the roof line, project over the third-floor windows of the tower.

12 Chapman House, late 1870s
309 Oakland Place
Eastlake with Italianate details; the house's eye-catcher is the pattern of open sawed work in its high-pitched gable ends.

13 Lee House, 1937
Foss and Company
Northeast corner Union Street N and Hazel
A brick Streamline Moderne box. A glass-walled living room with a half-circle bay looks out to the rear of the house. The front entrance is pressed in by the suggestion of a pair of wide, fluted columns; a narrow window of curved glass brick lights the stair hall.

13 Lee House.

NW-11 Hallock

On the way via Highway 75 across the open prairie to Hallock one passes through Kennedy, and on the east side of the highway a one-story commercial building (1906) designed by Bengt E. Sundberg seems to zoom out. Its rough tactile walls are of concrete block (in imitation of worked stone blocks). A corner entrance with a single Corinthian column, together with the stepped voussoir headers, draws attention to the building more effectively than could any sign.

Commercial building, Kennedy.

In Hallock itself, at the northwest corner of 3rd Street South and Birch Street, is the two-story brick city hall (1941); its closed appearance seems to betoken its readiness for its annual battle with winter winds and snow.

NW-12 Moorhead

Moorhead (originally called Burbank City) evolved quite early as a trading station on the Red River. Here the river could be forded, and yet on each side of the ford the water was deep enough for low-draft barges. The completion of the Northern Pacific rail lines to Moorhead in 1861 established the importance of the community, along with neighboring Fargo, North Dakota, across the river; the trains began to run by 1872. Since the 1870s the center of town has been the east/west railroad tracks, which sharply divide the town into a north half and a south half. Highways 10 and 94 run through town parallel to and adjacent to the railroad, further identifying the transportation element as the symbolic focus of the community. Only in recent years has this been partially modified by the freeway (Highway 94), which was built to the south, skirting both Moorhead and Fargo.

1 **Clay County Courthouse,** 1953–54
Foss and Company
807 11th Street N

A period piece of architectural fashion from the 1950s and 1960s, the courthouse is a three-story rectangular box composed of horizontal bands of windows and brick broken at the second-floor level by a solid stucco box that is cantilevered over the windows and doors below. This stucco box projection, with its lettering, and the entrance terrace below herald the building as dignified and civic rather than commercial.

2 **American Legion Building,** 1936
Carter and Meinecke
700 1st Avenue N

A PWA pavilion in stone; note the grillwork above the door, with the seated figure holding a torch.

2 American Legion Building.

3 **Log Cabin** ("Pioneer Log Cabin"), c. 1800s
Northwest corner 3rd Street S and 4th Avenue S

It looks too good to be true — this is how the nineteenth-century pioneers should have built their early log houses. This one works because it has been restored.

4 **Church of St. John the Divine (Episcopal),** 1898–99
Cass Gilbert
120 8th Street S

The architectural monument in Moorhead and without question one of Gilbert's most interesting churches. Like other nineteenth-century Episcopal churches in the United States, the Moorhead church creates a strange and remarkable play of scale, and it also brings together what would seem to be an impossible variety of past architectural styles. The sanctuary is a low shingled structure whose roof in places almost reaches to the ground. The tour de force of the design is the octagonal tower with its steeply pitched witch's-hat roof; the tower gives the impression of having been sawed off the roof of a large church and placed on the ground. Equally delightful is the thin octagonal chimney on the other side of the building; each corner of the octagon is articulated by the alternating pattern of projecting ends of the bricks.

4 Church of St. John the Divine.

5 **Comstock House,** 1883
Kees and Fisk
506 8th Street S

5 Comstock House.

This Minneapolis architectural firm produced a fashionable early Queen Anne Style house for their client, just the sort of design to be found in the early 1880 issues of the *American Architect and Building News.* The exterior of the house relies more on the placement of its various volumes than on a display of luxurious details from the saw and the lathe. A later and much more modest Queen Anne house (c. 1890) is located at 323 7th Street South.

6 **Concordia College,** estab. 1891
920 8th Street S

The Old Main Building (1906), a two-story raised-basement structure, is pure turn-of-the-century Beaux Arts. It has a five-part scheme with a projecting two-story portico in the center, balanced on each side with projecting corner pavilions. Also on the college grounds is an unusual three-story building, Bishop Whipple Hall, which appears to be a late nineteenth-century shingle house set on a series of high brick volumes (the hall was actually built as early as 1882).

NW-13 New York Mills

Although in the literature on Minnesota history New York Mills is often referred to as a Finnish town, its plan (a gridiron running parallel and perpendicular to the railroad) and its architectural image are typical turn-of-the-century forms.

There are a few small clapboard buildings which, because of their puritan simplicity, might be thought of as Finnish in spirit. Three of these can be found southwest of Front Street (Highway 10) on Walker Street.

1 **First State Bank Building** (now Mellin's Tailor Shop), 1904
Northwest side Main Street, northeast of Highway 10

A one-story Richardsonian Romanesque Revival building in brick with stone trim. The two arches opening on the front and the three on the side create a lively surprise pattern for the street.

2 **New York Mills Coop Lockers,** 1937
Northwest corner Highway 10 and Tousley Street

A brick Streamline Moderne design with glass bricks (some curved) and rows of white horizontal bands.

1 First State Bank Building.

NW-14 Park Rapids

Park Rapids was founded in 1880 on the rapids of the Fish Hook River. In the late nineteenth and early twentieth centuries the town's economy was based on lumbering, the production of plaster lath, and its function as a shipping point for agricultural products from nearby farms. Since the 1920s recreational activity has become increasingly important.

1 **Park Theatre,** c. 1938
107 Main Street S
Streamline Moderne, but of a strange concoction — the theatre itself seems to be of a design completely distinct from that of its entrance, marquee, and box-like rectangular sign.

2 **First Baptist Church,** c. 1906
101 Park Avenue S
A brick and shingle Craftsman church.

3 **Post Office,** 1938
Louis A. Simon
301 Park Avenue S
Colonial Williamsburg brought to the lake country of northern Minnesota. Note the authoritative Keep off the Grass signs.

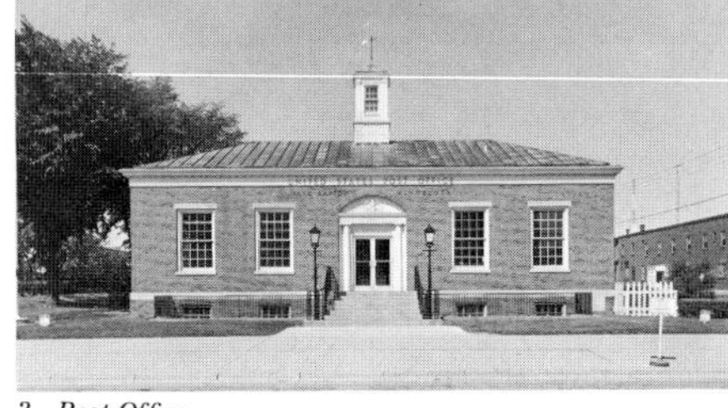

3 Post Office.

4 **Sebeka Log Cabin,** pre-1890
The small town of Sebeka is situated twenty miles south of Park Rapids on Highway 71, and the cabin is in a park just south of the junction of Highways 71 and 227. The walls are of hand-hewn logs, and the whole is covered with a single-gable roof.

NW-15 Pelican Rapids

The resort trade and agriculture form the economic basis of the town. Tourists probably remember as the image of the town the large concrete statue of a pelican that loyally guards the dam on the Pelican River. When the river is high, the bird, with its feet in the water, is even more convincing.

1 **Faith Evangelical Lutheran Church,** 1886, 1903
Northeast corner Broadway and 5th Avenue SE
The tower makes the building. In style, it is a late Medieval German tower, reduced in scale; from a distance it seems to be a large cathedral, but on closer view it turns out to be very small. The post–World War II addition, as is so often the case, constitutes an affront to the older building.

1 Faith Evangelical Lutheran Church.

2 **Blyburg House,** c. 1890s
22 5th Avenue SW

A large brick house, romantically situated on top of a hill. In style it is loosely Queen Anne/Colonial Revival, although certain of its details hark back to the Italianate.

3 **Service Station,** c. 1928
Southeast corner Broadway and 3rd Avenue SE

Pueblo Revival; an invasion from the Rio Grande Valley of New Mexico, with projecting vegas and all.

4 **Pelican Valley State Bank,** 1972
Eugene Hickey Associates
Corner Broadway and 1st Street SE

A near-perfect addition to the town: a low brick building with deeply recessed cutout openings.

5 **Village Hall,** 1899
East side Broadway, north bank Pelican River

Impossibly large volutes terminate the parapet of the street façade of the building. The composition of the volutes is supported at each corner by the suggestion of quoined engaged piers. The lower part of the façade has been ruined by recent remodeling.

6 **Statue of Pelican,** post-1945
East side Highway 59, north bank Pelican River

An effective programmatic advertisement for the town, just eye-catching and outrageous enough to attract considerable attention.

6 Statue of Pelican.

7 **Dunvilla Resort,** c. 1920
½ mile north of junction Highways 59 and 34

The enterprising motorist can purchase gasoline at the Pueblo Revival service station in Pelican Rapids, then travel north to Dunvilla and stay at the Mission Revival resort (arches with towers and so on). If all of this is too foreign, one can go across the road from the Dunvilla Resort and find a one-and-a-half-story "indigenous" log house dating from the late nineteenth century.

NW-16 Phelps

On the Otter Tail River, beside its own dam and millpond, is a late nineteenth-century rural gristmill (1889) complex that includes the mill building, a general store, and a log cabin. The three-story gambrel-roofed mill building is sheathed in clapboard, with a smaller three-story brick addition at the side. A covered lean-to porch (to shelter wagons delivering grain) runs along one side of the building.

West of Phelps Mill, at the junction of County Roads 1 and 35, is a finely crafted PWA stone school (1940). Three miles south, on the west side of County Road 35, is the Oswald Round Barn (c. 1900). A drive through Otter Tail County will reveal twenty-four additional round barns, all built at the turn of the century.

Phelps Mill.

School, near Phelps.

NW-17 Red Lake Falls

As one approaches Red Lake Falls from either direction on Highway 32, the Red Lake County Courthouse (on the northwest corner of Highway 32 and 1st Street) asserts its presence. Its hilltop location in an extensive park gives a prominence to the civic side of the community — an aspect which is seldom retained today in either small or large county seats. This Beaux Arts building (designed by Fremont D. Orff, 1910) has four end pavilions, each with its own drum and dome; a pedimented central entrance; and a square central volume that seems to be waiting for its own drum and dome. Within the central rotunda the two-story-plus space is really there. Arched openings provide views into the rotunda from the adjacent halls of the second floor. Small scenic murals have been placed in each corner.

The other monument of Red Lake Falls is the State Theatre (c. 1939), which is on Highway 32 just southeast of 1st Street. Below the marquee is a pair of doors, each with half-circle glass windows; the small ticket booth seems to pop forth from a curved vertical band of glass brick.

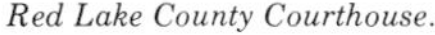

Red Lake County Courthouse.

State Theatre.

NW-18 Thief River Falls

The community's major contribution to architecture and the unusual is a building at 522 Red Lake Boulevard (east of Highway 32 off 6th Street). This structure (which was originally built as a hospital) ranks along with the Hurricane House at Osakis as an example of idiosyncratic folk architecture. Like the Hurricane House, this building is idiosyncratic only in a stylistic sense, for the basic form and details were undoubtedly arrived at through rational considerations. The building is a single rectangular volume covered by a sort of mansard roof. Rectangular flat-roofed bays protrude from the roof and the second-floor walls of the building; below, gable-roofed bays break up the otherwise plain walls.

House (522 Red Lake Boulevard).

To the west of Highway 52 at 415 Arnold Avenue South are the Skylite Apartments (1971) of Hodne and Stageberg. The design of this housing project for the elderly is a welcome change from the usual high-rise solution found elsewhere in the state. One-story wood-sheathed units are arranged around courts and patios. Skylights and high clerestory lighting in projecting shed-roof elements function internally to provide vertical space and externally to create a broken, picturesque form.

NW-19 Wadena

A visitor coming into the town from the north can experience it as a railroad visitor would have during the second and third decades of this century. South of the railroad tracks the passenger depot and the town's bandstand form the focal point in an open space of concrete, lawn, and trees.

1 **Wadena Village Hall,** 1912
North side Bryant Avenue, east of Jefferson Street
Similar in design to the city hall in Pine Island. All of the city's functions, both real and symbolic, are encompassed in the design. The large semicircular entrance proclaims the firehouse, and the roofed bell tower acts as a visual symbol of the village center. Here is an example of recent remodeling which has preserved the character of the building. Externally the only sign of the renovation is the placement of glass, with narrow horizontal mullions, in what used to be the doorway to the firehouse.

1 Wadena Village Hall.

2 **Cozy Theatre,** c. 1937
223 Jefferson Street S
The Streamline Moderne realized through the juxtaposition of curves and sharp angles.

3 **First Methodist Episcopal Church** (now First United Methodist Church), 1911
23 Dayton Avenue SE
English Gothic, of a sort; its thin volumetric form floats lightly over its stone foundation.

4 **St. Helena Episcopal Church,** 1895
1st Street SW and Dayton Avenue SW
A small fieldstone church in the Gothic mode. The steep roof seems to hover over, rather than be directly connected to, the stone walls below.

5 **Lustron House,** c. 1949
111 Dayton Avenue SW
These post–World War II prefabricated metal houses are rare in small communities, but here is one in pristine condition.

NW-20 Warren

As one drives through the flat plains adjoining the Snake River on Highway 75, the small town of Warren appears. Around it on all sides are well-kept farm complexes set in rich fields of wheat and alfalfa. The gridiron plan of the town follows the southwest/northeast axis of the railroad, although certain north/south, east/west corrections have been made.

1 **Marshall County Courthouse,** 1909
A. F. Ganger
208 Colvin Avenue E
A yellow-brick Romanesque Revival structure on a stone foundation. The frontispiece entrance, with its three arches and high pointed tower, seems an exotic addition to the plain H-shaped building.

2 **Old North Star College** (now Good Samaritan Center), 1911
410 McKinley Street S
A plain two-story raised-basement building in brick with little attached "architecture." Its character shows not in its styling but in the obvious antagonism between the building and its prairie site.

3 **Warren Theatre,** c. 1938
Johnson Avenue E at 2nd Street (Highway 75)

Like the State Theatre in nearby Red Lake Falls, the Warren Theatre has paired doors with half-circle glass windows, but it lacks the glass-brick centerpiece of the State Theatre. It somewhat makes up for this loss in the boldness of its curved neon sign and marquee.

4 **Historic Buildings**
Marshall County Fairgrounds, at east end of Johnson Avenue

Three historic buildings have been uprooted from their original sites and set down on the lawns of the fairgrounds: a clapboard church, a rural schoolhouse, and a cabin of hand-hewn logs with a shed-roof porch.

NW-21 Warroad

Warroad boasts that the "largest log church in the U.S." (St. Mary's Catholic Church) stands in its midst. The church is situated at the northeast corner of Roberts and Mackenzie Streets, north of Lake Street. This gable-roof structure and its brick tower were built in 1953. Its basic folk character battles with its pretense at "architecture" in such details as the stone entrance, the Latin cross window, and the tower. At the northwest corner of Lake and Roberts Streets is a Streamline Moderne theatre (c. 1937) — a brick-sheathed box.

St. Mary's Catholic Church.

NW-22 White Earth

The village of White Earth, on the White Earth Indian Reservation, houses one of Minnesota's really fine small rural churches — St. Columba's Episcopal Church (1889). This church is of the corner-tower type with a windowed gable section facing the street. The fieldstone walls of the church contrast with the Eastlake delicacy of its wood detailing.

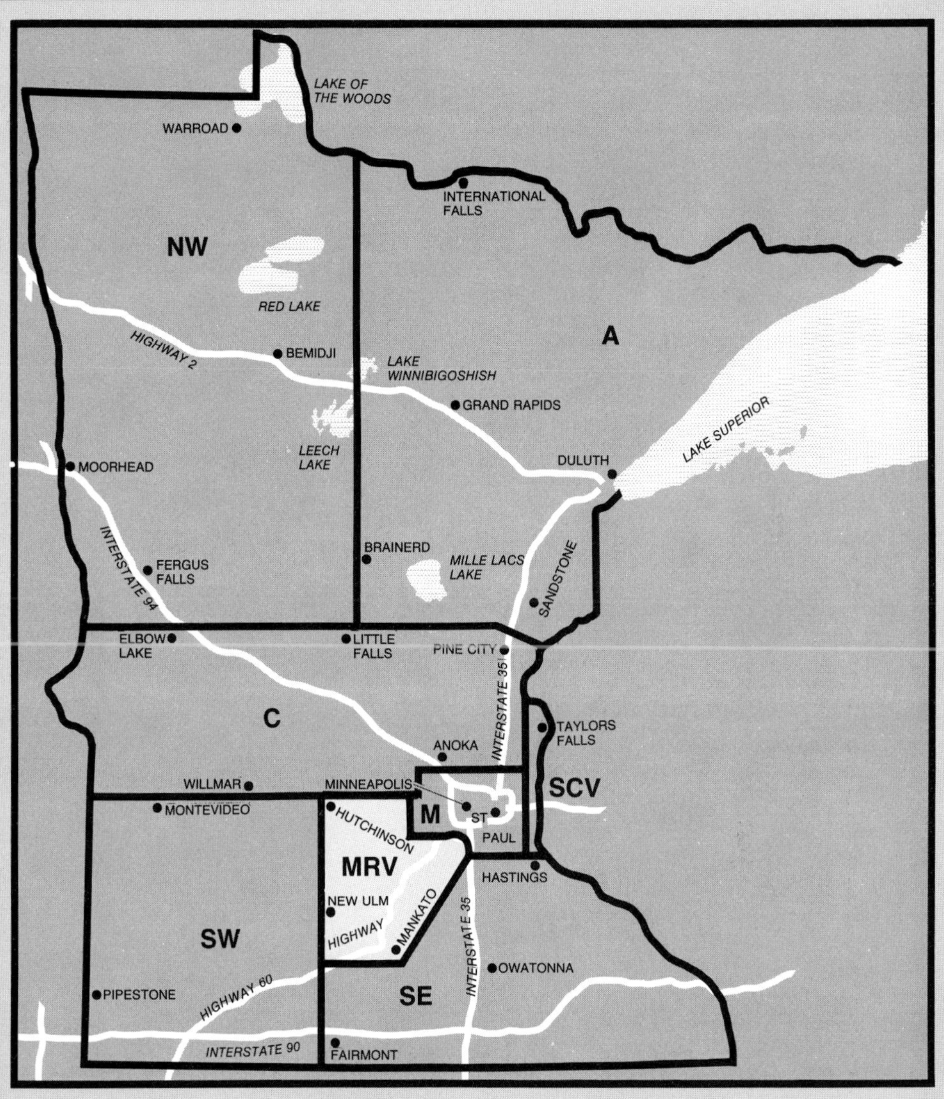
LAKE OF THE WOODS
WARROAD
INTERNATIONAL FALLS
NW
RED LAKE
A
HIGHWAY 2
BEMIDJI
LAKE WINNIBIGOSHISH
GRAND RAPIDS
LAKE SUPERIOR
LEECH LAKE
MOORHEAD
DULUTH
INTERSTATE 94
FERGUS FALLS
BRAINERD
MILLE LACS LAKE
SANDSTONE
ELBOW LAKE
LITTLE FALLS
PINE CITY
INTERSTATE 35
C
TAYLORS FALLS
ANOKA
WILLMAR
MINNEAPOLIS
SCV
MONTEVIDEO
HUTCHINSON
M
ST PAUL
MRV
HASTINGS
NEW ULM
INTERSTATE 35
HIGHWAY
MANKATO
SW
OWATONNA
PIPESTONE
HIGHWAY 60
SE
INTERSTATE 90
FAIRMONT

MRV-1 Arlington

Arlington was platted in 1856, and when the Chicago and Northwest Railroad reached it in the 1870s the town was replatted. In the downtown area are several commercial buildings which should be noted. At 302 Main Street West is a two-story gable-roofed commercial block (probably a bank originally) which is now used for law offices (c. 1890). In style it is loosely Romanesque with an arched entrance and small arched windows on the side and a grand arched window, articulated by light-colored voussoirs. The second-floor windows pierce through the upper entablature in a highly sculptural manner. Across the street at 309 Main Street West is a Streamline Moderne theatre, the Lido (c. 1939). The marquee and the surfaces of the theatre are plain, but the designer made up for this by the contrast of white glazed brick, bright blue glazed brick, and red trim. In the residential section of the town is the Foley House at 110 4th Avenue Northeast. This brick dwelling (c. 1880s) boasts a dramatic Eastlake porch, with the cantilevered roof supported by angled struts. At 212 2nd Avenue Northwest is the Queen Anne Bushey House (c. 1890). A delicate tracery of sawed and turned wood covers the front of the ground floor and the second-floor porches.

Bushey House, Arlington.

MRV-2 Belle Plaine

The small community of Belle Plaine on the east bank of the Minnesota River hides two churches of architectural interest. The First Presbyterian Church (219 Main Street West) is a small-scaled Gothic Revival church (c. 1870), built of stone with low, pronounced buttresses. The original entrance in front has been filled in and other changes have taken place, but the building still remains a gem among small church structures. Equally remarkable in design is the 1869 Episcopal Church (Walnut Street North between State Street East and Church Street East). The sanctuary of this church is Eastlake sheathed in clapboard and board-and-batten, and it has pointed windows. Off to the side is the entrance tower, a remarkable Eastlake design of open-work construction with a small bell tower perched on top.

Episcopal Church, Belle Plaine.

MRV-3 Carver

The town of Carver, north of the Minnesota River on Carver Creek, was settled in 1851–52 and was platted in 1857. The most interesting house in town is the Funk House (1902), a Queen Anne/Colonial Revival design with a round bay-tower topped by a conical roof. It can be found on the north side of County Road 40, just east of its intersection with County Road 147. One block south of that intersection, and three blocks west of downtown, is the Hilldale House (1871), a typical brick Italianate dwelling. High on the top of the hill overlooking the town, with its spire visible through the trees, is the St. Nicholas Catholic Church (1868) — more impressive and romantic when seen from afar.

MRV-4 Chaska

The town of Chaska was founded in 1854 by the Chaska Land Company. The townsite was platted on the northwest bank of the Minnesota River in the late 1850s, and by the 1880s the town was connected to the Twin Cities by railroad. At the northeast corner of Cedar Street and 2nd Street West is the brick Gothic Guardian Angels Catholic Church (1885). A somewhat more lively Gothic composition can be found in the open-towered Moravian Church (c. 1889), situated on the northwest corner of Walnut Street and 4th Street East.

MRV-5 East Union

In East Union, one of the earliest Swedish settlements in Minnesota, one finds a stone Lutheran church and a parish house which were built in 1858. The church is of the tower-entrance type, and the vertical emphasis of its high-pitched roof and its pointed windows places it within the Gothic. The interior in contrast is more akin to an eighteenth-century meeting hall, with its coved wood ceiling and plain walls. The church is located three and a half miles west of Carver on County Road 40. In nearby West Union is another Lutheran church of similar design, also dating from 1858.

MRV-6 Gaylord

• The Sibley County Courthouse (1917) by James A. Burner and William H. Macomber is probably the most handsome of the twentieth-century Beaux Arts courthouses in Minnesota. Its architectural background is midway between English and American Georgian and early nineteenth-century Greek Revival. An impressive pedimented portico with a raised basement projects from the front of the building. The walls behind and between the columns have been opened up with large glass windows. The proportions of the composition are as impressive as the detailing. The building is situated at the north end of 4th Street and Court Avenue.

MRV-7, MRV-8, MRV-9

MRV-7 Gibbon

The 1895 village hall in the Minneapolis and St. Louis Railroad town of Gibbon employs the image of a medieval castle in its design — a battered stone base with battered crenelated brick parapets, round arches, and an open belfry tower (which looks more like an afterthought than a part of the original design). The village hall is situated at the southeast corner of 1st Avenue and 12th Street, one block south of Highway 19.

MRV-8 Glencoe

The town was established in 1855, and in the 1870s the Chicago, Milwaukee, and St. Paul Railroad joined the community to the Twin Cities. At the southwest corner of 11th Street East (Franklin Street) and Ives Avenue South is the McLeod County Courthouse. The original courthouse was built in 1876, but what we see today is a 1909 Beaux Arts building in brick with quoined corners, entablatured windows, and a recessed central portico with two Ionic columns (Stebbins, Kinney, and Halden; additions in 1932–35 by Pass and Rockey). Next door (to the west) is the courthouse addition (1958) by Hammel and Green. The street elevation of the addition is a windowless brick wall with a stone base and cornice. The brick box is joined to the older building by a recessed glass section. On the whole this has worked out far better here than it has in courthouses elsewhere in the state.

On the northwest corner of 11th Street East and Ives Avenue South is the two-story brick Enterprise Building (c. 1880). The Enterprise sign is a perfect period piece of the 1920s. Farther west at 1011 Elliott Avenue South (off 11th Street) is the single-floor Streamline Moderne office building of the Glencoe Mills (c. 1940). Behind the office building stands a great bank of storage elevators.

MRV-9 Henderson

The town of Henderson on the Minnesota River was once the seat of Sibley County, but today it is only a small village with a few impressive remains of its past.

1 **Poehler Brothers Block** (now Henderson Mercantile Company), 1877
527 Main Street

A two-story commercial block in the Italianate Style. The first-floor front has been remodeled.

2 **Former Sibley County Courthouse,** 1879
Northwest corner Main Street and 6th Street S

A very plain but quite strong design in the Italianate Style. A suggestion of engaged piers divides the principal façade into three parts, and a small high-pitched gable brings added emphasis to the center entrance of the building.

2 Former Sibley County Courthouse.

3 **Poehler House,** 1882–83
George Pass
700 Main Street
A mixture of Eastlake and Queen Anne.

4 **Comnick House,** 1860s
104 8th Street S
Italianate, but in plan and elevation quite Greek/Federal. The house has round-headed windows above, segmented arched windows below, and an entrance with a transom and sidelights.

5 **Joseph R. Brown House,** 1856
317 5th Street S
A one-and-a-half-story cottage which utilizes both Gothic Revival and Italianate details.

6 **Cottage,** late 1870s
304 8th Street S
An extensive one-and-a-half-story French Second Empire dwelling situated on the hill overlooking the town. The sawed wood in the porch is derived from the Eastlake.

MRV-10 Hutchinson

The town was established on the south fork of the Crow River in 1855, but it was not incorporated until 1881. By 1880 the community was connected to the Twin Cities by the Burlington Northern Railroad.

1 **House,** c. 1880s
South side Highway 7 (Park Avenue), just east of railroad tracks
A square brick house with stone trim and a hipped roof that is flat in the center. The style is impossible to pin down — the bracketed roof hints at the Italianate, but nothing else does.

2 **House** (now McLeod County Historical Society), c. late 1890s
Southeast corner Jefferson Street and 1st Avenue SE
A two-story brick house. The porch, with its classical columns and balustrade, is Queen Anne/Colonial Revival.

3 **State Theatre,** c. 1937
North side Washington Avenue between Main and Hassan Streets
Angular Streamline Moderne with a circular central tower of glass and keyhole windows in the doors under the marquee.

4 **Public Library,** 1904
E. S. Stebbins
Northwest corner 1st Avenue SE and Hassan Street
A Beaux Arts Classical library with a pedimented recessed entry porch.

3 State Theatre.

5 **Medical Clinic,** c. 1939
107 1st Avenue SW
A small Streamline Moderne building in white stucco with a curved entrance of glass brick and corner windows.

6 **House,** c. 1905
406 Main Street S
The Colonial Revival in full force. The commodious brick dwelling has a two-story portico with four columns.

7 **Goodnow House,** 1913
Purcell, Feick, and Elmslie
446 Main Street S

A one-and-a-half-story brick and stucco house based upon Wright's *Ladies Home Journal* plan of 1906. The entry with its Richardsonian arch is on the ground level. Wide overhanging roofs with dramatic beam ends press the building onto the site. Finely leaded glass bookcases are situated at each side of the fireplace in the living room.

7 Goodnow House.

8 **Cottage,** c. 1870s
405 Franklin Street S

A one-and-a-half-story brick Eastlake Cottage with delicate sawed work on the front porch.

9 **St. Anastasia's Elementary School,** c. 1957
Traynor and Hermanson
400 Lake Street S

A Moderne building with a folded entrance canopy and occasional exposures of the steel frame. Highly colorful — the front brick panels are bright red, the glass blocks are clear and opaque white and there are touches elsewhere of royal blue and sea green.

9 St. Anastasia's Elementary School.

MRV-11 Kasota

Just south of St. Peter is the community of Kasota, which was platted in 1855 and incorporated in 1890. The town had a brief period of prosperity around 1890, and then it settled down to a quiet existence which has continued to the present. There are no street signs in the town, so the directions given here describe the location of buildings with reference to County Road 21.

1 **Kasota Township Hall,** 1889
On County Road 21

A plain brick building with just the slightest touch of stone detailing below the brick cornice and a series of projecting brick volumes (on both street façades) which are similar to the projecting base of Eastlake chimneys.

2 **Bank Building** (now Post Office), 1902
1 block south of County Road 21

A small brick building with brick and stone trim. The angled corner entrance with its engaged piers and arch is Romanesque.

3 **Village Hall,** 1899
1 block south of County Road 21 (1 block west of #2)
A two-story Eastlake building with brick and stone trim which stylistically is more nineteenth century than twentieth century.

4 **House,** c. 1860s
1 block north of County Road 21
The remains of a classic end-gable Greek Revival house with a side-hall plan. The entrance of this one-and-a-half-story house has a horizontal pediment, a suggestion of paneled side piers, and sidelights.

MRV-12 Le Sueur

Le Sueur was one of many towns established in the 1850s on the banks of the Minnesota River. The plats for the town were laid out in 1852 just below the junction of the Minnesota River and Le Sueur Creek. Milling and other activities were important in the early growth of the community, but the major economic activity since 1903 has been the Green Giant canning and processing plant. Through the 1950s Highway 169 crossed the river and went straight through town on Main Street. The new routing of Highway 169 west of the river has meant that the retail commercial aspects of the town can now be directed inward. A new pedestrian mall has been built on several blocks of Main Street, and new off-street parking has been provided.

1 **Mayo House,** 1859
118 Main Street N
A one-and-a-half-story central-pavilion cottage which blends the Greek, the Italianate, and the Gothic. Amazing changes of scale take place in the front elevation: The classical sidelighted entrance is far too large for the size of the cottage and for the gabled section above; equally out-of-scale with the volume of the house are the two large windows on each side of the central pavilion.

2 **Le Sueur Theatre,** c. 1937
209 Main Street S
The Moderne of the 1930s, more Zigzag than Streamline.

3 **Smith-Cosgrove House,** 1870
228 Main Street S
A French Second Empire house in brick. The central tower with its high-pitched hipped roof and small half-moon dormers and the long narrow window below are much closer to French than to American models.

4 **House,** late 1860s
129 2nd Street S
A central-hall plan Greek Revival house with Italianate details.

5 **Taylor House,** 1890
103 2nd Street S
A large and elaborately decorated (for Minnesota) Eastlake house with spindle work and sawed wood, encyclopedic in the changing textures of its wall surfaces.

6 **House,** c. 1905
228 2nd Street S
Turn-of-the-century Colonial Revival, rich in columns, arches, and bays.

6 House.

7 **Octagon House,** c. 1880s
224 4th Street S
A plain clapboard house of a single story in the shape of an octagon with appendages.

MRV-13 Mankato

In 1852 the Blue Earth Settlement Claim Association was formed in St. Paul to plan the settlement of Mankato. The site selected for the community was a reasonably wide, flat area between the Minnesota River and the hills which rise to the east and south on the east side of the river. By the time the city was incorporated in 1868 it had become an important center for flour milling and limestone quarrying. In 1868 a state normal school (now Mankato State College) was established in the city.

Front Street (both north and south) contains a number of nineteenth-century brick commercial blocks and also a Streamline Moderne theatre (the Grand Theatre). Along the elm-lined streets, especially in the southeastern section of the city, one finds an assortment of architectural styles from the late nineteenth and early twentieth centuries; few of these are grand houses, but the neighborhood atmosphere and the hilly site make this a very pleasant area.

Five miles west of Mankato on Highway 68 is the stone Seppman Mill, which was built in 1862–63. The mill, in Minneopa State Park, was wind-powered. Its conical form seems far more European than one expects to encounter in Minnesota. Nearby, also on Highway 68, one-half mile west of its junction with Highway 60, is a brick pipeline company building; its Streamline Moderne design (c. 1940) is identical to that of a building with a similar function in Alexandria.

Seppman Mill, near Mankato.

1 **First National Bank,** 1913
Ellerbe and Round
229 Front Street S

The first studies for the design of this Prairie bank were made in 1912 by Purcell, Feick, and Elmslie. The design provided for a landscaped forecourt and a deep Richardsonian arch at the entrance. This was rejected by the client, and Ellerbe and Round produced the design we see today — a design which closely follows that of Sullivan but which has none of the liveliness of a building by Sullivan or by Purcell, Feick, and Elmslie. Still, it is a good academic exercise in the Prairie Style, and it is certainly the most important single building in Mankato.

1 First National Bank.

2 **Union Block,** 1887
513 Front Street S

A three-story Eastlake/Romanesque Revival commercial block.

3 **Blue Earth County Courthouse,** 1889
Healy and Allen
204 5th Street S

The architects combined the Romanesque and the French Second Empire styles to produce an impressive and remarkably coherent design. On the northwest side of the building there are arched openings in the curved sides of the entrance porch. The interior of the building was remodeled in 1965.

4 **First Presbyterian Church,** 1893
220 Hickory Street E

In the late 1880s and early 1890s a number of architects borrowed forms and details from both the Romanesque and the Gothic and applied them as in the large serviceable interior auditorium of this church. The building is essentially Richardsonian Romanesque, but many of its details are Gothic.

5 **Cray House** (now YWCA), 1897–99
603 2nd Street S

Romanesque Revival in brick and stone, with a Colonial Revival entrance porch. The architect seems to have had a passion for numerous bands of coupled columns.

6 **Hubbard House** (now Blue Earth County Historical Society), c. 1870s
606 Broad Street S

A two-and-a-half-story French Second Empire house in brick (which is now painted). The building was remodeled in the 1880s. The Hubbard Carriage Barn (1891), in the Queen Anne Style, is presently located across Warren Street, but it is to be moved to a spot behind the Hubbard House and restored to its former condition by Miller-Dunwiddie Architects.

7 **House,** early 1880s
212 Liberty Street

An Eastlake/Queen Anne house of brick and wood. The vertical and horizontal patterning of the walls comes close to the Stick Style. Note the ornament in the entrance pediment of the porch and the metal cut-out flag with an M on top of the tower.

• 8 **House,** c. 1880
811 2nd Street S

A brick Eastlake/Queen Anne house culminating in a round corner stair-tower with a classic Eastlake window assemblage.

9 **Ray Cottage,** 1870–71
217 Lincoln Street

A one-and-a-half-story French Second Empire cottage. The front porch has delicate, very thin Ionic columns.

MRV-14 New Auburn

New Auburn houses another of Minnesota's Artstone creameries. The New Auburn Creamery (1929) has a stepped crenelated roof and makes a slight nod toward the Prairie School in its glazed brick decoration; the names of the creamery's board of directors appear on its cornerstone. The creamery is located one block west of Highway 22, which is the town's main street. Also on Highway 22 is a brick Streamline Moderne building (1945) which was originally a school; it now houses Al and Alma's Auburn Club. The small brick commercial building on the west side of Highway 22 (to the south) is now a residence. Brick has been used exclusively to create a patterned surface and a cornice for the building.

MRV-15, MRV-16

MRV-15 New Prague

In New Prague (founded in 1856) is the New Prague Hotel (1898) at 212 West Main Street. Cass Gilbert, who designed the building, modeled the two-story structure after late eighteenth-century English Georgian prototypes. Another commercial building of interest in New Prague is the former First National Bank Building (now the Fidelity State Bank) at 112 East Main Street. This terra-cotta building is a delicate, finely detailed version of Beaux Arts classicism.

New Prague Hotel.

MRV-16 New Ulm

The city was founded in 1854 by German colonists who came first from Chicago and later from Cincinnati. They chose for the site of their new city a terraced bench on the west bank of the Minnesota River, just above its confluence with the smaller Cottonwood River. The orientation of the Minnesota River at this point is northwest/southeast, and the city's gridiron was patterned accordingly. The plan of the city went far beyond the gridiron schemes which were developed in most Minnesota towns dating from the second half of the nineteenth century. Two extensive rectangular parks were laid out on top of the bluff overlooking the river. Two blocks away from the bluff a major street, Broadway, was developed as a residential street. Farther up the hill a block was set aside for the courthouse, and farther west on the terraced hill West Park and Monument Park were laid out. Other parks — North Park and the adjacent Brown County Agricultural Society Park — were added to the north, and South Park was added to the south. Still later Riverside Park was established along the Minnesota River at the east end of Center Street.

The general appearance of the community today suggests a balance between order and overt regimentation. The retail commercial area is assembled around Minnesota Street, the industrial and commercial center is on the river flats, and the residential district lies on both sides of Minnesota Street. The newer residential additions have been built near South Park and on the hill behind the Hermann Monument and Martin Luther College. From a planning point of view the major unresolved problem is still the use of Broadway as the city's link with Highways 14 and 68.

Architecturally New Ulm has often been referred to as a city of German-inspired architecture, but this is only marginally the case. By far the vast majority of its commercial, public, and residential buildings reflect the usual changes which have occurred in American architectural fashions. And in those instances in which the buildings do have a nineteenth-century European character, their styles point more to the lowlands and even northeastern France than to Germany and central Europe.

The extensive use of brick with its simplicity and plain surfaces does create a feeling of kinship with Europe more than with the typical wood Eastlake and Queen Anne architecture of the United States, but the interior and exterior detailing of these New Ulm buildings accurately reflects the various changes which have occurred in American architectural taste.

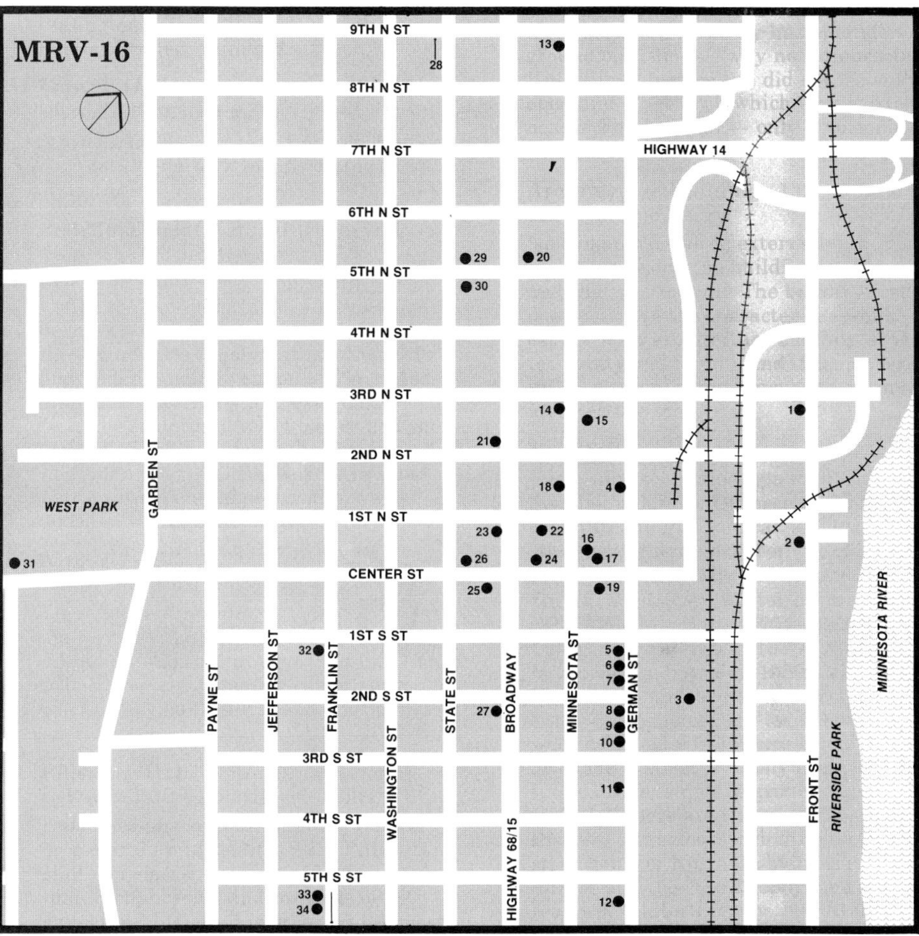

1 **Service Station,** c. 1928
Southwest corner Front Street N and 3rd Street N

A Hansel and Gretel image for a service station — half-timber walls, a swayed roof, and a chimney.

2 **New Ulm Machine and Iron Works Building,** c. 1870s
19 Front Street N

Cast-iron columns support three of the arches on the ground level of this Italianate commercial block. Near the top two pairs of round-hooded windows provide a false arcade.

3 **Chicago Northwestern Railroad Depot,** c. 1890s
Valley Street S between 1st and 2nd Streets S
A stone railroad station modeled after Richardson's suburban Boston stations. Low hipped roofs cover the open waiting area between the main block and the two end buildings.

4 **House,** c. 1936
115 German Street N
A two-story Streamline Moderne house with horizontal dark banding.

5 **House,** c. 1880
110 German Street S
A high brick rectangle covered by a flat-topped hip roof with dormers and gables. The detailing is Eastlake, but the form is anything but Eastlake.

5 House.

6 **House,** c. 1880
114 German Street S
Another large brick box, in this case with a gable roof which has been flattened on top. The detailing is Eastlake.

7 **House,** c. 1880
124 German Street S
A brick house with a mansard roof and wood detailing in the Eastlake Style.

8 **Schmidt House,** 1898
200 German Street S
A brick house whose detailing is classical (very late Italianate).

9 **Seiter House,** 1865
212 German Street S
A segmented arched porch runs across the front of this Italianate dwelling. The center portion is two-story, balanced by high single-story wings on each side.

10 **House,** c. 1890
Northwest corner German Street S and 3rd Street S
A Queen Anne Style house with turned woodwork.

11 **House,** c. 1890
312 German Street S
A commodious brick Queen Anne dwelling with elaborate woodwork in the high gable ends and on the porches.

12 **House,** 1870
508 German Street S
An Italianate Villa residence of brick (now painted). A band composed of a square within a square forms the entablature for the building.

13 **Niemann House,** c. 1900
827 Minnesota Street N
The house is a crenelated fortress, a fanciful and highly romantic image.

13 Niemann House.

14 **Commercial Block,** c. 1890
Southwest corner Minnesota Street N and 3rd Street N
The arched portion of the façade looks to the Romanesque, but the character of the proportions and the detailing is Queen Anne. Note the two-story commercial block across Minnesota Street (southeast corner of 3rd Street North); it is Eastlake in style.

15 Kiesling House and Park, 1861
220 Minnesota Street N

A small urban park has been created by Interdesign (1969–72) between this small clapboard house and the street. To the rear of the house is a partially underground meeting room. The house is now used by the chamber of commerce.

16 Historic Mural, 1972
16 Minnesota Street N (north wall)

The wall mural, "Life Sketches: New Ulm, 1850s" by Gordon L. Dingman, was sculptured in brick and then fired.

•**17 W. Boesch Building and Hummel Maltzahn Building,** 1890
10–12 Minnesota Street N

Four large bays and a balcony project from the second floor, and above them two false-fronted gables break up the skyline. Across the street (9–11 Minnesota Street North) is the three-story Romanesque Revival Masonic Block (1890).

18 Citizens State Bank of New Ulm, 1973
Vosejpka Associates
105 Minnesota Street N

The street façade of the bank is designed as a series of overlaid, interpenetrating rectangular forms. A gigantic clock on the left balances the deeply cut-out openings on the other side. A high arcade, leading from the rear parking lot to the street, is treated as a separate building. The interior of the bank has partially carpeted walls.

18 Citizens State Bank of New Ulm.

19 Georgia's Bar and Rock Room, c. 1941
Corner Center Street and German Street S

A Streamline Moderne establishment with a maroon-and-cream-colored sign.

20 Service Station, c. 1924
Northeast corner Broadway N and 5th Street N

A corner filling station. Two fat round towers enclose a single-story section. A hipped roof and latticework have been added at the front.

21 Armory, 1914
205 Broadway N

When viewed from down the street the building's square and hexagonal towers and crenelated parapets add a lively urban note to the streetscape.

22 New Ulm Theatre, c. 1938
517 1st Street N

A lukewarm Streamline Moderne theatre.

23 Public Library and Historical Museum, 1936
Albert G. Plagens
27 Broadway N

PWA Moderne, with a wonderful relief sculpture of a prairie schooner over the entrance to the museum. A new addition is currently being built.

23 Public Library and Historical Museum.

• 24 **Post Office,** 1909
James Knox Taylor
Center Street between Broadway N and Minnesota Street N

A fanciful horizontal pattern of white stone and red brick with stepped and scalloped gables. Supposedly inspired by German architecture, but in fact much closer to Dutch or Belgian design.

25 **House,** late 1890s
611 Center Street

This is one of a number of brick houses in New Ulm which have stepped gable ends—a visual device which reflects a self-conscious return to European forms.

26 **Lind House,** 1887
Frank Thayer
622 Center Street

A brick Queen Anne dwelling with a round bay tower.

27 **House,** c. 1880
200 Broadway S

A square tower adjoins a one-and-a-half-story mansard roof section; stone quoining on the corners and cast-iron railings adorn the house. A walk or drive farther south on Broadway will reveal numerous late nineteenth-century brick houses.

28 **Historic Buildings,** 1800s
Brown County Agricultural Society Park
Northwest corner State Street N and 12th Street N

Two buildings: a rural clapboard schoolhouse with an open bell tower and a cabin of hand-hewn logs.

29 **Convent, Holy Trinity Cathedral,** 1872
500 State Street N

29 Convent, Holy Trinity Cathedral.

A French Second Empire building has been joined to a somewhat later Gothic Revival (à la Ruskin) chapel. The chapel has a small cut-out metal spire.

30 **House,** c. 1935
422 State Street N

A Streamline Moderne box with a musical treble clef symbol between the two second-story windows. Note how the shed roofs of the entrance and the small projection next to the entrance have been stuccoed over to create a continuous surface for the roof and the walls.

30 House.

• 31 **Hermann Monument,** 1887–89
Alfonzo Pelzer; Julius Berndt
Northeast corner Center Street and Monument Street N

In the nineteenth century there was a passion for public monuments, and in Minnesota the Hermann Monument is the best of them all. Situated on a high podium is a ten-columned open classical temple crowned by a dome with a row of arched dormer windows; the culmination — in a Wagnerian fashion — is the statue of a Teutonic warrior by Alfonzo Pelzer. The temple itself was designed by Julius Berndt, who employed these classical fragments in a way no Roman or Greek could possibly recognize. Berndt also seems to have invented a new classical order in his columns. The whole extravaganza is 102 feet high.

32 **House,** c. 1889
100 Franklin Street S

The thin, lacy woodwork of this house is both Eastlake and Queen Anne.

33 **Gazebo, Hauenstein Brewery,** 1880s, 1891
Southeast corner Jefferson Street and 16th Street S

An Eastlake gazebo which now has a stone base; a built-in bench runs around the interior. The structure was rebuilt and enlarged in 1891.

34 **Schell Brewery and August Schell House,** 1889, 1885
West end 20th Street S (approached from 18th Street S and Broadway)

A nineteenth-century complex consisting of a brick brewery building (1889), the residence of the owner, various outbuildings, and a formal garden. The brewery is a plain building which boasts a few Queen Anne details. The house is European in character (more Belgian or French than German), and the two-story porch overlooking the south garden is Gothic. The garden, with its gazebo, walks, and terraces, forms a romantic transition between the house and the brewery.

MRV-17 Ottawa

The Minnesota River community of Ottawa was platted as early as 1856 (its original name being Minnewashta). Within town at the northwest corner of Buchanan and Bryant Streets is the Ottawa Township Hall (c. 1860s), a small building in the Greek Revival style. Another Greek Revival building is the Ottawa Methodist Church (1858) at the southwest corner of Liberty and Whittier Streets. This end-gable, entrance-tower church is built of a handsome pink stone. It is now used as the Le Sueur County Museum. The town also has several early stone dwellings. The cottage at the northwest corner of Sumner and Whittier Streets and the house at the northwest corner of Sumner and Kansas Streets are of particular interest.

MRV-18 St. Peter

In 1857, only three years after the small, still undeveloped town of St. Peter had been platted, it was selected by a majority of the state legislators to be the new capital of Minnesota, replacing St. Paul. In the end the capital city was not changed, but the event certainly helped put St. Peter on the map. St. Peter's site on the Minnesota River gave the city access to waterpower and boat transportation, and by the mid-1860s the city was connected to the Twin Cities by the St. Paul and Sioux City Railroad. These were important factors in the economic life of the city, which was based on flour milling, retailing, and marketing of farm products. The city's importance was further enhanced in the late 1870s by the growth of two institutions — Gustavus Adolphus College and a state hospital for the insane.

The original area of the city, from the river up to Washington Avenue and including the commercial area of Minnesota Avenue, still remains essentially as it was in the nineteenth century. Northward from Washington Avenue and toward the college post–World War II housing has been built. The usual strip commercial developments extend for a limited distance north and south of the city on Highway 169.

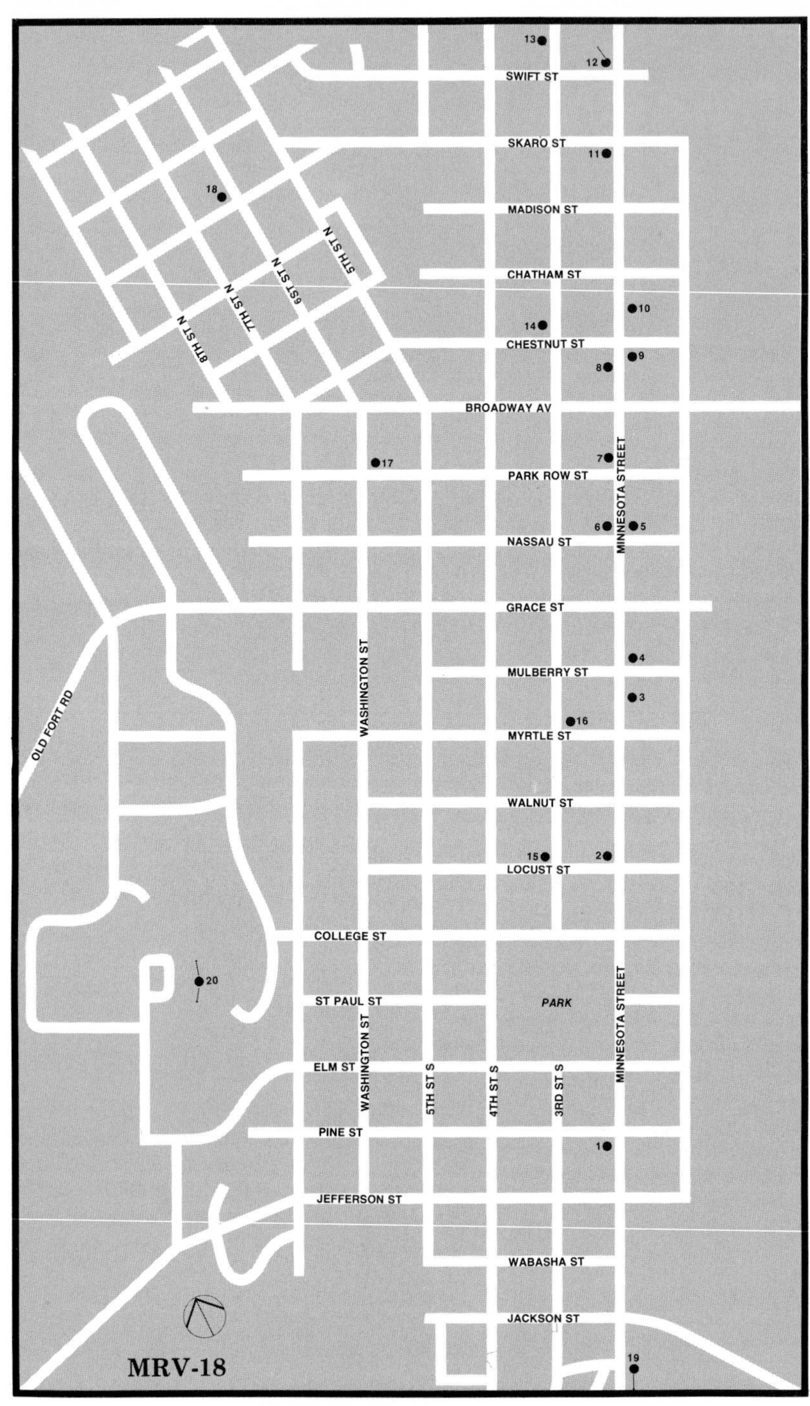
SWIFT ST
SKARO ST
MADISON ST
CHATHAM ST
CHESTNUT ST
BROADWAY AV
PARK ROW ST
NASSAU ST
GRACE ST
MULBERRY ST
MYRTLE ST
WALNUT ST
LOCUST ST
COLLEGE ST
ST PAUL ST
PARK
ELM ST
PINE ST
JEFFERSON ST
WABASHA ST
JACKSON ST
MINNESOTA STREET
WASHINGTON ST
5TH ST S
4TH ST S
3RD ST S
5TH ST N
6ST ST N
7TH ST N
8TH ST N
OLD FORT RD
MRV-18

1 **House,** c. 1880
1202 Minnesota Avenue S

Basically Eastlake in style, but the corner bay-tower is crowned by a complex mansard roof terminating in a large weather vane. There are Queen Anne features as well, including a horizontal oval window. Above the porch entrance are carved the initials "J. E."

2 **House,** 1873
Edward P. Bassford
720 Minnesota Avenue S

A brick Italianate house designed by one of Minnesota's early architects. The house was illustrated in Andreas's *Historical Atlas* of 1874.

3 **Nicollet County Courthouse,** 1880–81
Edward P. Bassford and E. S. Stebbins
Southeast corner Minnesota Avenue S and Mulberry Street E

Italianate with a high central tower. Some of the design elements are Romanesque. The mansard-roofed entrance which has recently been added almost destroys the original effect of the building.

4 **Public Library,** c. 1905
429 Minnesota Avenue S

A small raised-basement Beaux Arts composition. Little has been altered inside.

5 **First National Bank Building** (now Gannon's Restaurant), 1914
Alban Lockhart
225 Minnesota Avenue S

A classical façade of four Ionic columns on the front and eight engaged piers with Ionic capitals on the side. The conversion of the building to a restaurant is not as successful as it might have been, especially in the signing.

6 **Nicollet County Bank Building,** c. 1886
Northwest corner Minnesota Avenue S and Nassau Street W

An Eastlake/Queen Anne two-story commercial block, with a corner entrance and a corner bay-tower above. The addition to the building in 1925 was designed by George Pass.

7 **Nicollet House Hotel,** 1870s
Edward P. Bassford
Park Row Street W at Broadway

A large three-story block in the Italianate Style, with an oversized broken pediment in the center of the principal façade, bracketed eaves, and a projecting balcony.

• 8 **Church of the Holy Communion (Episcopal),** 1869
Henry M. Congdon
110 Minnesota Avenue N

The lines of the high-pitched roof continue down through the buttresses to the ground. A set of three small gable dormers pop out on the two sides of the roof. This is another of Bishop Whipple's miniature churches.

9 **Bornemann House,** c. 1860s
125 Minnesota Avenue N

A puritanical Federal/Greek Revival clapboard house, of the two-story central-hall plan. The windows on the front and side are pedimented; the present entrance porch is a late addition.

10 **House,** c. 1915
215 Minnesota Avenue N

A Prairie box, brought to the ground by its hovering, low-pitched hip roofs. The once-open porch has been enclosed.

11 **House,** c. 1880s
420 Minnesota Avenue N

A square stair-tower projects diagonally from one corner of the house, topped by a double roof — the lower one with a concave curve and the upper one with four small gables. The tower is mildly Eastlake, but the main portion of the house is Italianate.

12 **House,** c. 1870s
702 Minnesota Avenue N

A plain clapboard box with projecting pedimented windows on the first floor, hooded windows on the second floor, and a small entrance porch rich in Eastlake decoration.

13 **House,** c. 1870
620 3rd Street N

A two-story Italianate house with a porch across the front and a low hipped roof.

14 House, c. 1890
202 3rd Street N

The picture of a Victorian house. The porch wraps itself around a three-story tower with an odd roof.

15 Union Presbyterian Church, 1871
Locust Street W at 3rd Street S

Gothic Revival as it might have been envisioned by Charles Eastlake. The chimney on the south side of the church is treated as a Gothic pinnacle with a spire of metal.

16 Church of Immaculate Conception, St. Mary's (Catholic), 1889
3rd Street S at Myrtle Street

A brick church, basically Gothic Revival but with round arched windows.

17 House, c. 1890
525 Park Row Street W

Certainly one of the most unique corner towers to be found on a Minnesota dwelling. A layer of three drums, each smaller than the preceding one, culminates in a curved conical roof. To the left of the entrance one side of the porch roof is simply suspended in midair without a post. The imagination of the carpenter and/or owner is evident in the design of this house.

• **18 St. Julien Cox House,** 1871, 1873
500 Washington Avenue N

The most impressive example of a Gothic Revival dwelling still standing in Minnesota. (The composition also includes a separate stable.) On close inspection of the building one discovers that it is actually an Italianate cottage with Gothic detailing. The tower tucked into the L of the house, the bays, the round-hooded windows, and the paneled columns on the porch are Italianate features, and yet it all ends up being Gothic.

19 State Hospital for Mental Cases (now St. Peter State Hospital), estab. 1866
Off Highway 169, south of town

Most of the buildings on the hospital grounds, especially the recent ones, are totally bland. The first building (1866), however, is quite strong; it is a three-story raised-basement structure in stone with a gable roof. Its style is Greek, although it is a late product of the nineteenth-century Greek Revival.

19 State Hospital for Mental Cases (now St. Peter State Hospital).

20 Gustavus Adolphus College, estab. 1862
West end of College Street

The college was first established in Red Wing and then moved to East Union (near Carver). In 1876, after the completion of Old Main, the college was moved to St. Peter. The entire plan was both classical and romantic. Old Main was connected to 11th Street South by two parallel roadways, and the later buildings were loosely grouped around the resulting open space. In the 1930s William M. Ingemann drew up a master plan for the campus which suggested how some order could be imposed. (Little of this plan was carried out.) In the 1950s Magney, Tusler, and Setter prepared a new master plan which organized all of the new buildings west of Old Main.

Old Main, 1875–76
Edward P. Bassford

A three-story central pavilion and tower in Kasota stone; in style, French Second Empire.

Uhler Hall, 1929
William M. Ingemann

Collegiate Gothic of a neutral character. The inner space of the quadrangle works quite well. Ingemann and Bergstedt carried on the same style theme in Rundstrom Hall (1939) and in Wahlstrom Hall (1947).

Christ Chapel, 1961
Setter, Leach, and Lindstrom

A pencil-thin spire rises from a diagonal box.

Nobel Science Hall, 1963
Setter, Leach, and Lindstrom
A two-story relief sculpture adorns the center of the building.

Folke Bernadotte Memorial Library, 1972
Setter, Leach, and Lindstrom
A cut-into brick box with curved projecting volumes.

• **Schaefer Fine Arts Center,** 1971
Hammel, Green, and Abrahamson
Although varied forms are used, the fine arts complex is a quiet series of brick volumes, almost classical in feeling. The interiors of brick and wood convey the same quality.

MRV-19 Shakopee

Shakopee, situated on the southeast bank of the Minnesota River, was established in 1851 as a trading post. The town was platted in 1854 and eventually became the seat of Scott County. With the gradual spread of suburban Minneapolis to the west and south Shakopee is increasingly being drawn into the orbit of the Twin Cities metropolitan area. The Minnesota Valley Restoration Project, located two miles east of town on Highway 13 (near Memorial Park), includes a number of historic buildings which have been moved in from various locations.

1 **Faribault Trading Post,** c. 1844
A one-and-a-half-story log cabin.

2 **Burger Farm Complex,** c. 1850s
A group of early farm buildings constructed of logs.

3 **"Atwater" Cottage,** c. 1870s
A post-Civil War Gothic Revival cottage.

4 **Realander House,** 1862
A one-and-a-half-story house which is mildly Greek Revival.

5 **Blooming Prairie Church,** c. 1880
A typical Carpenter's Gothic Revival church.

6 **Pond Grist Mill,** 1875
A simple, direct structure of clapboard.

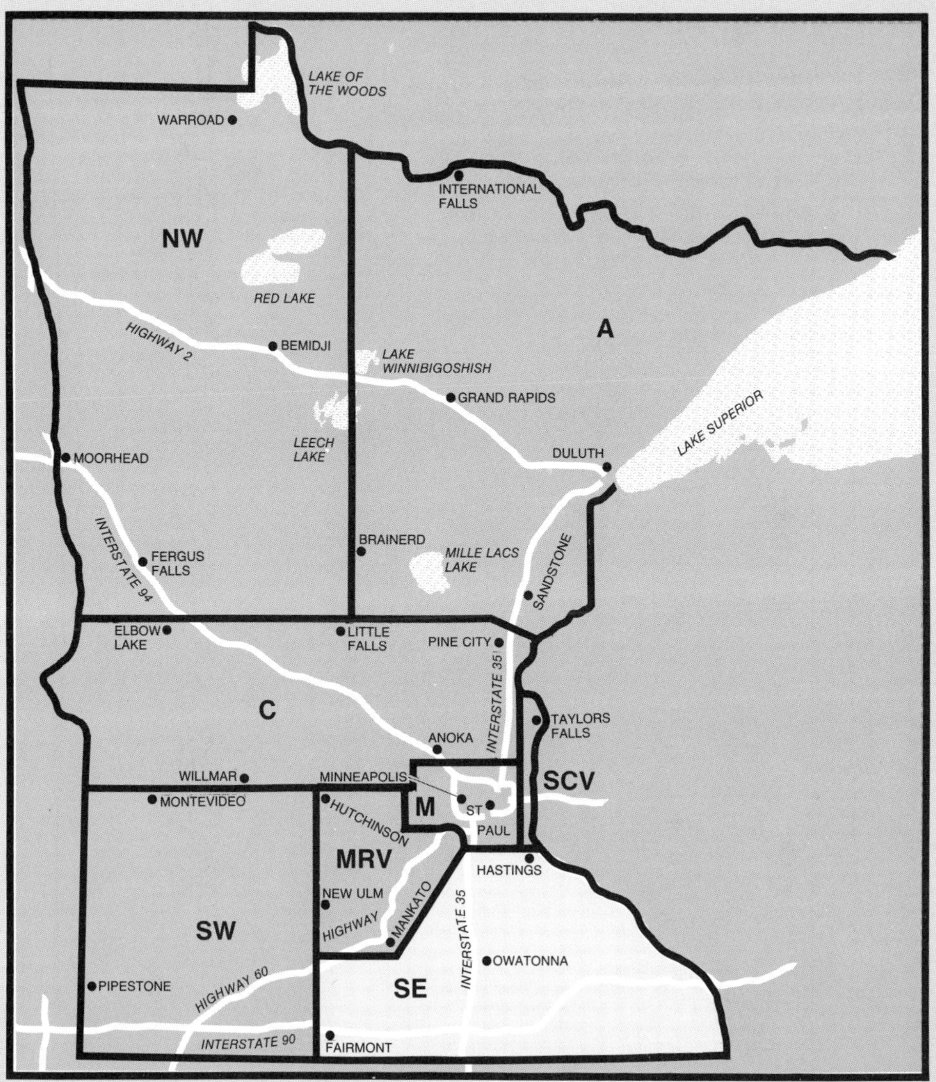
LAKE OF THE WOODS
WARROAD
INTERNATIONAL FALLS
NW
RED LAKE
A
HIGHWAY 2
BEMIDJI
LAKE WINNIBIGOSHISH
GRAND RAPIDS
LAKE SUPERIOR
LEECH LAKE
MOORHEAD
DULUTH
INTERSTATE 94
BRAINERD
MILLE LACS LAKE
FERGUS FALLS
SANDSTONE
ELBOW LAKE
LITTLE FALLS
PINE CITY
INTERSTATE 35
C
TAYLORS FALLS
ANOKA
WILLMAR
MINNEAPOLIS
SCV
MONTEVIDEO
M
ST PAUL
HUTCHINSON
MRV
HASTINGS
NEW ULM
HIGHWAY
MANKATO
INTERSTATE 35
SW
OWATONNA
PIPESTONE
HIGHWAY 60
SE
INTERSTATE 90
FAIRMONT

SE-1 Adams

This railroad village (platted in 1868) houses one of Purcell and Elmslie's small Prairie banks. The former First National Bank (now a municipal liquor store) is located on the northeast corner of Main and 4th Streets. The building was commissioned in 1917, but because of the war it was not completed until 1920. The building has an air of dignity and repose and at the same time an everyday domestic quality. The interior design includes a tent ceiling, brick wainscoting, a tile floor, and even a fireplace in the main business area. A number of changes have been made in the building; especially regrettable is the replacement of the stained glass windows over the entrance with glass bricks.

First National Bank Building (now municipal liquor store), Adams. Photo: William G. Purcell.

SE-2 Albert Lea

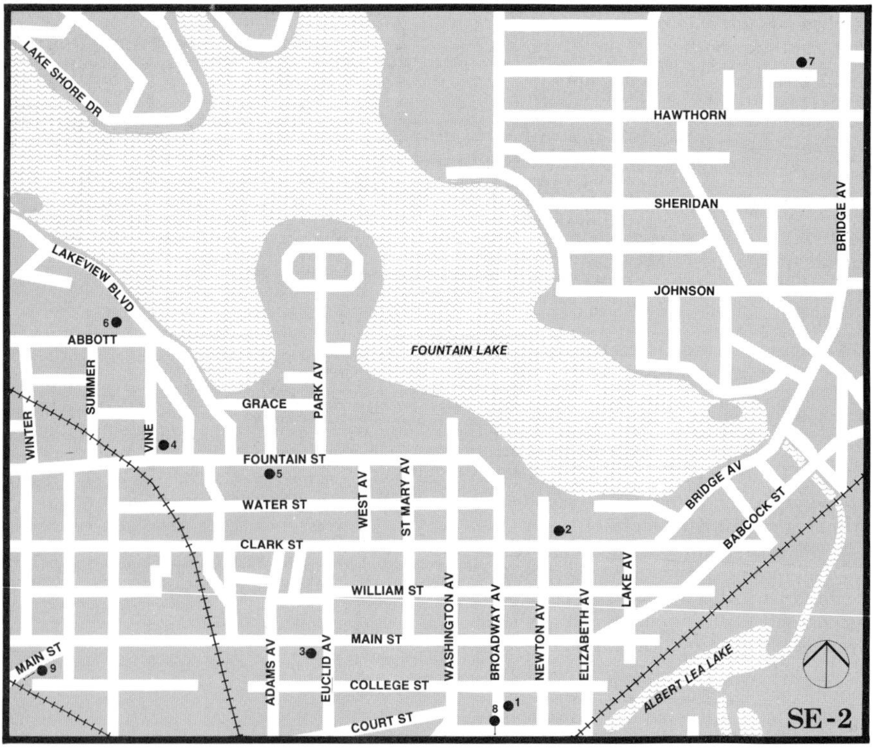

Albert Lea was one of the early railway towns on the Southern Minnesota Railroad. It was settled in 1855 and platted the following year. By the 1860s it had access to the Mississippi River by rail. The city's site encompasses a number of lakes, the largest of which are Lake Albert Lea and Fountain Lake. Main Street and the commercial district meander between the two lakes. The divided boulevards which carry the old highways through the town, the tree-lined residential streets, and the lakes with their parks create a pleasant suburban atmosphere. The new freeways skirt the city completely (Highway 90 far to the north and Highway 35 to the east).

1 **Freeborn County Courthouse,** 1887
C. A. Dunham
Southeast corner Broadway and College Street

A highly original essay in Richardsonian Romanesque, especially in the great tower and the sculpture of four "dogs of the Nile" ready to leap from the building. Banal recent additions (in 1954 by Bernard J. Hein and in 1975 by Foss, Engelstad, and Foss) now press in and around a building of real strength.

1 Freeborn County Courthouse.

2 **City Offices and Library,** 1968
Foss, Engelstad, and Foss
Northeast corner Newton Avenue N and Clark Street

There is a one-story wall, almost windowless, on the Clark Street side. A three-story Corporate International façade faces north toward the lake. The building has the blandness of the 1960s and little civic presence.

3 **United Pentecostal Church** (now Church of Christ), c. 1880s
Southwest corner Main Street W and Euclid Avenue

A carpenter's design in clapboard with a gabled roof. The arched windows have slightly emphasized hoods.

4 **Service Station,** c. 1928
Northeast corner Fountain and Vine Streets

A tiny Colonial Revival house with a chimney, shutters, and window boxes used as a service station.

4 Service Station.

5 **Hiller House,** c. 1905
609 Fountain Street

A dwelling of English half-timber and brick with an octagonal corner turret from the Queen Anne Style. It adds up to a picturesque silhouette.

6 **Lakeview Elementary School,** 1968
Haarstick and Lundgren
902 Abbott Avenue (at Lakeview Boulevard)

A rather neutral but still tasteful exercise in brick volumes and rhythmic patterns of deeply cut windows.

7 **Freeborn County Historical Park**
West of junction Bridge Avenue and Minnie Maddern Street

Several nineteenth-century historic buildings have been moved to this site at the south end of the county fairgrounds. They include a clapboard Gothic Revival church (1878), the Big Oak School, a log cabin, and several small commercial buildings of wood.

8 **Halverson Elementary School,** 1955–56
Hammel and Green
East corner Highway 65 and 11th Street E

A Miesian essay in steel frame with brick infilling. Note the suspended canopy, the underside of which is painted a bright sky blue.

9 **Southwest Junior High School,** 1957–58
Hammel and Green
Highway 69, 1 block south of Highway 16 at Frost Street

Three separate pavilions connected by glassed ramps.

9 Southwest Junior High School.

SE-3 Alden

The Alden Municipal Building (1938) was designed by William M. Ingemann of St. Paul, who worked in a wide variety of Period styles during the 1930s. The municipal building is an impressive exercise in the PWA Moderne. It has a central pavilion with matched wings on the sides; its most eye-catching elements are two brick pylons which terminate in stylized brick urns. The building is located at Broadway, just north of Main Street. North of it, at 215 Broadway North, is the brick high school (c. 1920) with its grouping of vertical attached piers which is reminiscent of the Prairie Style buildings of Purcell and Elmslie. South on Broadway, on the west side between 1st and 2nd Avenues, is a two-story dwelling with a balconied tower. In style it is Queen Anne with Eastlake details and proportions.

Municipal building.

SE-4 Altura

Round barns abound in and around Altura. Most of these barns were built around 1910 by one builder, who, according to local tradition, came from Kansas and built barns in a round form so that they could withstand cyclones. The barns were built on raised stone foundations, and their roofs were divided into two spherical segments with a small cupola on top. A good selection of these structures can be seen east of town on Highway 248 and then north on County Road 31 toward the town of Beaver. Near the southeast corner of County Roads 31 and 28 is a round barn which was remodeled in 1949; the new dome springs directly from the raised stone base, and a central silo projects from the center of the domed roof, creating a strange visual effect. Another of these barns exists on Highway 247, just east of Potsdam.

Round barn (c. 1910; remodeled, 1949).

SE-5 Austin

The city was platted in 1856 on the west bank of the Red Cedar River. It has grown appreciably, and it now houses the large Hormel meat-packing plant. As the city has expanded toward the west, it has abandoned the rectangular geometry of the gridiron scheme and replaced it with meandering curved streets. The east/west freeway (Highway 90) passes just north of the city.

1 **Paramount Theatre,** 1928
Ellerbe and Company
North side 4th Avenue NE at junction 1st Street NE
Some of the ornamentation and the tile work is Spanish Colonial Revival, but the sense of the building is Lowland, almost Dutch. A new marquee and a new sign have replaced the original ones.

2 **Northwestern Bank,** 1970
Warren W. Kane
Northwest corner Main Street N and 4th Avenue NW
A Wrightian building of great exuberance.

3 **Service Station,** c. 1930
Southeast corner 1st Drive NW and 5th Place NW
Smoothed-over classical with contrasting brick corner quoins.

3 Service Station.

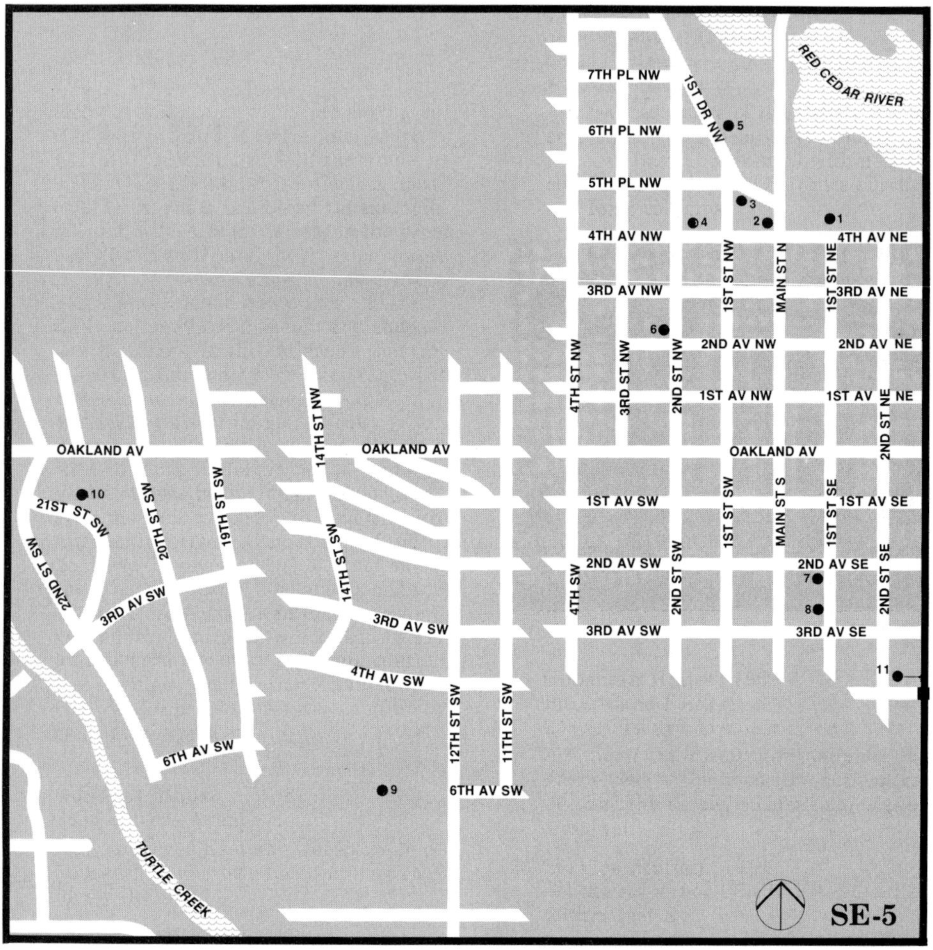

SE-5

4 **Hormel House** (now YWCA), c. 1905
208 4th Avenue NW

The Colonial Revival on a grand scale. A bold two-story pedimented porch with fluted Ionic columns faces the street.

5 **Red Cedar Inn** (now Holiday Inn), 1959–60
Hammel and Green
Northeast side 1st Drive NW at 6th Place NW

A dignified four-story box with precast metal fins, set on a low podium.

4 Hormel House (now YWCA).

6 **Crane House** (now Morreim Building), 1906
300 2nd Avenue NW

A commodious brick dwelling, obviously inspired by the turn-of-the-century work of the Prairie School architect George W. Maher.

7 **House,** c. 1870
300 1st Street SE

A side-hall Italianate house in brick with a wide, bracketed overhanging roof. The porch is a recent addition.

8 **House,** c. late 1870s
308 1st Street SE

A two-story Italianate house in clapboard with a wide central gable. The porch (probably not the original one) has Ionic columns.

9 **Historical Center**
Mower County Fairgrounds
West side 12th Street SW, opposite 6th Avenue SW

A historic park which seems to include just about everything — a log cabin (1861), the wonderful cupola from the nineteenth-century Mower County Courthouse (torn down in the 1950s), a church, a railroad depot, a house, a cement mixer, and a Sherman tank. All safely ensconced in locked-in quarters.

10 **Elam House** (now Plunkett House), 1950–51
Frank Lloyd Wright
309 21st Street SW

A Wright dwelling of stone, glass, and cypress. The butterfly roof seems to press the building down onto the site. The house reveals a remarkable play of scale between the low and intimate band of glass doors leading to the balcony and the glass area above. The rear terrace and the garage were added later.

10 Elam House (now Plunkett House).

11 **Ellis Junior High School,** 1957–58
Hammel and Green
4th Avenue SE between 15th and 16th Streets SE

An elegant and correct Miesian design for a single-floor school.

11 Ellis Junior High School.

SE-6 Blooming Prairie

When first settled in 1856 the community was called Oak Glen; it was renamed when the Chicago, Milwaukee, St. Paul, and Pacific Railroad reached the town. Almost hidden from view at the northeast corner of Highway 218 and 1st Street is a small stucco service station dating from about 1928 (no longer in use); it is in the English Cottage Style with a high-pitched roof. The Union Creamery (c. 1905) can be reached by driving west on 1st Street to 2nd Avenue Southeast and turning north (east side of the street). Concrete blocks in imitation of stone give the creamery its tactile surface. Farther north on Highway 218 and two miles east on Highway 30 is an Italianate wood barn (the date 1893 is conveniently painted above the door) with a four-gabled cupola.

SE-7 Blue Earth

The town was platted at the junction of the Blue Earth River with its east branch. During the 1870s the community was connected with the rest of Minnesota and with towns in Iowa by the St. Peter and Sioux City Railroad. The proposed route of the new freeway skirts the town on the north. At present one enters the downtown area through a pleasantly designed interchange situated in a parklike setting at the north end of town.

1 **Johnson House,** 1934–35
Paul Havens
115 2nd Street E

The Streamline Moderne as a box; two bands of five grooves go around the house horizontally and connect all of the windows together.

1 Johnson House.

2 **Faribault County Courthouse,** 1891
West side Main Street between 2nd and 3rd Streets W

Romanesque Revival with a seven-story tower. A strange Miesian stair, an entrance platform, and light standards have been placed before the handsome double-arched entrance.

2 Faribault County Courthouse.

3 **Post Publishing Building,** 1937
West side Main Street between 5th and 6th Streets W

PWA Moderne, very restrained; tastefully placed lettering on the front of the building.

4 First Farmers National Bank (now unused), c. 1938
West side Main Street between 6th and 7th Streets W

A Moderne bank of the 1930s, classical and formal but not heavy or monumental. A band of Moderne relief sculpture of stylized plants, leaves, and flowers.

4 First Farmers National Bank (now unused).

5 House, c. 1880
106 Holland Street (at 6th Street)

Eastlake with a remarkable tower. The tower is covered by two concave roof surfaces with gables at each end.

6 Presbyterian Church, 1897
Southwest corner Galbraith Street and 6th Street E

Numerous towers and gables portray this church as Medieval, but the heavy reliance on the round arch would seem to point to the Romanesque.

7 Housing for the Elderly, 1969
Miller and Melby
Southwest corner Galbraith Street and 7th Street E

This four-story, sixty-unit structure is designed in a horseshoe shape, with the covered unit entrances facing only a secluded garden courtyard.

8 House, c. 1930
309 7th Street E

A stone Colonial Revival house with a Tuscan-columned porch.

•9 Episcopal Church of the Good Shepherd, 1871
Northeast corner 8th and Moore Streets

A board-and-batten Gothic Revival church with wood buttresses and a four-stage tower.

10 Wakefield House (now Faribault County Historical Society), 1857
405 6th Street E

A brick side-hall Italianate house; round-hooded windows and an entrance with a semicircular fanlight and sidelights.

11 Octagonal Barn, c. 1900s
Fairgrounds (½ mile north of town on Highway 169)

An eight-sided wood livestock pavilion topped by an eight-sided clerestory section.

SE-8 Brownsville

Brownsville, an early steamboat landing, was settled in 1848 and platted in 1854. On the north side of Main Street between 3rd and 4th Streets is the board-and-batten Gothic Revival Emmanuel Evangelical Lutheran Church (c. 1857). The windows are pointed (V-shaped), and the steep form of the main gable is repeated in the small entrance vestibule. Farther west on County Road 3 is a two-story brick Italianate schoolhouse (1873). A concrete block entrance has been added recently. Approximately eight miles west of Brownsville on County Road 3 is a metal-sheathed round barn (c. 1910); the barn is situated on the south side of the road.

SE-9 Caledonia

The town (settled in 1851) sits on a flat plain with deep river and creek valleys running to the north, east, and south. At the northwest corner of Main and Marshall Streets is Hauser's Hotel (c. 1870s), a two-story brick building with a central gable. Its cantilevered porch roof over the ground level is supported by struts with circular patterns of sawed work. One block south on Marshall Street are the courthouse square and two stone buildings — the county jail (1875) and the Houston County Courthouse (1883). The courthouse, which has suffered from the usual bland additions and alterations over the years, is Romanesque (not Richardsonian Romanesque). The jail, architecturally the stronger of the two buildings, is Italianate mixed with Eastlake. At the northeast corner of Pine and South Streets is a Craftsman feed store (c. 1910), which is basically a bungalow court with a wide gable-covered entrance leading into the inner court.

Hauser's Hotel.

Feed store.

SE-10 Cannon Falls

Cannon Falls was founded as a milling town at the falls of the Cannon River. Like other southeastern Minnesota towns, it was a product of the immigration and real estate boom of the 1850s. First settled in 1854, it was platted on a gridiron plan in the following year and was incorporated in 1857. Its main street (4th Street) and its residential areas remain much as they were before 1900. On 4th Street there are a few exceptions — a Beaux Arts bank building (#2) and several storefronts — which reflect changes in design fashion in the 1920s and later. To the west of town there are a few new commercial developments and a limited number of post-1950 houses of the single-level ranch house variety. The section of town east of 4th Street is little changed; the only major new building is St. Ansgar's Lutheran Church (1970), a picturesque concrete structure built on open farmland at the edge of town on Highway 19.

1 **Yale Hardware Building,** 1887
Southeast corner 4th Street and Mill Street W

A two-story Eastlake building of brick, remodeled on the ground level. Note the cafe next door, whose image was modernized in the 1930s with glass brick and new lettering.

2 **Security State Bank,** c. 1920
111 4th Street N

A classical Beaux Arts bank with a recessed porch, one column on each side. As a commercial street design, the building works out well; the two sections on each side continue the line of the adjacent buildings, while the recessed entrance brings depth and thereby distinction to the structure.

3 **Masonic Temple,** 1883
119 4th Street S
A two-story Eastlake building in brick, with stores below and a meeting hall above.

4 **Cottage,** c. 1870s
318 4th Street S
A miniature cottage with pointed windows.

5 **Three Cottages,** c. 1870s
410, 414, and 422 4th Street S
These three small clapboard cottages are excellent examples of nineteenth-century speculative housing.

6 **Van Campen House,** early 1870s
307 Mill Street W
A simplified Italian Villa dwelling with a central cupola.

7 **Old Firehouse** (now Public Library), late 1860s
North side Mill Street W between 2nd and 3rd Streets
A small stone-walled building. The original stone lintels above the windows are Italianate in design. The glass brick by the entrance adds a needed note of modernity.

8 **Episcopal Church of the Redeemer,** late 1860s
Southeast corner Mill Street W and 3rd Street

8 Episcopal Church of the Redeemer.

The most impressive architectural monument in Cannon Falls. It asserts itself entirely through its basic shape, that of a rectangular volume covered by a high-pitched gable roof. There is a simple wood tower at the front and a row of narrow pointed-arch windows on each flank. The present entrance is new, and some remodeling has been done on the interior.

9 **Cottage,** c. 1870
Northeast corner Mill Street W and 2nd Street
A cottage with a slightly Gothic flavor.

10 **Congregational Church,** c. 1890
220 Main Street W
A rural English Gothic church with a heavily crenelated tower. The rough, tactile stonework of the walls and the fine-cut stonework around the windows and doors transform an interesting everyday design into a handsome building.

11 **House,** c. 1878
Southwest corner Main Street W and 2nd Street
A side-hall Italianate house with a porch across the front and a concave mansard roof. The recessed entrance with its curved transom light, the square-piered posts of the porch, and the pedimented windows represent the hand of a designer.

12 **St. Paul's Lutheran Church,** 1890s
Northeast corner Main Street W and Dow Street
A carpenter's turn-of-the-century wood Gothic church. This one is of the entrance-tower type, sheathed in clapboard.

13 **Cottage,** c. 1880
303 6th Street N
Certain details of this house are reminiscent of the Greek Revival; note especially the entrance with its transom and pair of sidelights.

14 **House,** c. 1880
311 6th Street N
A two-story gable-roofed rectangular box; unusual square-hooded windows and a small Eastlake entrance porch.

15 House, c. 1879
200 8th Street N
The front gable is dominated by a central composition of three arched windows.

16 House, c. 1895
Northwest corner 8th Street N and Hoffman Street
A conservative Queen Anne house, rich in turned wood, especially on the front porch.

17 First Baptist Church, c. 1895
Northeast corner Bridge Street N and State Street W
Right out of a builder's plan book; clapboard with a gabled steeple.

SE-11 Canton

The village was first settled in the 1850s, but it was not incorporated until 1887 (after the coming of the railroad). On the west side of Main Street (which runs north and south) is a small two-story Richardsonian commercial block (c. 1890). A deep entrance at one side on the ground level is balanced on the other side by an arched window. On the upper level an angled bay has been placed in the center of the façade. South on Main Street, also on the west side, is the firehouse (c. 1870s), apparently an early Greek Revival structure which has been remodeled for its current use. The Canton Church (c. 1870) is situated in the northwestern part of town, one-half block west of Main Street. In style it is Eastlake with a variety of tactile sheathing (vertical, diagonal, and horizontal). The bell tower on its aproned shingle base has a delicate pattern of sawed work. One block east of Main Street (and one block south of the church) stands a one-and-a-half-story Greek Revival cottage (late 1860s) with a sidelighted entrance.

Canton Church.

Firehouse, Canton.

SE-12 Chatfield

The town, which was platted in 1854, was laid out on a hillside overlooking the Root River. The community contains a number of brick and wood dwellings built in the 1860s and thereafter.

•1 **Lovel House,** c. 1892
218 Winona Street
A large-scale shingle house which is Queen Anne/Colonial Revival. A gambrel roof covers the main part of the house as well as the service wing, and a round bay becomes a tower with a bell-shaped roof. Diamond-paned windows cover the upper part of the double-hung windows. This is a classic example of what Vincent Scully has labeled the Shingle Style.

2 **"The Oaks,"** c. 1873
132 Winona Street
Italianate in brick. The side-hall entrance at the gable end looks onto an elegant porch.

3 **House,** c. 1870s
428 Fillmore Street
The Greek and the Italianate brought together in a single design. The windows have pediments, and the entrance is slightly recessed with sidelights, a transom light, and a heavy entablature and cornice.

4 **House,** c. 1870
Corner Winona and Prospect Streets
Greek Revival in clapboard. Narrow windows extending down to floor level lead onto the front porch and to the roof-balcony above.

5 **House,** 1870s
Corner Fillmore and Spring Streets
A two-story Italianate house in brick; side-hall plan.

6 **White House,** c. 1890
122 Burr Oak Avenue
When the Queen Anne Style was rendered in brick, it usually tended to be restrained, but that is hardly the case here. The front porch and the adjoining porte cochere are busy and spindly, and the oddly roofed tower, the bays, and the pediment keep everything from being quiet.

6 White House.

SE-13 Clark's Grove

Near Clark's Grove is the Lerdal Creamery. This brick building (c. 1895) displays the two usual hallmarks of a midwestern creamery — circular drum roof vents of metal and a tall brick chimney. The creamery is located three miles south of Clark's Grove on Highway 65 and three miles east on County Road 25.

SE-14 Clinton Falls

As the Straight River flows north from Owatonna, its gradient produces a series of rapids and thence waterpower for mills. The Clinton Falls mill building, now sheathed in corrugated sheet metal, stands on the west bank of the river. Just below it is a narrow iron-truss bridge (pre-1900) which is still in use. The road to the mill and the bridge runs east from Highway 218 through a forest; there are only a few houses on each side of the road. The whole scene is rustic and in a way is highly reminiscent of rural areas in the East. Like nearby Medford and Crystal Lake Clinton Falls has preserved a turn-of-the-century creamery. This gable-roofed brick structure is dominated by two large circular metal vents.

Creamery.

SE-15 Dakota

In town on County Road 12 stand two clapboard service stations (c. 1925) with hipped roofs. Both have covered service areas and short stubby Tuscan columns on piers. Behind the Mobil Station is a gable-roofed garage which was originally a blacksmith's shop (built c. 1890).

SE-16 Dodge Center

The community was platted in 1869 as a railroad village. In town the Hardin House at the northeast corner of Central Avenue and 2nd Street Northeast is a well-maintained Italianate building with a central gable (c. 1870s). Across the street at the northwest corner of Central Avenue and 2nd Street Northeast is the First Congregational Church (c. 1905), a Craftsman version of the Gothic. Another church, much plainer and older, is situated on the southwest corner of 2nd Avenue Northeast and 1st Street (c. 1870s). Its segmented arched windows are crowned by projecting pediments. Farther south on 2nd Avenue Northeast, on the west side between Main and 1st Streets, is a well-preserved Eastlake cottage (c. 1880).

SE-17 Dover

The town of Dover on the south fork of the Whitewater River was platted by the Winona and St. Peter Railroad in 1869. In town, two blocks east of County Road 10 and two streets south of the railroad, is a classic side-hall Italianate house (c. 1870s). Around 1900 a Colonial Revival porch terminating in an octagonal projection was built across the front of the house. The porch is supported on concrete piers with open segmented arches between them. Another house worth visiting is the Brown House, which is situated four streets south of the railroad and one block east of County Road 10. The street façade of the Brown House has an entrance (onto a porch) at the left, a bay at the right, and only one centrally placed window on the second floor. The house has stone trim, a stone foundation, and brick walls. One mile south of town on County Road 10 (on the east side of the road) is the Krause House (1870s), a two-story Italianate farmhouse in brick. Two and a half miles north of Dover on County Road 10 is an L-shaped two-story clapboard house (early 1870s) which suggests the Greek in the symmetrical arrangement of the windows and the use of a half-circle window in the front gable.

Italianate/Colonial Revival house.

SE-18 Dundas

This former milling town straddles the rapids of the Cannon River three miles south of Northfield on Highway 3. It was platted in 1857 and chartered in 1879. The Milwaukee and St. Paul Railroad reached the community by 1870. Today Dundas is made up of two blocks of small commercial buildings along the west side of Main Street and a few houses. Since there are no street signs, Main Street is the reference point for the directions to the buildings.

1 **Archibald Mill,** 1857
East side Main Street, south of bridge

Ruins in Minnesota and elsewhere in the United States are not very common. Here the "heavy atmosphere" of the past is pleasant but not too sublime. The visitor can wander among the crumbling stone walls of the mill, look at the interior (now overgrown with vines and shrubs), and walk through the old river raceway. The river at this point is calm and both shores are heavily wooded; the entire setting has an idyllic, almost unreal quality about it. Old engravings of the mill depict a simple two-story stone building covered by a low-pitched gable roof.

2 **Dundas Methodist Church** (now a residence), 1882–83
East side Main Street, ¼ mile south of commercial buildings

An example of Carpenter's Gothic with an unusual corner tower at an oblique angle to the adjacent walls. Recent modernization included the replacement of the original west windows with brilliant blue plastic.

3 **Archibald House,** 1860
East across bridge and turn right (south); east side of street

A well-preserved end-gable house of wood; Greek Revival in style.

4 **Ault General Store,** c. 1860s
East across bridge, south on County Road 20; west side of street

A two-story commercial building of stone. The store below has three arched openings facing the street.

5 **Church of the Holy Cross (Episcopal),** 1868
Jacob Goodman
East across bridge, south on County Road 20 4 blocks; east side of road

One of Bishop Whipple's stone Gothic churches. This church is similar in design to several which were illustrated in Richard Upjohn's *Rural Architecture* (New York, 1852). The tower has been placed at the rear of the church on the northeast corner, a plan which appears in several of Minnesota's Episcopal church buildings from the 1860s.

5 Church of the Holy Cross.

SE-19 Eitzen

Two miles north of Eitzen on Highway 76 a gravel road goes off to the south. In the distance one can see a grove of trees and within it • the Portland Prairie Methodist Church (1876). This clapboard church provides an impressive advertisement of architecture as a façade. In front of the simple gable-roofed structure is a wonderful two-dimensional Eastlake composition of a window, a door, a chimney, and even a small tower. The high point of the design is the chimney, which is treated as a major element — a Gothic pinnacle. In town, at the southwest corner of the major east/west, north/south streets is the two-story stone Bunge Store (late 1870s), which now houses the Eitzen Historical Society. The store's only decorative features are the thin wood vertical supports with slightly bracketed Eastlake tops at each side of the entrance. Across the east/west street to the north is the Eitzen State Bank (1908), a single-story brick building in vaguely Queen Anne design which has been brought up to date with inserts of metal and glass brick. Toward the east on the east/west street, also on the north side, is a wood Eastlake house (c. 1870s). A little farther to the east on the south side of the same street is the Eitzen School (c. 1900). This ashlar block raised-basement building has a low central entrance tower with crenelated battlements. Just south of the Bunge Store is a stone barn. The most impressive building in town is the former blacksmith shop (c. 1870s), which stands on the east side of the same

Bunge Store (now Eitzen Historical Society) and Eitzen State Bank.

street, just before it joins Highway 76. The building is actually a large stone barn; the composition of the main façade consists of a large arched entrance — just a little off-center — and a small segmented arched door at the side with a shuttered door/window combination above.

SE-20 Eyota

The town boasts one of the state's few remaining one-story octagonal houses. The sections of the roof project from a central chimney and extend out over a porch. The house (c. 1870s) is located on 5th Street East at the end of Center Street. Close by, at the corner of 5th Street West and Franklin Street, is a large one-and-a-half-story Eastlake cottage (c. 1880) with a fancy sawed pattern in its main gable end and an equally fancy ornamented front porch. On the northeast corner of South Avenue and 3rd Street East is a one-and-a-half-story clapboard house; with its partially sawed bargeboards and angled pointed windows, it could be catalogued as an Eastlake version of the Gothic. Farther down South Avenue at the southwest corner of 2nd Street East is St. Paul's United Church of Christ (c. late 1880s), also in Eastlake Gothic but with clapboard and fish-scale shingles.

Eastlake cottage.

SE-21 Fairmont

When first platted in 1857 the community was named Fair Mount because of its hilltop location overlooking a chain of lakes. The group of four lakes within the corporate boundaries of the city provides a natural open park setting. The Martin County Courthouse of 1906 (at Blue Earth Avenue and 2nd Street) is on a hill which looks toward the lake to the west and over the rest of the city to the east. The Minneapolis firm of Bell and Detweiler designed the building, producing a Beaux Arts design which is more Baroque than Neoclassical. The large faces of four clocks project from the dome; within are murals by T. Rohrbeck. Down the hill toward the east on Blue Earth Avenue is the red ashlar

Wohlheter House.

block Church of Christ (late 1890s) at the southwest corner of Blue Earth Avenue and Elm Street. This is a square structure which, notwithstanding its recessed pointed-arch entrance, is Romanesque Revival. In the residential district south of Sisseton Lake, is the Wohlheter House (1899) at 320 Woodland Avenue. Here is a Colonial Revival dwelling with both authority and personal idiosyncrasy: it is an encyclopedi of details used in the turn-of-the-century Colonial Revival, all put together in an improbable way.

SE-22 Faribault

"The town owes much of its attractiveness still to the charming natural scenery which so impressed even the untutored savage," according to the Faribault Citizens' Committee (*Faribault and Vicinity*, 1884). It is situated a little above the junction of the Cannon and Straight Rivers — the rivers which provided the waterpower for the early mills. Although the site was occupied at a much earlier date, the town was not platted until 1855; it was incorporated in 1872.

From the beginning Faribault was divided into two parts: the main commercial, manufacturing, and residential area to the west of the Cannon River, and the churches, schools, and other institutions high on the bluff to the east of the river. Like the people of most aggressive young communities in mid-nineteenth-century Minnesota, the citizens of Faribault were eager to see their town become the site of public and private institutions. By 1879 the city had managed to obtain six institutions. The largest of these were the State Institution for the Deaf and Dumb (1863, now the Minnesota School for the Deaf), Shattuck School (1865), St. Mary's Hall (1865, now St. Mary's School), and the State School for Feeble-Minded Children (1879–81, no longer in existence). "All of these," the author of the brochure noted, "have fine large buildings, of such character that they are not only an ornament to the town, but they give assurance of the future growth and improvement which are sure to come."

By the late 1870s a new and elaborate courthouse had been built (in the prevailing Italianate Style), and the community was connected with the Twin Cities and other parts of Minnesota by the Chicago, Milwaukee, and St. Paul Railroad and the Rock Island Railroad. Industry flourished with the establishment of flour mills, the Klemer Woolen Mill, the Faribault Foundry and Windmill Company, and the Faribault Wagon and Carriage Company and the opening of local limestone quarries.

Through the 1940s the principal north/south highway (Highway 65) traveled directly down Central Avenue, Faribault's main street. Since the construction of Highway 35 west of town however, the business and residential streets have been used primarily by local traffic. Highway 60, the east/west highway, still passes directly through town (4th Street North), accompanied by the usual strip developments. The new suburban Faribo Plaza Shopping Center is situated southeast of Division Street and Wilson Avenue (Highway 65).

The pattern for labeling the numbered streets in Faribault apparently was changed several times during the development of the city, and the original signing has not been modified to conform to a single consistent system. Because of this the labeling on the accompanying map should be noted with special care.

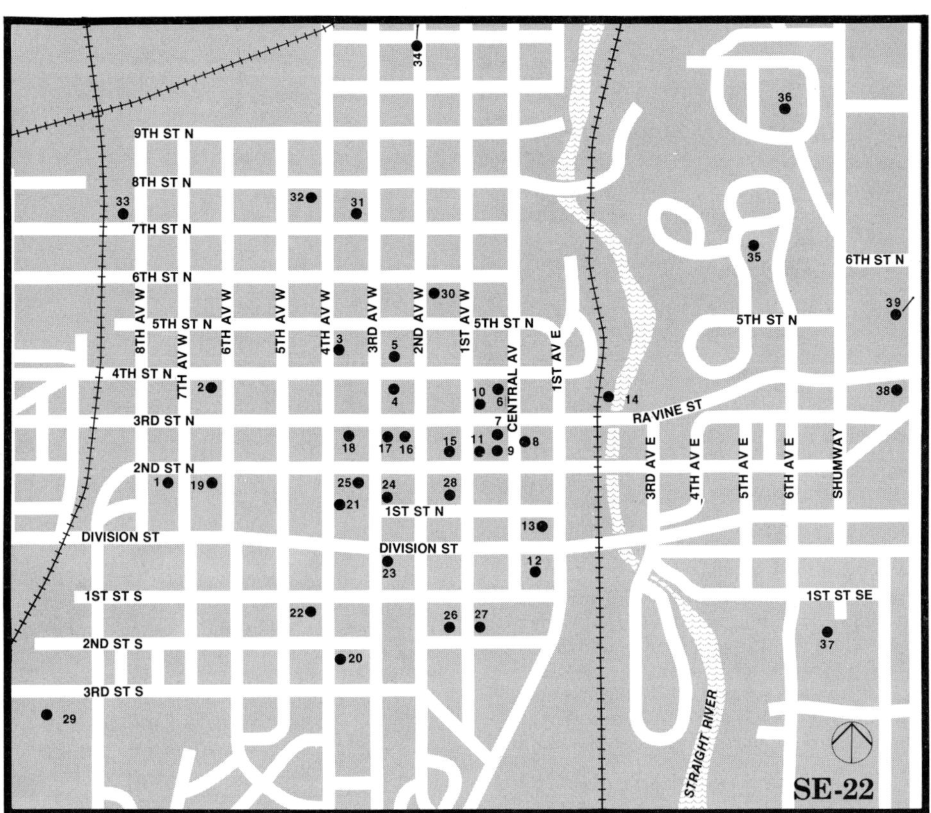

1 **House,** c. 1865
14 7th Avenue NW

Faribault contains a number of end-gable Greek Revival houses or cottages, of which this is a typical example. Other examples are to be found at 126 2nd Avenue West, 603 1st Street South, 427 5th Street West, and 331 3rd Street West.

2 **Godfrey House,** early 1880s
609 4th Street NW

House, 1880s
615 4th Street NW

Two turreted houses representing an odd mixture of Eastlake and Gothic Revival details. The house at 615 4th Street Northwest is Queen Anne in style.

3 **House,** late 1860s
328 4th Street N

A two-story brick Italianate house.

•4 **Rice County Courthouse,** 1932
Nairne W. Fisher
218 3rd Street NW

A near-perfect mixture of the classical and the Zigzag Moderne. Relief sculpture on the sides of the building along 4th and 3rd Streets extols civic virtue, industry, and farming. Within, a central rotunda is approached by a Zigzag Moderne staircase; Moderne metal and glass light fixtures abound.

5 **Lampert Lumber Company Offices** (now unused), c. 1920s
206 4th Street NW

Commercial vernacular — in this instance, wood clapboard Colonial Revival with an odd roof and gable.

6 Commercial Block, 1874
316 Central Avenue
A two-story brick business block in the Eastlake Style.

7 Commercial Block, 1878
216 Central Avenue
Much of the commercial architecture of the 1870s and 1880s resists the historian's passion for precise pigeonholing. Perhaps the best label for this building would be Victorian Eastlake.

8 Commercial Block, 1874
217 Central Avenue
A three-story brick structure in the Eastlake Style. Note how the four numerals of the date have been placed in each of the cornice cartouches.

9 Three Commercial Buildings
Northwest corner Central Avenue and 2nd Street N
The Lieb Building on the corner dates from 1882; the next two buildings (to the north) are loosely Eastlake in style and probably date from the end of the 1870s. Although the Lieb Building is later than its two neighbors, it is more classical (Italianate) in design.

Central Avenue business district, Faribault.

10 Store/Office Block, 1884
24 3rd Street NW
Victorian Gothic with very rich detailing of the street façade.

11 Village Theatre, c. 1950
20 2nd Street NW
The façade consists of thinly overlaid horizontal and flat planes.

10 Store/Office Block.

12 Thomas Scott Memorial Library, 1929
Charles W. Buckman
Southeast corner Central Avenue and Division Street
Bertram Goodhue's Los Angeles Public Library reduced in scale and Gothic in character rather than Classical and Byzantine. The light-colored limestone of the exterior presents a continuous, unbroken surface. Both within and without are numerous Zigzag Moderne (Art Deco) details. The main stained-glass window at the entrance is by Charles Connick of Boston, and the series of murals in the main reading room, extolling Greece's contributions to the world, were painted by Alfred J. Hyslep of Northfield. The multilevel plan, with openings and windows giving views into the various levels, is both visually and functionally quite ingenious.

12 Thomas Scott Memorial Library.

13 House, 1853
12 N 1st Avenue E
A Greek Revival house with end gables; side-hall plan. Its width makes it more rural and vernacular than most examples. Note the sawed wood design beneath the porch; it is pure Gothic Revival. The Totrault House at 224 2nd Street Northeast is a stone building with many of the same qualities, although it was built somewhat later.

14 Rock Island/Burlington Railroad Station, 1901
3rd Street NE at river
Of the two railroad depots in town this one, which is mildly Richardsonian Romanesque, has the strongest architectural character. Its setting on the river, with the business district to the west and the various public institutions across the river on the wooded heights, must have given passengers on the trains an inviting first view of the city.

15 City Hall, 1894
208 1st Avenue NW
Originally the building housed both the city hall and the library. Externally the building is mildly classical; the south entrance with its columns and niches is its most interesting feature. Within, the character of the spaces, the details, and even such fixtures as the fireplaces in the offices are Queen Anne.

16 House (now apartments), c. 1890s
211 3rd Street NW
A commodious Queen Anne dwelling with the usual extensive wraparound porch and corner bay-tower.

17 Congregational Church, 1867
227 3rd Street NW
An early stone church with Northern Italian overtones. The steeple with its high pointed tower is pure Mid-Victorian; four small dormers have been removed from the roof. The interior is unusual: The entrance is through the basement, which is on ground level on 3rd Street, and the sanctuary with its flat ceiling, classical cornices, and paneled walls conveys almost a secular image.

18 House, late 1890s
319 3rd Street NW
Queen Anne/Colonial Revival; a studied pattern of various shapes and sizes of windows has been used on the street façade. Note the rectangular picture-framed window assemblage at the left of the entrance. Also of interest is the wood barn in the rear and the pattern of sawed and turned work in its gables.

19 House, c. 1870s
128 N 6th Avenue W
In form, Greek Revival; in detail, both Greek and Italianate.

20 Carufel House, 1870s
201 S 4th Avenue W
A small stone cottage.

21 Cottage, c. 1890
111 N 4th Avenue W
A late Eastlake/Queen Anne cottage with a small fanciful tower.

22 House, c. 1860s
102 S 4th Avenue W
A stark, puritanical stone house. Italianate; side-hall plan with an arched entrance.

23 Immaculate Conception Catholic Church, 1870s
3 3rd Avenue SW
A stone church with a classical central entrance tower; a plain interior with a balcony and an exposed staircase at the rear of the sanctuary.

24 House, late 1870s
107 N 3rd Avenue W
Italianate house of light-colored brick with a central gable; side-hall plan. There is a one-story porch across the front.

25 Hutchinson-Johnson House, c. 1890
305 2nd Street N
A luxurious Queen Anne house — for Minnesota. It has an octagonal tower with small paned windows on the top floor, much sawed and turned work, and an extensive porch around much of the house.

26 **Buck House,** 1895
124 S 1st Avenue SW

Respectability with authority: A large Colonial Revival house with a two-story pedimented entrance porch and a carriage entrance at the side — all set down on a hillside with more than ample grounds.

27 **House,** c. 1870s
115 S 1st Avenue SW

A two-story brick house with a low mansard roof, a mixture of French Second Empire and Italianate.

28 **House,** c. 1870s
104 1st Street NW

The French Second Empire Style in full force. The house has a central curved roof gable with an elongated oval-framed window.

29 **Faribault High School,** 1958
Magney, Tusler, Setter, Leach, Lindstrom, and Erickson
330 9th Avenue SW

A two-story Miesian design of the 1950s; exposed concrete frame, infill brick walls, and a decorative cornice.

30 **Cathedral of Our Merciful Savior (Episcopal),** 1862–69
James Renwick; Robert Wiley
515 2nd Avenue NW

According to the church records, "plans furnished by James Renwick and Company of New York"; Robert Wiley of St. Paul was the supervisory architect. In quality of design this church is unquestionably one of the most impressive in Minnesota. In style it is English Gothic. There is a large, almost cathedral-like tower at the side and rear. Behind the church, at the corner of 6th Street North and 1st Avenue West, is the 1894 Memorial Guild house, a small-scaled Richardsonian Romanesque building.

31 **Cottage,** early 1870s
716 3rd Avenue NW

Cottage, 1870s
728 3rd Avenue NW

Grant House (now apartments), 1890
J. Walter Stevens
306 7th Street NW

House, c. 1910
724 3rd Avenue NW

These four houses present a revealing picture of four decades of domestic architecture in Faribault. The cottage at 716 3rd Avenue Northwest is Eastlake with an intricate pattern of turned and sawed woodwork on its entrance porch. The cottage at 728 3rd Avenue Northwest is of the usual end-gable Greek Revival type, but the banded concrete columns which support the porch date from the early 1900s. The Grant House is a bulky Queen Anne/Colonial Revival design. The stucco and shingle house at 724 3rd Avenue Northwest well represents the Craftsman tradition of the early 1900s.

•32 **House,** c. 1900
728 N 4th Avenue W

A gable-roofed Queen Anne/Colonial Revival house. If it had been completely shingled, it would fit comfortably into the Shingle Style.

33 **Faribault Water Works,** 1938
Long and Thorshov
North side 7th Street NW, west of 8th Avenue NW

A concrete PWA Moderne building; surface pattern of alternating horizontal and vertical rectangles (from the boards used as the forms for the concrete); within, one whole wall of glass brick.

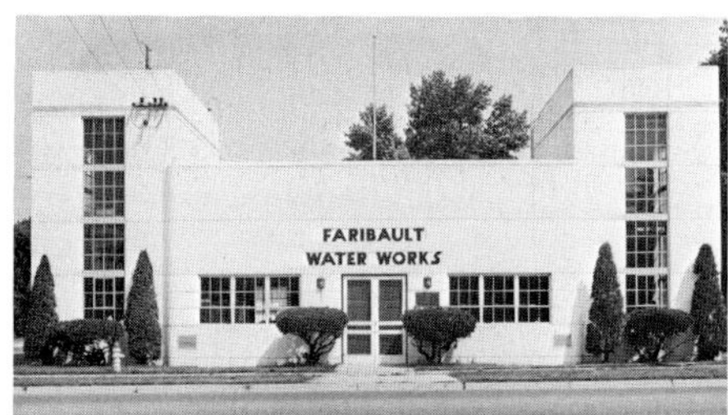

33 Faribault Water Works.

34 **Pleasant Valley Church of the Holy Innocents,** c. 1870s
Pleasant Valley Schoolhouse, 1887
Log Cabin, pre-1900
Faribault County Fairgrounds: North on 2nd Avenue NW (Highway 3) across Cannon River; on west side of road

Of the three the church is of the greatest architectural interest. It is a thin, narrow structure, and its verticality is accentuated by the surface pattern of board-and-batten.

35 **Minnesota School for the Deaf,** estab. 1863
Northwest corner 6th Avenue NE and 5th Street NE

A complex of Classical Revival buildings from the turn of the century and later, situated within an open English landscaped park. Noyas Hall (1902–10), by Charles H. Johnston, is Beaux Arts classical; Tate Hall, with its Williamsburg cupola, shuttered windows, and two-story portico, is Classical via Colonial (Georgian) Revival. The most engaging of the buildings is Pollard Hall (c. 1928) for children; its entrance is guarded by a large friendly sculpture of a dog and a cat, and above it a pair of romping children in relief sculpture look down on those who enter the building. The school has experienced much in the way of new construction, which is evident in the 1960s mansard roof style. The stonework of the new buildings is handsome, but the forced roof forms, which might work for a service station or a supermarket, do not work here. The best by far of the newer buildings is the heating plant, with its modular walls and its row of black chimney stacks.

35 Pollard Hall, Minnesota School for the Deaf.

36 **Shattuck School,** estab. 1865
Shumway Avenue, 1 block north of junction with 6th Street NE

The Gothic Revival at its best. Beyond the Gothic gateway (1926) a complex of three buildings can be seen across the open drill field. To the left (west) is the Morgan Refectory, and in the center is Shumway Hall; these were designed in 1887 by Willcox and Johnston. The crenelated building to the right (east) was designed between 1907 and 1910 by Cass Gilbert. West of the Morgan Refectory is the English Gothic St. James School for Boys (c. 1920s). The architectural high point of the place is • the Chapel of the Good Shepherd, designed in 1872–73 by Henry Congdon of New York. The stone church's tour de force is its tower, which is open at the base and has a spire of solid stone.

36 Shumway Hall, Shattuck School.

37 **Former Seabury Divinity School,** 1888
Willcox and Johnston
Southeast corner 6th Avenue E and 1st Street SE

A towering Romanesque/Gothic stone building, now somewhat lost at the edge of the new Rice County District No. 1 Hospital.

38 **Thurber House,** c. 1860s?
817 Ravine Street

A one-and-a-half-story stone house; with its tasteful remodeling it resembles a period house of the late 1930s. In style it is Greek Revival.

39 **Crystal Lake Creamery,** c. 1900s
2 miles northeast of town on Highway 20

Another example of the creamery as a building type at the turn of the century. This one, which is now abandoned, is of brick, and its detailing is classical.

SE-23 Frontenac and Old Frontenac

Old Frontenac, just north of Long Point on Lake Pepin was an early Indian trading post. It was settled in the mid-1850s and contains a number of important examples of the Greek Revival. In the 1870s Old Frontenac was described as one of the most charming resorts in the land, and it was forecast that the town would develop as a site of summer hotels and residences — something which never occurred. Frontenac itself was built a mile from the railroad, which ran along the Mississippi. The streets in Old Frontenac are unmarked but the town is so small that this poses no problem.

1 **Bank** (now Frontenac Cycle Sales), 1915
On Highway 61 in Frontenac
The classical cast-iron front of the building is identical to the front of the Security State Bank in Marine on St. Croix (#1).

1 Bank (now Frontenac Cycle Sales).

2 **Christ Episcopal Church,** 1869
On County Road 2 in Old Frontenac
One of Bishop Whipple's vertical board-and-batten Gothic Revival churches.

3 **St. Hubert's Lodge** (known as General Garrard House), 1856
Off County Road 2 in Old Frontenac
A balconied two-story porch runs across the front of this board-and-batten Greek Revival house. The house was added to and altered in the 1860s and later. In general appearance it is an informal building, and its designation as a lodge suits it well.

•4 **Westervelt House,** c. 1855
Off County Road 2 in Old Frontenac
A formal two-story Greek Revival house with entablatured windows and doors, paneled engaged corner piers, dentils, and enclosed pediments with round windows. Its L-shaped plan is unusual.

5 **Methodist Camp** (Old Frontenac Inn), 1860s
On lake in north part of Old Frontenac
In and around the camp are a number of wood clapboard houses, some mildly Greek Revival in style, others approaching the Gothic Revival.

6 **Villa Academy** (Villa Maria)
County Road 2, south of Old Frontenac, on west side of road
The model on the grounds is a replica of the original 1869 building. The existing Romanesque Revival building was built in the early 1890s and has been remodeled frequently since then.

6 Villa Academy.

SE-24 Garden City

This city situated on the Watonwan River was named Watonwan when it was established in 1856. It was renamed and replatted in 1858. The brick Baptist Church (1860s) is essentially a Greek Revival building. Its front is divided into three panels by the suggestion of brick piers and an entablature. The church is located on Highway 169, one-half block north of the Watonwan River. Near Garden City is the Fleming Round Barn, which has a conical roof (c. 1900); it is situated on the northeast corner of County Road 13 and Highway 169, one and a half miles south of Garden City. More difficult to find is the single-story octagonal house (probably late 1850s) on the Munter farm, which is located one and a half miles north of Garden City on Highway 169, one-quarter of a mile north of Milepost 42, then east on a gravel road and just past the intersection with a second gravel road coming from the south. The house is built of brick and has round-hooded windows.

Munter House.

SE-25 Good Thunder

The town was established on the railway between Mankato and Albert Lea in 1871. There are several simple brick houses in the town, but Good Thunder's architectural gem is the Daige House (late 1870s), which is located just north of the town's only bank. This one-and-a-half-story brick cottage is Gothic in form, with details such as round-hooded windows and corner quoining which are Italianate. All of this is supplemented by fine sawed work which is Eastlake. Two blocks south of the bank is a raised-basement brick schoolhouse, which has a fine tower with arched openings (1891).

Daige House.

SE-26 Grand Meadow

Grand Meadow was platted in 1870 when the railroad was built through this section of Mower County. On the northwest corner of Main Street and Railroad Avenue is the Exchange State Bank (now the First American State Bank), designed by Purcell, Feick, and Elmslie in 1910. This two-story brick bank and office building was the first Prairie Style bank designed and built by the firm. Large terra-cotta cartouches frame the window on the exterior side wall, and there is a rectangular band of tile and terra-cotta above the entrance. Originally the stairs at the entrance had rectangles of stone on each side, the arched entry at the side was approached directly by stairs, and no basement windows interrupted the stone base of the building. The interior of the bank has been considerably remodeled.

Exchange State Bank (now First American State Bank), Photo: William G. Purcell.

SE-27 Granger

The village of Granger lies right on the boundary between Minnesota and Iowa, and its major north/south street extends into Iowa. As one enters the town from the north on County Road 15, one sees a two-story clapboard schoolhouse (c. 1860s), which was once used as the city hall, on the west side of the road. It is a hipped-roof Greek Revival building with an Eastlake porch and a small bell tower; the entrance has sidelights and a transom. The architectural gem of Granger in the Granger Methodist Church (c. 1866), which is not really located in Granger but just across the border in the Iowa community of Florenceville (south on County Road 15 through Granger, then east on County Road 30 about one-quarter of a mile). The church stands on the south side of the road, which is the boundary between the two states. It has a superb entablatured entrance with double doors, segmented arched windows, paneled engaged piers at the corners, and a tower belfry over the front gable.

Granger Methodist Church.

SE-28 Harmony

One and a half miles east of Harmony on Highway 44 is the two-story Sunblad House (1886). This stone house has a pattern of large-scale quoining on the two front corners, and the two windows on each side of the central entrance have pediments cut out of single blocks of stone. The house was originally T-shaped, but later on wood-sheathed wings were added.

Sunblad House.

SE-29 Hastings

Hastings was one of the early pre–Civil War river towns of Minnesota. A trading post was established at the site in 1833, and the town was platted in 1853 and incorporated in 1857. The site had several advantages: it was located only a few miles above the confluence of the Mississippi and St. Croix rivers; the Vermillion River, which flows to the south and east, provided waterpower for a mill at its falls; and, finally, the terrain was high enough above the river so that the community was secure against floods and the dampness of the low river plain.

By 1871 Hastings was spoken of as one of the great wheat marts of the Northwest. The completion of two rail lines to the city (the Milwaukee and St. Paul and the Southern Minnesota) and the construction later of a railroad and automobile (carriage) bridge across the Mississippi River enhanced its importance as a shipping center for the surrounding rich farmlands. Various small-scale manufacturing enterprises were established at an early date. One of the most interesting of these was the Brownson Manufacturing Company, which began to produce a pre-cut house, "The Gopher State House," in the 1860s. Though aggressive in its desire to expand, Hastings grew slowly, and like many other Minnesota communities its present-day urban pattern and buildings are substantially of the nineteenth century. The changes — some positive, some negative — of the past quarter of a century have been limited. On the negative side Hastings has lost its really great public monument, the steel spiral bridge (built in 1895, destroyed in 1955) which was so beautifully scaled to the town. The new bridge, especially in its approach through town, is hardly an urban asset. Strip commercial development on Vermillion Street, the major north/south thoroughfare, has turned an attractive residential street into a jumble of often contradictory uses. The construction of the new County Government Center far to the west of the city, in what amounts to the image of a suburban shopping center, hardly does much to enhance the older city core. Since Hastings has so far not been plagued by the construction of an overscaled freeway, the automobile has been kept within reasonable bounds. The approach from the west on Highway 55 (8th Street West) through the main city park to Vermillion Street is a pleasant introduction to a small urban environment.

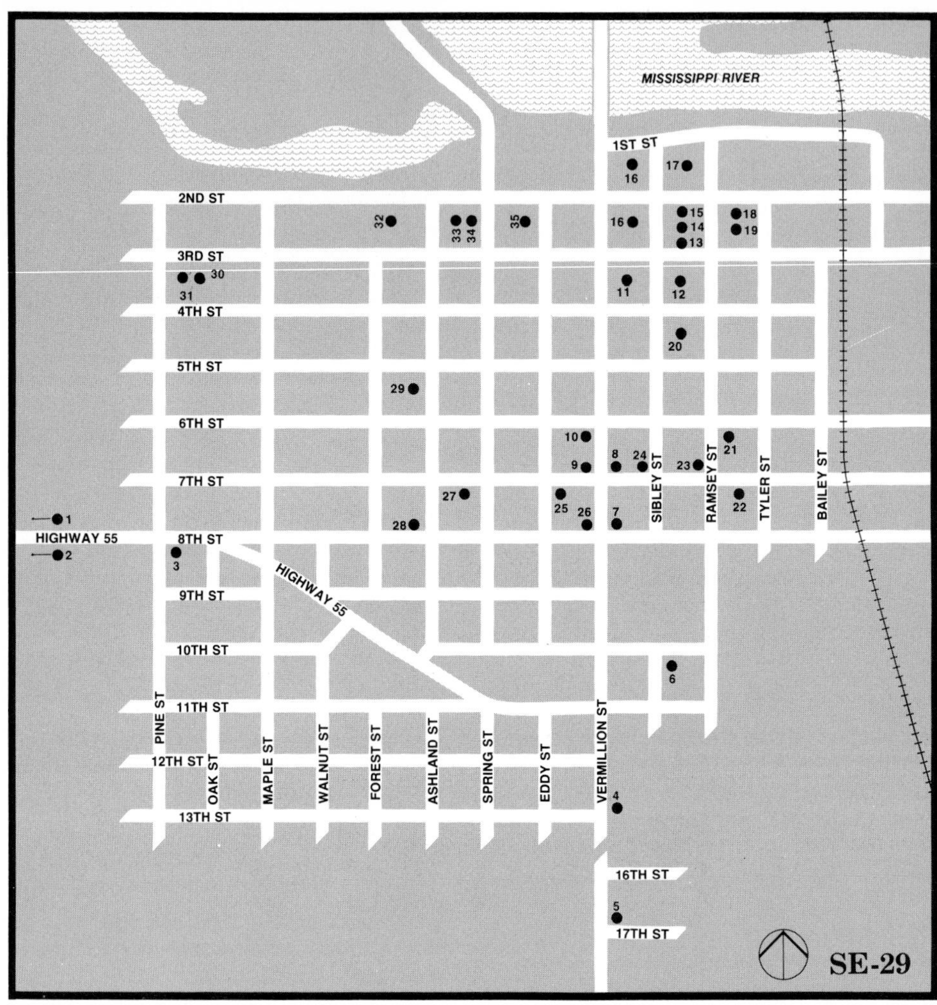
MISSISSIPPI RIVER
1ST ST
2ND ST
3RD ST
4TH ST
5TH ST
6TH ST
7TH ST
8TH ST
9TH ST
10TH ST
11TH ST
12TH ST
13TH ST
16TH ST
17TH ST
HIGHWAY 55
HIGHWAY 55
PINE ST
OAK ST
MAPLE ST
WALNUT ST
FOREST ST
ASHLAND ST
SPRING ST
EDDY ST
VERMILLION ST
SIBLEY ST
RAMSEY ST
TYLER ST
BAILEY ST
1
2
3
4
5
6
7
8
9
10
11
12
13
14
15
16
16
17
18
19
20
21
22
23
24
25
26
27
28
29
30
31
32
33
34
35
SE-29

1 **Dakota County Government Center,** 1973–74
Ellerbe Architects
West Highway 55 (north side of road)

A group of brick cut-out boxes starkly placed on a low hill, at present in the midst of agricultural fields. As a design the complex is sculpturally strong, especially when seen from a distance, but as an approach to rational civic planning it is problematic. Its location is predicated solely on the use of the automobile, and it is an open question whether productive farmland should be converted to such urban use. The esthetic image used seems purposely anonymous and ponderously serious and has the effect of overawing the citizen rather than enticing him into an environment which would reflect Hastings's small-scaled atmosphere.

1 Dakota County Government Center.

2 **Mississippi Valley Clinic,** c. 1972
955 Highway 55 (west of Prairie Street)

A single-story suburban medical building, sheathed in vertical cedar; a suggestion of depth is created by the use of square-hooded windows.

3 **Fasbender Medical Clinic,** 1957–59
Frank Lloyd Wright
Southeast corner Highway 55 and Pine Street

A perfect example of how a building can be modern and a strong work of art by an individual artist, fit beautifully into a specific environment, and carry on the existing urban scale of the community. The landscaped grounds of the building blend into the adjacent park. Since the building is almost buried in the ground, we are aware only of its folded roof and brick utility core. It is one of Wright's impressive late buildings.

3 Fasbender Medical Clinic.

4 **Barbaras House,** c. 1880s
1225 Vermillion Street

A marvelous potpourri of styles: Italianate balcony and hooded windows and door, Eastlake jigsaw work, and finally a Gothic high-pitched dormer.

5 **Le Duc House,** 1856–62
Augustus F. Knight
1629 Vermillion Street

The Le Duc House is one of the most widely known of Minnesota's nineteenth-century buildings. Its design was boldly lifted from A. J. Downing's *Cottage Residences* (1842); Knight's major contribution seems to have been that of simply reversing the plan. Downing described the style of the building as "a cottage in the Rhine Style." It is basically nineteenth-century Gothic Revival, with occasional touches of the Italianate. The original Downing House, built for J. T. Headley, was located on the Hudson, and with a stretch of the imagination Le Duc's hilltop location in Hastings could perhaps be thought of as analogous. Downing wrote that his design had been built "in a picturesque and highly appropriate position," where its steep roof-lines harmonized admirably with the bold hills of the Hudson highlands.

6 **Hanson House,** c. 1899
1007 Sibley Street

A commodious Queen Anne/Colonial Revival house which was moved to the present site from its original location at 903 Vermillion Street. The plan of the ground floor has a central octagonal living hall, off which, through wide openings, flow the secondary "public" rooms. Externally there is a round corner tower and an extensive porch which wraps itself around the tower and across the front of the house.

7 **Full Gospel Assembly Church,** c. 1890s
Northeast corner Vermillion Street and 8th Street E

Basically Gothic, but pure classical details are present, including engaged piers at the corners of the tower.

7 Full Gospel Assembly Church.

8 **St. Luke's Episcopal Church,** 1881
Northeast corner Vermillion Street and 7th Street E

A reserved gable-roofed Gothic church in brick with a central crenelated tower. A regrettable modern addition has been attached to the north side of the building.

9 **Van Dyke House,** 1868
612 Vermillion Street

A two-and-a-half-story French Second Empire mansion. The house has all the classic characteristics of the style: a projecting central pavilion with a high curved mansard roof treated as a tower element, round-topped dormer windows, bays, and a hooded entrance.

10 **First United Presbyterian Church,** c. 1890s
602 Vermillion Street

Classical Revival of a sort. The front façade is dominated by a centrally placed Palladian window.

11 **Dakota County Courthouse,** 1869–70
A. M. Radcliff
Vermillion Street and 3rd Street W

A French Second Empire composition with details that are reminiscent of late Italianate. The corners of the square building are articulated by small towers with curved mansard roofs. A classical dome dating from 1912 surmounts the center of the building. A characteristic, "insensitive fifties" addition (1955) has been awkwardly attached to the older building.

11 Dakota County Courthouse.

12 **Yanz House,** c. 1878
307 Sibley Street

This design well illustrates how stylistic modes often continued on long after they were out of fashion in the large urban areas. The basic form of the house is Greek Revival, but its central pediment, with a round window and other bold detailing, is Italianate.

13 **Masonic Block,** 1881
221 Sibley Street

An imposing three-story brick commercial building, basically in the Eastlake Style. It originally housed a bank on the street level with offices above and a lodge room for the Masonic Temple on the third floor. Next door at 219 Sibley Street is a two-story brick commercial structure, the Hageman-Humm Building, constructed in 1882.

14 "Ye Olde City Hall" (now a private office building), 1884
215 Sibley Street

A two-story Eastlake design; recently modified and made somewhat Colonial.

15 Stage 8 Theatre, c. 1938
213 Sibley Street

A small Streamline Moderne motion picture theatre.

16 Commercial Buildings
2nd Street E between Vermillion and Ramsey Streets

Both sides of 2nd Street East contain one-story and two-story commercial buildings of the late nineteenth and early twentieth centuries. In most cases the ground floors have been modernized, but the upper floors and entablatures often remain intact. Two of the most notable of these structures are the Mertz Building (1899) at 217 2nd Street East and the tall, narrow, three-story Finch Building (1880) at 201 2nd Street East.

17 Gardner Hotel, 1884
221 2nd Street E

A beautifully preserved three-story brick hotel, in style mildly Eastlake.

18 Post Office, 1936
Louis A. Simon (architect); Neal A. Melick (engineer)
Southeast corner Ramsey Street and 2nd Street E

A neutral, red-brick PWA post office, more classical than Moderne. Conservative classical Roman light standards contrast with the design of the relief sculpture above each of the windows, the subject of which is a stylized airplane motor and propeller.

19 Commercial Block, c. 1880
215 Ramsey Street

A double store and office building in the Eastlake Style.

20 Guardian Angels Catholic Church, 1865–68
216 4th Street E

Very late Greek Revival, in stone with quoined corners.

21 St. Boniface Catholic Church, 1869–71, 1892
520 Ramsey Street

A brick Gothic Revival church with a central entrance tower and spire.

22 Voight Cottage, 1870s?
316 7th Street E

A one-and-a-half-story Gothic cottage with central high-pitched gable and verge boards. The present enclosed front porch is not original.

23 Latto House, 1880–81
Northwest corner Ramsey Street and 7th Street E

A two-story brick residence in much simplified Queen Anne Style.

24 Rich House, 1868
117 7th Street E

A classic L-plan Italianate villa with a three-story tower in the middle of the L. Note the nineteenth-century iron fence which still surrounds the garden.

25 Nolan House, 1860s, 1889
121 7th Street W

The original house was Greek Revival with Italianate details. It has been modified by later additions.

26 Howes House, late 1860s
718 Vermillion Street

Like the Rich House (#24), this is an L-plan Italianate house with a tower in the middle of the L. The house is surrounded by ample lawns, gardens, trees, and shrubs, a perfect picture of a nineteenth-century residence.

27 Todd House, c. 1857
309 7th Street W

One of several two-story clapboard Greek Revival houses in Hastings which were moved from nearby Nininger.

28 Eckert House, c. 1857
724 Ashland Street

An often-encountered mid-nineteenth-century blending of Greek and Italianate styles. This two-story, side-hall plan house has engaged piers at the corners and a small Italianate cupola surmounting its hipped roof.

29 Johnson Cottage, 1870
401 5th Street W

A one-and-a-half-story cottage; basically Greek Revival, but the high-pitched roof is Gothic.

30 House, c. 1890
625 3rd Street W

A small Queen Anne house.

31 Thompson House, 1870s
Southeast corner Pine Street and 3rd Street W

A two-and-a-half-story French Second Empire house in brick; the centerpiece of the front is the two-story bay with its tall conical roof. As often is the case in houses of this type, the detailing is Italianate.

32 Pringle-Claggett House, late 1850s
413 2nd Street W

A large-scaled Italianate house placed on the edge of the hill overlooking the river.

33 Thorne House, 1861
319 2nd Street W

An impressive square Italianate house in stone with a central cupola. The Ionic-columned entrance porch is a sympathetic later addition.

34 Octagon House, 1857–58
Southwest corner 2nd Street W and Spring Street

A variation on the Brown house illustrated in O. S. Fowler's *A Home for All or the Gravel Wall and Octagon Mode of Building* (1854). Of this form Fowler wrote, "Since, then, the octagon form is more beautiful as well as capacious, and more consonant with the predominant or governing forms of Nature — the Spherical — it deserves consideration." Hastings's octagonal house rests on a high basement and is surmounted by a cupola. Its detailing is essentially Italianate.

34 Octagon House.

35 Reed-Strauss Cottage, 1875
207 2nd Street W

A French Second Empire cottage with a central pavilion tower, a central-hall plan, and round-topped dormer windows. The exterior porch has been removed, and the house is now stuccoed.

36 Ramsey Mill, 1857
South on Vermillion Street to 18th Street, east to Old Mill Park

The ruins of this three-story stone mill sit delightfully and romantically in the woods next to the falls of the Vermillion River. In the United States it seems that the only romantic, picturesque ruins which survive are utilitarian structures — factories, mills, bridges, and fragments of roads and railroad lines.

37 Nininger, 1856
Literally nothing remains of this community, which was promoted by one of the most fascinating of Minnesota's nineteenth-century personalities, Ignatius Donnelly. By 1857 Nininger contained over one hundred houses, and plans had been laid for a large hotel, a library, and a railroad (the never-realized Nininger, St. Peter, and Western Railroad). With the Depression of 1857 the city began to disappear as many of the houses were moved to Hastings or to the St. Paul area. Finally all that was left was Donnelly's own Italian villa (c. 1868), his second house in Nininger. The house stood intact until it was torn down after World War II; the library, the only room saved from the house, was given to the Minnesota Historical Society. Nininger was just one of hundreds of paper cities which were platted during the boom of the 1850s but did not survive.

SE-30 Homer

The Mississippi River town of Homer possesses two important architectural treasures: • the Gothic Revival Bunnell House (c. 1855) and the King House ("Rockledge"), designed by the Chicago Prairie architect George W. Maher in about 1912. The Bunnell House, situated on the north side of town above the river road, is a one-and-a-half-story Gothic cottage with a two-story porch which faces toward the river. The lower floor is sheathed in stone, and Gothic details abound — bargeboards and cornices with horizontal rows of cut-out crosses, step pediments with wood gables above the windows, and so on. The King estate is located 1½ miles south of Homer on Highway 14 (the river road). The estate consists of the main house, • a studio-house, and a caretaker's cottage. All are designed in Maher's personal version of the Prairie Style. The house exhibits Maher's characteristic monumentality, but the caretaker's cottage is a Prairie bungalow with a hipped roof. The studio-house is the most fascinating of the three buildings. It appears to be a combination of Pueblo Revival, Prairie, and Viennese Secessionist elements. Its central studio space is two stories high with a large north-facing window and a narrow band of clerestory windows along the sides. The King estate is not open to the public, but during the winter months it is possible to obtain glimpses of it from the river road.

"Rockledge" (King House).

SE-31 Janesville

The original town was founded in the 1850s, but when the Winona and St. Peter Railroad was located to the east, most of the town's buildings were moved to the new railroad site during the winter of 1869–70. On Main Street (perpendicular to Highway 14) are two commercial buildings worth noting — the Janesville Hatchery and Produce Building on the northeast corner of Main Street and 2nd Street (late 1880s) and the Miner Block on the southwest corner of Main Street and 1st Street (late 1890s). The first of these buildings

Janesville Hatchery and Produce Building.

St. John's Episcopal Church.

has a wood porch in the Eastlake Style across part of its front. The cornice with its small pediments and stubby pinnacles is also within the Eastlake tradition. The Miner Block is in the Queen Anne Style in a classical mood. Farther west on 1st Street near the northeast corner of Skookum Street is the board-and-batten St. John's Episcopal Church (c. 1872). This is another of Bishop Whipple's small Gothic Revival churches in wood.

At 305 Mill Street West is the Schuttloffel Cottage (c. 1871). This is a small, beautifully preserved brick cottage with a finely detailed entrance porch in the center and a large bay projecting off the side elevation of the house. At the north end of town, on the northwest corner of Main Street and Fourth Street, is the Holtz House (late 1890s). A round corner tower with a bulbous double roof projects from the Queen Anne/Colonial Revival structure.

SE-32 Kasson

The town was platted in 1865 when the Winona and St. Peter Railroad came through on its way to Winona. Since the railroad ignored the already established town of Mantorville to the north, most of the inhabitants of that town moved down to Kasson. Highway 14 passes along the south edge of town, and the business section on Main Street and in the residential area to the north remain intact. Although there are a few post–World War II buildings around, the town's dominant note is pre-1920.

1 **Kasson Municipal Building,** 1917
Purcell and Elmslie
122 Main Street W

An interesting but certainly not great Purcell and Elmslie building. Each of the façades of the building works out fine, but the overall design is unsatisfactory. On the whole the exterior today remains as built, except that the projecting rectangular vent next to the chimney has been removed. The interior has been drastically remodeled. Originally the building housed the fire department on its lowest level, the police department, other city departments, and the post office on the main level, and the council chamber and the public library on the second floor.

1 Kasson Municipal Building.

2 **Theatre** (now Mount Zion Lutheran Church), c. 1937
215 Main Street W

The glass bricks (Streamline Moderne) distinguish this otherwise plain, neutral building. On the ground level two curved walls of brick lead into the theatre entrance; above are two large glass-brick windows and a vertical glass-brick tower.

3 **Kasson Water Tower,** 1895
Southeast corner 2nd Street NW and 4th Avenue NW

The town's major landmark. A circular stone base with a metal spiral staircase wrapped around it and the tank on top — utility and romance, all in one.

3 Kasson Water Tower.

4 **Kasson School** (now a private house), late 1860s
Southwest corner 1st Street NW and 3rd Avenue NW

This two-story brick structure is severe and plain until suddenly it bursts forth in large-scale, really exuberant sawed work on both gable ends. The general pattern of the sawed work is Eastlake, but the design patterns are hardly typical.

5 **Leuthold House,** c. 1898
108 2nd Street NW

A good-sized Queen Anne/Colonial Revival house which relies on size and shape rather than on details to state its case.

6 **Cottage,** c. 1870s
Southwest corner 4th Street NE and 1st Avenue NE

Small cottages such as this are found throughout Minnesota, and most if not all were probably derived from designs found in one or another of the mid-nineteenth-century pattern books. This one is a small rectangular box topped by a second-story mansard roof.

7 **House,** c. 1880
207 Mantorville Road

A brick Eastlake house.

SE-33 Kenyon

Five miles southeast of Kenyon on Highway 56 and four miles east on County Road 11 is St. Rose's Catholic Church (1889). This stone church is of the entrance-tower type with a high wood belfry and spire. Round and arched windows suggest the Romanesque rather than the Gothic.

St. Rose's Catholic Church, near Kenyon.

SE-34 La Crescent

This village, across the Mississippi River from La Crosse, Wisconsin, was settled in 1851 and platted in 1856. At 433–35 7th Street South is the clapboard Cameron House (1871). The box-like volume of the house is completely dominated by a grand glassed-in belvedere. The recessed entrance with its engaged piers and entablature and the bracket roof are strong Italianate elements. Another Italianate house (c. 1870s), this one of brick, is located at 234 1st Street North. The house still retains its original entry porch and side porch.

Cameron House.

SE-35 Lake City

Lake City, situated on Lake Pepin, was settled in the early 1850s and was formally platted in 1856. The city is spread out thinly along the lake's west shore. A park adjoins much of the lake, and an enclosed harbor lies opposite Center Street. The railroad (Chicago, Milwaukee, St. Paul, and Pacific) defines the western boundary of the community.

1 **Pavilion** (Band Stand), c. 1910
City Park, northwest corner Center and High Streets

An open octagonal structure. The roof is supported by eight Ionic columns.

2 **Commercial Block,** c. 1880s
West side Washington Street between Center and Lyon Streets

The ground floor of this small two-story Italianate commercial building has been remodeled, and now the three arched openings provide a handsome portico. The thin, narrow columns have Corinthian capitals.

3 **Milliken House,** c. 1870s
220 High Street S

A two-story clapboard Italianate house with paired brackets supporting the wide overhang of the roof. The front porch has been enclosed, and the two bays at the side have been remodeled to include windows of glass brick.

4 **Patton House,** 1887
205 Marion Street

A plain but well-proportioned Queen Anne dwelling. Later additions include a Colonial Revival front porch.

5 **House,** c. 1870s
220 Oak Street S

A side-hall Greek Revival house with Italianate verticality of form and details; pedimented windows and sidelighted transom entrance. The posts of the porch have a delicate open pattern in sawed wood.

6 **House,** c. 1900
304 Oak Street S

The turn-of-the-century Colonial Revival at its best. A two-story porch with Ionic columns and a low balustraded terrace provide an impressive frontispiece for the dwelling.

7 **Stout Cottage,** c. 1890s
310 Oak Street S

A rather plain one-and-a-half-story cottage is given character by a Gothic/Islamic ogee window placed in the central gable.

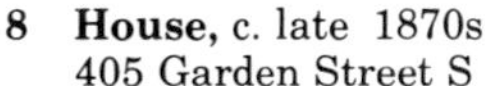

7 *Stout Cottage.*

8 *House.*

8 **House,** c. late 1870s
405 Garden Street S

One assumes that the inspiration was French Second Empire, but it is a fresh and original manipulation of the elements of the style in the tiny mansard tower with round dormers, arched dormers, and concave roof.

SE-36 Lanesboro

The village of Lanesboro was platted in 1868 when the Southern Minnesota Railway was extended across the south branch of the Root River. The town is located on a relatively flat plain situated at a bend of the river, which at this point lies in a deep gorge. The gridiron scheme has been applied to the site, but it is occasionally modified by the pattern of the river and the terrain of the hills south and east of the center of town.

1 **Fire Hall** (formerly town hall and fire hall), 1886
Southwest corner Coffee Street and Kenilworth Street N

A two-story stone building, much remodeled. Its small open Eastlake bell tower is probably the original one.

2 **House,** c. 1890
West side Kenilworth Street N, north of Coffee Street

Spindles have been formed into a spoked pattern of wheels on the first-floor porch of this Queen Anne house.

3 *Two Former Hotels.*

3 Two Former Hotels, c. 1870s
East side Parkway S, 1 block south of Coffee Street

These two wood-sheathed hotels are built into the steep hillside with three floors facing the street and two upper floors facing to the rear. Both have projecting cantilevered porches (on the second level) supported by Eastlake Style diagonal struts. One of the buildings is late Greek Revival in form, the other is Italianate.

4 Commercial Block, c. 1880
101 Parkway N

Finely cut smooth stone is used on the street front of this two-story office and store block. In style it is refined late Italianate.

4 Commercial Block.

5 Commercial Building, c. 1870s
West side Parkway S, corner Elmwood Street

An Italianate brick building with three arches. Fluted columns support the spring of the center arch and one side of each of the other two arches. Above the arches a central door is balanced by a window on each side.

5 Commercial Building.

6 Railroad Bridge, 1883
Chicago Bridge Company
West of Parkway S, 2 blocks south of Coffee Street

An early iron-truss railroad bridge. A similar bridge for automobiles exists at the north edge of the town on Ashburn Street (Highway 250).

7 Sons of Norway Lodge, c. 1900
200 Parkway S

The Colonial Revival in pressed metal (in imitation of ashlar blocks). A half-sunburst pattern dominates the gable end of the entrance porch.

8 Bethlehem Lutheran Church, 1868, 1917
200 Kenilworth Street S

A stone Gothic Revival church with an Eastlake tower spire. An embarrassingly "modern" addition (flat roofs and all) has been appended to the building.

9 St. Patrick's Catholic Church, 1872
400 Hillcrest Street (at Ridgeview Lane)

A stone church with a corner tower. Italianate with a suggestion of Gothic, particularly in the entrance, the belfry, and the spire.

10 House, c. 1870
Northwest corner Parkway S and Kirkwood Street

A brick Italianate house with a cruciform plan. The dramatic round-arched windows have wide projecting stone headers. The brackets of the roof are arranged in pairs.

11 House, c. 1880
500 Kenilworth Street S

A plain brick house, close to being styleless. The segmented windows hint at the Italianate.

12 United Methodist Church, 1889
507 Parkway S

A brick Gothic church with a corner tower.

13 House, c. 1890
500 Calhoun S

Queen Anne with a round corner tower and a spire.

•**14 House,** c. 1898
600 Calhoun S

The Queen Anne turning into the Colonial Revival. The house has a pair of abundantly decorated porches, one on the ground level, the other a balcony.

15 House, c. 1892
706 Fillmore S

Circular, oval, and moon-gate openings occur on the porches on the first and second floors. Shingles and clapboard sheathe this Queen Anne building.

16 House, c. 1892
708 Parkway S

A lively Queen Anne composition. The round corner tower, which becomes an open second-floor porch, is roofed by a double concave/convex roof terminating in a point. At each side of the entrance the walls project out as a freestanding segmented curve. The third-floor gables are highly ornamented.

16 House.

SE-37 Lenora

On the northeastern boundary of Lenora (founded in 1855) is the stone Methodist church. This gable-roofed Greek Revival church was built in 1856 and was rebuilt in 1865. Each of the sides has three large windows. A utilitarian entrance has been built at the front.

Methodist Church.

SE-38 LeRoy

Le Roy, on the Iowa and Minnesota division of the Chicago, Milwaukee, and St. Paul Railroad, was platted in 1867. Its claim to architectural fame rests on one building — the First State Bank of Le Roy (1914), designed by Purcell and Elmslie. This small gem of a Prairie bank is situated on the north side of Main Street. In front the bank presents a narrow façade organized around a deep-set arched entrance. On the east side a band of very small and narrow windows lights the office work area, and a large opaque window provides general lighting for the main banking room. Note the glass mosaic (with "P & E" worked into the design) in the lunette above the entrance.

First State Bank of Le Roy.

SE-39 Mantorville

Mantorville comes close to being a historic museum village. Although the town is still the seat of Dodge County, its economic base today relies more on the visitors who come to see its early buildings than anything else. Formerly its economy was centered on its mills on the Zumbro River and the granite quarries which lie south of the town. The community was platted in 1856. When the Southern Minnesota Railroad bypassed it in the late 1860s and went through newly founded Kasson, the majority of Mantorville's inhabitants moved to the railway town. In 1963 concern for the town's historic buildings led to the beginning of a restoration program which has continued to the present.

1 **Hubbell House (Hotel),** 1856
Northeast corner Main and 5th Streets
A flat-roofed stone hotel building of three stories. It has been made more authentic by the addition of white shutters and other Colonial details.

2 **Bank Building,** 1895
West side Main Street between 5th and 6th Streets
A diminutive Richardsonian Romanesque building.

•3 **Dodge County Courthouse,** 1865
E. Townsend Mix
East side Main Street between 6th and 7th Streets
A rare surviving example of the Greek Revival — the only county courthouse in this style still standing in the state. A flat-pedimented porch with Tuscan columns stands in front of the gable-roofed building.

4 **St. John's Episcopal Church** (now Grange Museum), 1869
West side Main Street between 6th and 7th Streets
A stone Gothic Revival church with a corner entrance tower. The upper section of the tower is certainly not original. Quoining occurs on all corners, and pointed headers are projected out above the small windows.

5 **Mantorville Opera House,** 1918
South side 5th Street between Main and Clay Streets

As a design the building seems to point to Vienna and the turn-of-the-century Secessionists seen through the eyes of a Prairie architect. A gable panel of cut stone is set in the middle of the second floor. Even the lettering style of the building's date seems Viennese.

6 **Severance House,** c. 1860s
Northwest corner 4th and Clay Streets

On the street side a two-story bay with round-headed windows and a bracketed roof establishes the Italianate character of this house.

6 Severance House.

7 **St. Margaret's Catholic Church,** 1862
Northwest corner 6th and Clay Streets

This church, originally built for a Protestant denomination, was consecrated as a Catholic church in 1910. The proportions and the eave detailing of the gable-roofed structure are Greek Revival. The pointed windows are Gothic Revival. An inharmonious entrance vestibule has been added to the front of this clapboard building.

8 **Cottage,** c. 1860s
Southwest corner 6th and Clay Streets

A Greek Revival façade in a one-story cottage — all delightfully pretentious in view of how little lies behind it. The central entrance consists of an engaged pier and a pedimented door, and there are elaborate fluted engaged piers at each corner of the front.

8 Cottage.

9 **Gates, Slingerland Park,** late 1890s
North side 5th Street between West and Walnut Streets

Two stone piers and between them a decorative metal sign with the park's name. A proto–Art Nouveau design rendered in a Classical guise.

10 **First Congregational Church,** c. 1864
West side Walnut Street between 5th and 6th Streets

Similar in concept to St. Margaret's Catholic Church (#7). A gable-roofed Greek Revival building in stone with pointed Gothic windows. A fanciful Eastlake belfry has been added at the side; the more recent stone additions are hardly fanciful or delightful.

SE-40 Medford

The Piper House (1877) represents a type of farm complex which was seldom built in Minnesota. Here the house is directly connected to the summer kitchen, woodshed, barn, and granary in true New England fashion. In style the house has an end-gable, side-hall plan which derives from the Greek/Federal Revival, but the detailing, both within and without, is Italianate. The house is located on the east side of the corner of Main Street South (Highway 218) and 5th Avenue Southeast. Another interesting building is the creamery (1914), located in the western part of town at 313 1st Avenue Northwest. It is a glazed brick structure; the large circular roof vent is accompanied by a tall cylindrical chimney.

Piper House.

SE-41 Millville

In the small village of Millville, on the Zumbro River, is the old Swedish Evangelical Lutheran Church (1874). This structure beautifully illustrates how impressive a simple form placed on the correct site can be. The church, situated on a low hill, has walls of stone and a plain gable roof; the entrance and the windows are pointed. The worked stone voussoirs of the entrance are pulled outward just enough to produce a delicate shadow pattern. The effect is that of a Greek Revival building with Gothic detailing.

Swedish Evangelical Lutheran Church.

SE-42 Minnesota City

The Stuart Hotel (c. 1860s) in Minnesota City is a stark two-story Greek Revival building with a simple detailed porch around the ground floor. South of the hotel is the Gothic Revival First Baptist Church (c. 1890). The hotel and the church are situated in the center of town, one-quarter mile south of Highway 248.

SE-43 Minnesota Lake

A visit to Minnesota Lake and the Nordaas American Homes establishment is an enjoyable way to spend an afternoon. Here is an architectural/landscape folly which should be preserved: The main building (1960s) is a dream version of Mount Vernon, surmounted by a triple-tiered drum, a dome, and a small replica of the Statue of Liberty. In the adjoining area are fenced statues of cows and horses. The nearby pond has a bridge, a fountain, and a battleship. The entrance gate consists of an open pergola supported by four fluted columns. On top is a baldachin holding a bell (perhaps representing the Liberty Bell). The theme is America and free enterprise.

Nordaas American Homes.

SE-44 Money Creek

The village was platted in 1856 at the junction of the Campbell and Wiscoy valleys. It consists of two main east/west streets and two smaller north/south streets. North of Main Street is the small ashlar block Methodist Episcopal Church (c. 1909). Its most telling feature is the stone corner tower with its open belfry and crenelated and parapeted roof. At the west end of the same block is a single-story wood store building (c. 1880), with a false front. To the west is a two-story brick side-hall house (c. 1870); the overall design is Italianate, but the entrance and the horizontal scale are Greek Revival. Money Creek is located four miles north of Houston on Highway 76.

Store building.

SE-45 Nerstrand

Two miles northwest of Nerstrand (Highway 246 north, then west on County Road 29), high on an open hill, stand two churches in the midst of a cemetery. The paired churches are approached through a metal gate which bears the name "Valley Grove." The churches face one another with a space of about seventy-five feet between them. One church bears the date 1862 and is a straightforward brick Greek Revival building with a low square tower. The newer church (c. 1880s) is clapboard Gothic Revival with a high open belfry and steeple. The strong impression which this scene conveys stems from the spatial relationship of the two churches, the picturesque melancholy of the graveyard, the gate with its metal arch and lettering, and the loneliness of the hilltop location.

Valley Grove churches, near Nerstrand.

SE-46 Northfield

The community was founded on the banks of the Cannon River in 1855 (the year it was platted), and by the end of the 1880s it had grown to a city of four thousand inhabitants. It had three large water-powered mills, and it was connected to the Twin Cities and other communities by three railroads. Among Northfield's chief assets are its two colleges — St. Olaf College (1874) in the western part of town and Carleton College (1866) in the northeastern section. For decades Northfield's motto was "Cows, Colleges, and Contentment," and in many ways the motto is as appropriate today as it was fifty years ago. According to the pamphlet *All about Northfield, Minnesota*, published by the *Northfield News* in 1889, "Northfield's nearness and ease of access to St. Paul and Minneapolis, her educational advantages, the natural beauty and healthfulness of her situation, the extreme cheapness of desirable building lots, all combine to invite busy men of business to come to her for quiet, inexpensive, beautiful and happy homes."

Northfield is one of the few river towns in Minnesota which have used the river itself as a visual focus. The presence of the Cannon River is apparent from various parts of Northfield, and Bridge Square (the hub of the city) faces onto a park bordering the river.

Division Street, the main business street, and many of the residential streets still have a nineteenth-century appearance. One of the town's original flour mills, which now operates as a cereal processing plant, stands on the west bank of the river, just south of the River Street bridge. On the east side of town are many houses from the 1860s through the 1890s, but most of these houses have lost much of their original character through remodeling. Many newer houses (built in the 1930s and thereafter) are to be found in the northeastern part of the town.

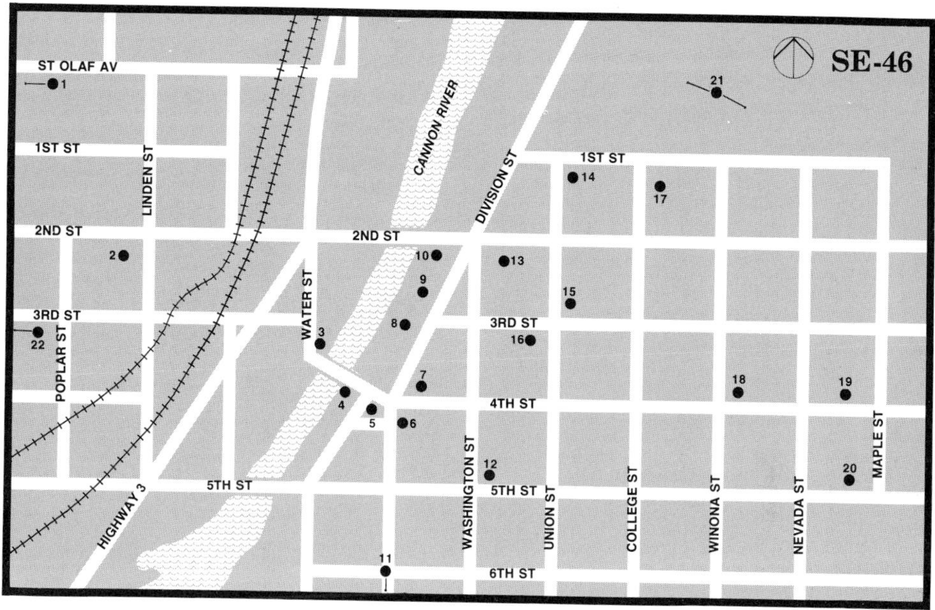

1 **St. Olaf College,** estab. 1874
West end St. Olaf Avenue

The college grounds command a magnificent view of the city and the surrounding country. Old Main, which is still standing, was built in 1877–78; it was designed by Long and Haglin. Like hundreds of late nineteenth-century American college buildings it is a stylistic mixture of Ruskinian Gothic and French Second Empire. The architectural vocabulary of Ytterboe Hall (Omeyer and Thori, 1900) was Chateauesque, but in Steensland Hall (Omeyer and Thori, 1902) it shifted to the classical — in this case a blend of Palladio and Jefferson. Eventually Collegiate Gothic (of the Ralph Adams Cram variety) was seized upon as the logical vocabulary for the college. Between the mid-1920s and the 1950s several well-designed English Elizabethan buildings were constructed on the campus. As designs, the most interesting of these is Holland Hall (Coolidge and Hodgdon, 1925), the west side of which encompasses a fine organization of windows and vertical stone walls. Other buildings which entail the same Gothic mode are Rolvaag Memorial Library (Lang and Raugland, 1942), Agnes Mellby Hall (Charles Hodgdon and Son, 1938), Thorson Hall (Lang and Raugland, 1948), the Boe Memorial Chapel (Lang and Raugland, 1953), and Hilleboe Hall (Lang and Raugland, 1951). All of these Gothic Revival structures with beautiful stonework seem to have been molded intc their hilltop locations.

In the 1960s the college's planners again shifted their stylistic grounds and decided to be modern — not the fashionable modern of the period, but mild modern in which there would be an effort to relate the new and the old, primarily through the use of similar masonry. Such compromises are not easy to carry off, and the results at St. Olaf have at best been mixed. The most successful of the new buildings are the two tower dormitories — the ten-story Mohn Hall (1967) and the thirteen-story Agnes Larson Hall (1964), both designed by Sovik, Mathre, and Madsen. The architects had the advantage of being able to look at Eero Saarinen's Morse and Stiles colleges, built at Yale in 1962. The later work of the firm in the Skoglund Athletic Center

(1967) and the Music Building (Sovik, Mathre, Sathrum, and Quanbeck, 1975) is not as successful. The new buildings do not fit into the site as well as the earlier Gothic buildings do, and the Skoglund Athletic Center in particular has a disturbingly bulky and overscaled appearance.

2 **Kingman House,** c. early 1880s
200 Linden Street S
Lightly Italianate with a pair of two-story bays on each side of the entrance porch.

3 **State Bank Building** (now a travel agency), 1910
Harry Jones
311 Water Street S
An architectural oddity — a masonry building with an Egyptian pylon at the entrance and a low glass dome over the central part of the building. The street façade of the building follows the curve of Water Street.

4 **Post Office,** 1936
Rand Laboratories; Louis A. Simon; Neal A. Melick (engineer)
Southeast corner Water Street W and Bridge Square
Collegiate Gothic in stone.

5 **Scrivers Building,** 1869
Southwest corner Division Street and 4th Street E
This stone building has been substantially altered over the years, but one can get some idea of how the original looked by examining the east section of the façade (facing Bridge Square). This façade was repeated on the west side. The large oval dormers, which were added over the flat roof of the Bridge Square façade in 1888, and the central gable are unusual adaptations of the Italianate. The building was acquired by the Northfield Historical Society in 1975.

6 **Central Block,** 1893
Southeast corner Division Street and 4th Street E
A Queen Anne commercial block. The round corner tower with its conical roof overlooks the central part of the downtown bridge.

7 **Nutting Building** (now First National Building), 1889
Northeast corner Division Street and 4th Street E
A three-story Eastlake block, remodeled on the ground level in 1956.

8 **YMCA** (now City Hall), 1885
Division Street at 3rd Street E
A knowing exercise in the English Queen Anne. A two-story windowed bay is the main element on the street façade. "Welcome" is carved in stone over the door. Next door is the original city hall, an Italianate/Eastlake building.

9 **Nutting Block,** 1893
220 Division Street (just north of intersection of Division Street and 3rd Street E)
Richardsonian Romanesque. Originally a woolen mill, the building has reinforced concrete floors.

10 **Archer House** (now Stuart Hotel), 1877
212 Division Street (just north of intersection of Division Street and 3rd Street E)
A four-story brick French Second Empire hotel with later additions on the northwest corner.

10 Archer House (now Stuart Hotel).

11 **Spriggs House,** c. 1880s
Northeast corner Division Street and Fremont Street S
Another architectural oddity, known locally as the "House of Seven Gables" because of the strong roof line; it is almost as if the extensively remodeled gables had been pasted onto a flat-roofed three-story building.

12 **All Saints Episcopal Church,** 1866
Northeast corner Washington and 5th Street E

One of Bishop Whipple's Gothic Revival Episcopal churches. This vertical board-and-batten church was enlarged in 1879, and the tower was replaced by the present tower spire. The building is similar in design to churches illustrated in Richard Upjohn's *Rural Architecture*, published in 1852.

13 **Stewart House,** late 1870s
208 2nd Street E

A two-story Italianate house in clapboard.

14 **Diebold House,** c. 1940–41
300 1st Street E

A Streamline Moderne house which in many of its details resembles the "modern" houses built in the San Francisco Bay area in the late 1930s and early 1940s. A house of similar design from the late 1930s is situated at 4 Walden Place (south of St. Olaf College, off Highway 19).

15 **Nutting House,** 1888–89
J. E. Cook
217 Union Street

A large, and (as it would have been described at the time it was built) "substantial" brick dwelling. In style, Eastlake/Queen Anne.

16 **First United Church of Christ,** 1881
Southwest corner Union Street and 3rd Street E

Gothic Revival in brick with a tall corner tower and spire.

17 **Ogden House,** late 1860s
107 College Street

An Italianate side-hall house. A similar house (c. 1870) is located at 118 College Street.

18 **House,** early 1870s
317 Winona Street E

Gothic Revival and Italianate. Note also the Stevens House (early 1870s) at 500 4th Street East.

19 **Pye House,** c. 1910
613 4th Street E

A Craftsman version of an English half-timber dwelling.

20 **Baire House,** 1961
Robert Warn
613 5th Street E

The carport, the entrance passage in the center, and the courtyard with its wood walls face the street. The shed roof of the carport and one side of the low gable of the house form a butterfly roof.

21 **Carleton College,** 1866

The site selected for the college lay on the northern boundary of the city. In contrast to the hilly location of St. Olaf, Carleton's site was low and flat. Willis Hall (Old Main) was constructed between 1869 and 1872; after a fire it was rebuilt in 1879. In style it is French Second Empire, but the verticality of the building and much of its detail give it a Gothic Revival character. Scoville Memorial Library (Fisher and Patton, 1896) was an adaptation of Richardson's numerous small libraries in the Romanesque Revival Style. The most interesting nineteenth-century building on the campus is the Goodsell Observatory, a Richardsonian Romanesque building designed in 1887 by J. Walter Stevens of Minneapolis (or perhaps by Harvey Ellis). After about 1910 Carleton's new buildings were Gothic (vaguely English Tudor), but they were dull in comparison with the handsome Gothic buildings at St. Olaf College. The only exception is Skinner Memorial Chapel (Patton, Holmes, and Flinn, 1916), which is an academic rendition of an English Gothic church.

After World War II Carleton began an extensive expansion. The buildings of the 1950s were gently modern; probably the best of them is Boliou Art Hall (Magney,

21 Goodsell Observatory, Carleton College.

Tusler, and Setter, 1949), which has some of the calmness one finds in the work of the elder Saarinen. In the early 1960s the college engaged Minoru Yamasaki, who placed tinselly pavilions, towers, and other buildings all over campus. They work best when seen as imaginary palaces, perhaps out of the *Arabian Nights* tales, situated in a distant landscape. The best of these buildings is the Goodhue Dining Hall, which should be viewed from the bluff or the southwest side of Lyman Lake. Other examples of his work are the Olin Hall of Science (1961), the Men's Gymnasium (1964), the Women's Recreation Center (1965), and Watson Hall (1964–66).

In 1971 another change in stylistic allegiance occurred as Harry Weese produced a pair of closed-in boxes with a greenhouse entrance for the Music and Drama Center. And in 1974–75 Sovik, Mathre, Sathrum, and Quanbeck added a stylishly up-to-date version of the brick cut-into box in the Sealy Mudd Science Center. All of these divergent architectural styles work together reasonably well because of the superb landscaping of the site which took place between 1920 and 1975 under the direction of the resident landscape architect, D. Blake Stewart.

22 Taft Cottage, c. 1860s
3 miles west of town on Highway 19 (south side)

A one-and-a-half-story Gothic cottage in wood.

SE-47 Owatonna

This south central Minnesota city was founded in 1854 in the midst of rich agricultural lands. The site was selected because of the confluence here of the Straight River and Maple Creek. By 1858 the community was incorporated as a town, and by 1865 it had officially become a city. In 1866 the Minnesota Central Railway (now the Chicago, Rock Island, and Pacific) reached Owatonna from the north, and the Winona and St. Peter line (now the Chicago and Northwestern) came from the east in the same year.

The gridiron pattern of the streets was modified to provide for Central Park. Cedar Street and Bridge Street to the west radiate out from two sides of the park. By 1900 the park had become the focal point of the town, with a good number of the public buildings, churches, and major commercial buildings either looking out on the park or being close by. Cedar Street North and Bridge Street early became the principal commercial strips of the town. To the west, a major residential area developed along Main, Broadway, and Vine Streets on a low hill. The two dominant landmarks in town were (and still are) the classical courthouse overlooking the park and the Romanesque Revival tower of the Owatonna State School (now the Pillsbury Baptist College) on the hill in the residential district. The residential streets are beautifully landscaped with large trees. Over the years the city has developed four additional parks, which now total over forty-three acres; the city's park board was created in 1908. Both of the major freeways (Highway 35 to the west and Highway 218 to the south) skirt the city, and the original urban fabric remains intact. Architecturally, the city has long been a mecca for students of architecture; among its main attractions are Sullivan's National Farmers Bank and two distinguished houses by Purcell and Elmslie.

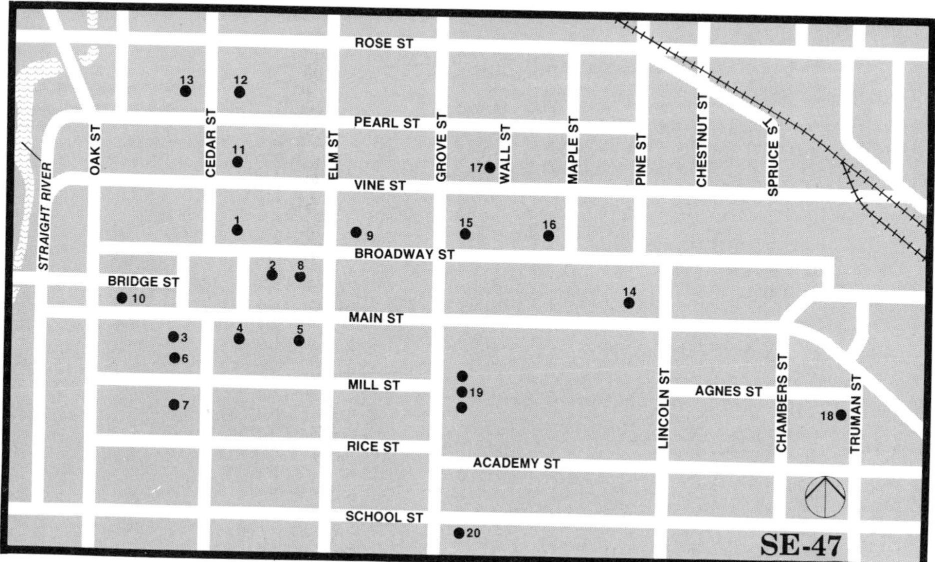

•1 **National Farmers Bank** (now Northwestern National Bank), 1907–1908
Louis H. Sullivan; George Grant Elmslie
101 Cedar Street N

Since its completion Sullivan's bank in Owatonna has been one of the points on any serious architectural pilgrimage in the United States, and the city's billboards let the visitor know that this is indeed the home of Sullivan's most famous bank. It is a building which one can return to again and again, and it remains as impressive as ever in its basic form and in the quality of its details. As in all of Sullivan's post-1890 buildings, the classical concept of order underlies the pristine cube, the great semicircular windows, the axial organization plan, the elevations, and the lively use of rich terra-cotta, sawed wood, and cast-iron ornamentation. It was fortunate in every way that when the building had to be modified and expanded in the late 1950s Harwell H. Harris was engaged to do the design (1957). He modified the interior but retained its basic Sullivan quality. The fitness of Harris's detailing is evident in the interior, but its presence has in no way compromised the original. The idea of the building as a jewel box set down in a prairie town, with a utilitarian two-story commercial building to the rear on Broadway, was completely Sullivan's. The sensitive realization of his idea and the superb ornamentation came from the hands of George Elmslie.

1 National Farmers Bank (now Northwestern National Bank).
Photo: Chicago Architectural Photographing Company.

2 **Northwestern Motor Bank,** 1964
Harwell H. Harris
Southeast corner Broadway Street and Park Square E

Here, across the corner from the great bank, is the new drive-in banking facility, low-keyed in profile so that it relates to, but does not compete with, the bank and forms a quiet backdrop for the adjacent Central Park. It is equally well related to the Sullivanesque Home of Federated Insurance Companies Building (#8), which adjoins to the east.

3 **City and Firemen's Hall,** 1907
107 Main Street W

During the decade 1900 to 1910 numerous municipal buildings of this type were built throughout Minnesota. All of the usual municipal functions were gathered together under one roof — the city hall with its offices, the council chambers, the police department, and the fire department. In style these buildings ranged from classicized Romanesque to full and open classic. They were not usually built in parklike settings but rather were placed directly on the street along with commercial buildings. Their street façades had one or more entrances, usually arched, for fire trucks and a low tower to house the town's fire bell. These were often the only outwardly visible indications that the buildings were civic rather than commercial. The Owatonna City Hall has all of these qualities; it differs from others only in being larger (three stories). In style it is lightly Romanesque.

4 **Steele County Courthouse,** 1892
T. D. Allen
111 Main Street E

In style, classicized Romanesque. Civic virtue is made emphatic by the large sculptured group set above the main entrance. Down Main Street (to the east), just beyond the First Baptist Church, is a small brick building. This was the first county courthouse building, which has now been refurbished to house the Chamber of Commerce.

5 **First Baptist Church,** 1885
123 Main Street E

A masonry Gothic Revival church which helps to establish the area around Central Park as the community center.

6 **St. Paul's Episcopal Church,** 1885
Northwest corner Cedar Street S and Mill Street W

Carpenter's Gothic, but with a strong Queen Anne feeling, especially in the variety of materials used to sheathe the building — shingles, board-and-batten, and clapboard. Its crowning glory is its open tower, topped by a conical spire.

6 *St. Paul's Episcopal Church.*

7 **Bungalow Court,** c. 1925
Southwest corner Cedar Street S and Mill Street W

A U-plan bungalow court of eight units, some with fireplaces. The design of this stucco building is Craftsman, c. 1910, rather than the period style of the 1920s.

8 **Home of Federated Insurance Companies Building,** 1923
Jacobson and Jacobson
129 Broadway Street E

A real discovery for those enamored with Prairie architecture. Above the entrance is a bold Sullivanesque ornamental pattern in bright terra-cotta. The design of the ornament on this building seems to be derived in part from Sullivan's work of the early 1890s and in part from Elmslie's ornamented designs, c. 1907–15. But the real tour de force lies within. Here one is confronted with a three-story brick hall resplendent with ornament in terra-cotta and leaded glass windows. It is as if Purcell and Elmslie's rotunda of the Woodbury County Courthouse in Iowa had been compressed into an eighth of its space — really remarkable.

•9 **Owatonna Public Library,** 1898–1900
Smith and Gutterson
105 Elm Street N

Most American library buildings at the turn of the century were inexpensive versions of Beaux Arts Classicism. The imagery of the Owatonna library is Greek and very strong.

10 **Tivoli Building,** 1876
135 Bridge Street

A small two-story Victorian Eastlake building, now remodeled on the ground floor. Note the adjacent building at 137 Bridge Street (1879), which still retains its unaltered façade on the ground floor.

11 **State Theatre,** c. 1937
215½ Cedar Street N

A neutral theatre building, with a late 1930s Streamline Moderne marquee, sign, entrance, and ticket booth.

12 **Zamboni Building,** 1929
Northeast corner Cedar Street N and Pearl Street W

A single-story retail commercial building whose two street façades are clothed in brightly colored terra-cotta. Its sixteenth-century Italian-derived design is a surprise to find in a southern Minnesota community. It is the sort of building which was popular during the 1920s in California and in the large Midwestern and Eastern cities but which is not often found in small communities.

13 **Commercial Block,** c. 1890
310 Cedar Street N

A severe three-story building in dark stone.

•14 **Buxton Bungalow,** 1912
Purcell, Feick, and Elmslie
424 Main Street E

A beautiful illustration of how the California bungalow could be radically revised functionally and at the same time transformed into a high art object. The kitchen (and its entrance) and the main entrance to the house face the street, and the living room overlooks the garden to the rear. Since the land slopes to the rear, the house is two stories high on the north side. Note the bank of brilliantly painted, stenciled ornament which ties the various front elements together.

15 **House,** c. 1912
306 Broadway Street E

A Queen Anne/Colonial Revival dwelling.

16 **House,** c. 1912
352 Broadway Street E

A brick Prairie Style house — a variation on Wright's $5,000 concrete *Ladies' Home Journal* house (1906).

17 **Adair House,** 1913
Purcell, Feick, and Elmslie
322 Vine Street E

In this house one can see the work of both of the principal designers — the high-pitched roof, the side screen porch, and the provisions for the garage are Purcell's; the fine detailing of the elevations, the brightly painted ornament, and the interior detailing are Elmslie's.

18 **House,** c. 1939
565 Agnes Street

A restrained Streamline Moderne residence.

19 **Owatonna State School** (now Pillsbury Baptist College), estab. 1885
315 Grove Street S

The campus comprises three buildings: the Romanesque Revival Administration Building (W. B. Dunnell, 1887) with its high tower; in the center Pillsbury Hall (1885), also Romanesque; and to the south a Classical porticoed building (c. 1900). The large Administration Building has been sensitively remodeled and restored, especially its entrance hall and staircase.

20 **"Village of Yesterday"**
Steele County Fairgrounds, southwest corner Austin Road and Park Street

Several nineteenth-century buildings which have been moved to a site in the fairgrounds. The most important of these by far is the Dunnell House (c. 1870), which is an elaborate, large Italianate house with a central cupola. Other buildings include a Catholic church (1876), which is a clapboard Carpenter's Gothic structure; the Bixby Railroad Depot (c. 1890s); and the usual pre-1900 log cabin.

SE-48 Pickwick

Pickwick (platted in 1857) sits in a small glade by Big Trout Creek. On the banks of the millpond adjacent to the dam is the Pickwick Mill (1856). This stone building is currently four stories high; originally it had six floors, but the upper floors were destroyed in a tornado in 1907. The façade facing the pond has a symmetrical disposition of windows on each side of a vertical series of doors, one on each floor. Pickwick is located two miles southwest of Highway 61 (the river road) at Lamoille on County Road 7.

Pickwick Mill.

SE-49 Pine Island

Pine Island is known for its dairy products, especially cheese. Since the town lies to the west of the freeway (Highway 52), its wooded residential streets and its principal commercial streets (still with diagonal parking) seem remote from the urban world of the 1960s and 1970s.

1 **City Hall,** 1909
Northwest corner Main Street S and 3rd Street SE
A brick municipal building originally designed to encompass council chambers, fire and police departments, and similar offices. It is a rather uninspired structure except for the arched tower with its four clock faces. Stylistically the building beautifully resists pigeonholing. There is a slight hint of Richardsonian Romanesque Revival and a pinch of late Medieval from northern Italy. A number of changes, such as the present entrance, have not added to the building's charm.

1 City Hall.

2 **L. F. Irish Block,** 1895
West side Main Street S, north of 3rd Street SE
A fine three-story Eastlake commercial block. The ground floor, with its steps and two arched openings, remains intact. The verticality of the second and third floors has been reduced, causing the building to look larger than it actually is.

3 **House,** c. 1870s
123 2nd Street SW
An Italianate house with a central pediment; side-hall plan.

4 **House,** c. 1900
Southwest corner 2nd Avenue SW and 2nd Street SW
A one-and-a-half-story Queen Anne/Colonial Revival house.

5 **House,** c. 1890
225 2nd Street SW
A strange, very narrow, elongated Queen Anne residence; not at all typical of the style.

6 **House,** c. 1889
314 2nd Street SW
An Eastlake residence brought up to date with Queen Anne fixtures.

7 **Pine Island Methodist Episcopal Church,** 1900
Northwest corner 1st Street NW and Main Street N
Gothic Revival, with a sense of the Craftsman movement. The name of the church is conveniently placed in the leaded, stained-glass window above the entrance.

7 Pine Island Methodist Episcopal Church.

SE-50 Pleasant Grove

Two and a half miles north of the village on County Road 1 is Fugle's Mill (1868). It is on the west side of the road just south of the Root River. The mill building is a narrow gable-roofed structure symmetrically punctuated with openings for double-hung windows and doors. Its stonework is especially fine.

Fugle's Mill, near Pleasant Grove.

SE-51 Preston

Preston was founded as a milling town on the north bank of the Root River in 1853. In the downtown area, on the north side of Fillmore Street between St. Paul and St. Anthony Streets is a two-story brick commercial block. As a design it is cleaned-up Eastlake. The date 1903, which is inscribed in the small central pediment of the cornice, is startlingly late for a design such as this. At 305 Fillmore Street is a two-story wood dwelling (c. 1870s) which combines the Italianate and the Eastlake. Partially hidden behind the tree at the southeast corner of Houston and Preston Streets is a boxy brick Italianate dwelling. Its overhanging roof has a pattern of paired and single brackets. A Greek Revival church (c. 1870s) with a wood entrance tower and pointed Gothic windows once stood across the street, but now all that greets the visitor is a stone foundation.

SE-52 Red Wing

The city of Red Wing is situated on the banks of the Mississippi River at the north end of Lake Pepin. A glance at the terrain will readily indicate why this site was selected, for it has an extensive area of flatland directly adjacent to the river, and the slope of the hills behind provides abundant space for residences. The site was originally the location of a mission to the Sioux (in 1837). Settlers began to arrive in 1850–52, and the town was incorporated in 1857. In the 1870s the town assumed much of its present status as a small manufacturing center, as a shipping point for agricultural products, and as a retail center for the farming area to the west. By 1871 Red Wing was connected with St. Paul to the north and west, and with Chicago to the east, by the Airline Railroad, which provided "speedy and constant communications."

The narrowness of the river flatlands at the west and east ends of the city currently pose planning difficulties, especially as far as the automobile is concerned. Both the west and east entries into town on Highway 61/63 have the usual commercial strip developments, which have tended to impinge on the hillside residential areas to the south. As long as the highway parallel to the river (Highway 61) is not a major freeway, Red Wing is safe; if this situation changes, there will be grave consequences for all the river towns.

The plan of Red Wing is the basic gridiron, except at the center of town where two parallel thoroughfares, East Avenue and West Avenue, form what amounts to the civic, religious, and cultural center of the community. The Goodhue County Courthouse, the civic auditorium, the post office, the library, and a number of churches are located here. Though these buildings represent a variety of styles, from the nineteenth-century Gothic Revival (Christ Episcopal Church, #7) to the 1930s PWA Moderne (Goodhue County Courthouse, #11), they all fit together very well, owing to their similarity of scale, the open parklike spaces between and around them, the heavy vegetation, and finally the slope of the hill down to the river.

The major residential area, which lies west of downtown on 3rd through 7th Streets, continues to be well maintained. Architecturally there are a number of real gems: the Lawther Octagonal House of 1857 (#30), the French Second Empire Sprague House of 1867 (#32), and one of America's impressive Prairie Style buildings, the Hoyt House of 1913 (#31). In addition to these major monuments, there is a fine stylistic array of nineteenth-century houses, especially on 3rd, 4th, and 5th Streets West. The commercial downtown area (on and around Main and Bush Streets) is ripe for sympathetic renewal, for it contains numerous late nineteenth-century and early twentieth-century buildings of real character, many of which could easily be recycled to new uses.

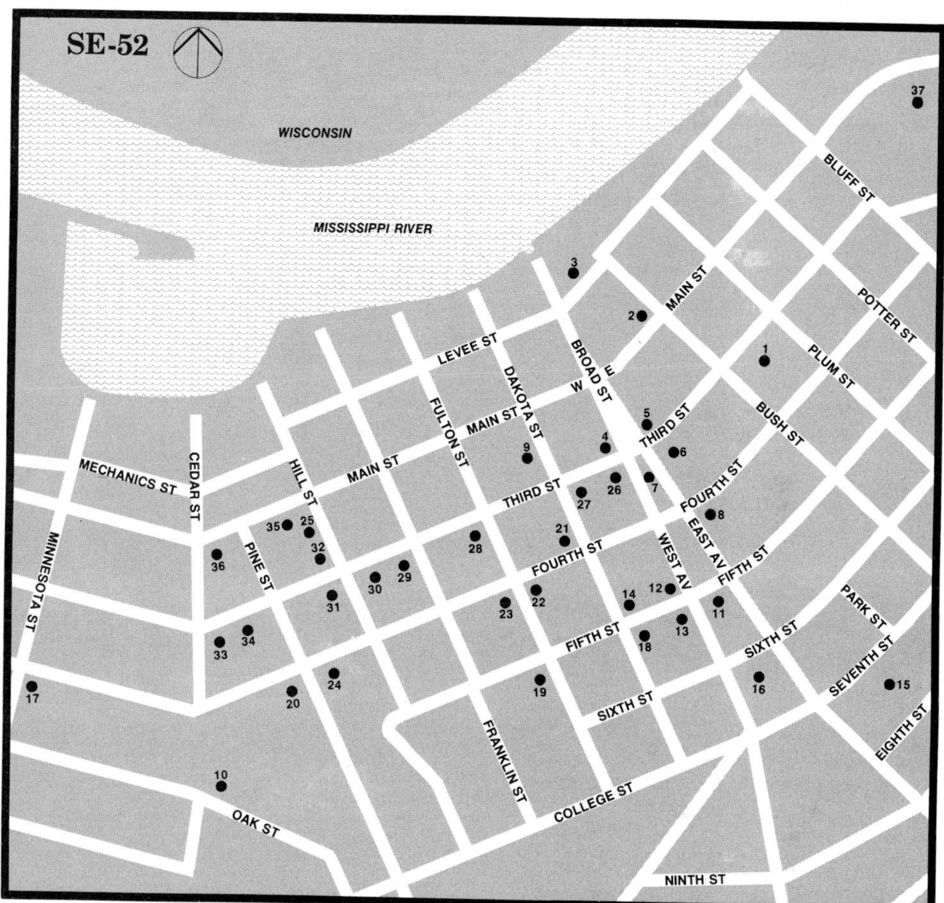

1 **Daily Eagle Building,** 1889
319 3rd Street E

Eastlake in flavor, with Queen Anne touches. Its cornice is of pressed metal. The date of the building is inserted in leaded stained glass in the upper part of its central window. The ground floor has been remodeled and now is completely anonymous. A downtown walk along Main and Bush Streets will turn up other nineteenth-century and early twentieth-century buildings such as the Gladstone Block, between 3rd and 4th Streets West.

2 **St. James Hotel,** c. 1880s
Northwest corner Main and Bush Streets

A major downtown commercial block; a four-story Italianate building with a Corinthian-columned entrance.

3 **Milwaukee Road Passenger Station,** c. 1890
Levee, corner Broad Street

Of interest here is not so much the station itself, which is basically classical, but its location alongside the small river park. This certainly is a very pleasant way (via train) to enter the town, with a view of the river on one side and the town and the hillside on the other.

4 **Post Office,** c. 1915
Northwest corner West Avenue and 3rd Street W

A classical Renaissance building; not great, but it does contribute to the civic feeling of West and East Avenues.

5 **Red Wing Public Library,** 1960s
225 East Avenue
The design of this contemporary stone and metal building, like that of the post office, is fairly run-of-the-mill, but its designer has responded to the location, and the building's low horizontal form carries on the scale of nearby buildings.

6 **T. B. Sheldon Memorial Auditorium/ Theatre,** c. 1912
L. A. Lamoreaux
443 3rd Street W
Simplified Beaux Arts classicism in light-colored brick.

7 **Christ Episcopal Church,** 1869–71; tower, 1898
Henry Dudley
3rd Street, corner West Avenue
This stone Gothic church is the civic, religious, and cultural center of the community.

8 **First United Methodist Church,** 1908
4th Street, corner East Avenue
Two crenelated towers look down on the stone Romanesque fabric of the sanctuary.

9 **House,** c. 1850s
210 Dakota Street
A surprise in this area directly adjoining downtown: a small Greek Revival saltbox, right out of early nineteenth-century New England.

10 **House,** c. 1860s
1160 Oak Street
A two-story Italianate house in brick.

11 **Goodhue County Courthouse,** 1931–32
Buechner and Orth; E. D. Corwin
5th Street between East and West Avenues
PWA Fascist Moderne. Its three-story bulk was successful in this case because of the extent of the landscaping around it and the park which lies across 5th Street. Its windows are organized into vertical bands; a suggestion of fluted engaged piers with sculptured figures on top brings a degree of visual emphasis to the main entrance.

12 **Insurance Company Building,** 1938
William M. Ingemann
426 West Avenue
A match for the courthouse, the insurance building poses as a public structure, clothed in PWA Moderne garb.

13 **First Lutheran Church,** 1895
615 5th Street W
A fanciful, highly picturesque version of the Gothic; more French than English. Beautiful light tan stone walls dramatically contrast with the details — cornice, finials, pinnacles, dormers — which are painted white.

14 **United Lutheran Church,** 1905
Northeast corner Dakota Street and 5th Street W
A stone Romanesque Revival church; Richardsonian with a suggestion of the Craftsman.

15 **Brooks-Sheldon House,** 1875
457 7th Street E
An Italianate house of the gable-end, side-hall plan type.

16 **House,** c. 1860s
521 6th Street
A symmetrical Italianate box of the Villa vintage.

17 **House,** c. 1860s
Southwest corner 5th Street W and Buchanan Street
A two-story Italianate house with pronounced brackets supporting its widely projecting roof.

18 **Cottage** (now an antique shop), 1854
Southeast corner 5th and Dakota Streets
A small clapboard cottage with many later additions. Its spirit is Gothic, although some of its features are Greek. A good example of mid-nineteenth-century vernacular.

19 **Pierce House,** c. 1860s
803 5th Street W
An Italianate villa of the central-gable type with a round window in the gable.

20 **House,** c. 1870
Southwest corner 4th Street W and Pine Street
A large Italianate house in stone, basically a square-box villa. The exterior porch is probably a later addition.

21 Taber House, late 1860s
706 4th Street W

A two-story Italian villa in brick with a central gable and a porch across the front.

22 House, c. 1870
725 4th Street W

Another Italian villa with heavily articulated brackets below the main roof and the porch roof. The house is now stuccoed.

23 Sheldon House, 1875
805 4th Street W

A good-sized Italianate house in brick with a central tower, an almost flat roof, and detailing that is often more Eastlake than Italianate.

24 Betcher House, c. 1910
1025 4th Street W

A Period Revival house of the early part of the century; in style, English Tudor rendered in stucco, half-timber, and brick.

25 House, c. 1870
212 Hill Street

A heavily bracketed Italianate box with a hipped roof; modest in size.

26 House, c. 1860s
609 3rd Street W

Greek Revival with a suggestion of the Italianate.

27 Smith House, c. 1870s
617 3rd Street W

This sort of architectural oddity is a delight to come upon. The house is of brick, with tall, narrow openings, and the gable ends extend as stepped parapets. The sense of the house is Dutch, although the design is hardly architecturally correct.

28 Wilder House, c. 1860s
807 3rd Street

An end-gable, side-hall Greek Revival house with a recessed entrance and sidelights.

29 House, c. 1860s
905 3rd Street W

Italianate, with a double-arched window on the second floor.

•30 Lawther Octagonal House, 1857
927 3rd Street W

The largest and most pretentious of Minnesota's octagonal houses. This brick dwelling was built as a pure octagon, with a porch around all sides, a central hall, and a spiral staircase that was lighted and led up to the small, windowed cupola. There are four chimneys on the exterior walls, and a metal fence tops both the house and the cupola. An addition was built to the rear in the 1870s and the plan was modified. Its hillside location and its raised basement to the front (facing north) dramatically set off its octagonal shape.

31 Hoyt House, 1913
Purcell, Feick, and Elmslie
300 Hill Street

One of Purcell, Feick, and Elmslie's most successful designs. The plan is a modified Prairie cruciform scheme with the entrance to the side on Hill Street. An enclosed porch, a living room, and a dining room go across the front; a library, a kitchen, and a service area are at the south side of the entrance hall. A long horizontal mural of a moonlit forest is above the living room fireplace. The connecting passageway and garage were planned in 1913, but they were not built until 1915. The sawed-work designs in wood for this house, especially the screen of the garage passageway, represent Elmslie's decorative ability at its finest.

31 Hoyt House.

32 Sprague House, 1867
1008 3rd Street W

A Charles Addams version of what a Victorian mansion should be. The Sprague house is situated on a large city lot with ample lawns, shrubs, and tall trees. It is a classic example of the French Second Empire Style, with concave mansard roofs, a tall tower, and heavy stone detailing that contrasts with the brick walls, arched windows, porches, and bays — it is all here, even to the pair of hitching posts along the street in front.

32 Sprague House.

33 House, c. 1870
1121 3rd Street W

Italianate with dramatic use of a central gable. The gable, which breaks through the projecting roof lines, has a small circular (vented) opening. Below, a porch with groups of double piers leads to a sumptuous entrance with sidelights and transom lights.

34 Williston House, c. 1870
1107 3rd Street W

An Italianate house of some size with narrow horizontal attic windows placed in the entablature. Much of the sawed and turned detailing in the pediment above the windows and on the first-floor bay window is Eastlake.

35 Cottage, c. 1860
1015 Main Street W

A one-and-a-half-story Gothic cottage in brick with verge boards in the gables.

36 Service Station (now automobile dealership), c. 1937
Southeast corner Main and Cedar Streets

A metal-sheathed Streamline Moderne station with not only rounded corners but also rounded parapets.

37 Minnesota Training School for Boys, estab. 1889
W. B. Dunnell
East of town on Highway 61

(Not on map.) The nineteenth-century image of a jail or a penitentiary was that of a medieval castle with its dungeons. Even a reformatory must strike a grim note. Here the main building, the chapel, the shops, and the boiler room were of heavy rusticated stone, all watched over by a three-story tower. In style Richardsonian Romanesque Revival.

SE-53 Rochester

Scattered hither and yon throughout the country are towns and cities that have developed for reasons other than the specifics of their geographic environment, and Rochester is one of these. There is no intrinsic logic of locale which in any way could account for this city's preeminence as an internationally known medical center. The emergence of the Mayo Clinic in the early 1900s slowly transformed what was a small, prosperous agricultural center into the type of urban environment we normally expect to encounter only in or around a large city. If one approaches Rochester from the northwest on Highway 52 or from the east on Highway 14, the city appears to be a large metropolitan area with industrial plants, freeways and their overpasses and underpasses, shopping centers, and in the distance high-rise buildings. But the truth is that present-day Rochester comprises not a unified environment but five separate ones — an urban freeway world to the west and south around Highways 52 and 14 (extending from the IBM compound to the north to the Apache Mall Shopping Center to the south); the medical center of the community around 2nd Street Southwest and 2nd Avenue Southwest and north of West Center Street; a small prairie city business district between 2nd Avenue Southwest and Broadway North; the original residential area (north of 2nd Street Southwest); and finally around the edges a scattering of upper-middle-class suburban houses (usually single-story) on ample parcels of land. Although these five worlds do to a degree melt into one another, they generally convey a sense of separateness.

The nineteenth-century urban and architectural history of Rochester is similar to that of other southern Minnesota communities. The site was initially selected because of its location on the rapids and falls of the Zumbro River. A gridiron scheme of streets was platted in 1855 with Broadway and Center Street as the base, and the town was incorporated in 1858. Although the geographic environs of the city embraced hills and valleys, the river, and a number of streams, the gridiron remained the preferred urban division pattern through the early 1940s. During the post–World War II years when suburban developments on the periphery were created on former farmland, the low density of housing made possible a curvilinear pattern of roads that proved to be very popular.

When the town was originally laid out, a public square was provided between 2nd Street Southwest and 1st Street Northwest but as the community developed the center shifted to the south. The original scheme also provided for the Courthouse Park on 2nd Street Southwest and an oval residential park (Cascade Park) on 2nd Avenue Northwest. Eventually extensive recreational areas were added along the eastern periphery — to the north Mayo Park and others along the Zumbro River and Silver Lake, and to the south Soldiers Memorial Field and the adjacent parkland along the river.

The key developments during the early years of the community's existence were the construction of the first wooden bridge over the Zumbro River in 1856 and the completion of the first iron bridge two decades later, the erection of the flour mills and the sawmills on the Zumbro and its tributaries beginning in 1856, the arrival of the Winona and St. Peter Railroad in 1864, and finally (at long last, from the city's point of view) the Chicago Great Western railroad connection to the Twin Cities in 1902. It was during the post–Civil War years of the 1860s and the early 1870s that Rochester began to develop its downtown business district and public buildings. From the late 1860s and on into the early 1890s the center of town was marked by the tall tower and vertical mass of the French Second Empire Style Central High School (1867–68) and the loosely Italianate Olmsted County Courthouse (1866) with its high drum and dome. Scattered near these two civic monuments were three low-seated church buildings. Education, government, and the church symbolically dominated the town. Slowly, though, the visual (and symbolic) importance of these public buildings diminished as commercial structures proliferated; by the early 1900s it was apparent to all that commerce was what really counted. But commerce in its turn symbolically gave way to medicine with the construction of the Mayo Clinic's Plummer Building, which was completed in the late 1920s. From that moment on the medical image maintained its dominance.

Architecturally, Rochester has sampled all the styles of the last half of the nineteenth century and the first three-quarters of the twentieth century. But, in contrast to other small southern Minnesota towns and cities, Rochester has not preserved much of its architectural past. On Broadway one can still find the remains of a number of brick commercial buildings dating from the late nineteenth and very early twentieth centuries, but the major monuments of the past — Central High School, the original courthouse, the Richardsonian Romanesque Revival public library, and St. Mary's Hospital — are all gone. There are a few scattered remnants of nineteenth-century domestic architecture, but like the public and commercial buildings most of the domestic structures either have been drastically remodeled or have been torn down. The visual impression conveyed to a visitor today is that of a small, very prosperous city of the 1950s and 1960s — a city of the present, not of the past.

1 **International Business Machines Corporation Building,** 1957–58
Saarinen, Saarinen, and Associates
Southwest of junction Highway 52 and 37th Street NW

A classic Corporate International Style building of the 1950s, set in its own industrial park and appropriately sited, directly adjacent to the freeway. A beautifully detailed period piece of an era now gone.

2 **Dayton Company Store Building,** 1972
Victor Gruen Associates
Apache Mall, junction Highway 52 and Apache Road SW

The undecorated box or grouping of boxes as the dominant note in a suburban shopping center, a form that Gruen, more than anyone else, has popularized since the 1950s.

3 **House,** c. 1889
713 2nd Street SW

A two-story Queen Anne Style clapboard house.

4 **Olmsted County Courthouse,** 1958
Daniel M. Robbins and Associates
Northwest corner 2nd Street SW and 5th Avenue SW

The 1866 courthouse was a civic monument that dominated the community, both in the town itself and from a distance. The current structure is purposely unobtrusive and hides itself alongside its extensive parking lot. Its image is down to earth and businesslike, and bureaucratic or civic virtue it does not celebrate.

5 **High School,** 1916
Miller, Fullenwilder, and Dowling
Northwest corner 2nd Street SW and 4th Avenue SW

A three-story brick complex that is of interest not so much in its overall design as in its detailing. The Chicago firm that designed the building rummaged through the latest avant-garde styles present in Chicago in about 1910 and brought together elements of the Midwest Prairie School and the Craftsman, with a touch of Viennese Secessionist. Note especially the metal light standards and the patterns in the leaded-glass windows.

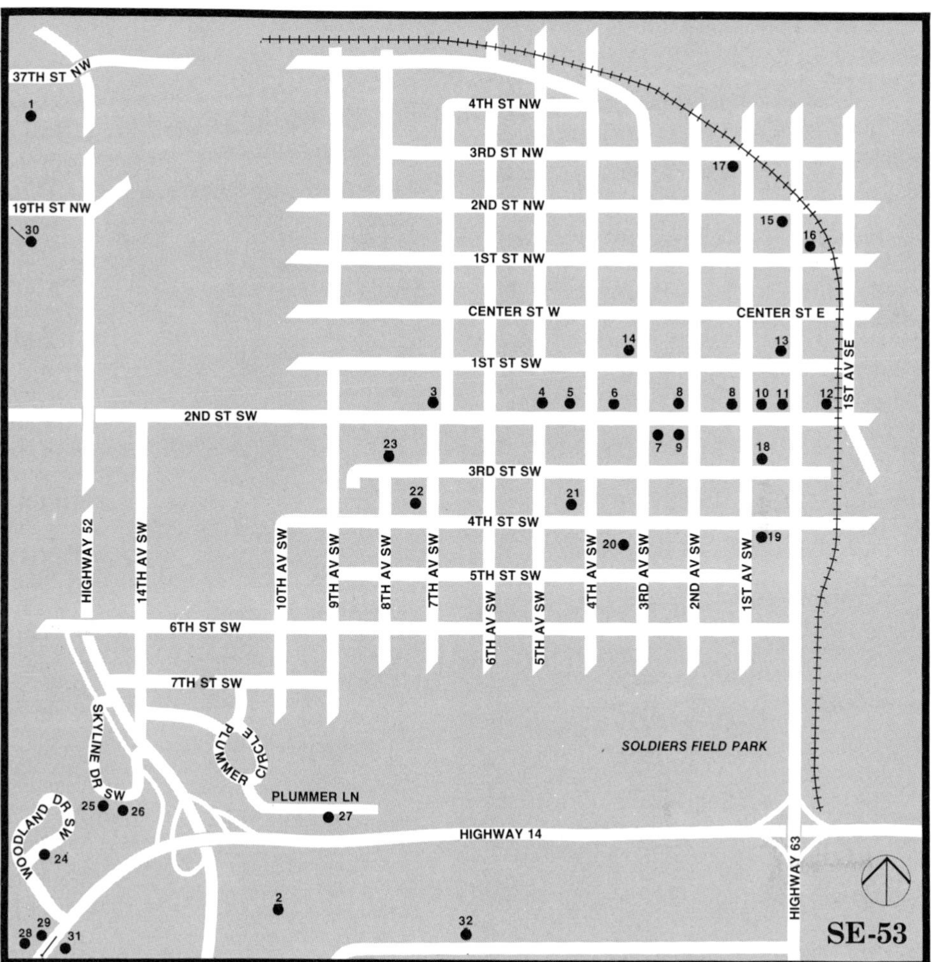
37TH ST NW
19TH ST NW
4TH ST NW
3RD ST NW
2ND ST NW
1ST ST NW
CENTER ST W
CENTER ST E
1ST ST SW
2ND ST SW
3RD ST SW
4TH ST SW
5TH ST SW
6TH ST SW
7TH ST SW
1ST AV SE
HIGHWAY 52
14TH AV SW
10TH AV SW
9TH AV SW
8TH AV SW
7TH AV SW
6TH AV SW
5TH AV SW
4TH AV SW
3RD AV SW
2ND AV SW
1ST AV SW
SKYLINE DR SW
PLUMMER CIRCLE
PLUMMER LN
WOODLAND DR SW
SOLDIERS FIELD PARK
HIGHWAY 14
HIGHWAY 63
SE-53

6 **Calvary Episcopal Church,** 1862
Northeast corner 2nd Street SW and 3rd Avenue SW

A gable-roofed brick church, originally with a small entrance porch to the south and six pointed windows on each flank. The entrance has been changed to the east side with the addition of a porch.

7 **Rochester Public Library** (now Student Center, Mayo Clinic), 1936–37

Harold H. Crawford and Peter P. Bross
Southeast corner 2nd Street SW and 3rd Avenue SW

The late English Gothic was frequently used for small public buildings, especially libraries and schools, during the 1920s and 1930s. This library, built with PWA funds, conveys the bookish mood we are expected to associate with the Middle Ages.

8 **Plummer Building, Mayo Clinic,** 1926–28
Ellerbe Architects
Northeast corner 2nd Street SW and 2nd Avenue SW

Diagnostic Building, Mayo Clinic, 1952–55
Ellerbe Architects
Northwest corner 2nd Street SW and 2nd Avenue SW

The Plummer Building, with its fifteen-story bulk and its high decorated tower, is still the visual landmark of the city. In style it is vaguely classical with details that are reminiscent of Northern Italian Gothic and even a hint of the Byzantine.

The Diagnostic Building is a competent but bland twelve-story interpretation of the Corporate International Style — bank upon bank of horizontal band windows and bland end walls; all elegantly and expensively detailed in marble. Mounted on the exterior of the building is a figure by Ivan Mestrovic; inside in the lobby is a large mural by the West Coast artist Millard Sheets.

The firm of Ellerbe Architects also designed the nearby Rochester Methodist Hospital (at 201 Center Street West), the John Marshall High School, the Franklin power substation, the airport terminal, and other buildings in Rochester.

8 Plummer Building, Mayo Clinic.

9 **Hilton and Guggenheim Laboratory Buildings,** 1973–74
Ellerbe Architects
Southwest corner 2nd Street SW and 2nd Avenue SW

The Ellerbe firm has always adroitly kept up with the latest fashions. In this concrete, glass, and steel complex it has taken over the grammar of the New Brutalism of the late 1950s and 1960s and has applied it in a vertical glass prismatic box — all competently handled.

10 **Commercial Building,** c. 1914
Northeast corner 2nd Street SW and 1st Avenue SW

A three-story Prairie building in brick. A tile pattern encases the recessed window sections, each of which is articulated by a pair of engaged columns. The ground level of the building has been remodeled.

11 **Olmsted County Bank and Trust Company Building,** 1918
Ellerbe Architects
Near northwest corner Broadway S on 2nd Street SW

A tasteful Beaux Arts temple façade in stone. Its scale and dignified image fit in well with the adjoining commercial buildings along 2nd Street Southwest.

12 **Railroad Passenger Station** (now a bus depot), c. 1880s
19 2nd Street SE at 1st Avenue SE

An Eastlake/Queen Anne wooden railroad station which has been recycled for a logical new use; well landscaped and restored.

13 Chateau Theatre, 1927
Ellerbe Architects
15 1st Street SW

The stage-set quality of its mansard roof suggests that the design is French, but the central group of three arcaded windows with their serpentine columns speak more of the world of Byzantium.

13 *Chateau Theatre.*

14 Post Office, 1932–34
Harold H. Crawford and John M. Miller; James A. Wetmore
Northwest corner 1st Street SW and 3rd Avenue SW

PWA classic, with fluted engaged piers. The buffalo heads used as the capitals of the engaged columns greet the entering visitor. Within is a 1937 Federal Art Project mural (appropriately enough, of oxen pulling logs) by David Granahan.

15 Rochester Armory, c. 1890s
Southwest corner Broadway N and 2nd Street NW

An aura of medieval militarism is evoked by a high, unbroken brick wall and a crenelated tower.

16 B. F. Goodrich Service Center, c. 1935
Northeast corner Broadway N and 1st Street NE

Rich in Moderne (Art Deco) terra-cotta and tile ornament.

17 Whiting House (now Heritage House), 1875
In Central Park (1st Avenue NW and 3rd Street NW)

A side-hall Italianate house which has recently been moved and renovated. On occasion open to the public.

17 *Whiting House (now Heritage House).*

18 City Hall, c. 1931
Northeast corner 1st Avenue SW and 3rd Street SW

PWA Moderne (actually late 1920s Neoclassical) with delicate metal light standards on each side of the main entrance and etched glass in the doors. The building is set back slightly from the street.

19 First National Auto Bank, 1973
Byron D. Stadsvald
Southeast corner 1st Avenue SW and 4th Street SW

A one-story drive-in bank facility of wood and brick; sensitively sited and designed for this downtown location.

20 Knowlton House (now B'nai B'rith Center and Synagogue), 1910
Purcell and Feick
306 4th Street SW

A substantial yellow-brick house designed by William Gray Purcell, one of the major Prairie School architects. The porch with its three arched openings serves as an entrance for both pedestrians and vehicles. Impressive stained-glass windows adorn the south wall of the entrance porch. An earlier house designed by Purcell is now gone, and two other houses designed by him in 1912 and 1928 were not built.

21 **House,** c. 1890
419 4th Street SW
Queen Anne, with an octagonal tower and fine spindle work.

22 **Mayo Foundation House,** 1915–18
Ellerbe Architects
701 4th Street SW
A forty-seven-room Tudor mansion of stone. A square five-story tower with attached columns (somewhat institutional in character) looks over the gable-roofed lower sections of the house.

23 **Crewe House,** 1914
Ellerbe and Round
3rd Street SW at end of 8th Avenue SW
A two-story Prairie Style house in stucco.

24 **McBean House,** 1957
Frank Lloyd Wright
1532 Woodland Drive SW
One of Wright's prefabricated houses, produced by the Marshall Erdman Company. The windows are arranged in horizontal modular units, and the main area of the house is capped by a wide (in profile) overhanging roof.

24 McBean House.

25 **Bulbulian House,** 1947–50
Frank Lloyd Wright
22 Skyline Drive SW
A typical post–World War II Wright product; its hovering low-pitched gabled roof gently rests on bands of glass, which in turn are set on concrete block walls.

26 **Keys House,** 1947; 1949–50
Frank Lloyd Wright
36 Skyline Drive SW
One of the most impressive of Wright's post–World War II Usonian houses. This one, built of concrete block, was developed from his scheme for World War II workers' houses, each of which was to be within a dirt berm. Since it is seen from above, the roof pattern — a hipped roof floating over a projecting flat roof — is as important a design element as the walls of the house.

26 Keys House.

27 **"Quarry Hill" (Plummer House),** 1924
Ellerbe Architects
1091 Plummer Lane (off Plummer's Circle)
A three-story English Tudor house of limestone stucco and half-timbering. The tapering circular water tower of stone was the first building to be constructed on the estate.

28 **Mayowood House,** 1910–12
Mayowood Hill Drive
A forty-room concrete house set on the brink of a hill. (Consult the Olmsted County Historical Society for information about guided tours.)

29 Olmsted County Historical Society Building, 1973
Joseph Weichselbaum and Associates
3103 Salem Road SW

A single-story concrete block building buried in its own dirt berm.

30 Fellows Barn, 1868
3210 19th Street NW (1 mile west of Highway 52, near corner of 19th Street NW and 32nd Avenue NW

A gable-roofed stone barn with a large arched doorway and a louvered cupola on the roof.

30 Fellows Barn.

31 Dodge House and Barn, c. 1861
3105 Salem Road SW

The balanced composition of the two-story stone house is mildly Greek. The barn and the accompanying shed are tucked into the hillside. The roof of the barn boasts an elaborately detailed cupola. The Dodge farm complex was illustrated in Andreas's 1874 *Atlas*.

32 Toogood Barns, c. 1860s
Near corner 16th Street SW and 6th Avenue SW (about ½ mile east of Apache Mall)

Two stone barns have been joined together by a single-story wood section. The larger of the barns has a hipped roof surmounted by a tall cupola.

SE-54 Rollingstone

The pre–Civil War community of Rollingstone is situated on the creek of the same name two and a half miles west of Minnesota City. The town's major monument is the Holy Trinity Catholic Church (1869). The church is of stone with buttressed side walls and has a central entrance tower. It is located at the west end of Main Street. The two-story brick Dietrich Block (1879) and the adjoining one-and-a-half-story brick structure (c. 1880) which now houses the Stoos Electric Company are also on Main Street. Both buildings have round-headed windows. The three-arched storefronts of the Dietrich Block have been filled in.

SE-55 Rushford

The village of Rushford was established in 1854 at the confluence of the Root River and the south branch of Rush Creek. The community assumed even more importance when the Southern Minnesota railway reached the town in the late 1860s.

1 **Chicago, Milwaukee, St. Paul and Pacific Railroad Passenger Station** (now Milwaukee Road Depot), c. 1880s
2 blocks west of Mill Street
The two-story station is sheathed in board-and-batten and clapboard. Its stylistic flavor is late Eastlake.

2 **Mill and Elevator Complex,** 1900
1 block west of Mill Street
A variety of vertical and horizontal volumes (some circular, others rectilinear), all tightly grouped.

2 Mill and Elevator Complex.

3 **Wagon Works,** c. 1870
Southwest corner Stevens Avenue and Elm Street
A completely anonymous two-story stone building — utilitarian and frank.

4 **Rushford Mill,** c. 1860s
West end Winona Street (south branch of Rush Creek)
A three-story stone mill building with deeply recessed arched doorways. The windows all have segmented arches.

4 Rushford Mill.

5 **United Presbyterian Church,** c. 1905
East side Mill Street, 1 block north of Elm Street
A Craftsman church with a corner tower. The round-arched windows refer lightly to the Romanesque.

6 **House,** 1870s
225 Stevens Avenue
Gothic in an Eastlake interpretation.

6 House.

7 **House,** c. 1859
417 Stevens Avenue
A stone home that has been much remodeled. The major additions (c. 1900) are Queen Anne/Colonial Revival.

SE-56 St. Charles

In the downtown area of St. Charles, on the west side of Whitewater Avenue between 10th and 15th Streets, there is a fine group of two-story brick commercial blocks dating from 1891 and 1892. In style these buildings waver between the Eastlake and the Queen Anne. At 1461 Whitewater Avenue is a two-story brick house (c. 1880s) which is somewhat Eastlake. The two-story brick dwelling (c. 1880s) at 1512 Whitewater Avenue is more Gothic than anything else.

SE-57 St. Clair

St. Clair is located on the site of the former Winnebago Indian Agency. One-half mile southeast of the town on County Highway 173 is the old Indian Agency House of 1855. Like other early classical houses in Minnesota it is more Federal than specifically Greek Revival in style. It is of the central-hall type and has two stories. The brick end walls are carried up to form a single wide chimney for several flues. Projecting bricks have been arranged in a horizontal band directly under the eaves to create a dentil effect.

SE-58 Saratoga

The village of Saratoga (founded in 1854) lies four miles south of St. Charles. It contains some romantic stone ruins along Trout Creek and a stone Greek Revival cottage (c. 1860). The one-and-a-half-story cottage, situated on the west side of Highway 74, is of the side-hall type; the entrance is recessed with sidelights.

Cottage.

SE-59 Spring Valley

Spring Valley, founded in 1855, is at the junction of the Chicago and Northwestern and the Chicago, Milwaukee, St. Paul, and Pacific railways. On the west side of Main Street south of Broadway is a striking two-story stone commercial block (1871). The Italianate building has a row of seven arches on the ground level with the two groupings of three arches at the side supported by narrow columns. On the upper level there is a row of arched windows and a dramatic bracketed cornice. Two blocks west of Main Street on Courtland Street West is a brick Methodist church (1876) which now serves as a museum. Except for its modernized raised basement the building is one of the outstanding Victorian Gothic churches in the state. Note especially the stone-trimmed brick tower and the high pointed roof. At the northwest corner of Grant Street West and Washington Avenue is a one-and-a-half-story Eastlake Gothic cottage (c. 1870s). Its arched porch is markedly Italianate.

Commercial block.

Methodist Church.

SE-60 Stockton

The village of Stockton, which lies five miles west of Winona, was platted in 1856. Water power from Garvin Brook provided the energy for a roller mill (c. 1890). The wood and stone mill, the dam, and the millpond are located one block south of Highway 14. In town on the north side of Highway 14 is the board-and-batten Grace Lutheran Church (c. 1870), an early Gothic Revival church with an entrance tower. Next door to the church (to the west) is the former blacksmith shop, which is sheathed in pressed metal in imitation of stone. North on County Road 23 (toward Minnesota City) one finds two turn-of-the-century round barns (c. 1910). One is located seven-tenths of a mile north of Highway 14; the other is two and a half miles north of the highway.

Roller mill, Stockton.

Round barn, near Stockton.

SE-61 Vasa

Vasa is a small pinpoint on the map midway between Red Wing and Cannon Falls on Highway 19. It was settled in 1855–56 as a Swedish Lutheran community. As one approaches the town from any direction the first building to come into view is the Vasa Lutheran Church (1869). This brick church is of the entrance-tower-and-spire scheme, and its hilltop location proclaims its preeminence over the surrounding countryside. The main street of the town, which lies parallel to Highway 19 and one block north of it, contains several early clapboard structures; most interesting are the chaste, almost Greek Revival Vasa Museum (c. 1860) and the Vasa School (c. 1860s), which boasts a few Italianate details. Down the hill the Vasa Creamery programmatically declares its purpose by the milk can mounted on its roof.

Vasa Museum.

SE-62 Veseli

The very small village of Veseli (incorporated in 1889) lies east of New Prague, off Highway 19. Its dominant architectural landmark is the Catholic Church of the Most Holy Trinity, built in 1905 from plans by Clarence H. Johnston, Sr. This brick church is Italian Romanesque with a separate campanile. Although it is plain on the outside, the interior is rich in ornamentation.

SE-63 Wabasha

This site on the floodplain of the Mississippi River has a long history of use as a fur-trading center. The city was established in 1843 and was platted in 1854. At the northwest corner of Main and Pembroke Streets is a two-story brick Eastlake block (c. 1880) which has recently been remodeled into offices. The tall narrow windows have been filled in with sheets of glass, and the verticality of the structure has been repeated in a new glass bay at the corner. The results of the remodeling are on the whole quite successful. A few blocks away, at the southeast corner of Main and Bridge Streets, is the Anderson Hotel, a plain three-story brick structure which has been remodeled and expanded since it was built in the 1890s. The stone Grace Memorial Church (c. 1900) can be found at the northeast corner of 3rd and Bailey Streets. The church is consciously modeled after English Medieval village churches, but its flavor is turn-of-the-century Craftsman. At the northeast corner of 3rd and Allegheny Streets is an elegant two-story house of the side-hall type. Its form is Italianate, but the detailing (particularly the sawed work) is Eastlake.

Eastlake office block.

Grace Memorial Church.

SE-64 Waseca

Waseca, just west of Clear Lake, was established as a railroad town in 1867. The town became the seat for Waseca County in 1870.

1 **Waseca County Courthouse,** 1897
Orff and Joralemon
West side State Street N between 3rd and 4th Avenues NW

Richardsonian Romanesque in brick with stone trim. Glass brick has been used to modernize the building and bring it up to date.

2 **Smith Hotel,** c. 1870
Northeast corner State Street S and 2nd Avenue SE

The proportions and much of the detailing of this two-and-a-half-story brick building convey the sense of a Federal Style building. The entrance has sidelights and a fanlight, and small pedimented dormers protrude from the low-pitched mansard roof.

2 Smith Hotel.

3 **First State Bank,** 1971
Vosejpka Associates
Northeast corner 2nd Avenue NE and 2nd Street NE

A circular domed structure with a round central skylight. The form and details are Wrightian.

4 **Phelps House,** 1867
402 2nd Avenue NE

A brick Italianate volume with a hipped roof and a central-hall plan.

5 **First Congregational Church,** 1953
Hills, Gilbertson, and Hayes
503 2nd Avenue NE

Inspired by the brick churches of Saarinen and Saarinen before and after World War II. The sanctuary is a single rectangular block; the vertical rectangular volume of the bell tower is connected to the sanctuary by a two-story glass bridge.

6 **Schaumkessel House,** c. 1880s
911 8th Street SE

A sparsely detailed two-story Italianate house with a hood over the door and a two-story bay at the side.

7 **Ward House,** c. 1905
804 Elm Avenue E

Turn-of-the-century Colonial Revival. The pedimented two-story porch has Ionic columns. There is a Palladian window in the gable.

7 Ward House.

8 **Masonic Temple** (originally a house), c. 1905
831 3rd Avenue NE

The bulky brick block is joined to its site by a wide spreading single-story porch. A Classical composition which looks to the Colonial Revival, the Italian Renaissance, and the Chicago work of George W. Maher.

SE-65 Wasioja

The village of Wasioja was platted on the Zumbro River in 1856. In the 1860s it had a population of one thousand, but its development was stymied by the fact that it failed to become the county seat; furthermore, after the Civil War the railroad bypassed the town. Now only a few scattered buildings and ruins remain. On the south side of 2nd Street between Mechanic and Mill Streets are the stone ruins of the Wasioja Seminary, which burned in 1905. At the southwest corner of Broadway and 1st Streets is a small gable-roofed stone bank building constructed in 1855; during the Civil War it was a recruiting station. At the northeast corner of Front and Mechanic Streets is a two-story stone schoolhouse (1868). This hipped-roof building was constructed (and probably designed) by the Doig brothers, two local carpenters. In style it is severely classical, more English than American. Nearby is the Greek Revival Baptist Church (1857–58), which stands on the northeast corner of Front and Miller Streets (two blocks east of County Road 9 and one-half block north of County Road 16). It is one of the handsomest and most complete Greek Revival churches in Minnesota. Finally, at 115 Main Street North is the one-and-a-half-story Doig House. This stone Greek Revival house was built in 1858.

Baptist Church.

SE-66 Waterville

This pre–Civil War town was founded in 1855 and was platted in 1856. The St. Andrews Episcopal Church at 210 Lake Streek West (1870–74) is a board-and-batten Gothic Revival structure. Its cross-gable tower is surmounted by a tall thin spire. On the northeast corner of 2nd Street South and Paquin Street East is the Union Hotel, a plain two-story building in brick, dating from about the 1870s.

SE-67 Weaver

The small railroad town of Weaver, just north of the confluence of the Whitewater and Mississippi rivers, was platted in 1871. On its main street is one of Minnesota's best-preserved two-story brick commercial buildings (1875). On the ground level the structure has a series of arched openings with windows which are articulated by a delicate pattern of circles and half-circles. On the second floor the windows are arched and have projecting brick hoods with stone keystones.

Commercial building.

SE-68 Wells

Often in the smaller towns of Minnesota one finds that the local bar and off-sale liquor establishments are combined with the civic municipal building, but Wells has further refined this approach by combining the theatre and municipal building into a single structure (1960) at 125–31 Broadway South. The building is a box with high and low elevations sheathed in polished granite; the single canopy has a vertical theatre sign at one end and in the middle "Municipal Building" in small letters which project above the top of the canopy — all tasteful and (one would assume) financially sensible. The building was designed by W. F. Wirtz. There are also two residences in Wells which are of interest: the Thompson House at 39 2nd Avenue, a two-story brick Italianate house (c. 1870s) with very dramatic segmented arched windows; and the Leland House at 410 2nd Avenue South, a Queen Anne dwelling with a pinnacled porte cochere.

SE-69 West Concord

West Concord contains two churches of interest. St. Matthew's Episcopal Church (c. 1870s) on Arnold Street, west of 1st Street, is a Gothic Revival church with a corner tower. The building is sheathed in narrow clapboard, and the tower is decorated with brackets and dentils. The Methodist Episcopal Church (c. 1907) on the southwest corner of Main and 2nd Streets is a wood structure with a few details which point to the Romanesque. Its most unusual feature is an angled corner tower.

Methodist Episcopal Church.

SE-70 Whalan

On a hill high above the railroad town of Whalan (founded in 1868) is the two-story clapboard village hall (c. late 1870s) with a small open belfry tower perched on top of its front gable dormer. East of town on Highway 16 and then one-quarter mile south on County Road 23 is the stone Walker Mill (c. 1870). Its doors and windows have immense stone headers.

SE-71 Winona

When Winona was platted in 1852, it was named Montezuma. Its name was changed the following year, and in 1857 the community was incorporated. "The shape of the town site," it was noted in 1858, "is that of a vast amphitheatre — bounded on the north by the broad 'Father of Waters,' and the bold bluffs of the Wisconsin shore, while on the east, south, and west, the magnificent verdure-covered hills form a beautiful but extensive curve, or semi-circle. Utility, beauty, and romance are so singularly blended in this charming spot, as to earn for Winona the appellation of the 'Queen City of Minnesota.' " (From *City of Winona and Southern Minnesota: A Sketch of Their Growth and Prospects*, published in 1858 by D. Sinclair and Company, Winona.)

By the 1860s Winona had over ten sawmills, had acquired a number of flour mills, and the new Winona and St. Peter Railroad was bringing grain from the western plains to be shipped downriver. By the late nineteenth century other industries had been added to its economic base, including limestone quarrying, brick manufacturing, and pharmaceutical manufacturing. The city early achieved prominence in the field of education and became the site of a state normal school in 1860.

The city's gridiron scheme was established parallel to the river, running on a NNE/SSW axis. A five-block levee park was developed between Washington and Walnut Streets, and on the south side of the city a park was established on the north shore of Lake Winona. On the hill south and above Lake Winona is Garvin Heights Park. Highways 14 and 61 run south of the lake, thus avoiding the city's oldest commercial and residential districts. Highway 43, which crosses over the bridge to Highway 54 on the Wisconsin side of the river, still winds through the city.

Efforts are being made to rejuvenate Winona's downtown area through the construction of a mall and the recycling and restoration of buildings.

1 **Chicago and Northwestern Railroad Swing Bridge,** 1898
Best viewed from Johnson Street and Levee Park

The swing section is a balanced pair of cantilevered truss bridges with a small control house in the center.

2 **Chicago and Northwestern Railroad Depot,** c. late 1880s
North side 2nd Street W, opposite Huff Street

A two-story brick station, mildly Queen Anne in style. A Greek cross pattern in brick defines the entablature.

3 **Anger's Block,** c. 1860s
East side Walnut Street between 2nd and 3rd Streets E

A two-story Italianate commercial block. The lower level has round-headed arches supported by thin engaged columns, and the upper level has simple round-headed windows in a horizontal band.

•4 **Winona County Courthouse,** 1888
Charles G. Maybury
Southeast corner Washington Street and 3rd Street W

Along with the Minneapolis City Hall/Courthouse the Winona Courthouse represents a high point in Richardsonian Romanesque in Minnesota. The deep central arch is balanced at the side by the square corner tower.

5 **Winona Hotel,** 1890
Southwest corner Johnson Street and 3rd Street W

The Romanesque Revival in a five-story brick and stone block. The center three floors are tied together vertically within an arched and pier order. The small arched windows on the top floor are arranged in groups of three. The exterior brick and stone have been painted.

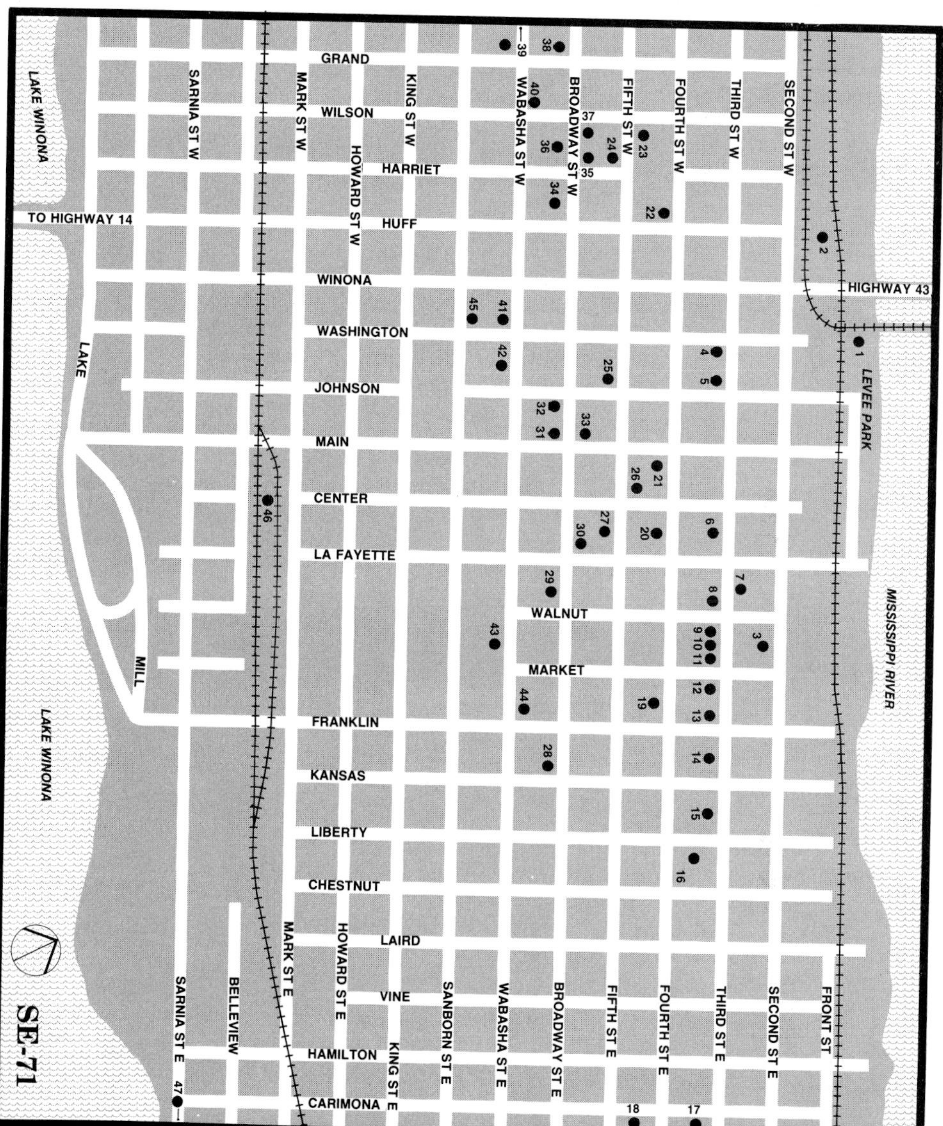
GRAND
WILSON
HARRIET
HUFF
WINONA
WASHINGTON
JOHNSON
MAIN
CENTER
LA FAYETTE
WALNUT
MARKET
FRANKLIN
KANSAS
LIBERTY
CHESTNUT
LAIRD
VINE
HAMILTON
CARIMONA
TO HIGHWAY 14
HIGHWAY 43
LAKE WINONA
LAKE
MILL
LEVEE PARK
MISSISSIPPI RIVER
SARNIA ST W
MARK ST W
HOWARD ST W
KING ST W
WABASHA ST W
BROADWAY ST W
FIFTH ST W
FOURTH ST W
THIRD ST W
SECOND ST W
SARNIA ST E
BELLEVIEW
MARK ST E
HOWARD ST E
KING ST E
SANBORN ST E
WABASHA ST E
BROADWAY ST E
FIFTH ST E
FOURTH ST E
THIRD ST E
SECOND ST E
FRONT ST
SE-71

6 Choate Building, 1889
A. E. Myher
Southeast corner Center Street and 3rd Street E

A four-story Romanesque pile with a high-pitched hip roof, corner towers, recessed balconies, and numerous arches.

7 Merchants' National Bank, 1911–12
Purcell, Feick, and Elmslie
102–104 3rd Street E

This bank is one of the great monuments of the Prairie School in Minnesota. Its basic form — a rectangular volume pierced by two glass walls, defined by filled-in corners and piers — came from Purcell; the glory of its ornamental work in terra-cotta and stained glass came from Elmslie. The terra-cotta lunette dominated by an eagle above the entrance represents the best of Elmslie's ornamental patterns. In 1969 plans were made to demolish the building and to replace it with a larger structure, but because of local and national concern the Purcell and Elmslie masterpiece was spared. The firm of Dykins and Handford expanded the building (1969–70) to the north and east, retaining the magnificent main banking space with its two glass walls and skylighted space. It is regrettable that the design of the Levee Plaza in front of the bank detracts from the front elevation.

7 Merchants' National Bank. Photo: William G. Purcell.

•8 German-American Bank of Winona (now Castle Dress Shop), 1892
129 3rd Street E

The Romanesque Revival with an irregular silhouette composed of a corner tower with a conical roof and two high pediments.

9 Pletke Grocery Store (now Brothers Pizza), 1886
151–155 3rd Street E

Eastlake and early Queen Anne are mixed in this two-story brick commercial block. Everything from the base of the second-floor windows down has been modernized.

10 Commercial Block, 1886
157-161 3rd Street E

The second floor has a pattern of projecting bays and gables, all in the Queen Anne Style. The two center bays have gable roofs, and the two end bays have half-conical roofs.

11 Strunk Building, 1890
173 3rd Street E

The upper façade is divided into five vertical panels with engaged piers which end in pinnacles. The pattern of light-colored stone contrasts dramatically with the dark brick surfaces.

12 Pelzer Block, c. 1890
207 3rd Street E

The narrow central window is balanced on each side by two projecting bays.

13 Bub Building, 1892
225 3rd Street E

A Queen Anne commercial block.

14 Rachow Block, 1886
251 3rd Street E

A concoction of Italianate and Eastlake. The street level fortunately has not been modernized.

15 Service Station, c. 1928
Southeast corner Kansas Street and 3rd Street E

A flat canopy projects from the simple brick box. The canopy is supported by two Tuscan columns set on low brick bases. The pumps themselves seem to be from the 1930s.

16 **J. R. Watkins Medical Products Company,** 1911, 1913
George W. Maher
150–178 Liberty Street

The company originated in Winona in 1868, and in 1911 it employed the Chicago Prairie architect George W. Maher to design its administration building. In 1913 Maher designed the adjoining ten-story manufacturing building. "The windows [of the Administration Building]," it was noted, "are of Art and stained glass typifying the beautiful landscape which surrounds Winona." The building has been well treated over the years, but changes have been made on both the interior and the exterior. The four light standards on the street are now gone, as are the vertical wall lamps which were situated on each side of the entrance.

16 J. R. Watkins Medical Products Company.

17 **East Side Fire Station,** 1891
Southeast corner 3rd Street E and Carimona Street

Romanesque Revival with a strong surface emphasis on the second-floor arches.

18 **St. Stanislaus Catholic Church,** 1894
Southeast corner 4th Street E and Carimona Street

A remarkable blending of the Baroque and the Romanesque. A drum and an oddly shaped segmented dome surmount the octagonal sanctuary, looking more like a large-scale lantern than a drum and dome.

19 **Mathews House,** c. 1870
205 4th Street E

It would appear that the original house was Italianate with a central tower and an arched window tower. Subsequent additions have created a bewildering composition.

20 **Exchange Building,** 1900
Southeast corner 4th Street E and Center Street

Designers in the 1890s made a noble effort to work in the Romanesque and Classical camps at the same time. This building is essentially Classical, but much of its detail is Romanesque.

•21 **Winona Savings Bank** (now Winona National Savings Bank), 1914
George W. Maher
Southeast corner 4th Street W and Main Street

The overall style is Egyptian Revival, but the plan and the detailing are of the Prairie School. The second floor contained a community exhibition room and separate meeting rooms for women and men. The usual richness of Maher's work abounds within in the beautiful polished inlaid stone and the windows of Tiffany glass.

•22 **Huff House,** 1857
Southwest corner 4th Street W and Huff Street

The Italianate house with its central gable seems modest beside the large three-and-a-half-story tower. At the front of the house is a Queen Anne Islamic porch.

23 **Hallenbeck House,** c. 1891
374 5th Street W

In this Queen Anne house various gable-roofed volumes sheathed in fish-scale shingles are pieced together.

24 **Bell House,** c. 1900
255 Harriet Street

Queen Anne/Colonial Revival. Note the large picture window to the left of the door.

25 Laird Public Library, 1897
W. P. Laird and E. V. Seeler
Southwest corner 5th Street W and Johnson Street

When the plans were published, it was stated that the "architecture will be of the Renaissance type." A fine Beaux Arts composition with a central pedimented porch and a central dome behind it.

25 Laird Public Library.

26 Younger Building (now Roher Medical Offices), c. 1935
North side 5th Street E between Main and Center Streets

The Streamline and Zigzag Moderne combined in a two-story brick building. The stepped pattern of the windows in the first-floor bay is a motif drawn from the buildings in the Century of Progress Exhibition in Chicago.

27 Keyes House, c. 1870
Southeast corner 5th Street E and Center Street

A commodious two-story brick Italianate house with a central gable. There are sharply angled stone pediments over the second-story windows and rectangular stone pediments on the windows below. The brickwork and stonework have been painted.

28 House, c. 1870s
277 Broadway E

Basically a side-hall Italianate house in brick, modified by a wide gambrel-roofed central gable.

29 Prentice House, c. 1870s
101 Broadway E

The curved stone window headers of this large Italianate house are almost Baroque in character. Note the richly bracketed roof.

30 St. Paul Episcopal Church, 1873–74
Northwest corner Broadway E and Lafayette Street

Originally described as English Gothic with a Norman tower. The crenelated tower is at the side of the gable-roofed structure. The side aisles are covered with a connected shed roof of a lower pitch.

31 House, c. 1870
65–67 Broadway W

An L-shaped Italianate house with a tower. It was transformed into a stucco Craftsman house in about 1905.

•**32 Sinclair House,** c. 1870s
73 Broadway W

A two-story Italianate house with a central gable. It still retains its elegant balustraded porch and paired columns. Notice the balustraded porte cochere at the side.

33 Central United Methodist Church, 1896
L. E. Wheeler and Charles G. Maybury
Northwest corner Broadway W and Main Street

The three-arched entrance and the superbly romantic tower are two of the finest Richardsonian Romanesque fragments to be found in the state. The main part of the church was redesigned by A. Hensel Fink and Eckert and Carlson in 1964.

33 Central United Methodist Church.

34 Buck House, c. 1870s
315 Broadway W

A handsome house but the style is elusive. The detailing of the porch and the window headers is Italianate; other elements seem to be of a much later date with overtones of the Queen Anne/Colonial Revival of the 1890s.

35 Hodgins-Tearse House, 1890
Charles G. Maybury
275 Harriet Street

Queen Anne Style in style, but almost Colonial Revival.

36 Prentiss House, c. 1900
369 Broadway W

A "correct" gambrel-roofed Colonial Revival house with a pair of balustraded bays at the side, wide Ionic columns on the entrance porch, and pedimented dormers in the roof.

37 First Baptist Church, 1888–93
Northeast corner Broadway W and Wilson Street

The round corner tower and the pattern of light and dark stone strongly establish the character of this church as Gothic Revival.

38 Gallager House, 1913
Purcell, Feick, and Elmslie
451 Broadway W

The living room is oriented around a five-sided corner bay window. The porch at the side has now been enclosed; originally the tan stucco and the wood detailing were not as strongly contrasted as they are today.

38 Gallager House.

39 Cotter Hall (now part of St. Theresa College), 1894
Northwest corner Wabasha (7th) Street W and Cummings Street

A highly restrained Queen Anne design in this three-story structure of brick and shingles.

40 Youman House, c. 1910
227 Wilson Street

The Colonial Revival realized in a brick American Georgian design.

41 Neviess House, c. 1895
203 Wabasha Street W

A two-story brick Queen Anne/Colonial Revival house with eaves supported by paired brackets. The extensive first-floor porch has a curved projection.

42 Laird House, c. 1900
167 Wabasha Street W

Queen Anne/Colonial Revival with a round corner turret topped with a bell-shaped roof. The third-floor dormers have unusual cut-in lunette windows. The house is sheathed in bands of wide and narrow clapboard and fish-scale shingles.

•**43 Watkins House** (now Watkins United Methodist Home), 1926
Cram and Ferguson
175 Wabasha Street E

The style of the house was described in the *American Architect* (August 20, 1928) as a modified English sixteenth-century form, "partially Tudor, practically Elizabethan." Cram, America's great Gothic Revivalist, organized the interior space around a two-story music room with a concert organ entirely hidden by a grille of carved wood. The setting of this mansion in the middle of a modest residential district is akin to that of a medieval castle with its dependent town.

44 Schmitz House, c. 1890
226 Wabasha Street E

The Queen Anne in all its exuberance with projecting bays, spindled porches, pedimented gables, a tower, and the usual surfaces of fish-scale shingles and clapboard.

45 Peregrine Cottage, c. late 1860s
204 Sanborn Street W
A one-and-a-half-story French Second Empire cottage with assertive three-dimensional detailing around the dormers and in the bracketed eaves.

46 Chicago, Milwaukee, St. Paul, and Pacific Railroad Passenger Depot, c. 1900
South side Mark Street at south end of Center Street
A picturesque brick passenger station with stone trim; in style, loosely Queen Anne.

47 House, c. 1950
718 Mankato Drive
A yellow Lustron prefabricated house with a few later additions.

SE-72 Wykoff

Wykoff was platted as a railroad town on the Southern Minnesota line in 1871. The streets are not marked, so only general directions can be provided. In the southwest part of town, one block west of Highway 80, is St. John's Lutheran Church (1899), a Craftsman Gothic building with an octagonal belfry and spire. Because of the small size of the windows in relation to the extensive surrounding clapboard surfaces, the scale of the building is deceptive. On the west side of Highway 80 just south of Wykoff's small commercial area is a strongly proportioned French Second Empire cottage; the date 1876 is placed in the center of the front façade. The brick walls have been carried up to the second-floor windowsills, and the mansard roof is extremely steep and high.

Cottage.

SE-73 Zumbrota

This small river community houses two fascinating architectural gems: the First Congregational Church, a pure Greek Revival building, and a covered bridge (the only one still standing in Minnesota). In nearby Canton Township are the stone ruins of the Oxford Flour Mill, and at Whiterock is the late nineteenth-century Miller Store Building.

First Congregational Church, c. 1860
455 East Avenue

New England transplanted to the Upper Midwest. The church boasts a pedimented front with four engaged piers, a triangular gable with a centrally placed round window, and a two-tiered tower with a steeple. Low-relief engaged piers occur on the two long flank walls. It seems a shame to find incongruous post-1945 slab doors and a concrete stoop with metal railing in what otherwise is such a finely detailed building.

First Congregational Church.

2 **United Redeemer Lutheran Church,** 1912
Southeast corner Central Avenue and 3rd Street W

Brick, turn-of-the-century Carpenter's Gothic, with fine stained-glass windows.

3 **Cottage,** c. 1870s
Southeast corner 6th and Main Streets

A Gothic-inspired cottage in clapboard.

4 **House,** late 1870s
208 3rd Street

A two-story French Second Empire design in wood.

5 **Two Houses,** c. 1865
207 and 233 3rd Street

A pair of Italianate houses of the side-hall plan.

6 **Covered Bridge,** 1863
Zumbrota Fairgrounds, north on Main Street across the Zumbro River

The bridge was originally located over the Zumbro River. Outwardly it resembles an elongated gable-roofed barn. Inside the 116-foot structure the heavy-timbered, latticed trusses of the two lateral walls are visible. Nearby are several other nineteenth-century buildings (a log house, a schoolhouse, and a railroad station) that have been moved to the fairgrounds from their original sites.

6 Covered Bridge.

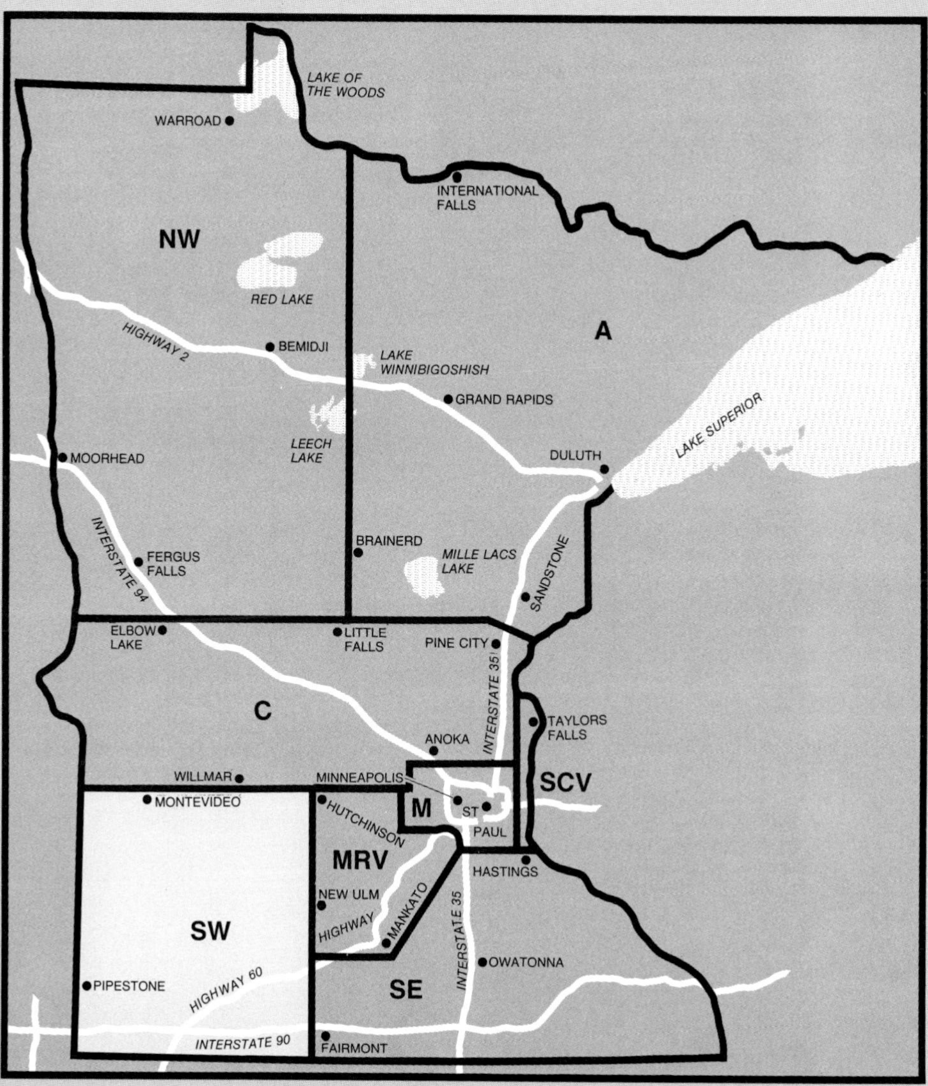
LAKE OF THE WOODS
WARROAD
INTERNATIONAL FALLS
NW
RED LAKE
A
HIGHWAY 2
BEMIDJI
LAKE WINNIBIGOSHISH
GRAND RAPIDS
LAKE SUPERIOR
LEECH LAKE
MOORHEAD
DULUTH
INTERSTATE 94
BRAINERD
FERGUS FALLS
MILLE LACS LAKE
SANDSTONE
ELBOW LAKE
LITTLE FALLS
PINE CITY
INTERSTATE 35
C
TAYLORS FALLS
ANOKA
WILLMAR
MINNEAPOLIS
SCV
MONTEVIDEO
M
ST PAUL
HUTCHINSON
MRV
HASTINGS
NEW ULM
MANKATO
HIGHWAY
SW
INTERSTATE 35
OWATONNA
PIPESTONE
HIGHWAY 60
SE
INTERSTATE 90
FAIRMONT

SW-1 Adrian

This agricultural community was platted in 1876 on the banks of Kanaranzi Creek.

1 **Slade Hotel,** 1891
Frank Thayer
Northeast corner Main and 2nd Streets
The openings on the ground level have arches of various sizes, and arches are used decoratively in the brick surfaces above. In style, a little Queen Anne, a little Romanesque.

1 Slade Hotel.

2 **Commercial Block,** 1891
Northwest corner Main and 2nd Streets
A square corner tower with a high-pitched pyramided roof and false-fronted pediments draws attention to this two-story block.

3 **St. Adrian's Catholic Church,** 1900
Northeast corner Main and 6th Streets
A non-Richardsonian Romanesque Revival church in brick with a two-tower façade. The taller of the towers can be seen for miles around.

SW-2 Belview

The Odeon Theatre (1901) is one of those small-town structures that are a delight to encounter. Its architectural character is reserved for its street façade, and the small curved roof at the front gable end may have been designed to carry a tower. A Colonial Revival doorway with a curved transom window is placed in a recessed entrance on the ground level. The name "Odeon" and the date are used decoratively. The theatre is located in town on the east side of Highway 273 (County Road 7).

Odeon Theatre.

SW-3 Canby

The town of Canby was platted in 1876, after the Chicago and Northwestern Railroad had laid its line through Yellow Medicine County to the Dakota border. Downtown, on the main street (Highway 75) between 1st and 2nd Streets East, is a group of one-story and two-story brick stores and commercial blocks, all of which date from the 1890s. In style they represent a mixture of the Queen Anne and the Romanesque. Note especially the two-story bank building (now housing a restaurant and a store) with its square corner tower. Next door is a two-story brick commercial block (1894) with wide arched windows (now filled in with glass brick) on the second floor. The single-floor Swenson Block (1895) displays an elaborate arched and pedimented parapet. A service station (c. 1926) with an English Cottage image is located on 1st Street East, one block south of Highway 75. At 109 St. Olaf Avenue North (Highway 75) is the Canby Theatre (c. 1936), in which PWA classical conservatism is blended with the Streamline Moderne. Farther down the main street at the north corner of 4th Street West is a Queen Anne dwelling (1890) with a corner bay-tower; the tower is partially surrounded by the curved porch on the second floor.

Service station.

SW-4 Dawson

The railroad village of Dawson on the west fork of the Lac qui Parle River was platted in 1884. Its major visual landmarks are the mass of rectangular and cylindrical volumes which make up the Dawson Mills and Elevators. These are located south of Highway 212 and west of 6th Street. On the west side of 6th Street, between Walnut Street and Chestnut Street, is the Streamline Moderne Grand Theatre (c. 1939). At the northwest corner of 6th Street and Chestnut is the brick Northwestern Bank Building (c. 1916); its details are classical, but in design it is similar to several of Louis Sullivan's small Prairie banks, especially the Adams Building in Algona, Iowa (1913), and the Farmers' and Merchants' Union Bank in Columbus, Wisconsin (1919). Unquestionably

First National Bank Building.

the most vigorous design in town is found in the First National Bank Building (1892) on the east side of 6th Street between Chestnut Street and Pine Street. In style this two-story brick pile is Romanesque, but the elements of the style have been sculpturally molded in a manner reminiscent of the mid-nineteenth-century work of the Philadelphia architect Frank Furness.

In the pleasant residential section west of the downtown area are two houses of special interest. At 712 Pine Street is a clapboard gabled house with a mansard-roofed corner tower (c. 1890). A block farther west at 816 Pine Street is a two-story central-hall dwelling (c. 1890); the basic form is Italianate, with late Eastlake/Queen Anne sawed and turned work.

SW-5 Fort Ridgely

The fort was built between 1853 and 1854 and continued to be used through 1867. There are numerous stone foundations at the site, but the only buildings still standing are the gable-roofed stone commissary (1853) and the rebuilt powder house of hand-hewn logs. Both brick and stone were employed as headers in the commissary; except for this feature, the building is simply an impressive utilitarian structure.

SW-6 Granite Falls

This community on the west bank of the Minnesota River was platted in 1872. A hydroelectric plant utilizes the thirty-eight-foot falls to provide electricity for the surrounding area. At 415 9th Avenue is the Yellow Medicine County Courthouse (designed by Frederick E. Hoover, 1889). This Romanesque Revival structure has suffered as a result of remodeling and additions in 1940 and again in 1960. North of the courthouse at 450 9th Avenue is the stone-trimmed brick school (1930). The remodeling of this building included replacement of the original windows with a band of horizontal metal-framed windows on the lower level and glass-brick infill above, but the changes in the windows and elsewhere have been carried off with great reserve and taste. At 210 9th Avenue is the clapboard United Church of Christ (1899), in which the round-arched windows and the broad open belfry with its pyramid roof are Romanesque instead of the usual Gothic. The Granite Falls Bank (1912) at 702 Prentice Street is a dignified Beaux Arts structure. The light-colored terra-cotta featured in the entablature, the door and window moldings, and the engaged piers contrasts with the darker brick surfaces.

The Upper Sioux Agency (now officially designated as a historic site) is located seven and a half miles southeast of Granite Falls on Highway 67. Several of the brick buildings have been restored.

Granite Falls Bank.

One is a double house (1859–60) which burned in 1862 and was rebuilt in 1866. The style of the house is Greek with central entrances, a hipped roof, and a gable-roofed wing on each side. Three and a half miles farther south on Highway 67 is the Gothic Revival Rockvalle Lutheran Church (c. 1890). This clapboard church has two towers with tall pointed spires; the shingles and the sawed and spindle work are Queen Anne. About three miles north of Granite Falls on Chippewa County Road 5 is a much remodeled version of O. S. Fowler's "octagonal mode" of building. The two-story octagonal Holt House (1875–79) has been stuccoed over and a new porch has been added.

Double house, Upper Sioux Agency, near Granite Falls.

Rockvalle Lutheran Church, near Granite Falls.

SW-7 Hector

At 206 Main Street is the Farmers and Merchants State Bank (now Security State Bank) designed by Purcell and Elmslie (1916–17). The structure was planned as a combined bank, printing plant, telephone exchange, and office building. In its exterior design this bank is markedly different from other Prairie banks by Purcell and Elmslie — the lower floor is sheathed in brick, but the upper floor has a smooth stucco surface with a projecting border of brick and terra-cotta around the windows. The ornament above the entrance represents a high point in George Elmslie's design in terra-cotta. A new section has been added at the rear of the building, and new signing has been placed in front. Two iron and glass light standards at each side of the entrance to the bank are now gone. The original terra-cotta clock face is hidden away behind the new bank sign.

Farmers and Merchants State Bank (now Security State Bank), Hector. Photo: William G. Purcell.

SW-8 Heron Lake

The Farmers State Bank Building (1895) at Heron Lake is an especially fine Richardsonian Romanesque Revival building by Peterson and Dachendorf. It is situated on the main street, one block southeast of Highway 60. The blocks of sandstone used to face the main floor and its projecting arched entrance are bold and large in scale; above, narrow vertical shafting suggests bands of engaged piers which are supplemented by a pair of polished engaged columns.

Many towns of southwestern Minnesota seem to be dominated by grain terminal elevators, most of which are of concrete. A new bank of these elevators can be seen on Highway 60, two miles southwest of Heron Lake.

Farmers State Bank Building.

SW-9 Ivanhoe

This town lies ten miles east of the South Dakota border. It was established in 1900, and it was named for the hero of Sir Walter Scott's novel of the same name. Two years after its founding the community became the seat for Lincoln County. In the courthouse square, at the northwest corner of Rotherwood Street and Rebecca Street, is a pristine example of a Beaux arts courthouse (designed by Howard Parsons, 1919). Above the entrance in the raised basement is a pedimented portico with six columns. The building has been remodeled, and the original windows have been replaced with glass bricks and plate glass. Since the original window openings are intact, the new window patterns do not distract from the original design. Just south of the courthouse is the county jail (c. 1903), a mildly Romanesque brick building with a low crenelated tower. At the southwest corner of Saxon Street and Norman Street is a commercial building (c. 1904) which represents the usual turn-of-the-century mixture of the Romanesque and the Classical. Its most unusual feature is a row of small round windows placed just below the cornice on both street façades. Across the street at 402 Norman Street North is the former Ivanhoe Co-op Creamery (now the Mid-Town Feed and Supply Store). This 1929 creamery building, like so many others in Minnesota, is constructed of Artstone structural bricks in red, yellow, and green. The glazed bricks and the terracotta elements were produced during the 1920s in New Ulm. A few miles north of Ivanhoe is the small village of Wilno, which is oriented around the St. John Cantius Church (c. 1883). This brick Romanesque church presents a façade of twin towers with the gabled sanctuary in the middle. The spires of the towers have been removed. Wilno can be reached by traveling north of Ivanhoe on Highway 75 to County Road 17 and one and a half miles east.

SW-10 Jackson

The Jackson County Courthouse of 1900 indicates the major shift in images in the late 1890s from Richardsonian Romanesque to Beaux Arts classicism as the most appropriate form for a civic building. Buechner and Orth, who designed a number of Minnesota's courthouses, give us in the Jackson County Courthouse a correct and highly respectable classical building with a Roman pedimented entrance, a square drum with pediment and columns, and a segmented dome. The courthouse is at the southwest corner of Sherman Street and 4th Street. On the west side of 2nd Street, between Sherman Street and Grant Street, is another exercise in the Beaux Arts, the Jackson State Bank (c. 1910). North of the downtown area, in Ashley Park (west of the junction of State Street and Riverside Drive), is the pre-1860 Olson-Staabakken log cabin. The walls of hand-hewn logs and the stone chimney of the cabin are played off against the precisely carved memorial obelisk nearby.

Jackson County Courthouse.

SW-11 Jasper and Kenneth

Like Pipestone, Jasper is a community whose major public buildings are constructed of red quartzite. The town's main street exhibits a number of two-story buildings in this beautiful red stone. One block east of downtown on the main street (there are no street signs) is the Lutheran Church (1901) with walls of stone and an open shingled tower. In style the building is a Craftsman version of the Gothic; an unfortunate mansard roof addition has recently been built in front of the tower. Opposite the church is a boxy, all stone Craftsman house (c. 1901). One block farther east is the stone Jasper High School, which is composed of three sections built in different periods. The 1938 PWA Moderne addition is most impressive. Directly north of the high school is the United Methodist Church (originally the Fowler Methodist Episcopal Church), a raised-basement cubical composition with a smaller cubical entrance tower (1900).

Lutheran Church.

The town of Kenneth is southeast of Jasper on Rock County Road 3. The town hall, which was formerly a school (c. 1890s), is a two-story clapboard building with a bell tower over its central pediment and a metal spiral fire escape slide on the side.

SW-12 Kinbrae

Southwest of Kinbrae in Maco Oicu Park (on West Graham Lake) is a group of open park shelters designed as prototypes in 1966 by Hodne Associates. The structure shown in the photograph is a lacy, high wood truss suspended over a pair of stone pylons and wood piers. The shelters are located thirteen miles north of Worthington on Highway 59, five miles east on County Road 18 to Kinbrae, and one mile south into Maco Oicu Park.

Park shelter, Maco Oicu Park, near Kinbrae.

SW-13 Lake Benton

The town of Lake Benton nestles in and among the trees which grow along the shores of Lake Benton. The surrounding area is an open treeless prairie with low hills. The town was organized in the 1870s, and for a period of twenty years (between 1882 and 1902) it was the seat of Lincoln County.

1 **Opera House,** 1896
Benton Street between Fremont and Center Streets
It is not easy to catalogue this building stylistically. Its composition is classical, but its parts are not. The balcony projecting over the three entrance doors is supported by four engaged piers; on each side are long, narrow windows, the upper portions of which are circular.

2 *Methodist Church.*

2 **Methodist Church,** c. 1890s
Northwest corner Bluff and Center Streets
A delicate shingled tower placed in the open L of an unadorned, barnlike building.

• 3 **Barn,** c. 1890s
Near northeast corner Bluff and Grant Streets
A Queen Anne barn in clapboard and shingles. On each of the two sides there is a horizontal pattern of four round windows.

4 **House,** c. 1900
Southwest corner Bluff and Center Streets
A Queen Anne/Colonial Revival house. The three-story round corner bay-tower is sheathed in shingles in a variety of different patterns.

5 **Cottage,** c. 1890
212 Fremont Street
A stylistically late French Second Empire cottage; its detailing in turned and sawed wood is early Queen Anne in style.

6 **Brown's Trading Post,** c. 1870s
Hole in the Mountain Park (just west of junction of Highways 14 and 75, northwest of Lake Benton)

This cabin of hand-hewn logs was built on the nearby Anderson farm and later was moved to its site in the park.

6 Brown's Trading Post.

SW-14 Lamberton

Lamberton, situated south of the Cottonwood River, was first settled in 1873 with the coming of the Winona and St. Peter Railroad. It was incorporated as a town in 1879. The site is excellent for its gridiron pattern of streets because it is flat and uninterrupted by any major waterway.

1 **Farmers and Merchants State Bank,** 1941, 1955
A. Moorman and Company
120 Main Street S

The fashion of the 1950s at its best in a dignified and restrained small-town bank building.

1 Farmers and Merchants State Bank.

2 **Bank Building** (now Sanger's Bakery), c. 1890s
200 Main Street S

A Romanesque Revival building in brick with a corner entrance.

3 **IOOF Building,** 1898
301 Main Street

The second floor with its parapet, central gable, and pinnacles gives the building a vaguely Eastlake atmosphere. The remodeling of the lower floor (including the shingled awning) is unfortunate.

4 **Lamberton Food Products Building,** 1929
305 Main Street

Although a product of the late 1920s the styling of the façade of this structure points back to the Midwestern Prairie School of 1910. The parapet is composed of stepped projections accentuated by a rectangular pattern of tile.

5 **House,** c. 1890s
Northwest corner 2nd Avenue E and Birch Street S

Queen Anne with an octagonal corner tower. The tower has a high-pitched roof.

SW-15 Luverne

Luverne was settled after the Civil War and was officially platted in 1870. By 1880 the town was connected with North Dakota, Iowa, and the rest of Minnesota by the St. Paul and Sioux City Railroad. As in other southwestern Minnesota communities the economic orientation of Luverne is agricultural. Near the town are quarries from which handsome red granite is taken, and many of the nineteenth-century and early twentieth-century buildings in town are constructed of this material.

1 **Commercial Block** (now Montgomery Ward Store), c. 1890s
123 Main Street E
A narrow single-story commercial block of rough sandstone masonry in the Romanesque Revival mode. The architect put in as much in the way of a cornice, entablature, and brackets as he could in a small store building.

2 **Commercial Block,** late 1890s
North side Main Street, west of Cedar Street N
A rusticated two-story masonry building with two bays on the second floor. Originally there were three arches on the lower level.

3 **Public Library,** 1903–1904
W. E. E. Greene
205 Freeman Avenue N
A classical pedimented entrance cut at a forty-five-degree angle into the corner of the building conveys the effect of a false-fronted store. It all adds up to a turn-of-the-century Beaux Arts exercise, similar in plan to the public library at St. Peter.

3 Public Library.

4 **Rock County Courthouse,** 1888
T. D. Allen
Between Cedar Street N and McKenzie Street N at Luverne Street
Romanesque Revival. The high open tower has a conical roof; at the base of the tower is a double-arched opening into the building.

5 **Kniss House,** 1879
209 Estey Avenue N
A brick Italianate house with Eastlake details in wood. A columned classical porch was added at a later date (c. 1900).

6 **Museum - Hinkly House,** 1892
217 Freeman Avenue N
The front elevation is composed of double gables with a paneled effect; below it in the center is a classical columned porch. The walls of the house are of rusticated stone.

7 **Maplewood Cemetery,** c. 1890
On Warren Avenue about ¾ mile west of Kniss Avenue S
One first sees a shingled Gothic Revival chapel and porte cochere. Within the cemetery, posing as a prehistoric monument, is a red stone pile which is the Hinkly Mausoleum (c. 1900). The Hinkly name is spelled out in the pattern of the stone blocks.

7 Hinkly Mausoleum, Maplewood Cemetery.

• 8 **A & W Root Beer Stand,** late 1950s
702 Kniss Avenue S
Three creatures from the wilds of Disneyland, each holding up a hamburger and a mug of root beer.

SW-16 Madison

Madison was platted in 1884 as a village on the Minneapolis and St. Louis Railway. Its only major claim to architectural fame was the Madison State Bank designed by Purcell and Elmslie in 1913. This charming and very tiny Prairie bank with ornamental ironwork, light standards, and leaded glass was destroyed in 1968. It was replaced by a fake-mansard-roofed building which radiates emptiness. Out in the country east of Madison is the • Thoreson-Lind House (c. 1889), one of the most delightful spindled Queen Anne dwellings in Minnesota. Behind the house is an octagonal summerhouse with an open central cupola, and south of it is the Holton House (c. 1890), a Queen Anne dwelling equipped with two bay-towers. Neither of these houses is yet open to the public.

1 **Lac qui Parle County Courthouse,** 1889
Buechner and Jacobson
600 6th Street

A beautifully preserved Richardsonian Romanesque Revival courthouse. A high central tower with an open arcade below the roof stands over the front entrance. Note the use of river boulders as sheathing for the raised basement of the building.

2 **Carnegie Public Library,** 1906
401 6th Avenue

A raised-basement Beaux Arts design. The portico has paired Ionic columns and an ornamented pediment. The quoining is very dramatically emphasized in this building.

3 **Minnesota Valley Lutheran Church,** 1881
7¼ miles north of town on County Road 19, 3 miles east on County Road 32, and 1 mile north on County Road 67

The playful metal weather vane on the church's spire proclaims the 1881 date of this clapboard Gothic Revival church. The upper section of the tower, with its belfry surrounded by four tall pinnacles, is splendid. At some point in its history the church was placed on a new brick raised basement, altering its general appearance.

4 **Lac qui Parle Lutheran Church,** c. 1885
9 miles east of town on Highway 40 (continuing on County Road 20) and ½ mile south

A clapboard Gothic Revival church with later additions. Note especially the small square towers at the corners of the gabled side entrance.

SW-17 Marshall

With the coming of the Chicago and Northwestern Railway the city of Marshall was platted in 1872 and incorporated in 1876. The city's grid, which lies northeast/southwest, crosses the Redwood River several times. Southwest State College is situated east of the city on College Drive (Highway 19/68).

1 **Student Housing, Southwest State University,** 1968, 1970, 1972
Parker, Klein Associates
Northwest corner College Drive E and Highway 23

A formidable brick monument set in an open prairie. Projecting wing walls press and hold the enclosed volumes together.

1 Student Housing, Southwest State University.

2 **House,** c. 1920
102 Hill Street S

A crenelated rectangular bungalow in stone and stucco. The image is a little strong for a small suburban dwelling.

3 **Chicago and Northwestern Railroad Passenger Depot,** c. 1890
Northwest corner Depot Street and 1st Street

The long, low rectangular form of the station is broken by matched projections on the northeast side and by angular bays projecting onto the train platform. Mildly classical, with a backward glance at the Queen Anne.

4 **Masonic Temple,** 1917
325 Main Street W

A two-story Egyptian Revival pylon, partially ruined by the remodeling of the storefront on the ground floor.

5 **Lyon County Courthouse,** 1892
West corner Main and 6th Streets

Romanesque (not Richardsonian) in brick with stone trim and a raised stone basement. Its most romantic feature — a tower — has been removed. There is a new addition on the south side.

SW-18 Minneota

Minneota is on the south branch of the Yellow Medicine River. Architecturally the town is noted as the site of the Anderson House (c. 1892), which was designed by Cass Gilbert. The house exhibits an odd quality in its thin verticality and, above all, in its tall shingled octagonal tower — a tower which is at once Queen Anne and Romanesque. The rest of the house is committed to the Queen Anne/Colonial Revival. The Anderson House is located at 402 2nd Street East. Just south of 1st Street and Grant Street is St. Paul's (Icelandic) Church (1875), a Carpenter's Gothic church with a tower located on one side.

Anderson House.

The body of the church is high compared to the width and the length. Three blocks north on 2nd Street East is the O. G. Anderson Opera Hall and Store Building (1901), a two-story brick building in Queen Anne/Romanesque (very late for this style). Stores occupy the ground level, and the hall is on the second floor with an entrance at the side. One block west (on Highway 68) is the former Farmers' and Merchants' Bank, which now contains offices and a store. This 1916 Beaux Arts bank building boasts two street façades lined with engaged fluted Ionic columns. In the small town of Ghent (northwest of Marshall on Highway 68) is a raised-basement commercial building that was probably a bank when it was built in the late 1890s. A pair of stubby, wide Romanesque arches open into the entrance and what was once a large glass window (now partially filled in).

SW-19 Montevideo

Chippewa City, the predecessor of the city of Montevideo and the original seat of Chippewa County, was laid out on the west bank of the Chippewa River in 1868. In 1870 Montevideo was platted on the east side of the river and became the county seat. Except for part of the commercial district most of the city sits high on a bluff overlooking the confluence of the Chippewa and Minnesota rivers. Recently a drive-through (one-way) plaza has been built on 1st Street North between Sheridan Avenue and Nichols Avenue.

1 **Chippewa Bank Building,** 1903
300 1st Street N

A two-story Romanesque Revival (cleaned up by the classical) block in brick. Its corner bay-tower has an eye-catching bell-shaped dome.

2 **First Federal Savings and Loan Association,** 1964
William Cann
209 1st Street N

With a Spanish name (the only thing Spanish about it) Montevideo needs more of a Hispanic flavor. Here, what looks like the stern of a Spanish galleon, with arches and supporting columns of turned wood, has been set in front of a simple brick façade — all well done and quite urbane.

3 **Post Office,** 1927
James A. Wetmore
202 1st Street N

A Georgian design in brick with stone trim and a hint of Spain in the hipped tile roof.

2 First Federal Savings and Loan Association.

4 **Public Library** (now private residence), c. 1905
3rd Street at west end of Sheridan Avenue

A small Beaux Arts building in brick. Double Ionic columns support the central gabled portico.

5 Bungalow, c. 1924
514 3rd Street N

Another indication of Montevideo's Spanish architectural inheritance — a Pueblo Revival bungalow.

6 Eliason House, c. 1900
215 5th Street S

A commodious brick dwelling which points to the Colonial Revival.

7 Christ Lutheran Church (Gospel Fellowship Church), c.1905
Northeast corner 6th Street N and Eureka Avenue

Carpenter's Romanesque realized in concrete blocks in imitation of ashlar stone with shingled gables and tower and arched and round windows.

8 Chippewa County Courthouse, 1956
Thorshov and Cerny
11th Street and Washington Avenue (Highway 7)

The Corporate International Style made monumental in one of the most satisfactory of Minnesota's courthouses from the 1950s. At the front the second floor is projected out as a windowless volume supported on four piers which form a dignified (classical) entrance portico.

8 Chippewa County Courthouse.

9 Pioneer Village
Northeast quadrant at junction of Highways 7, 59, and 212

Several nineteenth-century buildings have been laid out to suggest a village scene. Among the buildings are a log cabin (c. 1870), a Lutheran church (1882), a schoolhouse, houses, and stores.

9 Pioneer Village.

SW-20 Mountain Lake

Mountain Lake was platted in 1872. Its environs hide two rare prizes — the Jacob Harder House in town and the Glen Harder House several miles away. Both were designed in the 1970s by Bruce Goff. The Jacob Harder House (1973) is located on the west side of 8th Street between 2nd and 3rd Avenues. Like most of Goff's productions this house is almost beyond description. Its basic form is circular, somewhat like a pregnant spaceship, and it is sheathed in fish-scale shingles which really look more like chicken feathers. The shingles, painted pea green, contrast with the suburban ranch house brick elements. •The Glen Harder House (1970–72) can be reached by driving east of Mountain Lake to County Road 1, then four and a half miles south to County Road 13, east for two miles, then south on a gravel road from which the house is visible. Three gigantic tree-trunk chimneys of river boulders project upward, each topped by an upturned piece of metal, and between them floats the house in birdlike (turkey?) fashion. The roof is covered with bright orange indoor/outdoor carpet.

Another (though far more conventional) nod toward modernity and the twentieth century is located in Mountain Lake at 1313 2nd Avenue. It is a white stucco Moderne box (late 1930s) with a corner stair window of glass brick. The trim and flashing are painted a deep midnight blue.

Jacob Harder House.

Stucco Moderne house.

SW-21 Olivia

The railroad town of Olivia was platted in 1878. Just off Highway 212, on the north side of DePue Avenue between 5th and 6th Streets, is the Renville County Courthouse (1902) by Fremont D. Orff. This City Beautiful courthouse plays on several classical themes at once. Its central entrance portico is Georgian while the end pavilion scheme and the segmented central dome are French Second Empire. The Second Empire is also suggested in the red brick, the yellow trim, and the blue-green copper roof. Inside the building a rotunda rises to the central drum and dome. Farther west on DePue Street, at the southwest corner of DePue Avenue and 9th Street, is the 1904 Faith Methodist Episcopal Church (now the Faith United Methodist Church). It is a Shingle Style version of the Romanesque with Craftsman detailing. The St. Aloysius' Catholic Church (1925), at 302 10th Street South, is also noteworthy. It is a rather clean interpretation of Italian Romanesque with a tall arched arcade in front and a separate campanile at the side.

SW-22 Pipestone

An important southwestern Minnesota railroad town where the Great Northern, the Chicago, Rock Island, and Pacific, and the Chicago, St. Paul, Minneapolis, and Omaha rail lines join. The city (platted in 1876) has the conventional gridiron pattern, only in this case the blocks are square rather than rectilinear. In the center of town, between 3rd and 4th Streets Southwest and Hiawatha and 2nd Avenue Southwest, is a large two-block square set aside for the county courthouse. The red quartzite for which Pipestone is famous has been used in many of the buildings.

1 **Water Tower,** 1919–22
L. P. Wolff
2nd Street NE at 6th Avenue NE

A duplicate of the Brainerd water tower (1918–21), which was designed by the same engineer. The concrete tower, an inverted milk bottle in shape, is imposed on top of a concrete shaft which flares out before the juncture.

2 **Calumet Hotel,** 1888
C. Smith; William Frost
104 Main Street W at Hiawatha

A four-story stone structure with a crenelated parapet on the Main Street façade and a Richardsonian Romanesque arch below.

3 **Three Commercial Buildings**
Main Street W (north side) between Hiawatha Avenue S and 2nd Avenue SW

The two-story IOOF Building (c. 1890) exhibits a peculiar window pattern on the second floor: the three windows to the left have headers which are in the form of a segmented arch; the four to the right are articulated as arched and pedimented Gothic windows. In the center is the former First National Bank Building (1898), which is classical. The building on the right, now housing the Madsen Drug Store (1899), has a suggestion of the Romanesque

3 Three Commercial Buildings.

4 **Old City Hall** (now Pipestone Museum), 1896
113 Hiawatha Avenue S

A rusticated building in Sioux quartzite and jasper.

5 **Moore Block** (now The Shoe Box), 1896
102 Main Street E at Hiawatha

A rusticated two-story stone building (Romanesque, perhaps) which is loaded with sculptured relief panels and cartouches depicting a wild and delightful assortment of animals, monsters, maidens, Indians, elves, and bearded gentlemen.

6 **Public Library,** 1904
217 Hiawatha Avenue S

Romanesque, with a Gothic pointed-arch entrance. A small relief panel above the entrance depicts an open book.

7 **Pipestone County Courthouse,** 1900
George Redman
4th Street SW between Hiawatha Avenue S and 2nd Avenue SW

Although classical in design, the heavily rusticated masonry and the numerous wide arches give the building a Romanesque feeling. The most charming element of the building is the small dome on top of the classical tower with its sculptured maiden keeping watch over the town.

8 **St. Leo's Church,** 1969
Sovik, Mathre, and Madsen
106 4th Street SE at Hiawatha

A two-story rectangular concrete form with an infill of brick panels projecting a few inches beyond the frame; glass (some of it stained) has been inserted into certain areas of the frame.

9 **First Presbyterian Church,** 1900
Pass and Scheppel
301 2nd Avenue SE

A two-dimensional Romanesque design with a fanciful crenelated tower.

10 **St. Paul's Episcopal Church,** 1892
221 4th Street SE

Multicolored stone and shingles in a Gothic Revival design.

8 St. Leo's Church.

SW-23 Redwood Falls

The city was platted in 1865 at the high falls of the Redwood River, about three miles above its confluence with the Minnesota River. Below the falls the Redwood River flows through a picturesque gorge before it emerges onto the flat plain of the Minnesota River. The grid plan of the city lies west of the falls and the gorge.

1 **Redwood County Courthouse,** 1891
E. P. Bassford
Courthouse Square, 3rd and Jefferson Streets

What was once a respectable Romanesque Revival building has been so drastically remodeled and expanded that little of the original remains. The "modern" additions are at best painful.

2 **Public Library,** 1904
Rockey, Church, and Pass
334 Jefferson Street

A City Beautiful classical library. It has a rough stone base with brick above it and exceptionally large plate-glass windows.

3 **Falls Theatre,** c. 1936
South side 2nd Street between Jefferson and Washington Streets

The Streamline Moderne intermingled with the PWA Moderne. The sharp angular lettering in the theatre's name is very nice.

2 Public Library.

4 **Armory,** c. 1916
North side 2nd Street between Jefferson and Washington Streets

The two-story brick building exhibits some elements of the Prairie School, particularly in its entrance screen.

5 Commercial Building, c. 1898
North side 2nd Street between Washington and Mill Streets

The façade presents a wide, low Richardsonian Romanesque arch which springs from two low piers of rustic stone.

5 Commercial Building.

6 Service Station (now Firestone store), c. 1929
Southeast corner 2nd and Mill Streets

A one-and-a-half-story station with a domestic image. The main part of the building is brick, and the upper part is stucco. A large dormer projects out of the tile roof. The adjacent store (facing 2nd Street) is Streamline Moderne.

7 Chollar House, 1878
Northeast corner Minnesota and 4th Streets

An elegant clapboard Italianate house with a slightly projecting central pavilion and gable.

8 PCA Building, 1967
Winslow E. Wedin
Northeast corner Highways 19 and 71 (Main Street) and County Road 101 (east of town)

A low-slung brick hexagon cantilevered out over its site. The low-pitched roof terminates in a glass skylight.

9 Ebbesen House, 1965
Winslow E. Wedin
410 Lincoln Street N

A "modern" house cantilevered out over a hillside site. The glass walls strongly contrast with the sculptural treatment of the stuccoed buttresses and other surfaces.

• **10 St. Cornelia's Episcopal Mission Church,** 1860
5 miles east of town, off County Road 24 (Lower Sioux Indian Reservation)

A stone Gothic Revival church with a central rose window in the front gable and a small crenelated tower toward the rear. Another impressive architectural monument created by Bishop Whipple.

11 Stone Warehouse, 1861
2 miles southeast of Mission Church (#10) on County Road 2 (former Lower Sioux Agency)

A two-story stone structure with a gable roof. The basic proportions are Greek.

SW-24 Renville

The railway village of Renville (platted in 1878) exhibits a remarkably complete sampling of the architectural styles in use since the mid-1890s. All of the buildings listed are on Main Street.

1 **Service Station,** c. 1925
Northwest corner Highway 212 and Main Street
This double-pier station has a hipped roof with false brackets and a Mission Style parapet. The original curved drive and brick piers are still there.

2 **United Methodist Church,** c. 1906
123 Main Street N at Bryant
A small, delicate French spire arises from the center of the church. The main sanctuary has large circular windows. In style, pure turn-of-the-century Craftsman.

3 **Palms Ball Room,** c. 1912
221 Main Street N at Colfax
Mission Revival in stucco. The original windows have been filled in with glass bricks.

4 **Revilla Theatre,** c. 1937
319 Main Street N
The L-shaped sign with its curved profile visually relates the marquee to the body of this Streamline Moderne theatre.

5 **City Hall and Municipal Liquor Store,** c. 1950
Henry Davis
329 and 325 Main Street N
Post–World War II Streamline Moderne with a curved glass-brick entrance, horizontal band windows of glass brick, and thin Roman brick used for the wall.

6 ·**Security Bank** (now Bottge's Department Store), 1896
Southwest corner Main Street and Dupont Avenue
A single-floor brick buiding with stone trim. Stylistically it is somewhere between the late Queen Anne and the turn-of-the-century Classical Revival.

SW-25 St. James

St. James, an 1870 town on the St. Paul and Sioux City Railroad, lies just east of Lake St. James. The town's original gridiron reflected the northeast/southwest orientation of the railroad; later additions to the town are oriented north/south, east/west. At 220 1st Avenue is a large and sumptuously detailed Queen Anne dwelling equipped with a keyhole window at its stair landing. Across the street (1st Avenue) near 4th Street is a post–World War II building in glazed brick, still advertising (with the original sign) Studebaker cars and trucks. The Watonwan County Courthouse at the southeast corner of 7th Street and 2nd Avenue South is Richardsonian Romanesque (1895). Its stone entrance arcade is especially impressive. At the southeast corner of 7th Street and 3rd Avenue South is the Presbyterian Church (Ernest H. Schmidt, 1946), in which rural Gothic has been simplified to produce a highly abstract source of forms. Finally, at 701 Armstrong Boulevard is a Moderne duplex (c. 1938) in white stucco with glass bricks at the corner and single bands connecting the headers and the window-sills horizontally.

House.

SW-26 Slayton

The county seat for Murray County was moved to Slayton in 1889, and two years later the new courthouse was completed (1891). The central tower with its peculiar segmented dome is classical, but the building below is Romanesque. A new addition has been built onto the rear (1974). The courthouse is located at the end of the main street at 28th Street and Broadway Avenue.

SW-27 Sleepy Eye

The town of Sleepy Eye lies on the southeast shore of Sleepy Eye Lake. It was founded in 1872 when the Winona and St. Peter Railroad was built south of the lake.

1 **Masonic Temple,** 1948
North of Main Street on 2nd Avenue NW
The Streamline Moderne carried over into the post-World War II years. A small stone frontispiece with curved walls leads into the entrance; an L-shaped pattern of bricks decorates the surrounding brick surface.

2 **Dyckman Free Public Library,** 1900
Southeast corner Main Street and 4th Avenue SW
According to local tradition the design of the library was modeled after the donor's former house in New Jersey, and indeed it is more domestic in feeling than institutional. Its central dormers with an arched window, the dentils of the cornice, and the columned porch make the building an example of the Colonial Revival.

3 **Union Congregational Church,** 1902
Northwest corner 2nd Avenue SW and Walnut Street

3 Union Congregational Church.

One would suspect that the design is supposed to be Romanesque, but the patterning of the windows and the French Second Empire domed tower take it off in some other direction. All in all a highly inventive design.

4 **St. John's Evangelical Lutheran Church,** 1902
Southwest corner 3rd Avenue SE and Walnut Street
A brick church with spires in nineteenth-century Gothic.

5 **Smith House,** c. 1880
101 Linden Street SE
An Italianate side-hall plan house with an Eastlake porch.

6 **Sleepy Eye Greenhouse,** c. 1927
Northwest corner Prescott Street and 4th Avenue NW
Artstone employed for the offices of a greenhouse; the raised brick decorative patterns have been derived from the Prairie Style. The porch of glass brick and metal, needless to say, is not original.

7 **House,** c. 1937
610 1st Street NE
The Moderne as a series of rectangular boxes of different sizes worked into a single composition. The white awnings with their dark edging add much to the total effect.

7 House.

8 St. Mary's Catholic Church, 1904
1st Avenue N between Willow and St. Mary's Streets

The two narrow and very tall towers and spires can be seen from afar, making the church the city's landmark. One of the towers has a clock. In style, German Gothic with a trace of French influence.

9 Heyman House, 1961
John Randall McDonald
657 3rd Avenue NW

A Wrightian house of concrete blocks with wood detailing. A cantilevered glass bay overlooks the lake.

9 Heyman House.

SW-28 Springfield

In downtown Springfield (especially on Central Avenue) there are several well-preserved late nineteenth-century storefronts. At 2 Marshall Street South is the two-story State Bank of Springfield (1906), which is partly Romanesque and partly Classical Revival. Just off the northwest corner of Central Avenue and Marshall Street is a single-story bakery, the sign for which is a handsome product of the 1930s. In the residential area at the northeast corner of Sanborn Avenue and Marshall Street North is a vigorous brick Colonial Revival house (c. 1900) in which English Georgian details are employed in a highly original manner. Across the street at 310 Marshall Street North is a stucco house (c. 1930) which is both Spanish Colonial Revival and Moderne.

House (c. 1900).

SW-29 Tracy

This community developed as a shipping point on the Chicago and Northwestern Railway. It was platted in 1875 and was incorporated as a village in 1881. Its gridiron was laid out parallel to the railroad, not according to a north/south, east/west orientation.

1 **Service Station,** c. 1925
Northeast corner Craig Avenue (Highway 14) and Center Street
A river-boulder cottage, chimney and all, for a service station.

2 **St. Mark's Episcopal Church and Museum,** 1902
Corner Center Street and 2nd Street
Medieval, but not specific; as usual with Episcopal churches, quite small in scale.

3 **Municipal Building,** 1938
P. C. Bettenburg
Morgan Avenue between 3rd and 4th Streets
A plain brick rectangle with a heavy PWA Moderne entrance.

4 **Public Library,** c. 1928
117 3rd Street
A library as a storefront building with a sophisticated and highly refined classical design in brick and stone.

4 Public Library.

5 **Commercial Block,** 1894–95
101 3rd Street
A bold, well-controlled interpretation of Richardsonian Romanesque. Large arched windows are used on the lower level, and smaller arched windows are used above.

6 **De Smet Welders,** c. 1940
Southeast corner 6th Street and Craig Avenue
A remarkable Streamline Moderne building in brick with a curved corner and a curved window on the second floor. There is a rhythmic pattern of four small windows along the upper part of the main façade with large areas of glass bricks on the lower part.

6 De Smet Welders.

SW-30 Tyler

Tyler, another southern Minnesota railway town, was laid out in 1879. It is known primarily for the Danebod community (#3) located at the south edge of town.

1 **State Bank of Tyler** (now Citizens State Bank), 1919
111 Tyler Street N
A Prairie Style bank in brick with cast-concrete details. The front and side are articulated with a row of thin engaged piers and a rhythmic pattern of tall, narrow windows. It all adds up to an academically cool building.

2 **Municipal Building,** 1946
Southeast corner Tyler Street and Bradley Avenue
A municipal building in the image of a utilitarian (but well-designed) factory. This mildly PWA Moderne structure houses the city offices, the firehouse, the municipal power plant, and a gymnasium/auditorium.

3 **Danebod**
South of town off Tyler Street, one block south of Highway 14
Danebod, a closely-knit religious community, was founded by a group of Danish Evangelical Lutherans. The symbolic form of the cross (or variations thereof) constitutes the basis for each of the community's public buildings.

Danebod Lutheran Church, 1893–95
A cruciform clapboard building with a square placed obliquely in the middle. The tower in the center is carried at a forty-five-degree angle to the arms of the cross. The exterior and interior detailing of the church is Eastlake.

Stone Hall, 1889
A single-floor stone building in the form of a Latin cross. Its entrance wing is crenelated Medieval, but the rest of the building with its pedimented windows comes close to being Greek Revival.

Gym Hall, 1904
Another cruciform clapboard building. The two sides of the entrance arm of the building project forward to the eaves, and the sides plus a small roof enclose the entrance.

3 Danebod Lutheran Church.

3 Stone Hall, Danebod.

3 Gym Hall, Danebod.

Folk School, 1917
The gable ends are carried up as parapets on this three-story brick building. The four-story crenelated corner tower and the pointed arches at the entrance suggest both Gothic and the native architecture of Denmark.

SW-31 Watson

This Chicago, Milwaukee, and St. Paul Railroad village is the site of the Watson Farmers Elevator (1886), reputed to be the oldest structure of its kind in the United States. It is a tall and narrow clapboard structure with a gable-roofed clerestory rising above two shed roofs. The elevator is situated just northeast of Highways 59 and 7 and the railroad tracks. On the southwest side of the highway, just before the main street into town, is a building that once functioned as a service station and a garage (c. 1924). The station itself is a small gable-roofed cottage. The attached garage has a shed roof, and the front wall has two windows with doors below them in the do-it-yourself commercial vernacular of the 1920s. East of the railroad tracks on the southwest corner of the community's two major streets is a pressed metal bank building (1903) which now serves as a meat locker. The selection and the placement of the pressed metal parts suggest turn-of-the-century classical styling.

Watson Farmers Elevator.

Service station and garage.

SW-32 Windom

Windom was platted in 1871 on a bend of the Des Moines River. The 1904 Cottonwood County Courthouse (designed by Omeyer and Thori) is an end-pavilion building of brick and stone located at the corner of 9th Street and 3rd Avenue. The principal façade poses a grand pedimented porch with Corinthian columns in front of the building. Above it a narrow octagonal drum supports a segmented dome with a figure on top. Inside in the central rotunda are painted murals. At the southeast corner of 9th Street and 3rd Avenue is Richard B. Vosejpka's Windom State Bank (1973). It is vaguely but not specifically Wrightian; its most interesting feature is its sunken courtyard. The classic two-story Queen Anne house (c. 1890s) at 856 5th Avenue has cusp arches in the porch, oval and pedimented windows, and fine turned work on the porch and in the third-floor gables. The Riverview Apartments (Miller, Hanson, and Westerbeck, 1974) at 906 6th Avenue are set near the river in a park with trees. Although this concrete and brick complex for the elderly is seven stories high, its height seems to match that of the trees along the river bank. The salient feature of the design is the horizontal layering of cantilevered concrete balconies, all of which have an excellent view of the river. In Island Park (off 6th Street) is the Monson and Chester Log Cabin (1869), which was moved to Windom in 1940. Originally it was one story high, but later it was remodeled into a one-and-a-half-story dwelling.

Riverview Apartments.

SW-33 Worthington

The Nobles County Courthouse (designed by Albert Bryan, 1894) conveys the impression that economy was the prime consideration in the minds of the elected officials of the time. It is a Romanesque building with its top shaved off, nothing more, situated in a wooded square at 10th Street and 3rd Avenue. At 819 10th Street is the seven-story Atrium high-rise (housing for the aged) designed in 1970 by Miller, Melby, and Hanson. It is a hefty urban image for a small urban environment, but it has plenty of parklike open space around it. At 925 2nd Avenue is a handsome period mode building of the twenties, the Masonic Temple (1925). It is a brick volume which has been made Medieval by a two-dimensional pattern in stone which runs across the brick façade. At 1311 4th Avenue is the Dayton House, a large turn-of-the-century Colonial Revival house.

Photohistory

1 *SCV-2 Arcola. Mower House, c. 1850.*

2 *SE-23-4 Old Frontenac. Westervelt House, c. 1855.*

3 SE-30 Homer. Bunnell House, c. 1855.

4 SE-52-30 Red Wing. Lawther Octagonal House, 1857.

Photohistory 5

5 SE-71-22 Winona. Huff House, 1857.

6 SW-23-10 Redwood Falls. St. Cornelia's Episcopal Mission Church, 1860.

7 SE-39-3 Mantorville. Dodge County Courthouse, 1865. E. Townsend Mix.

8 *SCV-7-8 Stillwater. House, late 1860s.*

9 *MRV-18-8 St. Peter. Church of the Holy Communion, 1869. Henry Congdon.*

10 *SE-22-36 Faribault. Chapel of the Good Shepherd, Shattuck School, 1872–73.* Henry Congdon.

11 *MRV-18-18 St. Peter. St. Julien Cox House, 1871, 1873.*

Photohistory 12

12 SE-19 Eitzen. Portland Prairie Methodist Church, 1876.

13 *C-28-5 Litchfield. Trinity Episcopal Church, 1871–72, 1879. Attributed to Richard Upjohn.*

14 *MRV-13-8 Mankato. House, c. 1880.*

15 M-2i-35 St. Paul. Laurel Terrace, 1884. William H. Willcox and Clarence H. Johnston, Sr.

16 MRV-16-31 New Ulm. Hermann Monument, 1887–89. Alfonzo Pelzer.

17 SE-71-4 Winona. Winona County Courthouse, 1888. Charles G. Maybury.

18 SW-16 Madison. Thoreson-Lind House, c. 1889.

19 M-2h-13 St. Paul. German Presbyterian Bethlehem Church, 1890. Cass Gilbert.

20 MRV-16-17 New Ulm. W. Boesch Building and Hummel Maltzahn Building, 1890.

21 SE-71-8 Winona. German-American Bank of Winona, 1892 (now Castle Dress Shop).

22 A-9d-3 Duluth. Traphagen Double House, 1892. Traphagen and Fitzpatrick.

23 *SE-12-1 Chatfield. Lovel House, c. 1892.*

24 *SW-13-3 Lake Benton. Barn, c. 1890s.*

25 *C-29-15 Little Falls. Williams Barn, c. 1890s.*

26 *C-37-6 Ortonville. Larson Round Barn, c. 1900.*

27 M-2a-9 St. Paul. Old Federal Courts Building, 1894–1904. J. Edbrooke Willowby.

28 NW-3 Barnesville. Old Stone House, c. 1895.

29 SE-47-9 Owatonna. Owatonna Public Library, 1898–1900. Smith and Gutterson.

30 *A-9d-15 Duluth. House, 1903.*

31 *A-23 Two Harbors. Lake County Courthouse, 1905. James Allen MacLeod.*

32 MRV-16-24 New Ulm. Post Office, 1909. James Knox Taylor.

Photohistory 33

33 SE-47-1 Owatonna. National Farmers Bank, 1907–1908 (now Northwestern National Bank). Louis H. Sullivan.

34 A-24-12 Virginia. House, c. 1908.

35 A-24-13 Virginia. Musakka House, c. 1910.

Photohistory 36, 37

36 *SE-47-14 Owatonna. Buxton Bungalow, 1912. Purcell, Feick, and Elmslie.*

37 *SE-30 Homer. "Rockledge" studio, c. 1912. George W. Maher.*

38 SE-71-21 Winona. Winona Savings Bank, 1914 (now Winona National Savings Bank). George W. Maher.

39 A-11 Eveleth. Manual training school, 1914. Bray and Nystrom.

40 M-16-4 White Bear Lake. Bankers Building, c. 1915.

41 C-2-4 Alexandria. Bank Building (now Bob's Clothes Shop), 1919–20.

42 M-1o-14 Minneapolis. Quinlan House, 1924. Frederick Ackerman.

43 A-16-11 Hibbing. House, c. 1927.

44 A-13 Grand Marais. Naniboujou Lodge, 1928–29. Holstead and Sullivan.

45 M-1n-29 Minneapolis. House, 1928. Purcell and Strauel.

46 M-13 Lake Minnetonka. Hunt House, 1931. Frank Joseph Forster.

47 SE-22-4 Faribault. Rice County Courthouse, 1932. Nairne W. Fisher.

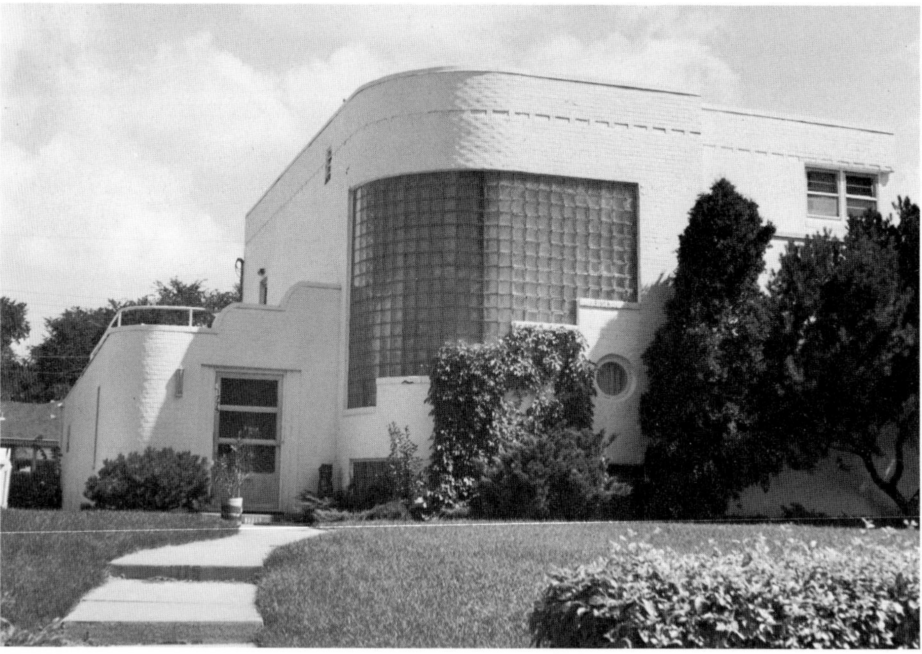

48 M-2j-27 St. Paul. House, 1939.

49 NW-9-5 Detroit Lakes. House, c. 1940.

50 A-22 Tower. Brick commercial building, c. 1940.

51 A-24-2 Virginia. Maco Theatre, c. 1940.

52 *A-23 Two Harbors. Lakeshore house, 1939–42. Edwin H. Lundie.*

53 *M-13 Lake Minnetonka. Private residence, 1952. Edwin H. Lundie.*

54 M-1l-8 Minneapolis. Christ Lutheran Church, 1949–50. Saarinen and Saarinen; Hills, Gilbertson, and Hayes.

55 M-2e-8 St. Paul. St. Columba Church, 1949–51. Barry Byrne.

56 M-1o-35 Minneapolis. Neils House, 1950–51. Frank Lloyd Wright.

57 M-10-1 Edina. Southdale Shopping Center, 1954–56. Victor Gruen and Associates.

Photohistory 58, 59

58 SW-15-8 Luverne. A & W Root Beer Stand, late 1950s.

59 A-16-14 Hibbing. St. Louis County Courthouse, 1954. Jyring and Jurenes.

60 *C-16-7 Collegeville. St. John's Prep School and Dormitory, 1961–62. Hanson and Michelson.*

61 *M-13-1 Lake Minnetonka. Cowles House (now Spring Hill Conference Center), 1961–63, 1972. Edward L. Barnes.*

62 M-13 Lake Minnetonka. Private residence, 1964. Ralph Rapson.

63 SW-20 Mountain Lake. Glen Harder House, 1970–72. Bruce Goff.

64 M-1a-22 Minneapolis. Crystal Court, IDS Center, 1968–73. Philip Johnson and John Burgee; Edward F. Baker.

Photohistory 65, 66

65 *M-1c-9 Minneapolis. "Chapel on the Street," St. Olaf's Catholic Church, 1971–72. Frederick Bentz–Milo Thompson and Assoc. Photo: Ken Smith.*

66 *MRV-18-20 St. Peter. Schaefer Fine Arts Center, Gustavus Adolphus College, 1971. Hammel, Green, and Abrahamson.*

67 A-23 Two Harbors. Cabin, 1971. Times Annex Architects.

68 M-13 Lake Minnetonka. Private residence, 1973. Frederick Bentz-Milo Thompson and Associates. Photo: Eric Sutherland.

Glossary of Architectural Styles

Glossary

One of the joys and banes of architecture is the question of style — not only for historians of architecture but also for architects and for those who simply enjoy and experience buildings. During the 1920s and 1930s the exponents of modern architecture sought to eliminate the study of history so that the architect and society would be able to create buildings which were not concerned with style. But it quickly became apparent that the "modern" architects themselves were creating a new and very impressive style (the International Style), thus proving all over again that style is the vocabulary and ultimately the language of architecture, and we can eliminate it only by eliminating architecture itself.

Catalogs of architectural styles generally fall into two groups — those that make finer and finer distinctions and those that tend to lump numerous stylistic episodes into a few broad categories. In this glossary we emulate the latter group, but in the text of the volume we point out the many individual buildings which exhibit elements of two or even three styles. We reject, or at least tentatively set aside, certain style categories which have been coined in recent times (for example, the Stick Style and the Shingle Style of Vincent Scully). We also indicate our reservations about the single term Art Deco to describe both the Moderne of the 1920s and the very different Moderne of the 1930s.

The nineteenth century was rather loose — and delightfully so — when it came to definitions of style. This is beautifully expressed in an old volume on architecture, *Picturesque California Homes* by Samuel and J. C. Newsom (published in San Francisco in 1887), in which the authors note that "the majority of buildings now being erected . . . are designed in the Free or Knickerbocker, Picturesque, Eastlake, Queen Anne, Colonial and Renaissance styles; with Moorish embellishments." We may all have a general idea of what Eastlake, Queen Anne, Colonial, and Renaissance might imply, but most of us would have some trouble recognizing the other styles. For the reader who wishes to look further into the history of architectural styles, we would recommend Marcus Whiffen's *American Architecture since 1780* (M.I.T. Press, Cambridge, 1969) and Charles Jencks' *Modern Movements in Architecture* (Doubleday, New York, 1970).

The styles listed in this glossary are generally arranged chronologically, although one must always be aware that one style often overlapped with another, and occasionally several styles existed side by side. The date range given with each of the styles indicates the period during which the style was poular in Minnesota.

Greek Revival Style (1840s to 1860s)

The Greek Revival Style ceased to be fashionable in the large urban areas of the east after 1850, although it continued as a provincial style in rural and small-town areas in the east well into the 1860s. Many structures labeled as Greek Revival are in fact very late examples of the Federal Style of 1800.

Characteristics

- rectilinear gable-roofed volumes, horizontal in character; roof of low pitch
- symmetrical or balanced plan and disposition of windows and doors (the side-hall plan being simply one-half of a symmetrical unit)
- wide entablatures, occasionally with dentils
- gable ends forming classical triangular pediments with horizontal eaves or roof cornices carried across the gable end
- engaged corner piers
- flat entablatured or pedimented windows and doors
- Doric (occasionally Ionic) columns
- entrances with sidelights and transom lights

Winslow-Scott House. SCV-8-6 Taylors Falls.

Gothic Revival Style (c. 1850s to 1900)

The Gothic provided one of the most intense of the picturesque styles which developed in the United States during the nineteenth century. The style can be divided into three phases: the Literary Picturesque Gothic, the Victorian Gothic, and the archaeological Gothic which developed toward the end of the century. The early examples of the style in Minnesota were all relatively simple, relying on only a few elements to suggest the style. The earliest Gothic Revival churches and houses in Minnesota were often classical Greek Revival buildings with horizontal emphasis to which Gothic details were added later. In the Victorian Gothic phase (1870s and 1880s) the volumes and all of the details accentuated the vertical.

Episcopal Church of the Good Shepherd. SE-7-9 Blue Earth.

Characteristics

- high-pitched roofs
- bargeboards on gable cornices
- lancet windows
- open Tudor arches, especially in the porches
- split pilasters (posts) on porches
- occasional crenelated parapets
- projecting pinnacles
- board-and-batten walls (employed most often in early examples)
- multicolored bands, especially on brick buildings (Victorian Gothic)
- elements of the English Perpendicular predominating (archaeological Gothic), especially surface paneling

Italianate Style (1860s to 1870s)

Sinclair House. SE-71-32 Winona.

The Italianate Style represented the best of two worlds — classical order and control and picturesque elements. The style developed in the mid-1830s and continued in popularity in the large urban centers of the east through the early 1860s. In the midwest and far west it continued into the 1880s and beyond. Its sources are to be found in late eighteenth-century paintings which depict northern Italian houses and landscapes; more direct sources for American architecture were the work of John Nash and others in England and English architectural pattern books. The Italianate can be divided into two phases: the Italianate Villa and the High Victorian Italianate. The first mode is fundamentally a rural or suburban form, usually characterized by an irregular mass; its hallmark is a campanilelike tower placed within the L of two major wings. The High Victorian Italianate tended to employ a single volumetric form, richly articulated by sharp, angular details.

Characteristics

- emphasis on the vertical in volumes and details
- broadly projected roofs supported by elaborate brackets with three-dimensional patterns
- round, segmented, straight-sided, rectangular, or arched windows; groups of double-arched windows
- angular bays
- heavy articulation of headers over windows and doors
- quoined corners
- thin attached colonnettes (almost Gothic)
- classical spindeled balustrades
- towers with low-pitched hipped roofs

Glossary

French Second Empire Style (1870s to 1880s)

The style was derived from the public and private architecture developed in France during the 1850s. It came to be used extensively for public buildings and commercial blocks and also for houses ranging from small cottages to large mansions. The style took hold in the United States in the late 1860s and continued through the early 1880s. It was often mixed with the Italianate. The style was not widely used in Minnesota except for large-scale townhouses, many of which were built in Minneapolis and St. Paul.

McKusick House. SCV-7-12 Stillwater.

Characteristics

- emphasis on verticality
- tower pavilions, central pavilions, and corner pavilions
- high mansard roofs, sometimes gently convex or concave in form, usually flat on top with the summit surrounded by a cast-iron railing
- a wide variety of domes and domelike forms
- pedimented dormers, rounded-arch dormers, and circular dormers with surrounding cartouches (oeils-de-boeuf)
- dormers were both wall dormers and roof dormers
- surfaces (in elaborate examples) rich in three-dimensional classical detailing; superimposed orders with entablatures and cornices; projecting windows with pediments and semicircular tops and bold side framing and sills; rusticated masonry on lower floor or basement
- heavy projecting roof cornices with brackets
- entablatures filled with a variety of classical details
- sculpture, particularly high-relief sculpture, used externally
- porch balustrades with thick turned spindles

Late Carpenter's Gothic Revival Style (c. 1870s to 1900)

First Baptist Church. C-6 Atwater.

The designs for most of Minnesota's late nineteenth-century churches were drawn from the numerous architectural pattern books which were published throughout the nineteenth century. Sometimes the carpenter (along with the local parson and the building committee) would recreate the designs of buildings they had seen in the east, working out free adaptations of the plans in the pattern books. During the 1870s and 1880s these churches were almost always simple rectangular gable-roofed structures with a central entrance tower attached to the front gable end of the building. Later on variations with double towers, side towers, and the like began to appear. Detailing in wood and glass was frequently derived from other popular contemporary styles, especially the Eastlake and the Queen Anne. At the end of the century elements of both the Colonial Revival and the Craftsman Arts and Crafts mode were employed in these buildings.

Characteristics

- rectangular gable-roofed volumes with entrance towers or (later) with paired towers and corner towers
- lancet windows
- main entrance usually with segmented arch or lancet arch
- tower normally broken into volumes superimposed on one another; belfry openings usually of lancet type; roof of tower generally with pointed spire

Eastlake Revival Style (1870s to 1880s)

It is said that this style had its origins in the writings and drawings of the English architect Charles Eastlake, although he strongly denied he had anything to do with the style. Eastlake's *Hints on Household Taste* was first published in London in 1868 and then in New York in 1872, and it served as one of the major sources of this style. The Eastlake Style was not widely popular in Minnesota, and there are only a few pure examples of it still around. Usually the elements of this style were mixed with those of other styles (especially the Queen Anne). The stylistic features from the 1850s and 1860s which the historian Vincent Scully attributes to the Stick Style share a number of similarities with early Eastlake.

Public Library Building. SCV-8-1 Taylors Falls.

Characteristics

- thin, tenuous vertical volumes, surfaces, and details, all fragile in nature
- exposure of structural members such as posts, dentils, bracing (curved, straight, or corner bracing), and angled struts
- surfaces divided into panels with each area defined by flat board molding; inner surfaces of panels covered with lap siding, tongue-and-groove siding, diagonal or vertical siding, or occasionally shingles
- profusion of jigsaw and lathe work in wood
- ornamentation often rendered in cut-out patterns, drilled holes, and thin layers of wood with very sharp edges
- ornamentation often confined to gable ends, porch posts, and entablatures
- projecting turned knobs as single or repeated decorations

Queen Anne Revival Style (1885 to 1900)

The Queen Anne Revival Style originated in England in the late 1860s in the work of Richard Norman Shaw. The first American architect to take up the mode was Henry Hobson Richardson in the mid-1870s. The American Queen Anne was *the* picturesque style in the late nineteenth-century American city, small town, and rural area. The form of these buildings was highly irregular, and special emphasis was given to the picturesque silhouette produced by gables and dormers, high chimneys, towers, turrets, and pinnacles. Round or hexagonal corner towers (often bay-towers) with conical pointed roofs and extensive porches which often wrapped themselves all the way around the house were characteristics of the style. In plan, the best of these houses were of the living-hall type with wide openings from the hall into the other family living spaces. All of the detailing tended to be directly or indirectly classical. By the early 1880s certain architects began to simplify the picturesque form, surfaces, and detailing of the Queen Anne, and out of this developed the Colonial Revival or Shingle Style.

House. SE-36-14 Lanesboro.

Characteristics

- irregular plans, elevations, and roof silhouettes
- vertical emphasis (later becoming increasingly horizontal)
- surfaces covered with a variety of tactile patterns in clapboard or shingles (especially fish-scale shingles)
- extensive wraparound porches on first floor
- balconied porches cut into second floor or third floor attic
- corner towers (sometimes bays), with conical, segmented concave, bulbous, or other roof shapes
- classical detailing in columns, dentils, scrolls, engaged columns, and piers
- tall chimneys with recessed panels
- leaded stained-glass windows, especially on stair landings

Richardsonian Romanesque Revival Style (late 1880s to early 1900s)

This highly personal version of the Romanesque first came into existence in Henry Hobson Richardson's design for Trinity Church in Boston (1872). By the early 1880s the Romanesque was a style of great prestige and was used for churches, governmental buildings, business blocks, large-scaled private residences, and multiple-family housing. Most examples of the Richardsonian Romanesque in Minnesota were built between 1886 and 1905. It was highly favored as a style for county courthouses in the state.

Three Row Houses. M-2i-34 St. Paul.

Characteristics

- weight and mass essential ingredients
- medieval and picturesque qualities realized by minimal number of elements
- rough masonry walls with detailing, arches, and dentils of smoother, more polished stone (often of a different color)
- arches, especially the early Christian arch from Syria, which seems to spring from the ground, used for doors, windows, and porches
- rectangular window openings divided by stone mullions and transoms into smaller rectangles; windows of large buildings grouped between tall narrow piers and arches; windows occasionally grouped horizontally (with either arched or flat headers) as a band directly under projecting roof soffit
- gable ends carried up to form a parapet
- round towers with pyramidal or convex roofs
- bands of engaged colonnettes

Chateauesque Revival Style (c. 1880s to early 1900s)

This style, derived from the hunting lodges and castles built during the reign of King Francis I (1515–47) of France, was popularized in the eastern United States by Richard Morris Hunt. It was infrequently used in Minnesota, although some elements of it were occasionally mixed with other styles. The few examples built in Minnesota were designed at about the turn of the century. Like the original French style, which was a combination of the late Medieval and the early French Renaissance, the American version was controlled and picturesque at the same time.

Union Depot. A-9a-3 Duluth. Photo: John R. Ulven, Jr.

Characteristics

- irregular, nonsymmetrical plans and silhouettes, with an open play between horizontal and vertical volumes and surfaces
- high-pitched roofs, wall and roof dormers with pedimented parapets, tall chimneys, and high pinnacles
- smart cut-stone wall surfaces
- projecting round corner turrets with thin conical roofs
- windows with either round arches or flat lintels and classical detailing
- some doors and windows of Gothic segmented arch pattern
- detailing (in stone) both classical and late Gothic

Glossary

Colonial Revival Style (1890 to 1915)

House. SE-22-32 Faribault.

Very early the American Queen Anne architects began to substitute eighteenth-century American Georgian and Federal elements for the Queen Anne classical elements which had been used by the English designers. The Shingle Style, which combined elements of the Queen Anne and the Colonial Revival, was the first major return in architectural styling to the simplicity and puritanism of America's early years. By the 1890s the Colonial Revival was fully on its way. At first this meant that the picturesque Queen Anne designs were simplified and classical Georgian and Federal detailing was substituted for the loosely classical features which had been used earlier. By 1900 the Georgian and Federal Revival styles had fully developed in form, plan, and detail. By 1915 the Colonial Revival buildings had become increasingly "correct" in their reproduction of Colonial packaging. Minnesota abounds with examples of the Colonial Revival. The Shingle Style was the only aspect of the style which never caught on (except in the impressive designs of Harvey Ellis, none of which was ever realized in Minnesota).

Characteristics

- simple rectangular volumes covered by gabled or hipped roofs
- symmetrical, balanced disposition of windows and doors
- surfaces covered with shingles (later clapboard or brick)
- classical Colonial detailing in columns, engaged piers, cornices, entablatures, shuttered windows
- double-hung windows with small panes; Palladian windows

Beaux Arts Style, City Beautiful Classicism (1890s to 1930s)

Sibley County Courthouse. MRV-6 Gaylord.

Beaux Arts Classicism embraces a variety of historic classical modes which came to be used in the United States in the early 1890s, continuing into the 1930s. The great buildings which are associated with the style are a mixture of late nineteenth-century Parisian Neo-Baroque, Italian Renaissance buildings, and a renewed fascination with grandiose Roman imperial architecture. The American Beaux Arts also embraces the late nineteenth-century Renaissance Revival and what could be called the Neo-Classical Revival. It became the one and only form of packaging for public buildings ranging from the smallest of public libraries to state capitols and the almost universal form for railroad stations, skyscrapers, and banks. In Minnesota it entered the scene very early in Cass Gilbert's scheme (1894) for the State Capitol. By the 1920s almost every Minnesota town of any size had a library, probably a post office, and almost always one or more banks in the style.

Characteristics

- formal and ponderous; purposely without reference to any scale
- symmetrical and balanced façade
- columned drums and domes (with interior rotundas)
- major emphasis on sequences of interior spaces (halls, corridors, staircases, public meeting chambers)
- monumental staircases
- central projecting pavilions
- classical porticos, usually with Ionic or Corinthian orders
- later Beaux Arts (Neo-Classical) buildings increasingly correct, relying for major visual effect on broad areas of undecorated surface

Late Gothic Revival Style (1895 to 1940)

The buildings of the late Gothic Revival are architecturally more accurate (also drier and more pretentious) in their forms and details than are the picturesque Gothic buildings of the nineteenth century. The stylistic sources for church and other public buildings were the late English Perpendicular Gothic and the late northern French Gothic, whereas in domestic architecture the borrowing was from the Tudor and French Norman traditions. The religious aspect of the late Gothic Revival movement was derived from the parsonages of the Boston architect Ralph Adams Cram. The late Gothic Revival Style was used most frequently for churches, educational buildings, skyscrapers, and dwellings. The style was widely used in Minnesota, where a number of important buildings in the style were produced by Cram and by his partner Bertram G. Goodhue.

Watkins House (now Watkins United Methodist Home). SE-71-43 Winona.

Characteristics

- correct use of volumes and details derived from English and French examples
- simple smooth surfaces of stone (often both inside and out)
- terra-cotta for details, especially in churches and commercial buildings
- elaborate windows of leaded stained glass
- stucco and half-timbering, brick, and stone in houses and small institutional buildings (libraries, clubs)
- round conical roof tower within L of two major wings
- buildings generally low and molded to irregularities of site

Craftsman (Arts and Crafts) Style (1895 to 1920)

The Craftsman Style was almost exclusively a domestic style associated with suburbia and the middle class. Although its ultimate source was the English Arts and Crafts movement and the architecture of M. H. Baillie Scott and Charles F. A. Voysey, the architectural forms developed in the United States were generally quite different fr(their English prototypes. The style became widely known from designs published in *The Craftsman*, a magazine issued between 1901 and 1917, and in the emergence of the woodsy California bungalow. In a broad sense all of the innovative designs from 1900 to 1910 were examples of the Craftsman esthetic (including the Midwestern Prairie School). The specific design sources for the style were complex, ranging from the English (Medieval) Cottage forms of Voysey and Scott to the early Queen Anne Shingle Style and the traditional wood Japanese house. The Craftsman Style came to be extensively used by contractors, and all large Minnesota communities have block upon block of these houses, usually stucco boxes covered by low-pitched hipped roofs with projecting screened porches or sun porches and exposed roof timbering.

House (now funeral home and chapel). A-24-9 Virginia.

Characteristics

- simple boxlike shapes with low-pitched roofs
- informal plans and nonsymmetrical elevations
- even large houses intimate and informal in scale
- usually stucco sheathing but sometimes clapboard or shingles; occasionally river boulder sheathing on lower portion of walls
- brick (especially clinker bricks) occasionally employed for foundations, parapet walls of porches and terraces, and chimneys
- exposure of structural members, especially rafters, struts supporting roof, and projecting beam ends
- screened porches, sun porches, and sleeping porches
- in best examples, buildings low and molded to irregularities of site

Glossary

Prairie Style (1905 to 1920)

The Prairie Style came into existence at the turn of the century in the Chicago work of Frank Lloyd Wright. By 1910 it had become an established style and was employed by architects and builders across the country. The form most often used was the low box design which Wright first published in 1906 in the *Ladies' Home Journal*. But each of the major Prairie architects developed a personal version of the style, ranging from the classical monumental designs of George W. Maher to the loose, highly varied designs of William G. Purcell and George G. Elmslie. Although one tends to think of the Prairie Style as a domestic style, a commercial and institutional counterpart (occasionally described as Sullivanesque) was used in small-scaled banks, libraries, schools, churches, and public buildings. A number of the major monuments in this style were built in Minnesota.

Fridholm House. M-2j-14 St. Paul.

Characteristics: Domestic Style

- usually stucco boxes with an emphasis on the horizontal
- windows and doors arranged in horizontal patterns; bands of windows placed directly under roof soffit
- façades (especially on street side) symmetrical and balanced
- usually one or more open or closed one-story porches projecting symmetrically from house; second-floor sleeping porches often present
- patterns of boards, especially horizontal boards (usually stained), connect windows, doors, and other elements
- casement windows in elaborate examples

Characteristics: Commercial and Institutional Style

- usually single brick-sheathed box
- façades almost always balanced and symmetrical
- freestanding engaged piers (no entablature) used to create a pattern in depth for the façades
- Richardsonian Syrian arches
- Sullivanesque patterned ornamentation in colored terra-cotta
- leaded stained-glass windows and skylights with geometric patterns

Mission Revival Style (1900 to 1912)

The Mission Revival began in California in the early 1890s and by 1900 the style was in use across the country. Outside of California the Mission Style (occasionally with an Islamic overtone) was utilized for recreational buildings, amusement parks, railroad stations, and occasionally for single-family and multiple-family housing. Minnesota would hardly seem the most likely place to encounter Mission Revival buildings, but a surprising number of them were built and many are still standing.

Pavilion, Loring Park. M-1a-33 Minneapolis.

Characteristics

- plain white stucco walls
- arched openings — usually with the pier, the arch, and the surface treated as a single smooth plane
- tile roofs of low pitch
- gable ends scalloped and parapeted
- paired bell towers, often covered with hipped tile roofs
- quatrefoil windows, especially in gable ends, often with surrounding cartouches
- occasional domes
- ornamentation (if any) cast in terra-cotta on concrete; patterns usually Islamic and/or Sullivanesque

Glossary

Period Revival Styles (1900 to 1941)

Domestic buildings during the first forty years of this century borrowed historical garb from various periods. The most frequently used styles were the following:

American Colonial (American Georgian and Federal)
English Georgian
English Elizabethan (Tudor) with half-timbering
French Norman Farmhouse
Spanish Colonial Revival (or Mediterranean)
Pueblo (Rio Grande) Style

Although the same general styles were used in, say, 1910 and again in the 1920s and the late 1930s, period buildings from 1910 still convey either a Queen Anne or Craftsman atmosphere and are readily distinguishable from the sharp, angular, thin, and brittle period buildings of the 1920s and the openly nostalgic period buildings of the 1930s which reflect America's eighteenth-century past. The Minnesota buildings from each period also reflect different historical antecedents, predominantly Medieval between 1924 and 1936 with a shift to Colonial between 1930 and 1941.

House. M-1o-20 Minneapolis.

Moderne (Art Deco) Style (1920 to 1941)

The Moderne divides itself into two distinct phases: the Zigzag Moderne of the 1920s and the Streamline Moderne of the 1930s. The Zigzag Moderne developed out of the classical designs of Bertram G. Goodhue and the vertical Gothic schemes of Eliel Saarinen, the forms and ornamentation of the Paris Exposition des Arts Décoratif of 1925 in the designs of Frank Lloyd Wright, and finally the influence of the newly developing International Style. The Streamline Moderne was an outgrowth of the machine esthetic, particularly the aerodynamic imagery of the airplane and the intensified influence of the International Style. The term Art Deco has recently been employed to describe both phases of the Moderne, but this does not take into account the diversity of stylistic sources or the major differences between the Moderne of the 1920s and the Moderne of the 1930s.

Characteristics: Zigzag Moderne (Art Deco)

- smooth-surfaced volumes with windows arranged in sunken vertical panels; no Classical or Medieval termination at top of building
- symmetry and balance in each elevation
- central tower with summit receding in a stepped pattern
- flat roof, usually headed by parapets
- buildings often monumental, formal, and heavy
- ornamentation of zigzags, chevrons, sunbursts, spirals, stylized motifs of plants and animals

Characteristics: Streamline Moderne

- stucco boxes, often with rounded corners and parapets
- emphasis on the horizontal in surfaces and band windows
- curved projecting wings
- generally nonsymmetrical compositions of volumes and elevations
- glass brick for walls and windows
- round windows
- steel railings for stairs, roof decks, and balconies
- brightly colored vitrolight

Wayzata Theatre. M-13-4 Lake Minnetonka.

Greyhound Bus Depot. A-3-3 Brainerd.

PWA Moderne Style (1930 to 1941)

During this period architects merged the Beaux Arts Classical (Neo-Classical phase) with the Zigzag and Streamline Moderne. The PWA Moderne Style is most closely associated with the architecture of federal government buildings, but it was also used for private commercial buildings. These buildings were fundamentally classical and formal, but enough Moderne details were injected to convey a contemporary feeling along with the traditional authority of the classical. Many PWA Moderne structures were built in Minnesota during the 1930s.

Farmers and Mechanics Bank. M-1a-17 Minneapolis.

Characteristics

- symmetrical form and classical horizontal proportions
- piers (used instead of columns) occasionally fluted but generally with no capitals or bases
- windows arranged as recessed vertical panels
- surfaces usually smooth and flat with terra-cotta ornamentation
- smooth stone sheathing; polished marble, granite, and terrazzo within and without
- relief sculpture and interior murals

International Style (1935 to 1942)

The International Style which developed in Europe in the 1920s in the hands of Le Corbusier, Gropius, and Mies van der Rohe did not begin to affect the Minnesota scene until the end of the 1930s. If one is precise in defining the style, one could argue that there were no examples of the International Style in Minnesota until after 1945. The work of a few Twin Cities architects such as Robert Cerny and Elizabeth and Winston Close approached the style, but these pre-1945 examples came closer to the regional woodsy examples from the San Francisco Bay area by William W. Wurster and others.

Starkey House. A-9d-29 Duluth.

Characteristics

- light horizontal volumes (often cantilevered)
- horizontality strongly emphasized
- walls and glass surfaces in same plane
- stucco walls
- flat roofing, usually without parapets
- extensive use of glass
- hospitallike image in white walls, tile, and metal

Glossary

Corporate International Style (1945 to 1960s)

In the United States the Lever House (1951–52) in New York, designed by Skidmore, Owings, and Merrill, was the first full realization of this style. The concept of clothing a building in a thin modular skin of metal and glass was directly derived from the 1920s designs of Mies van der Rohe and other European modernists. In the early examples of the style the repeated pattern of sheathing was simple and rectilinear, but by the end of the 1950s innumerable variations on this theme had been developed. In general the Corporate International Style sought to convey anonymity and the precision image of the machine. Minneapolis and St. Paul acquired a large number of these buildings, and the style is still in use.

General Mills Headquarters Buildings. M-14-2 Golden Valley.

Characteristics

- vertical box, with a suggestion of being set above the ground on stilts
- windows, spindles, and vertical surfaces all on the same plane
- buildings fragile in appearance
- horizontal layering of floors and repetitious cell-like character of interior spaces visible in exterior fenestration

The New Brutalism (1950–)

The name of this style was originally coined to describe the work done in the 1950s by certain British architects who created an esthetic based on the blunt exposure of a building's frame (concrete or steel), sheathing (often brick), and all of its "innards" (pipes, ducts, and so on). But very quickly the term began to be applied to the monumental rough concrete buildings of Le Corbusier and others which represent a revolt against the Corporate International Style. The Brutalist building is heavy, monumental, and emphatically permanent. Concrete is used in a deliberately crude fashion, and all of the inner workings of the building are visible. The end result is that as in traditional architecture the building has once again become a monumental piece of sculpture — one which is purposely not beautiful. Minnesota began to acquire its rash of Brutalist structures in the late 1960s.

Dormitories, St. John's University. C-16-4 Collegeville.

Characteristics

- a picturesque variety of forms — volumes projecting horizontally and vertically, contradicting shapes, shed roofs, cylinders
- walls and structure of concrete are united
- where wall and structure are separate, the walls as infill do not hide the structure (the structure, not the infill, predominates)
- openings as holes; occasional use of random holes
- concrete surfaces exposed within and without; tactile quality produced by pattern of wooden forms
- pipes, vents, ducts exposed

The New Formalism (1960–)

The New Formalism (or Neo-Palladianism) represents yet another twentieth-century effort to have the advantages of tradition and also the full advantages of modernity. In this compromise the Miesian esthetic of the Corporate International Style returns to the classical. Symmetry, classical proportions, arches, and traditional rich materials such as marble and granite are used. In form the building often tends to be a pavilion set on its own podium. The style came about in the hands of Edward D. Stone, Philip C. Johnson, and Minoru Yamasaki. Minneapolis and St. Paul have many examples of this recent fashion.

Olin Hall of Science, Carleton College. SE-46-21 Northfield.

Characteristics

- usually single volumes
- buildings separated from nature and usually set on a podium
- often exotic Near Eastern or Indian overtones
- suggestion of classical columns (piers) and entablatures
- arches in elliptical and other forms
- wall surfaces smooth, often elegantly sheathed in stone
- delicacy in all details; no heavy or monumental qualities
- external grilles of polished metal, concrete, and stone
- formal landscaping with pools and fountains; monumental High Art sculpture

Vertical Mine-Shaft School (1960–)

The vertical shed-roofed box, usually thinly sheathed in stucco or wood, has become a modish fashion throughout the United States since the late 1960s. The source of this rapidly accepted fashion was the design of the Sea Ranch condominiums (1965–66) in California by Charles Moore (Moore, Lyndon, Turnbull, and Whittaker). The numerous intellectual organizations characteristic of Moore's work have been dropped, and only the stylistic features remain. The interaction of history, humor, and satire inherent in Moore's work is almost never seen in the few examples of the style to appear in Minnesota in the 1970s.

St. John's Episcopal Church. C-45-19 St. Cloud.

Characteristics

- high and low rectangular volumes placed on end to create vertical forms usually covered with shed roofs
- monitor roof units
- sheathed in wood (plywood or shingles) or stucco
- window and door openings casually placed
- buildings light and fragile in appearance
- chimneys often tall metal stacks
- occasional bisection of rectangular form by diagonal walls and spaces
- organization of building around vertical core
- pipe and duct work often exposed, but playfully, not seriously

Cut-into Box (1965–)

The Cut-into Box, which is currently very popular in Minnesota, emerged out of the New Brutalism, the classical element in the New Formalism, and specifically the designs of Louis I. Kahn. In most examples the horizontal imagery of the International Style is maintained, but the building as a whole is transformed into something monumental and permanent and the traditional separateness of interior and exterior space is cultivated. Design elements such as Kahn's vertical service stacks or his diagonal splitting of volumes and Moore's unifying cores are now employed as style devices, devoid in most instances of their original conceptual origin. In Minnesota almost all examples of the style are completely sheathed in brick, and in only a few of them are any elements of the concrete or steel frame left exposed.

Mathematics and Science Building, St. Cloud State University. C-45-11 St. Cloud.

Characteristics

- usually several rectangular volumes, articulated horizontally
- brick sheathing, hiding structure
- windows and other openings deeply cut into the surface, usually with slanted apron sills
- exteriors usually of one color and a single tactile material

Suggested Readings

The literature listed here has been selected to provide the reader with a general survey of architecture and planning in Minnesota. For a sense of what America and Minnesota were like at the time of the 1776 centennial one should read John Brinckerhoff Jackson's *American Space: The Centennial Years, 1865–1876* (1972). Donald R. Torbert's *A Century of Architecture in Minnesota* (1958) presents a perceptive introduction to the architecture of the state in a single volume. Eileen Michels has written on such major Minnesota figures as Harvey Ellis and Edwin H. Lundie, and in her recent background study of the Minneapolis Institute of Arts she describes how a major building came into being and how it has subsequently been expanded and modified. Roger Kennedy, who has a deep fondness for Minnesota and its architecture, has written extensively on its domestic buildings.

Other major sources of information on planning and architecture in Minnesota are the promotional books, pamphlets, and other materials from the nineteenth and twentieth centuries issued by railroad companies, investors and land speculators, the State of Minnesota, and other private and governmental groups. The total number of such publications is impressive. Those listed here were found to be the most valuable. Other sources which are only briefly represented in the list are the numerous periodicals dealing with architecture in the state and the region which have been published over the years. Among these are *Architecture Minnesota; Bellman's Magazine; Keith's Magazine; Northwest Architect; Northwest Magazine; Northwest Builder, Decorator and Furnisher; Northwest, An Illustrated Journal of Literature, Agriculture, Western Progress;* and *Western Architect*.

In addition, to serve the new interest in the architectural past of the state many local historical societies and city and county planning departments have issued guides and publications focused on their respective areas. For instance, the Ramsey Hill Association has published an excellent guide for a walking tour of Ramsey Hill, and the Community Service Department of St. Paul has issued a series of brief guides to churches, houses, mercantile establishments, and sculpture in the downtown loop. The Washington County Historical Society's publication, *Stillwater's Priceless Heritage*, presents a tour of twenty-one nineteenth-century residences in Stillwater.

The suggested readings are divided into a list of publications which are arranged alphabetically by author and a list of anonymous publications which are arranged chronologically. Many of the publicatiaons in both sections are difficult to find, even in libraries. The best sources for these publications are the library of the Minnesota Historical Society, the Minneapolis Public Library, the St. Paul Public Library, and the University of Minnesota Library.

Suggested Readings

General Readings

Aguar, Charles E. *Exploring St. Louis County Historical Sites*. St. Louis County Historical Society, Duluth, 1971.

American Association for the Advancement of Science (publisher). *Handbook of Minneapolis*. 32nd annual meeting. Minneapolis, 1883.

Anderson Corporation (publisher). *Field Trip: Architect Seminar*. Bayport, Wisconsin, 1974.

Andreas, Alfred Theodore. *Illustrated Historical Atlas of Minnesota*. A. T. Andreas, Chicago, 1874.

Appell, Frederick W., Jr. "The Merchants National Bank of Winona." *Northwest Architect*, vol. 27, January/February 1974, pp. 8–11, 23.

Atwater, Isaac. *History of the City of Minneapolis*. 2 vols. Munsell and Co., New York, 1895.

Atwater, Isaac, and Stevens, John H. *History of Minneapolis and Hennepin County*. 2 vols., Munsell and Co., New York, 1895.

Beck, Catherine, and Gove, Gertrude B. *St. Cloud, Minnesota, from Log Cabin to Mobile Homes, 1855–1973*. Privately published. St. Cloud, 1973.

Bennett, Carl K. "A Bank Built for Farmers." *The Craftsman*, vol. 15, no. 2, November 1908, pp. 176–85.

Bennett, E. H. "Preliminary Report of the Minneapolis Civic Commission." *Western Architect*, vol. 17, February 1911, pp. 17–19.

———. *Preliminary Plan of Minneapolis*. Ralph Fletcher Seymour Co., Chicago, 1911.

Bill, Ledyard. *Minnesota, Its Character and Climate*. Wood and Holbrook, New York, 1871.

Bishop J. W. *History of Fillmore County, Minnesota*. Holley and Brown Printers, Chatfield, 1858.

Blegen, Theodore C. *Minnesota, a History of the State*. University of Minnesota Press, Minneapolis, 1963.

Borchert, John R. "The Twin Cities Urbanized Areas: Past, Present, Future." *Geographical Review*, vol. 51, no. 1, 1961, pp. 47–70.

Bowe, R. J., ed. *Historical Album of Minnesota*. Historical Publications, Inc., Minneapolis, 1957.

Breckenfield, Gurney. "How Minneapolis Fends Off the Urban Crisis." *Fortune*, vol. 93, January 1976, pp. 130–41; 180–82.

Bromley, Edward A. *Minneapolis Album — A Photographic History of the Early Days in Minneapolis*. Edward L. Thresher, Minneapolis, 1890. Republished in 1973 by Voyageur Press, Minneapolis, under the title *Minneapolis, a Portrait of the Past*, with a new introduction by Ervin J. Ganes.

Bushnell, David I., Jr. "Native Villages and Village Sites East of the Mississippi." Bureau of American Ethnology, Bulletin 69, Washington, 1919.

———. "Ojibwa Habitations and Other Structures." *Annual Report*. Smithsonian Institution, Washington, 1917.

Chicago and Northwestern Railroad (publisher). *Olmsted County, the Garden County of Minnesota*. Chicago, 1884.

Chicago, Rock Island, and Pacific Railroad (publisher). *The Land of Plenty*. Chicago, 1885.

Christison, Muriel B. "LeRoy S. Buffington and the Minneapolis Boom of the 1880's." *Minnesota History*, vol. 23, 1942, pp. 219–32.

Cleveland, Horace W. S. *The Aesthetic Development of the United Cities of Saint Paul and Minneapolis*. St. Paul, 1883.

———. "The Parks of the City." In *The History of St. Paul*, ed. by C. C. Andrews. D. Mason and Co., Syracuse, 1890.

———. *Suggestions for a System of Parks and Parkways for the City of Minneapolis*. Johnson, Smith, and Harrison, Minneapolis, 1883.

Coffin, Charles Carleton. *Seat of Empire*. Fields and Osgood, Boston, 1870.

Cox, Kenyon. "The New State Capitol of Minnesota." *Architectural Record*, vol. 18, August 1905, pp. 95–113.

Dean, William B. "A History of the Capitol Buildings of Minnesota with an Account of the Struggles for Their Location." *Minnesota Historical Society Collections*, vol. 12, 1905–1908, pp. 1–42.

Drury, John. *Historic Midwest Houses*. University of Minnesota Press, Minneapolis, 1947.

Dunn, James Taylor. *The St. Croix, a Midwest Border River*. Holt, Rinehart, and Winston, New York, 1965.

Eckbo, Dean, Austin, and Williams. *Minneapolis Parkway Systems*. San Francisco, 1971.

Empson, Donald. "Highland-Groveland-Macalester Park: The Old Reserve Township." *Ramsey County History*, vol. 10, Fall 1973, pp. 13–19.

Flanagan, Barbara. *Minneapolis*. St. Martin's Press, New York, 1973.

Folwell, William W. *A History of Minnesota*. 4 vols. Minnesota Historical Society, St. Paul, 1921–30.

Fowler, O.S. *A Home for All, or the Gravel Wall and Octagonal Mode of Building*. Fowler and Wells, New York, 1854.

France, Jean R. *A Rediscovery — Harvey Ellis: Artist, Architect*. University of Rochester and the Margaret Woodbury Strong Museum, Rochester, 1972.

Gebhard, David. *William Gray Purcell and George Grant Elmslie and the Early Progressive Movement in American Architecture*. Unpublished Ph.D. dissertation, University of Minnesota, Minneapolis, 1957.

———. *Work of Purcell and Elmslie, Architects*. Prairie School Press, Chicago, 1965.

Gilbert, Cass. "The Greatest Element of Monumental Architecture." *American Architect*, vol. 36, August 5, 1929, pp. 140–41.

———. "Revealing the Minnesota Capitol." *Architectural Record*, vol. 18, December 1905, pp. 480–81.

Goldberg, Paul. "Orchestral Hall's Design: A Rebuke to Red Velvet." *New York Times*, October 23, 1974, p. 38.

Goldfield, David R. "Historic Planning and Redevelopment in Minneapolis." *Journal of the American Institute of Planners*, vol. 42, January 1976, pp. 76–86.

Great Northern Railway (publisher). *Valley, Plain, and Peak*. St. Paul, 1894.

Harmon, Ralph L. "Ignatius Donnelly and His Faded Metropolis." *Minnesota History*, vol. 17, September 1936, pp. 262–75.

Hartshorne, Richard. "The Twin City District: A Unique Form of Urban Landscape." *Geographical Review*, vol. 22, 1932, pp. 431–42.

Heilbron, Bertha L. *The Thirty-Second State: History of Minnesota*. Minnesota Historical Society, St. Paul, 1958.

Heritage Preservation Commission, City of Minneapolis (publisher). *Washburn–Fair Oaks: A Study for Preservation*. Minneapolis, 1975.

Hewitt, Girart. *Minnesota, Its Advantages to Settlers*. St. Paul Press Printing Co., St. Paul, 1869.

Hoffmeyer, Albert. "In Conversation with Mr. Lundie." *Northwest Architect*, vol. 33, May/June 1969, pp. 20–47.

Holloway, Dennis, and Curl, Huldah, eds. *Winona: Towards an Energy Conserving Community*. School of Architecture, University of Minnesota, Minneapolis, 1975.

Holmquist, June D., and Brookins, Jean A. *Minnesota's Major Historic Sites: A Guide*. Minnesota Historical Society, St. Paul, 1963.

Hudson, Horace B. *Hudson's Dictionary of Minneapolis & Vicinity*. Hudson Publishing Co., Minneapolis, 1903.

———. *A Half Century of Minneapolis*. Hudson Publishing Co., Minneapolis, 1908.

———. *Hudson's Dictionary of Minneapolis*. Hudson Publishing Co., Minneapolis, 1916.

Immigration Department, State of Minnesota. *The Agricultural, Manufacturing, and Commercial Resources and Capabilities of Minnesota*. St. Paul, 1881.

———. *Great Opportunities in Minnesota*. St. Paul, 1910.

———. *Minnesota: Its Progress and Resources*. St. Paul, 1870, 1871, and 1872.

———. *On the Line*. Minneapolis, c. 1906.

Ingemann, William M. *Architecture and Design*. Vol. 2. December, 1938.

Ingram, E. W., Sr. *"All This from a 5-Cent Hamburger": The Story of the White Castle System*. The Newcomen Society in North America, New York, 1970.

Jackson, John Brinckerhoff. *American Space: The Centennial Years, 1865–1876*. Norton, New York, 1972.

Jacobsen, Christina. *The Burbank-Livingston-Griggs House: Historic Treasure on Summit Avenue*. Minnesota Historical Society, St. Paul, 1970.

Jacobsen, Hazel. *Car Tour: Some of Historic Hastings, 1850–1973*. Privately published. Hastings, 1973.

Jarchow, Merrill E. *The Earth Brought Forth: A History of Minnesota Agriculture to 1885*. Minneapolis, 1949.

Johnston, A. Walfred. "The Physical Geography of Minnesota." *Journal of Geography*, vol. 14, February 1916, pp. 161–231.

Jones, Harry W. "The Work of Harry W. Jones." *American Architect*, vol. 98, October 19, 1910.

Jones, Thelma. *Once upon a Lake*. Ross and Haines, Minneapolis, 1969.

Suggested Readings

Karni, Michael, and Levin, Robert. "Northwoods Vernacular Architecture: Finnish Log Buildings in Minnesota." *Northwest Architect*, vol. 96, May/June 1972, pp. 92–99.

Kennedy, Roger G. "Houses of the St. Croix Valley." *Minnesota History*, December 1963.

———. "Long, Dark Corridors: Harvey Ellis." *Prairie School Review*, vol. 5, nos. 1 and 2, 1968, pp. 5–18.

———. "The Long Shadow of Harvey Ellis." *Minnesota History*, vol. 40, Fall 1966, pp. 97–108.

———. *Minnesota Houses*. Minneapolis, c. 1967.

———. "Some Distant Vision." *The American West*, vol. 5, March 1968, pp. 16–23, 72–74.

Kieffer, Stephen A. *Transit and the Twins*. Twin Cities Rapid Transit Co., Minneapolis, 1958.

Koeper, H. F. *Historic St. Paul Buildings*. St. Paul Planning Board, St Paul, 1964.

Lathrop, Alan. "Augustus F. Knight, Architect, 1831–1914." *Northwest Architect*, vol. 38, no. 6, November/December 1974, pp. 274–75.

Long and Kees. *Architecture of Long and Kees*. Minneapolis, 1891.

Long and Thorshov. "The Architect and His Community: A Case Study — Minneapolis, Minnesota." *Progressive Architecture*, vol. 20, March 1948, pp. 47–51.

Loring, Charles M. "History of Parks & Public Grounds of Minneapolis." *Minnesota Historical Society Collections*, vol. 15, 1915, pp. 599–608.

McClure, Harlan E. *Twin Cities Architecture: Minneapolis and St. Paul*. Reinhold, New York, 1955.

McLean, Robert C. "Architecture in the Twin Cities." *Western Architect*, vol. 27, September 1918, pp. 75–76, 77–79.

Marlin, William. "America's Ten Most Livable Cities." *Christian Science Monitor*, June 18, 1975, pp. 14–15.

———. "Summing Up: A Big Old Warehouse Uncrates a Rich Mixture of Activities and Amenity." *Architectural Record*, vol. 158, December 1975, pp. 108–12.

Michels, Eileen (Manning). *The Architectural Designs of Harvey Ellis*. Unpublished M. A. thesis, University of Minnesota, Minneapolis, 1953.

———. *An Architectural View: 1883–1974*. Minneapolis Institute of Arts, Minneapolis, 1974.

———. *Encounter with Artists, Number Nine: Edwin Hugh Lundie, F.A.I.A. (1886–1972)*. Minnesota Museum of Art, St. Paul, 1972.

Minneapolis Board of Trade (publisher). *History and Growth of Minneapolis, Minnesota*. Minneapolis, 1884.

Minneapolis Industrial Exposition Association. *Reports for 1886 and Prospectus of the Second Annual Exhibition*. Swindurne and Co., Minneapolis, 1887.

Minneapolis Planning and Development Department (publisher). *Metro Center '85*. Minneapolis, 1970.

Minnesota Historical Society (publisher), *Historic Preservation in Minnesota: 1974–75*. St. Paul, 1974, 1975.

Morell and Nichols. *Plan of Stillwater*. Minneapolis, 1918.

Morgan, William T. *The Politics of Business in the Career of an American Architect: Cass Gilbert, 1878–1905*. Unpublished Ph.D. dissertation, University of Minnesota, Minneapolis, 1972.

Newman, M. W. "Minneapolis: City of Waters and Skyways." *Saturday Review*, vol. 3, August 21, 1976, pp. 14–16.

Noonan, Dana. *Some Notes on the Development of the Suburbs (Twin Cities)*. Unpublished paper. University of Minnesota Gallery, Minneapolis, 1974.

Northern Pacific Railroad (publisher). *Guide to the Lands of the Northern Pacific Railroad in Minnesota*. Minneapolis, 1872.

———. *Minnesota*. Minneapolis, 1924.

O'Connor, William Van, ed. *A History of the Arts in Minnesota*. University of Minnesota Press, Minneapolis, 1958.

Olsen, Russell L., Nelson, Edwin H., and Howarth, Fred. "Twin Cities Lines." *Interurban Special*, vol. 14, no. 2, December 1953, Los Angeles.

Palliser and Company. *Palliser's American Cottage Homes*. New York, 1878.

Peabody, Lloyd. "History of the Parks and Playgrounds of St. Paul." *Minnesota Historical Society Collections*, vol. 15, 1915, pp. 609–30.

Pederson, Kern O. *The Story of Fort Snelling*. Minnesota Historical Society, St. Paul, 1966.

Pond, Samuel W. "The Dakota or Sioux in Minnesota as They Were in 1834." *Minnesota Historical Society Collections*, vol. 12, 1908, pp. 319–501.

Radford, Robert A. "Activities of the Public Works Administration in Minnesota." *Northwest Architect*, vol. 1, November 1936, pp. 10–12.

Ramsey Hill Association (publisher). *Historic Ramsey Hill Yesterday and Today*. St. Paul, 1974.

Ridge, Martin. *Ignatius Donnelly: The Portrait of a Politician*. University of Chicago Press, Chicago, 1962.

Robinson, Charles M. "Ambitions of Three Cities." *Architectural Record*, vol. 21, May 1907, pp. 337–46.

Root, John W. "The City House in the West." *Scribner's Magazine*, vol. 8, September 1890, pp. 416–34.

St. Paul Community Services Department (publisher). (1) *Discover Saint Paul: Historic Churches*. (2) *Discover Saint Paul: Historic Houses*. (3) *Discover Saint Paul: Mercantile Architecture*. (4) *Discover Saint Paul: Sculpture in the Loop*. St. Paul, 1973–74.

St. Paul and Duluth Railroad (publisher). *"The Land of Promise."* St. Paul, 1893.

St. Paul, Minneapolis, and Manitoba Railway (publisher). *Red River Valley, the Land of Golden Grain*. St. Paul, 1882.

St. Paul and Sioux City Railroad (publisher). *Southwestern Minnesota, Land of Promise, a Soil of the Valleys with a Climate of the Mountains*. St. Paul, 1880.

Scarborough, Ray S. "The Lesser Cities of Minnesota." *Journal of Geography*, vol. 14, February 1916, pp. 233–36.

Scherer, Herbert. "Moderne in the Twin Cities." *Journal of the Society of Architectural Historians*, vol. 31, October 1972, p. 231.

Schmeckebier, Laurence E. *Art in Red Wing*. University of Minnesota Press, Minneapolis, 1946.

Schuyler, Montgomery. "Glimpses of Western Architecture: St. Paul and Minneapolis." *Harpers Magazine*, vol. 83, October 1891, pp. 736–55.

Scott, James A. *Duluth's Legacy, the City of Duluth: Vol. 1, Architecture*. Duluth Department of Research and Planning, Duluth, 1974.

Steinhauser, Frederic. "St. Anthony Park: The History of a 'Small Town' within a City." *Ramsey County History*, vol. 7, no. 1, Spring 1970, pp. 3–11.

Sullivan, Louis H. "National Farmers Bank, Owatonna." *Western Architect*, vol. 12, November 1908.

Szarkowski, John. *The Face of Minnesota*. University of Minnesota Press, Minneapolis, 1958.

Thompson, Neil B. *Minnesota's State Capitol: The Art and Politics of a Public Building*. Minnesota Historical Society, St. Paul, 1974.

Torbert, Donald R. "Advent of Modern Architecture in Minnesota." *Journal of the Society of Architectural Historians*, vol. 13, March 1954, pp. 18–23.

———. "Architecture and the City." *Everyday Art Quarterly*, no. 22, 1952, pp. 2, 3, 52.

———. *A Century of Architecture in Minnesota*. Minneapolis Institute of Arts, Minneapolis, 1958.

———. *Minneapolis Architecture and Architects, 1848–1908: A Study of Style Trends in Architecture in a Midwestern City Together with a Catalogue of Representative Buildings*. Unpublished Ph.D. dissertation, University of Minnesota, Minneapolis, 1953.

———. *Significant Architecture in the History of Minneapolis*. Minneapolis Planning Commission, Minneapolis, 1969.

Traphagen, O. G. *O. G. Traphagen, Successor to Traphagen and Fitzpatrick, Architects*. Chicago, n.d.

Tselos, Dimitri. "The Enigma of Buffington's Skyscraper." *Art Bulletin*, vol. 26, March 1944, pp. 3–12.

Upham, Warren. *Minnesota Geographic Names: Their Origin and Historic Significance*. Minnesota Historical Society, St. Paul, 1920; reissued by the Minnesota Historical Society in 1969, with a new introduction by James Taylor Dunn.

Warner, George F., and Foote, Charles M. *History of Hennepin County and the City of Minneapolis*. North Star, Minneapolis, 1881.

———. *History of Ramsey County and the City of St. Paul*. North Star, Minneapolis, 1881.

Washington County Historical Society (publisher). *Stillwater's Priceless Heritage*. Stillwater, c. 1974.

Willard, J. A. *Blue Earth County: Its Advantages to Settlers*. Mankato, 1868.

Williams, J. Fletcher. *A History of St. Paul and the County of Ramsey*. Minnesota Historical Society, St. Paul, 1876.

Winchell, N. M. *The Aborigines of Minnesota*. Minnesota Historical Society, St. Paul, 1911.

Winona and St. Peter Railroad (publisher). *A Guide to the Choicest Farming Lands in the New Northwest*. Chicago, 1882.

Suggested Readings

Wirth, Theodore. *Minneapolis Park System 1883–1944*. Board of Park Commissioners of Minneapolis, 1945.

Works Progress Administration. *Minnesota: A State Guide*. Viking Press, New York, 1938.

———. *Minnesota Arrowhead Country*. Albert Whiteman and Co., Chicago, 1941.

Zellie, Carole. "The Fabric of a Neighborhood." *Northwest Architect*, vol. 38, no. 6, November/December, 1974, pp. 272–73.

Zellie, Carole, and Lutz, Thomas J. *Saint Paul Architecture*. St. Paul Planning Department, St. Paul, 1975.

Miscellaneous Readings (in chronological order)

City of Winona and Southern Minnesota: A Sketch of Their Growth and Prospects. D. Sinclair and Co., Winona, 1858.

Mankato Weekly Record (publisher). *Blue Earth County: Its Advantages to Settlers."* 1868.

Picturesque Minnesota: A Guide for Tourists, Sportsmen and Invalids. Sioux City Route, Minneapolis, 1879.

Tribune Handbook of Minneapolis. Minneapolis Tribune, Minneapolis, 1884.

Faribault & Vicinity. Citizen's Committee of Faribault, Faribault, 1884.

The Zenith City — Duluth Illustrated. Art Publishing Co., Duluth, 1887.

Minneapolis Illustrated. Minneapolis Board of Trade, Chicago, 1889.

Pen & Sunlight Sketches of Minneapolis. Minneapolis Realty Co., Minneapolis, c. 1890.

St. Paul: The Queen City of the Northwest. Phoenix Publishing Co., St. Paul, 1890s.

Minneapolis: A Study. Tribune Job Printing Co., Minneapolis, 1891.

Art Work of Minneapolis. W. H. Parish Publishing Co., Chicago, 1896.

St. Paul History and Progress. Phoenix Press Co., St. Paul, 1897.

Red Wing Yearbook, 1902. Argus Press, Red Wing, 1902.

Great Opportunities in Minnesota. Office of the State Auditor, State of Minnesota, St. Paul, 1905.

Picturesque Lake Minnetonka. S. E. Ellis, Minneapolis, 1906. Republished in 1974 by the Excelsior–Lake Minnetonka Historical Society, Excelsior.

"The Minneapolis Spirit: The Story of a City of Lakes and Gardens." *American City*, vol. 6, 1912, pp. 398–404.

The Twin Cities Today. Twin Cities Line, Minneapolis, 1917.

"Twin Cities." *Fortune*, vol. 13, April 1936, pp. 117–19, 178, 183–84, 186, 190, 193–94, 197; vol. 14, July 1936, pp. 86–88, 142.

"Replanning Moves Forward in St. Paul." *American City*, vol. 53, March 1938, pp. 41–42.

"Twin Cities Vote on Recent Architectural Examples." *Architectural Record*, vol. 87, June 1940, pp. 20, 22.

Minnesota Presents. Minnesota Resources Commission, St. Paul, 1947.

"Architects Workshop Exhibition and Panel Discussion." *Everyday Art Quarterly*, no. 22, 1952, pp. 1–16.

"Architecture in Early Minneapolis." *Minneapolis Institute of Arts Bulletin*, vol. 41, January 1952, pp. 9–10.

"Fantasia in Glass and Iron: Metropolitan Building." *Architecture Forum*, vol. 103, August 1955, pp. 120–21.

Historical Building Survey for the Minneapolis Model City. Minneapolis Model City Housing Bureau, Minneapolis, 1971.

"The Gideon Pond House." *Northwest Architect*, vol. 36, January/February 1972, pp. 32–33.

Minneapolis People/City. University of Minnesota, School of Journalism and Mass Communication, Minneapolis, 1973.

Nicollet Island and East Bank Urban Renewal Project. Minneapolis Housing and Redevelopment Authority, Minneapolis, 1974.

"Twin Cities Renaissance: An Architectural Guide." *Architecture Minnesota*, vol. 1, no. 2, July/August 1975, pp. 5–51, 58–59.

General Index

General Index

General Index

General Index

General Index

General Index

General Index

General Index

General Index

General Index

General Index

General Index

General Index

General Index

General Index

General Index